MAKING A CHRISTIAN LANDSCAPE

Making a Christian Landscape is an important new interpretation of early medieval patterns of landscape development.

Sam Turner's new book traces landscape change in south-west Britain from the introduction of Christianity to the Norman Conquest (AD *c.* 450–1070). It stresses the significance of political and religious ideology in both the 'Celtic' west (especially Cornwall) and the 'Anglo-Saxon' east (especially the Wessex counties of Devon, Somerset, Wiltshire and Dorset). Combining innovative new research methods with archaeology, place-name evidence, historical sources and land-use patterns, it challenges previous work on the subject by suggesting that the two regions have much in common.

Employing modern mapping techniques to explore land-use trends, Turner advances a new model for the evolution of ecclesiastical institutions in south-west Britain. He shows that the early development of Christianity had an impact on the countryside that remains visible in the landscape we see today.

Accessibly written with a glossary of terms and a comprehensive bibliography, the book will appeal to both veterans and newcomers to landscape archaeology.

Sam Turner is lecturer in archaeology at Newcastle University and editor of the *Devon Archaeological Society Proceedings*.

MAKING A CHRISTIAN LANDSCAPE

The countryside in early medieval
Cornwall, Devon and Wessex

Sam Turner

UNIVERSITY
of
EXETER
PRESS

First published in 2006 by
University of Exeter Press
Reed Hall, Streatham Drive
Exeter, Devon EX4 4QR
UK

www.exeterpress.co.uk

British Library Cataloguing in Publication Data
A catalogue record for this book is
available from the British Library

HARDBACK ISBN 10: 0 85989 774 5
ISBN 13: 978 0 85989 774 7

PAPERBACK ISBN 10: 0 85989 785 0
ISBN 13: 978 0 85989 785 3

Front and back cover images by Mick Sharp.

Typeset in 9.5/12pt Plantin
by Exe Valley Dataset Ltd, Exeter

Printed and bound in Great Britain by
J. H. Haynes & Co Ltd, Sparkford, Yeovil

To Cathy, Grace and Libby,
with love

CONTENTS

*Detailed captions with cross-references to the main text are provided on the
pages immediately before and after the colour plates*

Plates, figures and tables

Front cover

St Piran's Cross, Perranporth, Cornwall. The cross stands close to the remains of the ruined churches of Perranzabuloe and St Piran's Oratory. It is probably the cross mentioned in the charter boundary clause of Tywarnhayle in AD 960 (S684).

Colour plates (between pp. xvi and xvii)

Black and white figures

Tables

Acknowledgements

I have incurred many debts in writing this book. It is mostly based on research undertaken for my PhD thesis while I held a University of York research studentship. Several employers provided flexible arrangements and support, and I am particularly grateful to Mike Green and Marion Bond.

I have been influenced by some wonderful teachers, including Phil Hull, Susan Herbert, the late Brian Hartley and especially my York supervisor Martin Carver, who always provided incisive, encouraging and entertaining comments on work in progress. Also at York, Lawrence Butler, Tania Dickinson, Jon Finch and Steve Roskams kindly read and commented on various chapters. My former colleagues at Devon County Council Archaeology Service kindly put up with me trying out endless hypotheses on them, and I am particularly grateful to Bill Horner and Ann Richards. My new colleagues at Newcastle have been unfailingly helpful and I am grateful to them for their ideas and advice, particularly Jim Crow, Chris Fowler, Kevin Greene and Mark Jackson. The University of Exeter Press's anonymous readers made many useful suggestions which have greatly improved the text. Anna Henderson at UEP, provided extremely helpful and detailed criticism of the draft version which has made the book much better and more readable. I am also very much indebted to other scholars who have helped me, especially John Blair, Harold Fox, Bjarne Gaut, Peter Herring, Tomás Ó Carragáin, Oliver Padel, Ann Preston-Jones, Julian Richards and Barbara Yorke.

The staff of the Cornwall SMR (particularly Steve Hartgroves), Somerset SMR (especially Chris Webster) and Devon SMR have kindly provided data and illustrations, and I am also grateful to the staff of the Cornwall Record Office, Devon Record Office and Wiltshire SMR for providing access to their records.

Many friends have influenced my work and my grateful thanks are due to all of them, but in particular to James Barret-Miles, Robert Bourke, Lawrence Hanson, the Kempsons, Mo Murthi, David Petts, Andrew Reynolds, Sarah Semple, Victoria Thompson, Matthew Webster and Howard Williams, and especially to my late cousin David Turner, who will remain an inspiration for much longer than the short while we had to get to know him.

My greatest debts are to other members of my family. In particular Margaret and Ray Aplin have been unflaggingly kind, generous and hospitable throughout the time I have been writing this book. Most of all to Cathy, Grace and Libby: with love, and thanks.

Newcastle,
December 2005

Definitions, Glossary and Abbreviations

Period Definitions

All dates cited in the text are AD, unless otherwise indicated. Chronological periods are referred to in the following ways:

Iron Age	*c.*800 BC—AD *c.*50
Roman	AD *c.*50—AD *c.*400
Romano-British	AD *c.*50—AD *c.*400
late Roman	the third and fourth centuries AD
post-Roman	from the beginning of the fifth to the end of the sixth century AD
late Antiquity	from the mid-fourth century to the end of the sixth century AD
medieval	from the fifth to the mid-sixteenth century AD
early medieval	from the fifth to the mid-eleventh century AD
pre-Conquest	before the Norman conquest (AD 1066) and after the fifth century AD
early Saxon	from the fifth century to the seventh century AD
middle Saxon	from the seventh century to the late ninth century AD
conversion period	in Cornwall the mid-fifth to seventh centuries AD; in Wessex the seventh and early eighth century AD
pre-Viking	before AD *c.*800
late Saxon	the tenth and the first half of the eleventh centuries AD
late pre-Conquest	the tenth and the first half of the eleventh centuries AD
late medieval	from the late eleventh to the mid-sixteenth century AD
post-medieval	from the mid-sixteenth to the late nineteenth century AD

Glossary and Other Definitions

Anglo-Saxon England	In this book, the area of Britain controlled by the Anglo-Saxon kingdoms, or (by the eleventh century) the kingdom of England (in this book, reference to 'Anglo-Saxon England' generally excludes Cornwall, though of course Cornwall was part of the kingdom of England by the eleventh century)
*bod	Old Cornish place-name element meaning 'dwelling' (Padel 1985: 23-6). The asterisk indicates that the word following it is presented in a hypothetical form rather than one known from a documentary source.
boundary clause	The description of the boundaries of a land unit, mentioning features that marked points along the boundary, and usually found in the text of a charter
Brittonic	The language sub-division including Welsh, Breton and Cornish
charter	A document granting land or privileges
Cornwall	Since the tenth century, Cornwall has been the south-westernmost county of England. Since the seventh or

	eighth centuries it had been an independent British kingdom, and before this probably comprised the western part of the kingdom of Dumnonia
Dumnonia	A post-Roman British kingdom of the fifth to seventh centuries, probably encompassing most of the historic counties of Devon and Cornwall
glebe	Land and/or other property supporting a clergyman, and forming part of his benefice
Hiberno-Saxon ornament	Decoration such as interlace and knotwork characteristic of Irish or English pre-Conquest art styles
hundred	A medium-sized late Saxon administrative unit, below the level of a shire
*lann	Old Cornish place-name element meaning 'enclosed cemetery' (Padel 1985: 142-5). See Chapter 1, pp.5-11
minster	An ecclesiastical centre, normally used interchangeably in this book with 'monastery'. See Chapter 1, pp.11-13
monastery	An ecclesiastical centre, normally used interchangeably in this book with 'minster'. See Chapter 1, pp.11-13
multiple estate	A landholding comprising a centre (or centres) having rights over a range of resources such as rough grazing and woodland, and linked to outlying settlements that owed various rents in kind to the centre(s)
Old Cornish	The ninth- to twelfth-century predecessor of the Middle (twelfth to sixteenth centuries) and Modern (seventeenth and eighteenth centuries) Cornish languages
parochia	Hypothetical Anglo-Saxon units of ecclesiastical administration. Parochiae are thought to have been centred on minsters or monasteries, and though typically larger that medieval parishes they are thought to have been their forerunners
reaves	Stony banks bounding long, narrow Bronze Age fields, now most commonly visible as earthworks. The best-known examples are on Dartmoor, but similar boundary systems occur elsewhere in the South West (Fleming 1988)
round	The name given to the enclosed settlements of Cornwall dating from the later Iron Age, Roman and post-Roman periods
royal vill	A royal settlement with a number of functions, including that of semi-permanent residence for members of the royal family and their entourages. They were also centres for royal estates and played an important role in the collection of royal dues, the administration of the rural landscape and the provision of justice
S321	Sawyer 1968, charter no. 321 (Sawyer, P., 1968. Anglo-Saxon Charters: an Annotated Handlist and Bibliography (London: Royal Historical Society))
terrier	A written survey or inventory of land or other property
tre	Cornish place-name element meaning 'estate, farmstead' (Padel 1985: 223-32)

Wessex	A kingdom of Anglo-Saxon England, comprising (from the eighth century at least) the historic counties of Devon, Somerset, Dorset, Wiltshire, Hampshire and (at times) Berkshire; Sussex, Surrey, Kent and Essex were added in the early ninth century
Western Wessex	In this book, the historic counties of Devon, Somerset, Dorset and Wiltshire

(For the definition of many more terms used in this book, see Lapidge et al. 1999.)

Abbreviations

CAU	Cornwall Archaeological Unit
CHES	Cornwall Historic Environment Service (before 2002 = Cornwall Archaeological Unit)
CRO	Cornwall Record Office
DCC	Devon County Council
DRO	Devon Record Office
EEA Exeter	Barlow, F. (ed.), 1996. *English Episcopal Acta* XI: *Exeter* 1046-1184 and *English Episcopal Acta* XII: *Exeter* 1186-1257 (2 vols, pages numbered consecutively)
ES	*Electronic Sawyer*
Electronic Sawyer	Kelly, S., (ed.) *The Electronic Sawyer: an online version of the revised edition of Sawyer's Anglo-Saxon Charters [S 1-1602]* (British Academy/Royal Historical Society Joint Committee on Anglo-Saxon Charters), http://www.trin.cam.ac.uk/sdk13/chartwww/eSawyer.99/eSawyer2.html (last consulted 22 Sept. 2005)
GIS	Geographical Information System. GIS computer programmes allow the presentation and analysis of spatial data
HER	Historic Environment Record
HLC	Historic Landscape Characterisation
ICS Index	Institute of Cornish Studies, University of Exeter: Cornish Place-Names Index
Lake 1	Polsue, J., 1867-73. *Lake's Parochial History of the County of Cornwall, Vol. 1* (Truro: W. Lake)
Lake 3	Polsue, J., 1867-73. *Lake's Parochial History of the County of Cornwall, Vol. 3* (Truro: W. Lake)
RCHMES	Royal Commission on the Historical Monuments of England
S	Sawyer, P., 1968. *Anglo-Saxon Charters: an Annotated Handlist and Bibliography* (London: Royal Historical Society)
SMR	Sites and Monuments Record
TRE	Domesday Book abbreviation for 'In the time of King Edward' (i.e. in 1066)

Colour Plates

Key to Plates 1-8
(see p.xvii for details of plates 9-16)

1. **St Just in Roseland church, Cornwall.** The church has been dedicated to a saint called *Iust* since at least the eleventh century (Orme 1996a). The churchtown was recorded as *Lansioch* (**lann* plus a personal name, Syek) in 1204 (Padel 1988: 101). [Photo: Mick Sharp]. (see p.7)

2a. **Wells Cathedral, Somerset.** The Anglo-Saxon church(es) seem to have stood just to the south of the present cathedral's south transept. The Lake, in the foreground, is fed by some of the springs that give the place its name (Rodwell 2001: fig.385). (see pp.51-3)

2b. **Earls Barton, Northamptonshire.** The church tower is a fine example of late Saxon architecture, and probably part of a thegn's manorial complex (Reynolds 1999: 96). (see pp.151-5)

3a. **St Laurence's Chapel, Bradford-on-Avon, Wiltshire.** The chapel probably dates to the beginning of the eleventh century, but is part of an ecclesiastical complex whose early origins are suggested by late seventh- or eighth-century sculpture discovered in the adjacent church of Holy Trinity. (see pp.66, 119-20)

3b. **Anglo-Saxon sculpture from West Camel, Somerset.** This cross-shaft, perhaps of ninth-century date, is decorated with interlaced plants and the bodies of long, sinuous animals (Foster 1987: fig.3). (see p.166, and also Plate 12)

4a. **Tintagel: the 1985 survey of the Island by the RCHM(E).** The earthworks of many small buildings cover the top and sides of the promontory and are thought to date principally to the post-Roman period. [© Crown Copyright. NMR]. (see pp.55-6)

4b. **General view of Tintagel Island,** looking north from Glebe Cliff. (see pp.55-6)

5. **Reconstructed sub-rectangular buildings on the terrace at 'Site C', Tintagel Island.** The top and flanks of the Island are covered in the remains of such structures; archaeological evidence suggests the majority date to the fifth to seventh centuries. (see pp.55-6, and also Plate 4a)

6a. **Interior of Madron Well, Cornwall.** The date of the chapel is uncertain, though the structure bears similarities to some likely pre-Conquest buildings such as St Helen's Oratory, Scilly [Photo: Mick Sharp]. (see pp.132-3)

6b. **Inscribed stone at South Hill, Cornwall.** The text, which runs vertically from top to bottom and is surmounted by a *chi-rho* symbol, reads *cumregni fili mauci*, '[the stone] of Cumregnus, son of Maucus' (Okasha 1993: 264-6; Thomas 1994: 278, fig.17.5). (see pp.140-3)

6c. **Part of a cross-shaft** probably dating to the ninth century at St Neot, Cornwall, with a fragment of a cross-head balanced on top. (see pp.49-50)

7. **The inscribed stone at Cardinham, Cornwall.** The inscription on this very weathered granite pillar is now extremely hard to decipher accurately (Okasha 1993: 88-90; Thomas 1994: 265). The medieval cross-head was added in the later nineteenth century. [Photo: Mick Sharp]. (see pp. 141-2)

8a. **An aerial view of the village of Shapwick, Somerset**, and surrounding fields. [Photo: Devon County Council/Somerset SMR No. SCCHER10847: taken 27/7/1994]. (see pp.103-5)

8b. **Aerial view of the landscape of the Blackdown Hills, Devon,** looking west across Luppitt Common. The sinuous medieval enclosures lie on the valley sides and valley bottom; straight-sided post-medieval fields have been laid out on Luppitt Common above (part of the Common still lay unenclosed at the beginning of the twentieth century). The settlements of Greenway Farm (centre left, with smoke rising) and Luppitt (extreme right) were both first mentioned in Domesday Book, where they were recorded as small estates of one and two hides respectively in 1066 (Thorn & Thorn 1985: 23,19 and 23,20). [Photo taken 15/11/2005]. (see p.149)

Plate 1: St Just in Roseland (see p.7)

Plate 2a:
Wells Cathedral
(see pp.51-3)

Plate 2b:
Late-Saxon Earls Barton
church (see pp.151-5)

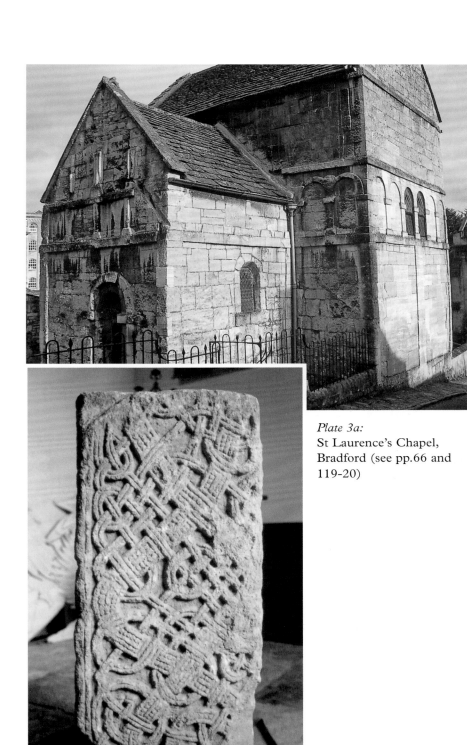

Plate 3a:
St Laurence's Chapel,
Bradford (see pp.66 and
119-20)

Plate 3b:
Anglo-Saxon sculpture,
Somerset (see p.166 and
Plate 12)

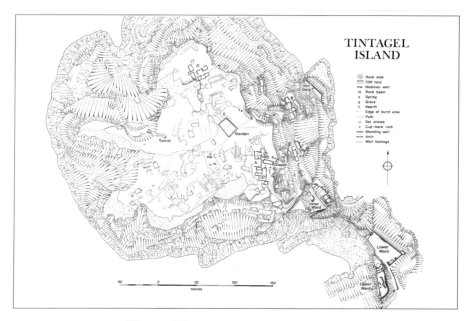

Plate 4a: Plan of Tintagel (see pp.55-6)

Plate 4b: General view of Tintagel (see pp.55-6)

Plate 5: Rectangular structures at Tintagel site
(see pp.55-6 and Plate 4a)

Plate 6a: Interior of Madron Well (see pp.132-3)

Plate 6b: Inscribed stone, South Hill, Cornwall (see pp.140-3)

Plate 6c: Part of cross-shaft, St Neot (see pp.49-50)

Plate 7: Inscribed stone, Cardinham (see pp.141-2)

Plate 8a: Aerial view of Shapwick, Somerset (see pp.103-5)

Plate 8b: Aerial view of the Blackdown Hills, Devon (see p.149)

Plate 9a: Glastonbury Tor (see p.146)

Plate 9b: Glastonbury town (see pp.51-3)

Plate 10a: Porth Chapel, looking east (see p.158)

Plate 10b: St Julitta's chapel (see p.161)

Plate 11a: Late Saxon cross, Lanivet, Cornwall (see p.162)

Plate 11b: King Doniert's Stone, St Cleer (see p.163)

Plate 11c: Hogback stone at Lanivet (see p.162)

Plate 12: Fragments of cross, Dolton, Devon (see p.166)

Plate 13a and b: St Jean at Poitiers (see p.184)

Plate 14a: St Kew church (see pp.48-9)

Plate 14b: Lanteglos by Fowey church and the landscape of southern
Cornwall (see pp.40-1)

Plate 15a: Four Hole Cross,
St Kew (see p.163)

Plate 15b: Three Hole Cross,
St Neot (see p.163)

Plate 16: Bodmin Moor in winter (see pp.86-91 and 188)

Key to Plates 9-16

(see p.xv for details of plates 1-8)

9a. **Aerial view of Glastonbury Tor,** site of post-Roman occupation and subsequently a probable late Saxon hermitage [Photo: Devon County Council/Somerset SMR No. SCCHER14171 (=2_023_0564), taken 5/7/1989]. (see p.146)

9b. **Glastonbury town** with the ruins of St Mary's Abbey, the main monastic focus at Glastonbury during the early middle ages. [Photo: Devon County Council/Somerset SMR No. SCCHER14387: taken 25/7/1995]. (see pp.51-3)

10a. **Porth Chapel, St Levan, looking east.** The ruins of St Levan's early chapel lie at the extreme bottom left of the photograph on the cliff above the beach; St Levan's holy well is higher up the cliff to the north. (see p.158)

10b. **The ruin of St Julitta's chapel on Tintagel Island, looking west.** The chapel probably incorporates the remains of post-Roman buildings in its lower courses. (see p.161)

11a. **A late Saxon cross** now in the graveyard at Lanivet, Cornwall. (see p.162)

11b. **King Doniert's Stone, Cornwall,** which stands with its taller partner the Other Half Stone in a small enclosure off the road from St Cleer to St Neot. The inscription reads *Doniert rogavit pro a[n]ima,* 'Doniert asked [for me] for his soul'. It probably dates to the later ninth century. (see p.163)

11c. **The moss-covered hogback stone at Lanivet, Cornwall.** Monuments like this stone and the cross (11a) may have been used to express the social status of a new class of English thegns in late Saxon Cornwall. (see p.162)

12. **Fragments of an Anglo-Saxon cross-shaft from Dolton, Devon,** probably dating to the late eighth or early ninth century. The bodies of beasts intertwine on the upper fragment, which has been inverted and hollowed out to act as the church font. (see p.166)

13a and 13b. The baptistery of St Jean at Poitiers. Probably first established in late Antiquity as part of an intra-mural episcopal complex, the baptistery underwent remodifications in the Merovingian period and the eleventh century (Février 1996). (see p.184)

14a. **St Kew church, Cornwall.** The church is the likely site of the earliest documented Cornish monastery, mentioned in the seventh-century *First Life of St Samson* as 'the monastery which is called Docco.' An inscribed stone bearing the name *Iusti* in ogam and Latin letters was found in 1924; it had been built into a bridge over the stream that flows past the churchyard along the valley bottom (Okasha 1993: 248; Olson 1989: 14-5). (see pp. 48-9, 125)

14b. **The Cornish landscape,** medieval and later: the church of St Wyllow, Lanteglos by Fowey, and the view across the later medieval fields of the Fowey valley to the 'Cornish Alps.' These great spoil heaps resulted from the nineteenth- and twentieth-century china clay industry. (see pp. 40-1)

15a. Four Hole Cross, St Neot. The cross stands beside the A30 on Bodmin Moor, close to its earliest recorded site on the northern boundary of St Neot parish. This late Saxon monument is decorated with plant scroll and triquetra knots on the arms of the cross head; the inscription 'GLW' relates to its use as a bound stone in the post-medieval period by the neighbouring Great Lord's Waste farm. It probably lost the upper part of its head some time in the eighteenth century, when it was apparently used for target practice by the local militia (Langdon 1996: 72). (see p.163)

15b. Three Hole Cross, St Kew. The cross is similar to St Piran's Cross at Perranporth, and may also date to the late Saxon period. It stands not far from the parish boundary between St Kew and Egloshayle, on a major road running east from the lowest crossing of the River Camel at Wadebridge. (see p.163)

16. Bodmin Moor in winter, looking south from the north-east corner of the St Neot study area (SX 225 765) along the course of the Withey Brook. (see pp.86-91, 188)

1

Introduction

Churches and the
early medieval landscape

The kingdom of Wessex was probably first converted to Christianity in the early seventh century, and the rulers and people of the British kingdom of Dumnonia[1] (including Cornwall) had probably been converted around 150 years earlier. Bede recorded only the barest details about Wessex in his *Ecclesiastical History*, including the names of Birinus and Cynegils, supposedly the first bishop and the first Christian king of the West Saxons.[2] The exact mechanisms and influences that brought about these events are far from clear; it seems possible that there were some Christians among the population before this, particularly in western regions that had only recently been conquered by Wessex such as Devon. As for Cornwall, the names of the protagonists are lost to history forever, as no written account survives. Whoever convinced these men and women to convert and whatever their motives, the religion they promoted was to exert a massive influence on the form of both early medieval society and the early medieval landscape.

This book is an investigation of the early Christian landscape of south-western Britain from the conversion period to the Norman Conquest (AD *c.*450-1070). Rather than focusing on individual sacred sites, it aims to study the impact of Christianity across the whole landscape. Changes in the structure of the landscape are inferred from sites, monuments, place-names and the wider patterns of fields and farms. These changes are mapped and studied, and then interpreted as reflecting the social, political and ideological changes that resulted from a range of practical adaptations to the new religion. The foundation of

---

[1] Dumnonia is the name of the British kingdom that probably encompassed most of Devon and Cornwall in the early sixth century. The name is derived from the tribal grouping known as the *Dumnonii*, which had controlled the region in the later Iron Age and which appears to have maintained a regional cultural identity throughout the Roman period. Devon became part of the Anglo-Saxon kingdom of Wessex some time during the seventh and eighth centuries.
[2] Bede *Ecclesiastical History*, III.7 (Farmer 1990: 153).

1

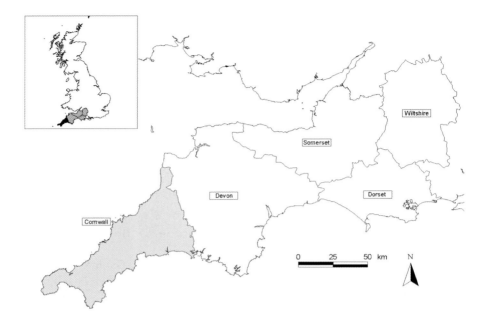

Fig. 1: The counties of south-west England.

churches is the most obvious of a range of changes that encompass the structure
of agricultural resources, distributions of settlements, and patterns of minor
sacred and ritual sites.

The study focuses on the early medieval ecclesiastical landscapes of Cornwall
and western Wessex, here defined as Devon, Somerset, Dorset and Wiltshire
(**Fig. 1**). For many people today, these two neighbouring regions of south-western
Britain have historically and culturally distinct identities. The modern county of
Cornwall forms the long tapering western end of the south-western peninsula.
The Cornish language was spoken here until the eleventh or twelfth century AD
in the east and until the eighteenth or nineteenth century AD in the west. This
language was a close relative of Welsh and Breton, and all three appear to have
developed from the same Brittonic root. In fact, archaeological and linguistic
evidence suggests the culture of Cornwall remained fairly stable in the first half of
the first millennium. Whilst it was part of the Roman Empire, Cornwall was never
as thoroughly integrated into the Roman world as most of eastern England: there
are no Roman towns in Cornwall, for instance, and only one small villa-like
settlement has ever been discovered (O'Neill 1933). Today a 'Celtic' Cornish
identity is reinforced by a pattern of distinctive place-names which contrast
sharply with the English place-names of Devon to the east. By contrast, Wessex
saw several major episodes of cultural and political transformation in the first
millennium. First, it was integrated into the Roman Empire much more fully than
most of western Britain, with all the attendant trappings of Roman culture
including towns, villas, a road system and a money economy. After the fall of the
western Empire, it witnessed the establishment of the new kingdom of Wessex
under a Germanic warrior aristocracy whose immediate ancestors had come to

Britain from continental Europe. Wessex became an Anglo-Saxon heartland, and it was under the kings of Wessex that a united kingdom of England eventually emerged. Thus the early history of the two regions is quite different: Cornwall was part of the 'Celtic' west that included other British kingdoms in Wales and Brittany, whilst Wessex was an Anglo-Saxon kingdom sharing more in common with others in the east of Britain like Sussex, Kent and East Anglia.

Despite the differences between the Anglo-Saxons of Wessex and the Britons of Cornwall, the dividing line between them was not fixed. At the time Cornwall was converted, Wessex did not really exist and the British kings of Dumnonia probably still controlled much of Devon. The conquest of the South West by Wessex was a gradual process, beginning in the sixth century and not complete until the tenth century at the earliest. Various regions counted in this book as parts of Wessex (particularly Devon and western Somerset) are in some ways transitional, since certain key developments in the landscape like the establishment of the very earliest ecclesiastical centres may have taken place under British rather than Anglo-Saxon kings.

Scholars of early medieval Britain have historically been divided into schools of 'Anglo-Saxon' and 'Celtic' studies. This may in part be due to the scholarly difficulties involved in undertaking literary studies and documentary history in several ancient languages, though the strong influence of nineteenth- and twentieth-century nationalist traditions are probably also significant. Although some scholars studying medieval Cornwall have recently begun to break down these divisions, others were content for their work to rest in the 'Celtic' category. Likewise, scholars of Wessex and Anglo-Saxon England have only rarely ventured into the 'Celtic' west. Whilst this separation is not always inappropriate, a lack of comparison between neighbouring regions can sometimes lead to the over-emphasis of local distinctiveness and a failure to appreciate how regional changes relate to the wider world.

This book uses early medieval Cornwall and Wessex as neighbouring regions that can be usefully compared and contrasted. The study of early landscapes in Cornwall and Wessex suggests that the development of ecclesiastical structures in the 'Celtic' west and 'Anglo-Saxon' east were rather more similar than some of our current models allow. These models have sometimes explained differences in the ecclesiastical landscapes of early medieval Britain with reference to ethnicity and predisposition towards certain forms of religion. It is hoped that the comparative landscape approach adopted here will allow a better understanding to emerge which explains changing practice in terms of social and political adaptations to the new Christian ideology. By analysing the early medieval countryside it is possible to see converging trajectories of landscape change in the centuries after the conversion to Christianity.

Making a Christian Landscape

An important theoretical principle for this book is the concept that changes in religious or political ideology, like the conversion of Britain to Christianity, can result in physical changes to the structure of the landscape. The way the people who live in a landscape understand it results from a range of influences. The natural environment is one of the most important: climate, topography, geology and soils all affect what activities will be possible in a landscape and the ways people will support themselves. Some scholars have chosen to stress the importance of environmental limitations and mundane activities like food production in the shaping of the landscape, and it is clear that the nature of agricultural production will deeply affect it (Williamson 2003). However, within these constraints it is the extent and nature of human action that will determine the appearance of the 'cultural' landscape, and the long-term history of a country like Britain shows that there are many different ways the same landscape can be inhabited and structured. It is clear that the things people believe and the way they express their beliefs have influenced not only people's perceptions of the landscape but also its physical form.

A few examples will show the impact of different societies' beliefs on different types of landscapes. Some groups have made little in the way of physical alterations, even if landscapes are of fundamental importance to their ideas and beliefs. The cosmology of the North American Mescalero Apache explains the physical and spiritual worlds as two parallel dimensions. Natural features such as rock outcrops, springs and caves act as special places where one dimension can be accessed from the other. Whilst these sites are regarded as very potent, they are normally not altered in any physical way (Carmichael 1994: 92-5). In Scandinavia, Saami sacred places encompass a similar range of locations. Whilst they tend to occupy distinctive positions in the landscape, they were often neither elaborated nor altered by the people who used them (Bradley 2000a: 5-13); nevertheless, they could provide an important vehicle for the expression of Saami identity (Welinder 2003). Richard Bradley has also suggested that Saami beliefs about nature and the world provide an appropriate analogy for those of people in Mesolithic Europe (Bradley 1998: 33).

In contrast to these examples, the belief systems of many other societies have resulted in significant alterations to the physical landscape. At the end of the Mesolithic period, there was a great change in some European landscapes when people began to build monuments. This seismic shift should probably be seen as a reflection of changing ideas about the world and how it should be ordered (ibid. 160-4):

> They were changing their attitudes to nature and the wild by domesticating plants and animals, and they were changing their whole conception of place by building megalithic tombs. Both attest a similar change of attitude, but the link was in the mind, not in the ploughsoil.
>
> (Bradley 1993: 17)

In India, the sacred geography of great Hindu holy sites like Benares have been reproduced at smaller scales in hundreds of lesser places, which take on some of their sanctity through imitation (Gold 1988; Coleman and Elsner 1995). Similarly, epigraphic evidence from west Africa shows how early Muslims in the region Islamicised the landscape, to the extent that one town came to be considered as a mirror of Mecca (Moraes Farias 1999). Idealised landscapes are occasionally realised in concrete form. In central America, elements of the landscape around the Classic Maya settlement of La Milpa in Belize appear to have been organised according to a 'cosmogram', which placed satellite pyramid and plaza groups at regular intervals around the central city (Tourtellot et al. 2002). Although complete reorderings of the landscape sometimes occur, it is more common for utopian models to be adapted to accommodate pre-existing features, whether mental or material. Normally, existing features are not wholly cleared away, but are given new meanings according to the guiding ideology (Snead and Preucel 1999). The cosmology of the Keres people of the northern Rio Grande region envisages a series of nested regions containing different landscape resources; at the centre lies the village, and at the margins a dangerous region inhabited by powerful supernatural creatures. Snead and Preucel's case studies show how this model could be adapted to fit local topographical settings and pre-existing patterns in the 'natural' and 'cultural' landscape (1999: 176). Other examples are provided by the ways early medieval Muslim societies Islamicised elements of Christian and pre-Christian religious landscapes (Carver 1996), or the way East Asian Buddhists assimilated local ideas about sacred mountains into Buddhist ideology, resulting in the creation of new kinds of Buddhist sacred landscapes (Barnes 1999). Changes of this kind are certainly a feature of the early Christian landscapes of Europe, where previous sacred topographies were altered to accommodate the new ideology rather than being swept away in a wholesale fashion (Orselli 1999: 186).

The sources and methods used in this book to investigate religious change and its wider impact are those of landscape archaeology. Whilst some recent studies have approached the religious traditions of early medieval Britain from literary and theological points of view (e.g. O. Davies 1996), the relative scarcity of relevant material makes this difficult for the South West and for Cornwall in particular. Previous studies of the region have often used archaeological or topographical approaches (e.g. Preston-Jones 1992; Thomas 1994), and one of the advantages of a landscape study is that it allows direct comparisons to be made with previous work.

Chapter 2 outlines a methodology for combining these sources and illustrates the way they can be used to investigate changes in the landscape. Chapters 3 to 7 discuss the role of Christianity in the developing landscape of early medieval south-west Britain by analysing the relationships between churches and other sites using archaeological information, place-names, maps and written sources. Chapter 8 explores the reinvented Christian 'ideology of settlement' which emerged from the new contexts created when the late Roman world was converted to Christianity.

The remainder of this chapter touches on some of the topics that will be investigated later in the book and discusses some of the previous work that has addressed them.

The *lann Model of Church Development in Western Britain

The most influential model for the development of ecclesiastical sites in western Britain was developed over thirty years ago by Charles Thomas (1971a: 49-51). It envisages that after the conversion to Christianity, traditional unenclosed burial grounds underwent a series of changes. First, a site would be enclosed with a small curvilinear boundary (sometimes known as a *lann[3]), and in time it would be further embellished with the addition of a cross, a chapel, and then a parish

---

[3] The asterisk (*) indicates that the word following it is presented in a hypothetical form rather than one known from a documentary source (see Padel 1985: xli).

church (ibid.: 49-51). Some scholars have suggested that this process took place early in Cornwall. On the north coast, for example, various churchyards are thought to have originated as Christian settlements founded by travellers from Wales or Ireland (Preston-Jones 1992: 122; see also Pearce 1982; Brook 1992). Although Ann Preston-Jones has pointed out that not all medieval churches with burial grounds have very early origins, the suggestion that the *lann-sites date to the early post-Roman period has been frequent (Pearce 1978: 92; Preston-Jones 1992: 105; Thomas 1994: 305-326):

> With Christianity came a whole package of ideas…associated site-types, place-names, monuments…

and:

> The earliest Christian foundations, or *lanns*, were settlements of people dedicated to a religious life.
>   (Preston-Jones & Rose 1986: 155, 160)

Recent work has continued to examine the form of early medieval cemeteries in the South West. Examples include the recently discovered site in Kenn parish (Devon) where post-Roman dug graves with east–west alignments may represent Christian burials (Weddell 2000). In Cornwall, St Endellion and nearby Treharrock are similar sites, both with apparently linear cemeteries of long-cist burials which in the case of St Endellion follow the course of the adjacent road. Although the later parish church stands near the site, the cemetery is far more extensive than its graveyard and crosses the parish boundary, showing that it is likely to pre-date the division of the area into two ecclesiastical units (Trudgian 1987). No evidence suggests that these cemeteries were enclosed at any date.

Recent research by David Petts on early medieval burial in western Britain has questioned the relevance of Thomas' model to the period before AD *c.*800 (Petts 2001, 2002a). Although several sites in Wales have been excavated and radiocarbon dated, such as Tandderwen (Clwyd), Atlantic Trading Estate (Glamorgan) and Plas Gogerddan (Dyfed), there appear to be very few examples of western British cemeteries that were enclosed in the post-Roman centuries (Petts 2002a). Similarly neither in Cornwall nor in Devon does excavated evidence suggest that any simple cemeteries were enclosed before the ninth century. Thomas' own excavations at St Dennis and Merther Uny show that these sites were only used for Christian burial from the tenth century at the very earliest (Thomas 1965, 1968b). Even on the Isles of Scilly, where several early church sites were investigated in the mid-twentieth century, there is little evidence to prove that fully developed local churches had appeared before AD *c.*800 (Thomas 1980, 1985; Ratcliffe 1994).

It has been argued that the presence of an inscribed stone and a *lann, either in name or enclosure form, indicate the existence of an early Christian site (e.g. Thomas 1994: 312). Archaeologists in Ireland have shown that the presence of stone sculpture often relates to a particularly prosperous period in the history of a site (Ó Floinn 1995; Ó Carragáin 2003). This could also be the case in Britain. However, around half the known monuments in Cornwall are not at ecclesiastical sites, and it is worth bearing in mind the possibility that other stones could have been moved to churches during the middle ages. Examples such as the St Clement stone (whose head was later recut as a cross) suggest that their significance was still understood long after they were first created, and many inscribed stones were incorporated into the building fabric of medieval churches (see Okasha 1993 *passim*). Whilst the occurrence of inscribed stones is certainly suggestive, it cannot be taken as *proof* of early origins for ecclesiastical sites.

In western Ireland the existence of numerous early ecclesiastical sites has been confirmed by archaeology. However, the evidence seems to suggest that many ecclesiastical sites were founded primarily as small settlements rather than being scattered burial grounds that were later enclosed as churchyards (Ó Carragáin 2003: 129-30). So the *lann* model has also been called into question here, but for a different reason. In Ireland, Wales and elsewhere, archaeologists have recognised that early medieval ecclesiastical sites could have originated in many ways (Edwards & Lane 1992: 10).

Place-names

Documents and place-names have been used to support the model of early enclosed burial grounds in Britain, but their evidence is hardly any more supportive than the archaeology (Petts 2002a). The Cornish place-name scholar Oliver Padel suggests that the *lann* element does not necessarily refer to ecclesiastical enclosures in Cornwall; for example, *lann*-sites without specifically ecclesiastical associations occur at Lewarne and probably at Lampen in the parish of St Neot, which was itself an important pre-Conquest ecclesiastical community (Padel 1985: 142-4). The earliest recorded use of a name in *lann* in Cornwall is possibly in a ninth-century charter granting land at Lawhitton (Sawyer 1968 (henceforth referred to as 'S') no. 1296; Padel 1988: 108; Hooke 1994a: 16-17). The late ninth-century *Life of St Paul Aurelian* includes a reference to a *monasterium* in Brittany called *Lanna Pauli* (Olson 1989: 23). Otherwise the earliest *lann* names in Cornwall are from tenth-century charters (e.g. *Landochou* (St Kew): S810; this site is the earliest recorded Cornish monastery, but in the seventh-century *First Life of St Samson* it was just called *Docco*: Olson 1989; Flobert 1997). Wendy Davies has suggested that some of the charters from south-east Wales in the *Book of Llandaff* could be dated to as early as the sixth century (Davies 1978). The 159 charters contain references to many estates with *llan* names (the equivalent in Welsh of *lann* in Cornish). However, scholarly opinion on these documents is far from united: whilst some of these grants have early origins, it seems likely that the actual *names* of the estates concerned were recorded in their twelfth-century form since the charters were being used at that time to bolster the claims of a new bishop of Llandaff. The *Book of Llandaff* is therefore unlikely to contain reliable evidence for early *llan*-names (J. Davies 1998: 45-6).

The Irish equivalent of *lann* is *cell.* (often *kill-* or *kil-* in modern place-names). There are numerous examples from the seventh century and some from earlier. However, this was neither the earliest type of place-name associated with church sites, nor was its use limited to the early period, and places were still being given *cell* place-names up to the twelfth century (Flanagan 1984: 31-4; Charles-Edwards 2000: 184-5). In addition, it is important to remember that there is no particular reason why the development of the early Christian landscape in Ireland should necessarily have been directly comparable to that of western Britain.

Padel has noted that *lann* may have been used to coin new names in Cornwall up to AD *c.*1200 **(Plate 1)**. It is therefore possible that ecclesiastical sites with *lann* names could have been given them relatively late. This is a particularly tempting interpretation in the light of Padel's observation that very few Christian sites that did *not* gain parochial status in the later middle ages (e.g. chapels or minor burial grounds) have names in *lann*, hinting that they were specific to churches of a certain status at the time the parish system was developing (Padel 1985: 144).

Dedications to Saints

There is another type of material that has become associated with the *lann* model through its occurrence in place-names, namely records of dedications to saints with Celtic names. As Padel has recently observed, dedications to Celtic saints formed a highly distinctive aspect of the ecclesiastical culture of Cornwall, not just in the later middle ages when over half the parish churches in the county had dedications to Celtic saints, but also during the period before 1100, when recorded dedications to Celtic saints are more than ten times as numerous as dedications to universal saints (between 34 and 39 to Celtic saints and only three to universal saints; Padel 2002: 330). Many churches have a Cornish place-name that incorporates the name of the saint to whom they are dedicated (e.g. *lann*-x dedicated to St X), though some are different (*lann*-x, dedicated to St Y; see Padel 2002: 311-13). Saints' names are compounded in Cornish place-names not only with the element *lann*, but also with elements such as *eglos* ('church'), *merther* ('saint's grave, place with a shrine for relics': Thomas 1971a: 89) and *alter* ('altar') (Padel 2002: 310-16). A very small number of the saints commemorated in Cornish dedications have hagiographical material dating to the early medieval period itself (e.g. St Samson of Dol, St Paul Aurelian; Flobert 1997; Cuissard 1881-3). Many others have later medieval *Lives* connected with them that commonly place their exploits in the earliest Christian centuries (Padel 2002: 319-20).

For Cornwall and Wales this hagiographical material was studied in the earlier part of the twentieth century by Doble, who published a long and invaluable series of booklets on the Cornish saints (later edited and collected together by D. Attwater and partly republished in six volumes as *The Saints of Cornwall* by the Dean and Chapter of Truro Cathedral: Doble 1960-97). Whilst he acknowledged the length of time between the period they were supposed to have lived and the composition of the saints' *Lives*, Doble did not in general question whether these figures had indeed existed in an early 'Age of Saints'. In this he was followed by later writers such as E. Bowen, who used the distribution of saints' names and dedications to write history about the early Christian period (e.g. Bowen 1969). However, such work is largely based on the assumption that the saints in question were actually present during the sixth century and that their presence at that time and in those places led directly to the dedications found in the later middle ages. As Davies has noted, this approach had already been questioned in the 1950s by Chadwick on the grounds that dedications first recorded in the later middle ages were not necessarily the direct result of the presence of individuals who might have lived over eight hundred years before (Davies 2002: 364; Chadwick 1954). In the early 1970s Susan Pearce argued that many of the Celtic dedications of Cornwall and south-west England could have arisen after the so-called 'Age of Saints' as a result of later developments and cultural contacts with Wales, Brittany and England (Pearce 1973). More recently a number of other scholars have pointed out that church dedications and ecclesiastical place-names could have been given over a long span of time during the early middle ages and later, and that a dedication to an 'early' saint does not necessarily imply the existence of an early church site, even though it will sometimes do so (e.g. Sharpe 2002: 153; Davies 2002: 390-4).

In Ireland the Martyrologies record hundreds of individuals revered as saints in the ninth century, but even here it is highly unlikely they all lived in the early Christian period and the rapid growth of their cults seems to have been largely a development of the seventh century and later (Thacker 2002: 34-7; Stokes 1905). In Cornwall, the earliest documentary evidence for widespread saints' cults is even later. It takes the form of a list of Brittonic saints' names compiled in the earlier tenth century and is now preserved in the Vatican Library (Olson & Padel 1986). This document almost certainly records the names of at least twenty-four saints venerated in Cornwall in the early tenth century. As noted above, Padel has shown that the cults of at least thirty-four Celtic saints were maintained in Cornwall before 1100, and it is beyond doubt that many further cults existed by this time though they are not recorded in surviving documents. Padel has suggested that the 'most economical assumption' about many of these names, particularly those recorded at only one or two sites, is that they had been the names of real people, perhaps priests or church founders (Padel 2002: 312-14). These localised cults form an important and distinctive part of Cornwall's religious history.

Nevertheless, dedications to these or other more widespread Celtic saints are hard to employ as a historical source to help explain the development of ecclesiastical structures in the period before A.D. *c.*1000, mainly because there is normally no way of discovering when they were first used at any specific site. Padel cites the example of *Entenyn*, with cult centres at St Anthony-in-Meneage, St Anthony-in-Roseland and possibly Ventontinny (Probus) (Padel 2002: 332-5). He suggests on linguistic grounds that the personal name-form 'Entenin' must have been coined before the ninth century in Cornwall (ibid. 334-5), but whether the figure commemorated at these sites lived much before this date and when each of the cult centres were first established is not clear from the evidence presently available. Only one or two dedications are reliably recorded in the ninth century or earlier (ibid. 329), and examples such as St Martin in Meneage, St Kew, Padstow and perhaps Bodmin show that the dedications of ecclesiastical sites ranging from the least to the most important could change over time (ibid. 311, 322; see Chapters 3 & 7). It also seems certain that dedications to saints with Celtic names would have been given to churches of varying status founded over several hundred years, as was probably also the case in south Wales (Davies 2002: 384-94). Dedication to a unique Cornish saint or to a 'regional' or 'inter-Celtic' saint found elsewhere in Wales, Cornwall or Brittany does not seem to reflect anything about the status of an individual church, since such dedications were given at both major and minor ecclesiastical foci (Padel 2002). For these reasons, this book will not rely heavily on church dedications to provide evidence for the location or history of the earliest ecclesiastical centres.

Adapting the *lann* Model

The *lann* model and related theories thus present several problems. Most importantly, recent research has shown that there is very little evidence for the enclosure and 'development' of cemeteries in western Britain before the eighth or ninth centuries (Petts 2002a). This conclusion makes a reconsideration of the development of the early church in Cornwall necessary. Any reassessment also provides an opportunity to deal with other important points which have been marginalised in the *lann model. For example, the suggestion that relatively large numbers of sites were founded in the post-Roman period has sometimes obscured potential differences between them, not only of date but also of status (Preston-Jones & Rose 1986: 157-8; Thomas 1994: 310-11). Finally, there is the question of the relationship between ecclesiastical sites and wider society. This is crucial to understanding life in early medieval Cornwall, but as in other parts of Britain and Ireland, it is a subject in need of further research (Monk 1998; Aston 2000a: 61-2).

These criticisms do not mean that the *lann model should be rejected outright. Sites such as Capel Maelog in Wales show that the sequence could have occurred much as Thomas suggested, but that it took place over a period encompassing the whole of the early middle ages (Britnell 1990; Petts 2001). It is also clear that there were sites in Britain at an early date which comprised settlements of people dedicated to religious lives. They occupied centres which were sometimes enclosed and which accommodated activities such as Christian burial. However, these were rather fewer in number than suggested by the *lann model, and as a group they appear to have comprised early monasteries of superior status: examples include Llandough and Berllan Bach in Wales and the early ecclesiastical sites of Cornwall discussed in Chapter 3 (Thomas & Holbrook 1994; James 1992: 100-1).

Most discussions rely on the *lann model to provide a framework in which to discuss the social context of early Christian sites in Cornwall. Preston-Jones and Rose have noted that the distribution of *lann-names concentrates in areas of fertile soils in south Cornwall which were likely to have been heavily settled in the early middle ages (Preston-Jones and Rose 1986: 156). In this model, early ecclesiastical settlements of largely undifferentiated status serve as local spiritual centres for groups of surrounding hamlets (ibid. 143, 160). Susan Pearce has outlined a similar model for the development of *lann-sites in pre-Anglo-Saxon Devon, although she stressed local lordship as the determining factor in the location of early ecclesiastical sites (Pearce 1982).

Numerous small Christian centres such as these suit agricultural models like that proposed by Harvey, who also regards early medieval Cornish society as relatively 'horizontal' and as lacking any strong central authority (Harvey 1997). This conclusion is based on an investigation of the tithing structure of West Cornwall (tithings were local units of legal administration). Although the evidence for the tithings comes from later medieval documents, Harvey speculates that it was in place early in the post-Roman period and provided the basis in relation to which Christian missionaries could locate their settlements (*lann-churches) (ibid. 20). There are two main problems with this argument: first, it assumes that the *lann-churches were established in large numbers at an early date, which may not have been the case, as discussed above. Secondly, it assumes that in early medieval Dumnonia there was an 'evolution' from a simple (horizontal and egalitarian) to a complex (hierarchical) society (see also Herring 1999b, 1999c).

However, there is a considerable body of evidence to suggest that there was a hierarchically structured society in Dumnonia throughout the early middle ages. In the earliest post-Roman centuries, the inscribed stones are the work of an elite consciously identifying themselves as such, sometimes with some literary sophistication (e.g. Howlett 1998; Thomas 1998; Knight 1992). Imported material from the Mediterranean and Gaul may also be evidence for an exchange system run by an elite capable of raising and trading a surplus (Campbell 1996), and there is even some written evidence in Gildas: Ch. 28, 1-2 for the names of Dumnonian kings (Winterbottom 1978). In the middle of the period, there are literary and historical references to kings of the region (e.g. Aldhelm's letter to Geraint; Lapidge & Herren 1979), and in the later pre-Conquest era, charters show there was a class of land-holding minor nobles (W. Davies 1982, 1998; Hooke 1994a). In Anglo-Saxon England emergent hierarchies and kingdoms are detectable in the archaeological and historical sources from the sixth and seventh centuries onwards (Carver 1989: 152). Societies in the west of Britain appear to have been structured in similar ways, as suggested, for example, by the comparability of 'British' and 'Anglo-Saxon' social orders in Ine's laws, which probably date to the late seventh century (Wormald 1999: 103; Attenborough 1922).

Other Theories of Church Development

John Blair and Patrick Hase have suggested that the prime consideration of church founders in Anglo-Saxon England was to provide a regular system of pastoral care for those living within royal administrative territories (Hase 1994: 61; Blair 1988a: 37-8; though see also Blair 1995c: 207). This theory has roots in a body of scholarship that deals with the structures of the early church in Britain and across Europe.[4] It has been challenged by Eric Cambridge and David Rollason who argue that this 'minster hypothesis' places too great an emphasis on the role of monastic foundations in the provision of pastoral care, and excludes bishops and priests who may have operated from local churches (Cambridge and Rollason 1995: 95). In his essay on the early church in County Durham, Cambridge has suggested that churches primarily founded to provide pastoral care filled in the gaps between monastic centres not concerned with this activity (Cambridge 1984), although Blair has argued that the archaeological evidence discussed by Cambridge fails to provide satisfactory grounds to differentiate between different classes of church (Blair 1988a: 36-7). This debate has highlighted one of the more difficult aspects of the study of the early medieval church in Britain, the problem of establishing the status of churches. It seems that almost any ecclesiastical establishment referred to in the documentary sources could be described as a *monasterium* (Blair & Sharpe 1992: 4-5). Although different sorts of churches are widely acknowledged to have existed, they are hard to detect by the terms used to refer to them (Cambridge and Rollason 1995; Campbell 1979).

There has been some debate over the most appropriate terminology to describe important early ecclesiastical centres in Britain (see Blair 1995c). As far as is known, none of the Cornish churches recorded in Domesday Book were 'monastic' in the normal later pre-Conquest sense (i.e. they had not been reformed according to the Benedictine Rule in the tenth century; see Yorke 1995: 210-25; Pitt 1999: 18). However, the majority of those identified by Olson had communities of priests or clerks in the eleventh century. As Olson notes, there was

---

[4] e.g. David 1947: 7-18; Stancliffe 1979; Constable 1982; Brooke 1982; Foot 1989.

a tendency in the early middle ages for communities to change from strictly 'monastic' houses with monks and an abbot to 'secular' clerical establishments comprising a group of priests (Olson 1989: 3-4). This has also been observed elsewhere in Britain, for example in Wales (Charles-Edwards 1970-2) and Anglo-Saxon England. Which monastic or clerical Rules may have been followed in early British ecclesiastical communities, and where the dividing line lay between 'monks' and 'clerks' is very unclear. For example, the foundation at St Germans is described as a *monasterium* in an eleventh-century text, despite the fact that it was also the seat of the bishop of Cornwall at the time (the so-called 'Lanalet Pontifical' **(see Fig. 10 on p.42)**; Olson 1989: 62-3). Shortly afterwards the community staffing the foundation is referred to as *canonici* in Domesday Book ('canons'; Thorn & Thorn 1979a: 2, 6). All over southern Britain the possibility of episodes of reform and refoundation exists, and attempting to use specific vocabulary to denote particular types of churches is likely to be unprofitable. Early churches will therefore be referred to in this book by a range of names including 'monasteries' and 'minsters'; no particular distinctions are implied (following Blair 2005: 3). The word 'church' is generally used to refer to a church building.

Martin Carver has suggested that three main types of economic infrastructure were available to Christians in early medieval Britain, and that these are also familiar from more recent usage: the episcopal, the monastic and the secular or private. The choice between them was essentially a political one, signalling acceptance of certain political ideas (Carver 1998a). He has argued that it is possible to distinguish which of the three categories of Christianity had been adopted by a particular group using archaeological evidence, 'not withstanding the tendency of the documents to pretend, improbably, that all operated together as one harmonious project'. Carver has suggested that one of the three 'options' generally tended to become dominant in any given society, and that different types of ecclesiastical centre were generally funded in different ways: monastic foundations through grants of land, episcopal systems by the payment of tithes, and 'secular' churches dependent upon 'the income and attitude of a local lord' (ibid. 22). The fact that episcopal, monastic and secular infrastructures required different economic commitments meant that a given community might find one system easier to accept and implement than another. Carver cites the example of east Yorkshire, where the evidence of pre-Conquest sculpture suggests that a system based on monasteries in the seventh and eighth centuries was replaced by one of small secular churches in the ninth to eleventh centuries, under the influence of Viking political ideology (ibid. 26).

One of the major problems with the 'minster hypothesis' is the inflexible way it has been applied (Cubitt 1995: 116-17). For example, the minster model may obscure differences between churches by demanding that they be interpreted as equivalents in the context of an ecclesiastical administrative system. Carver's suggestion about the different sources of support which different types of churches drew on may provide a useful way to approach the problem of difference (Carver 1998a).

However, it is clear from Richard Sharpe's re-analysis of early Irish sources that the 'episcopal', 'monastic' and 'secular' elements could be present as constituents of a complex system, perhaps not always harmonious, but nevertheless part of a whole (Sharpe 1984; Charles-Edwards 2000: 241-64). In England, some research has shown that elements of the pre-Viking ecclesiastical administrative system survived the 'Christian-to-Christian conversion' described by Carver in the Yorkshire area, so that 'monastic' and 'secular' systems would have been operating side by side (Palliser 1996), and other work has investigated the interaction between episcopal authority and monastic foundations through documents recording Anglo-Saxon church councils (Foot 1989; Cubitt 1995: 191-202). It seems unlikely that 'monastic', episcopal' and 'secular' structures were adopted as a singular prescription in Anglo-Saxon England or elsewhere in Britain (Blair 1995c: 210-11).

In the absence of comprehensive written records or plentiful archaeological evidence, it is likely that an analysis of the relationships between ecclesiastical centres and certain other elements of the landscape may allow interpretations about the status and role of the church in contemporary society. For example, if a church can be shown to have shared a location with a royal vill (or royal centre) and not to have possessed substantial independent estates, then it is likely that it would have been dependent for its status on the royal vill, as suggested by Hase (1994). By contrast, it seems likely that a church with extensive estates that was distant from a royal centre would have had a different status—perhaps 'monastic' in the sense that Glastonbury was.

In Chapters 3 to 7 the relationships between ecclesiastical sites and the secular elite in Cornwall and Wessex will be investigated. This analysis will include the relationships between churches and royal vills (Chapter 3), secular administrative structures and churches' *parochiae* (Chapter 5), and the nature of ecclesiastical estates (Chapter 5). In Chapter 7 the various types of churches established by different groups at different times will be considered. The exploration of these topics will build up a body of evidence on which conclusions about the nature of developing religious institutions, royal power and social structure in Cornwall and Wessex can be based.

A group of related questions focusing on changes in the structure of the wider landscape will also be considered in relation to church sites, and the new Christian 'ideology of settlement' they ushered in. John Blair and Richard Gem have described the major ecclesiastical sites of early medieval Britain as 'Holy Cities' (Blair 1996a; Gem 1996). Their model, which regards ecclesiastical centres as central to the worldview of early medieval people, will be discussed in Chapter 8. Using the material presented in Chapters 3 to 7, it will be argued that early medieval churches did indeed become central places in early medieval society, not only in terms of ideological self-understanding, but also in the landscapes of production, consumption, settlement and belief.

The long-term perspective afforded by a landscape archaeology approach allows changing patterns in the countryside to be investigated. The sequence of settlement patterns and changes in the geographical distribution of agricultural resources can be used to illuminate social and cultural changes (Alcock 1993: 55-72). The Cornish evidence is particularly well suited to this kind of analysis, since the archaeology and place-names of Cornwall can be used to build up a reliable image of the changing landscape in the early middle ages. In Chapter 4 three detailed case studies of parts of Cornwall will examine what relationships existed between the development of rural settlement and the establishment of ecclesiastical centres. In Wessex the settlement and place-name evidence is harder to interpret and simply not well enough understood to map development over time, so Cornwall receives more detailed treatment in this respect. However, the available evidence from Wessex does suggest that, as in Cornwall, changes in settlement patterns and in the structure of the landscape between the fifth and tenth centuries can be interpreted as reflecting social, political and ideological change resulting in part from the establishment of Christianity.

2

Studying early medieval landscapes in south-west Britain

Landscape Archaeology

The methods and sources used in this book to study the landscapes of the early middle ages combine to create an interdisciplinary method that uses place-names, historical sources and archaeological evidence at a range of different scales. This chapter introduces a technique for integrating these sources using GIS (Geographical Information Systems) known as Historic Landscape Characterisation (HLC). In the past HLC has mainly been used for landscape management and spatial planning, but recently scholars have begun to develop it as a way of researching medieval and later landscapes.

'Landscape archaeology' is characterised by work which collects information about ancient landscapes and the histories of land use. Archaeological sites are located and recorded and the relationships between them are studied. Scholars have stressed the importance of studying the whole landscape, rather than just concentrating on individual aspects such as 'sacred' sites (e.g. Dommelen 1999: 284; Given et al. 1999; Given & Knapp 2003: 3-4). This is because the whole landscape both affects and is affected by people (Knapp & Ashmore 1999: 20-1; Crumley 1999: 270). To approach past societies convincingly through their landscape it is necessary to have as much information about past landscapes as possible.

The methodological implications for studying the south-western landscape are that information has to be assembled from the widest possible range of sources before being subjected to specific questions. This must include interdisciplinary work and investigation of evidence such as historical documents and place-names, as well as archaeological sources (Moreland 1992; Bender 1993: 3).

This position has not always been accepted in archaeology. The New Archaeology movement which began in the 1950s largely rejected the use of historical texts as a source of evidence suitable for archaeologists. In the 1980s, postprocessual archaeology sought to stress the 'textuality' of material culture and also of the practice of archaeology (Hodder 1986; Shanks & Tilley 1987: 16), but as Ian Morris has commented it often kept 'history' at the most theoretical level and failed to engage profitably with written material (Morris 2000: 24; Feinman 1997: 372). In part as a result of this, considerations of context and longer-term changes have sometimes been marginalised (Parker Pearson et al. 1999: 234). Since the early 1990s, however, scholars like John Moreland have outlined how those interested in investigating whole landscapes can use written texts and material culture in a practical way (Knapp 1992b; Moreland 1992, 1998: 90-9; 2001)). They argue that just as material culture is in a recursive relationship with people, so too are texts or images: people decide their content, and in turn that content affects people's future actions. Texts and artefacts can therefore be regarded as similar categories of things, and can be encompassed by the same discussions.

The work of Ian Morris and John Moreland draws on the important twentieth-century historical tradition of *Annalisme*. A loosely defined method rather than a coherent 'school', *Annalisme* is history with a concern for interdisciplinary analysis of a wide variety of social and historical subjects, via the 'thick description' of specific contexts (Morris 2000: 24-5; Knapp 1992a: 6-8). Landscape archaeology and *Annales* history share many concerns. For example, landscapes need to be analysed in as much detail as possible; similarly, *Annales* history demands that context is described as fully as possible. One starting point for this book is the belief that all aspects of the historical context both affected and were affected by people, including material culture, written documents and images, and verbal culture (such as place-names). It is therefore crucial that all the available categories of data receive thorough and balanced treatment as important sources for early medieval cultural history.

Categories of data: place-names

As Christopher Tilley has stressed, place-names become crucially important elements of the landscape; named places and things 'become captured in social discourses and act as mnemonics for the historical actions of individuals and groups' (Tilley 1994: 18). Landscape historians have appreciated this significance for a long time, and place-names have been used in particular for discussions of population movements and ethnic change. For example, scholars once accepted equations between the appearance of names in a given language and the settlement of invaders speaking that language, with controversy centring on questions such as the number of settlers (Stenton 1971: 519-24; *cf.* Sawyer 1957-8). However, there are other possible contexts for continuities or changes in naming practice, and it is now argued that this kind of work sometimes relied on narrow assumptions about the use of language by different ethnic groups and their social relationships with each other (Hadley 1997). In the south-west peninsula, Cornwall provides an interesting example: minor place-names continued to be coined in the west of the county in the Cornish language throughout the late- and post-medieval periods, despite effective control by the English kingdom of Wessex and its successors from the tenth century onwards. In central Cornwall around Bodmin Moor, however, English administrative control was established slightly earlier and place-names were generally given in the English language from the eleventh or twelfth centuries (Austin et al. 1989). The use and adoption of place-names are governed by complicated patterns of influence and cultural interaction, not simply 'ethnic' factors.

Place-names contain a great deal of information, and historians and archaeologists have been keen to use them to illustrate historical processes. Many names are associated with topographical features, and Margaret Gelling has shown how names can be related to specific landscape features (Gelling 1984, 1998). This can be useful, but is sometimes deceptive: places bearing the name of a feature are quite often neither at nor even close to that feature, but instead may be part of a land unit that also includes it (see e.g. Faull 1984). In Cornwall for example, there are around fifteen places with the name *pen gelli ('grove's end': Padel 1985: 180). It has been suggested that this reflects the extent of woodland loss since these place-names were established: none is now nearer than a quarter of a mile to a wood (Rose & Preston-Jones 1995: 53). However, it is also possible that the name applied to the area of land attached to the farmstead as much as to the specific location of the settlement (for a Yorkshire example see Faull 1984: 139).

Another valuable type of information contained in place-names refers to tenurial status. Rosamond Faith (1997) has pointed out that different English place-name elements were given to settlements with different service obligations. Thus a place-name with the generic element *tun* represented a different type of settlement to one containing *worth* (Faith 1997: 141, 173-7). In Cornwall, Oliver Padel has noted that there may have been a difference in legal status between places with *bod names compared to those with *tre* names (Padel 1985: 25). Such differences are important, but must be used with care, because names are coined in specific social contexts. By the time Domesday Book was compiled, both *bod and *tre* names were applied to estate centres, indicating that any legal differences had probably become unimportant by the late eleventh century (Thorn & Thorn 1979a; but see Padel's comments on *bod place-names and medieval tithing names: 1985: 25). It is important not to apply certain values to place-names anachronistically when analysing relationships between settlements in any given period.

The relative chronologies of place-names present a related problem. Scholars have sometimes used the distributions of different place-name elements to track the geographical expansion of settlement, leading to complicated descriptions of landscape development. However, as Thomson has shown for Orkney, it is critical that the relative chronology and relationships between place-names are understood before this technique will produce valid results (Thomson 1995). Place-name evidence rarely gives the chronological definition which can sometimes be provided by documentary records or excavated archaeological evidence.

Relatively little modern place-name study has been undertaken on the modern counties that cover the Anglo-Saxon kingdom of Wessex. Whilst Dorset's place-names have been the subject of recent English Place-Name Society volumes (Mills 1977, 1980, 1989), the volumes on Devon and Wiltshire are now in need of revision and no definitive study has been published for Somerset or Hampshire (Gover et al. 1932, 1939). Fortunately, the place-names of Cornwall have been subject to very thorough study by Oliver Padel and his team, resulting in the *Index of Cornish Place-Names* (*ICS Index*; Padel 1985). The analysis in this book uses a limited number of Cornish place-name elements to illustrate different periods of landscape development (see Ch. 4). They generally follow the chronological limits suggested by Padel's linguistic analysis. These limits are not hard-and-fast, but provide an approximate guide to the periods when elements such as *tre* were commonly in use (Padel 1985: 223-4).

Despite this careful modern work, there are still problems. Whereas many Cornish settlement names have surviving medieval forms, most minor place-names (e.g. field, road and street names) do not. In the case of field names, most were not recorded until the production of the nineteenth-century tithe maps and awards. Nevertheless, these names still form a valuable source of evidence and often relate to the location of archaeological sites. In western Wessex, work in Somerset has suggested that habitative place-name elements preserved as field names in medieval documents may relate to the sites of long-abandoned early medieval settlements (Aston et al. 1998; Aston and Gerrard 1999). However, when early name forms are lacking, the identification of a site made on the basis of a minor place-name must be treated with caution.

In addition, it is not always possible to match recorded place-names with the sites to which they refer (e.g. where names are then recorded only once or twice in medieval or earlier documents forgotten locally). Place-names can also sometimes move about, referring to different locations in different periods. These problems can be particularly acute for landscape archaeologists who want to develop an in-depth understanding of a particular locality at particular times, rather than produce generalised distribution maps at very small scales (see e.g. Bennet 1998). Although some scholars have been able to link archaeological sites to place-names by drawing on surviving oral tradition and analogies with other sites, the reliability of these techniques is hard to demonstrate if names are not recorded independently in written sources (Stummann Hansen & Waugh 1998). It is therefore necessary to exercise considerable caution before attributing 'lost' settlement-names recorded in medieval documents to archaeological remains or to surviving settlements now known by other names.

In some ways, there are similarities between place-names and more conventional archaeological sources such as survey data derived from fieldwalking.[1] Neither indicate the complete settlement pattern in any given period, and both could be said to suffer 'erosion' from 'post-depositional' processes. Similarly, neither place-names nor survey data demonstrate clearly the status or size of the sites to which they refer, although both may suggest general hierarchies within settlement patterns. Neither data necessarily give the exact location of sites; instead, both suggest the approximate area of a settlement. The two types of data are far from completely analogous, but it is true that there are various problems in common between the two methods. These have not stopped critically aware archaeologists making effective use of survey data (e.g. Alcock 1993), and they should not stop them using place-names, nor from incorporating place-name evidence into studies of landscape archaeology.

Categories of Data: Written Sources

Historical documents provide all sorts of crucial information for landscape archaeologists in addition to place-names. For present purposes they can be

---

[1] Fieldwalking normally involves an archaeological team walking over the land collecting and identifying artefacts whose location is then recorded and plotted. For methodology and discussion of survey techniques see Davis et al. 1997; Given et al. 1999.

divided into three categories. First, there are documents that relate to defined areas of the landscape; secondly, documents containing information about the status and chronology of individual sites; and finally there are sources which provide general frameworks for the cultural history of the early medieval South West.

Into the first category fall documents such as Anglo-Saxon charter boundary clauses (Finberg 1964a; Hooke 1994a) or post-medieval glebe terriers (Potts 1974). In this book, these have been used for two main purposes. First, they provide information about specific sites (e.g. features used as markers in descriptions of estate boundaries). Secondly, they allow the extent of estates or other units of land to be mapped. Where they exist (and can be interpreted) documents such as Anglo-Saxon charter boundary clauses are of great value to landscape archaeologists, as they often contain detailed information about topographical features, land use, routeways and certain types of archaeological monuments that were prominent in the early medieval landscape (Hooke 1981: 20-2; Hooke 1998).

In the second category pre-Conquest documents can contain useful information relating to both the status and chronology of specific sites. Documents such as charters and Domesday Book can confirm the existence of (and provide a *terminus post quem* for) any places which are mentioned, and sometimes also indicate the status of sites. However, this information normally only relates to high-status sites such as royal vills or major churches (for royal vills see e.g. Gelling 1978: 184-5; Sawyer 1983; Faith 1997: 32; for churches see e.g. Olson 1989; Blair 1985). Associations with specific individuals may also suggest status or dates. Later medieval documentary records can provide information about the relationships between a mother church and its dependent chapelries that may be helpful in modelling earlier structures of ecclesiastical organisation. These sources can add valuable social and temporal dimensions to the analysis of historic landscapes.[2]

Finally, documents such as the *Anglo-Saxon Chronicle* (Swanton 1996) and the corpus of charters have provided historians with the main sources for a narrative history of events such as the Saxon settlement and Viking incursions. Classic contributions to the debate on the significance of this material include those by H.P.R. Finberg (1953a) and W.G. Hoskins (1960), and more recent syntheses of the region's early medieval history have been produced by Charles Insley (1998) and Barbara Yorke (1995). A major problem with the narrative sources is that they are very few. This means that many important issues are almost completely omitted (e.g. the migration of British-speakers from Dumnonia to Armorica in the post-Roman period; Fleuriot 1980), and even those that are mentioned—such as the 'conquest' of Cornwall by Wessex—generally receive very short entries in the sources (Svensson 1987: 3-7). The omissions and indeed the content of the entries underline the fact that the *Chronicle* and comparable sources were produced in specific historical contexts for specific audiences. Methodologically speaking, this problem underlines the necessity of interdisciplinary studies which incorporate evidence from a range of sources.

A wider variety of historical sources are important for analyzing the social and

---

[2] For a recent summary and application of methods for identifying minster churches in Wessex see Hall 2000: 4-29.

cultural context (Andrén 1998). The problems of combining documents and archaeology to this end include the danger of anachronism: it is critical that the sources under consideration relate to the same contexts. For example, it would not be methodologically sound to relate descriptions in the *Odyssey* to the archaeology of the Mycenean Peloponnese: though they purport to describe the same contexts, the two sources are the result of different periods and differing worldviews (Davis 1998: xxxv–xxxvi). This highlights the importance of 'thick description' (in the *Annaliste* sense) and the thorough investigation of context.

Categories of Data: Archaeology

Landscape archaeologists use evidence from the full range of available archaeological sources, including excavations, air and ground surveys, analysis of standing buildings or surviving monuments and environmental studies. Relatively few excavations have taken place on early medieval sites in south-west Britain, and many of these present considerable interpretative problems relating to the age of the excavations, the standard of recording, or financial and time pressures on the excavators. It is also common for investigations to encompass only small parts of any site, so that the character and extent of the deposits remain unclear pending further work (as at Tintagel churchyard: Nowakowski & Thomas 1992). The limited number of excavated sites in Devon and Cornwall in particular has had knock-on effects on topics such as our understanding of early medieval pottery typologies, and dating sites through pottery finds can be difficult (Thomas 1968a; Quinnell 2004; Turner & Gerrard 2004). Another result of this uncertainty is that pottery of the period may not be recognised or reported when found; there are certainly relatively few sites which are known to have produced grass-marked or bar-lug pottery of the 'native' types (see Hutchinson 1979; Bruce-Mitford 1997: 71-80).

The small number of excavations means it would be impossible to understand the early medieval landscape in the South West using data from excavated sites alone. Fortunately, a range of other archaeological sources can be brought to bear on questions of interest to landscape archaeologists. Standing buildings of the pre-Conquest period are extremely rare in the South West. Although those that do survive are undoubtedly of great importance, they are hard to interpret owing to a lack of standing or excavated comparanda in the region. The status, date and significance of churches in the far west like St Piran's Oratory in Cornwall are presently not completely clear (Olson 1989: 35-6). In central Wessex there are a few more buildings that preserve pre-Conquest fabric (e.g. Alton Barnes, Wiltshire; Taylor & Taylor 1965), but even here there are few well-understood buildings dating from before the tenth century. Individual stone monuments of the early medieval period are considerably more common. About seventy inscribed stones survive (or are reliably recorded) in the counties of Devon and Cornwall, mostly dating to the period between the fifth and seventh centuries (Okasha 1993). In addition, there is a large corpus of later pre-Conquest crosses and sculptural fragments bearing characteristically pre-Norman decoration (possibly as many as fifty in Cornwall alone; Okasha & Preston-Jones, in prep; Cramp 2006).

Survey methods including air photography and earthwork survey have been used extensively in southern England to complement the limited data from

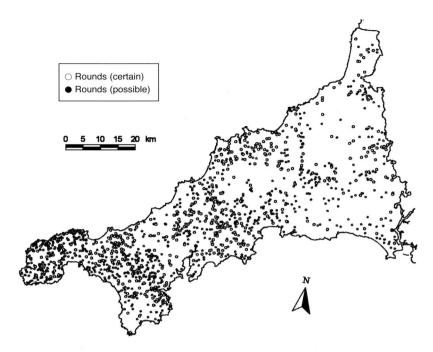

Fig 2: 'Rounds' in Cornwall (Data: Cornwall SMR).

excavation (e.g. Salisbury Plain: McOmish et al. 2002; Exmoor: Riley & Wilson-North 2001; Bodmin Moor: Johnson & Rose 1994). The archaeology of certain periods and regions is particularly visible to such techniques, for example the late Iron Age and Romano-British settlements of Cornwall (the 'rounds', of which around 1,400 are known: **Fig. 2**). Whilst this kind of information is extremely valuable for landscape archaeology, it must be used cautiously. Most importantly, sites are commonly identified on the basis of earthwork or cropmark morphology, so their date range will always remain uncertain. By analogy with excavated sites, the rounds recorded through air and field survey could date to any time from the fourth century BC to the sixth century AD (Johnson & Rose 1982; Rose & Johnson 1983; Rose & Preston-Jones 1995). In addition, it is likely that some sites will have been mis-identified, and/or mis-attributed to the Iron Age/Roman period, despite belonging to other eras (Griffith 1994: fig. 2). Surface artefact collection has made a relatively small impact on the early medieval archaeology of southern Britain, despite being a standard survey method in parts of Europe (Barker 1995; Millett et al. 2000; Given & Knapp 2003). This may change in the future as programmes like the Portable Antiquities Scheme make metal detector finds increasingly visible to archaeologists. Until now research projects such as the East Hampshire Survey, the East Berkshire Survey and the Kennet Valley Survey (also Berkshire) have all failed to locate significant quanitites of pre-Conquest pottery, probably because it is fragile and decays quickly when subjected to ploughing (Oake & Shennan 1985; Ford 1987; Lobb & Rose 1996). The Middle Avon Valley Survey surveyed fields for several kilometres to either side of the River Avon in western Hampshire, and succeeded in retrieving a small number of early medieval ceramics (Light et al. 1994). At Shapwick (Somerset), a ten-year field project applied a battery of techniques including intensive fieldwalking, place-name analysis and regressive map analysis to a single parish, and the results have begun to show the value of an interdisciplinary approach (Aston & Gerrard 1999; below, Ch. 4, 103-5).

The potential of environmental techniques including pollen studies have recently begun to be realised for the post-prehistoric South West, though relatively few projects have been undertaken to date away from the uplands of Dartmoor and Bodmin Moor (Caseldine & Hatton 1994; Fyfe et al. 2004). One of the main problems with these techniques is that they tend to provide only a generalised picture of landscape and land use, rather than one that can be related unambiguously to individual sites. Samples taken from large raised bogs or valley mires like those on parts of Dartmoor do not allow the reconstruction of normal medieval farming landscapes (Geary et al.1997: 208), although the increasing use of small mires means it is sometimes possible to suggest the occurrence of specific types of land use in closely defined areas (Fyfe 2006). Such research provides data that can confirm or question patterns identified through techniques such as Historic Landscape Characterisation or the analysis of settlement patterns.

Historic Landscape Characterisation

Historic Landscape Characterisation (HLC) is a method for understanding and mapping the landscape with reference to its historical development (McNab & Lambrick 1999: 54; Rippon 2004a). The technique is different to traditional archaeological mapping methods because it assigns 'historic character' to the whole landscape rather than just selected monuments or small areas.

In the early 1990s there was a growing realisation that despite some success in the conservation and management of individual sites and monuments, the broader historic landscape was not receiving adequate protection and management (Fairclough et al. 2002: 69-70). English Heritage therefore commissioned a project to evaluate and compare different methods for understanding and valuing the historic landscape. These encompassed both 'top-down' techniques, where experts delimited areas of landscape with historical and archaeological characteristics they considered of particular significance, and 'bottom-up' methods, including those that presented interpretations of the historic character of the whole landscape (Fairclough et al. 1999; for a 'top-down' approach see e.g. Darvill et al. 1993; for 'bottom-up' Herring 1998: 7-8). The first modern HLC work was commissioned as part of this project from the Cornwall Archaeological Unit, which mapped part of Bodmin Moor in late 1993. The Cornish project was extended to cover the whole county in 1994 (Cornwall County Council 1994, 1996), and since then methods have been developed and applied in many other regions (Fairclough et al. 2002; Clark et al. 2004; Turner 2005; for a similar but earlier approach see Finberg 1951 and **(Fig. 3)**). At around the same time, Steve Rippon developed an interdisciplinary approach that is closely related to HLC using regressive map analysis to deal with relatively large blocks of coastal wetlands (Rippon 1997: 18-30).

HLC draws on techniques which have long been used in other disciplines, for example in geology to show soil-type or in ecology to map habitats. Just as all parts of the landscape are forms of habitat, HLC recognises that the whole landscape has historical significance which results from human activity and use over the millennia. Herring has explained the basis of the Cornish method as follows:

> Closer examination [of the landscape] reveals that particular groupings and patterns of components which recur throughout the county can be seen to have been determined by similar histories. Cornwall's historic landscape can, therefore, be characterised, mapped and described, using a finite number of categories or types of 'historic landscape character'.
>
> (Herring 1998: 11)

The present-day landscape is examined using sources such as vertical air

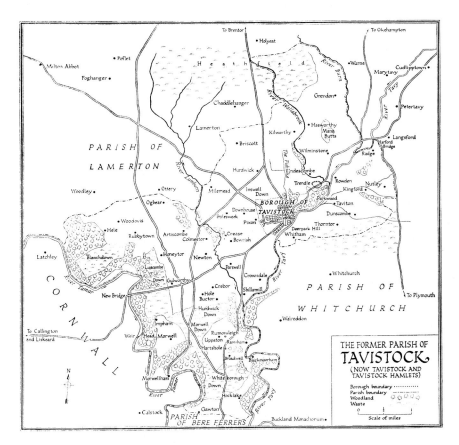

Fig 3: 4. H.P.R. Finberg's map of Tavistock. Finberg's map presents a characterisation of the landscape in the medieval parish of Tavistock based on eighteenth-century map sources and earlier documents. It shows Tavistock at the centre of an area of cultivated land, with extensive tracts of moorland and woodland lying at its margins. (From: H. Finberg, 1951. *Tavistock Abbey* (Cambridge), facing page 41. Reproduced by kind permission of Cambridge University Press.)

photographs, modern and historic maps and divided into landscape 'types'. These HLC types are normally classified in advance of the characterisation mapping. The distinctive characteristics exhibited by areas of land with similar histories of use are identified and a list of HLC types is defined. In the Cornwall assessment, seventeen types of landscape were used:

1. Rough ground
2. Prehistoric enclosures
3. Medieval enclosures
4. Post-medieval enclosures
5. Modern enclosures
6. Ancient woodland
7. Plantations and scrub woodland
8. Settlement (historic)
9. Settlement (modern)
10. Industrial (disused)
11. Industrial (active)
12. Communications
13. Recreation
14. Military
15. Ornamental
16. Water (reservoirs etc.)
17. Water (natural bodies)
(Herring 1999a: 21)

HLC types are then mapped, usually using a GIS (Geographical Information System; see e.g. Wills 1999). In different areas of the country, different types may be appropriate because of differing landscape histories, or because the landscape characterisation has been designed to be used at larger or smaller scales, or to reflect a more or less detailed range of HLC types. The method can therefore be very flexible. In recent characterisations of the Peak District and Hampshire, for example, many different types were used which related specifically to the landscape histories of the areas under consideration: no less than eighty-five in Hampshire. In Cornwall, characterisations of localised areas have been undertaken at 1:10,000 and 1:2,500 scale using project-specific HLC types (Barnatt 1999; Lambrick 1999; Herring 1998: 20-1).

One problem for earlier HLCs was that some areas may have more than one major landscape component contributing to overall character, so that it was unclear which was the dominant type and the one that should be mapped. This consideration also leads to problems associated with 'time-depth'; a 'recent' landscape (e.g. one created by nineteenth-century enclosure) may conceal strong elements of another kind of landscape (e.g. prehistoric enclosures; Herring 1998: 106-9). Various techniques have been used to overcome these problems. In the Cornwall HLC, text was written to accompany the HLC and alert users to the many potential historic components of a given HLC type. The use of GIS now provides a flexible solution to this problem (Herring 1999a: 22). Using a GIS allows each character area or 'polygon' to be given more than one descriptive characteristic (each 'polygon' is normally a geographically coherent block sharing the same historical development, and is mapped in the GIS as one HLC type)

(Wills 1999: 38-9). In current landscape characterisations, the database linked to the GIS allows many attributes to be given to individual 'polygons'. Interpretations of present and previous HLC types can be recorded for each individual 'polygon' in the GIS database (e.g. Turner 2005). This is potentially one of the most useful research applications of HLC: although the starting-point for most HLC maps is the historic character of today's landscape, it allows the researcher to construct interpretations of past landscapes in the GIS and use them to model how the landscape might have changed over time. When used for landscape research, tailored GIS-based HLCs can be designed to produce characterisations linked closely to questions concerning landscape change.

HLC has certain additional advantages over other techniques for mapping historic landscapes. The coverage of archaeological databases such as British county Sites and Monuments Registers (SMRs) tends not to be even, but to vary between and within counties. Plotting SMR entries on maps to try and present a picture of the historic landscape often gives an imbalanced picture—for example, it would commonly show medieval field boundaries that have been destroyed, but ignore those that are still *in situ* (N. Johnson 1999: 121). Furthermore, the location of an archaeological site as a point on a map (so-called 'point' data) also detracts from the value of the feature as part of a historic landscape; concentration on 'discrete features does not clearly reflect historic landscape character' (Herring 1998: 9, fig. 10). HLC is a significant methodological improvement because it allows the historic landscape to be given archaeological significance on a wide scale. As discussed above, it is crucial to build up an in-depth understanding of the whole landscape before investigating its constituent elements. The whole landscape has been the context for past action, and it is necessary to comprehend as much of it as possible (Darvill 1999; Knapp & Ashmore 1999). Using HLC maps helps to allow a 'break-out from the site-based myopia' of the past (Herring & Johnson 1997: 54)

In Chapter 4 (below) Historic Landscape Characterisations of case-study areas are used as starting points to examine the landscape and the relationships between different types of site. Purpose-built interpretative maps using an adapted form of the HLC method provide the essential spatial structure for the analysis of data gained from different sources. Johns and Herring (1996) have pioneered this approach in Cornwall through a detailed examination of part of St Keverne parish on the Lizard peninsula which combines conventional archaeological and historical data with HLC to interpret and describe the historic landscape of the area. Their study was fairly generalised and intended to answer questions for management and conservation purposes, but a similar technique has been applied more recently in pursuit of more closely defined research objectives. Ann Preston-Jones and Andrew Langdon have been able to map the locations of medieval stone sculpture against a basic HLC 'time-slice' depicting the medieval landscape of St Buryan (Cornwall). They were able to cast new light on the possible extent of St Buryan's medieval sanctuary and the role of sculpture in relation to early medieval land use (Preston-Jones & Langdon 2001). In Somerset, Steve Rippon has used a similar method to help illustrate the development of the landscape of Meare (Rippon 2004b). Such approaches are developed in this book. Using HLC, analyses of different types of data at different scales have been combined in a GIS to create a more comprehensive picture of the way medieval sites fitted into their landscape contexts, and of the relationships between them (see also Turner 2003a, 2003b).

As discussed above, HLC works by identifying and mapping coherent blocks of land that have shared historic land uses. For example, a group of nineteenth-century enclosures or an area of open strip fields might be mapped as individual 'polygons'. The method is particularly useful for medieval landscape studies in areas of 'ancient countryside' where the basic structure of the historic landscape is very old. Much of Cornwall, Devon, western Somerset and parts of Dorset have landscapes that have changed relatively little since the later middle ages (Rackham 1986: 1-5), and if there have been significant alterations, these can often be clearly discerned (e.g. the enclosure of heathland in the eighteenth and nineteenth centuries; Turner 2004a). The simple characterisations presented in the following chapters are divided into three historic landscape character types: medieval farmland, rough ground and woodland. As such they are undoubtedly over-simplifications, and they clearly do not convey the detailed texture of real medieval landscapes. Even so, because the South West is a region of 'ancient countryside' there are good reasons for believing that these HLCs do reflect a fairly accurate picture of the basic structure of the later medieval landscape.

Medieval Farmland

The 'medieval farmland' HLC type represents land that was cultivated in the middle ages, including that which has subsequently gone out of agricultural use. This includes several different types of land use including arable fields, watermeadow, orchards and gardens. The development of medieval fields and crop rotations in the South West is increasingly well-understood (Herring 2006a, 2006b). Whilst the particular form of 'convertible husbandry' practised in the region is known from later medieval documents (Fox 1991), palaeoenvironmental evidence hints that it may have been adopted during the early middle ages (Fyfe 2006) and there is both archaeological and documentary evidence for strip-field farming before the Norman Conquest (Fowler & Thomas 1962). A good example of the latter illustrates the long-term stability of some south-western landscapes. Peter Herring and Della Hooke have published a convincing solution to the late Saxon boundary clause of Trerice in St Dennis (S1019). They suggest that the 'heathfields' mentioned in the boundary clause of this tiny estate were still rough ground in the later nineteenth century (Herring & Hooke 1993). At Trerice there seems to have been been little change in the organisation of the landscape since the charter was written, and Hooke states that 'the enclosing banks of the fields have probably changed little since Anglo-Saxon times' (Hooke 1994a: 68).

Medieval enclosures have been identified by their highly characteristic irregular sinuous boundaries. There are a number of clearly identifiable sub-types relating to date of enclosure and type of land use, though these have not been mapped separately (Herring 1998: 27-8, 78-9). By far the most common fields included in the 'medieval enclosure' category are those derived from open strip fields **(Fig. 4)**. The existing field boundaries result from the enclosure of former open strips and bundles of strips that made up cropping units (Austin et al. 1980; Herring 2006b). Examples of open strip fields survive at Forrabury on the north Cornish coast and at Braunton in Devon (Finberg 1969a). Such survivals are the exception, though, and the vast majority of strip-field systems in Cornwall, Devon, and west Somerset were enclosed in the late medieval or early post-

Fig. 4: Leper fields, Little Torrington. The whole field system was originally enclosed from medieval strip fields, though only two of the characteristic long narrow strip enclosures remain today. Pottery found eroding from their boundary-banks suggests they were enclosed in the thirteenth or fourteenth centuries (source: Devon SMR). In the later nineteenth century there were many other strip enclosures here, but these were destroyed in the twentieth century.

medieval periods (Flatrès 1949; Fox & Padel 1998: lxviii-c; Herring 2006b). It is likely that the 'medieval farmland' character type mapped by the HLCs of these areas corresponds closely to the actual area under cultivation in the later middle ages. Areas of earthwork ridge-and-furrow which probably indicate periodic outfield/rough ground cultivation have also been included in this character type, even though they probably only represent very sporadic use for arable (e.g. on Bodmin Moor: Austin et al. 1989; Fox 1973).

Much of eastern Somerset, Dorset and Wiltshire lies in a zone with a rather different landscape history (Rackham 1986: 1-5). Here open fields may also have been established in the early middle ages, but they surrounded large nucleated villages and commonly remained unenclosed well into the post-medieval period. Even so, map regression analysis combined with HLC makes it possible to identify the areas that were formerly medieval fields, as shown by work at Shapwick in Somerset (Aston 1994b).

Rough Ground

The 'rough ground' HLC type consists of areas that were used predominantly as pastures and fuel-grounds in the medieval period. They were normally unenclosed, or divided only by long sinuous boundaries, some of which were already in existence by the end of the prehistoric period (Johnson & Rose 1994). A good deal of rough ground has survived in the south-western counties from the middle ages without significant alteration. It is typified by modern habitat types such as heath, bracken, gorse, scrub, unimproved grassland and wetlands (Herring 1998: 25). A large amount of land has been taken out of the 'rough ground' type since the middle ages and enclosed for agriculture (Herring 1998: 29; Herring 2004). These enclosures can generally be identified on the basis of their field boundary morphology and in the HLCs presented in this book they have been included in the 'rough ground' type. They are typified by field boundaries that are perfectly straight, having been laid out using post-medieval surveying techniques. Sometimes evidence suggests post-medieval field systems replaced earlier enclosures of medieval type (Turner 2004a: 30). Where this has been identified through archaeological or cartographic evidence the area has been included in the 'medieval farmland' HLC type. Relict prehistoric enclosures cover extensive parts of Bodmin Moor and Dartmoor and also exist in some coastal areas. Unless there is evidence to suggest they have been reused in the middle ages they have been included in the 'rough ground' type (Johnson & Rose 1994; Johns & Herring 1996).

Woodland

Most areas mapped in the 'woodland' HLC type have been derived from the historic map sources. In some cases woodland boundaries with distinctive morphology also indicate the extent of former woodland, particularly in steep-sided valleys. Identification of 'woodland' has also made use of English Nature's inventory of ancient woodland (English Nature 2005), although historic maps were relied on in preference to this source where the two were certainly contradictory.

The characterisations themselves were prepared at a scale of *c.* 1:10,000.[3] The sources for the Cornish case studies included relevant archaeological surveys showing relict field systems (Johnson & Rose 1994; National Mapping Programme data in Cornwall SMR), and all available early estate maps, tithe maps, and historic Ordnance Survey maps (Turner 2003a). These provided a range of sources dating to before the mid-Victorian High Farming period and mid-twentieth-century agricultural intensification, which have significantly altered the countryside in many areas.[4] Other characterisations are based on data from HLC projects sponsored by English Heritage in Somerset (Aldred 2001) and Devon (Turner 2005). It is important to note that the characterisations were all performed without reference to place-names or other types of documentary or settlement evidence (e.g. locations of deserted medieval settlements).

Nevertheless, the HLCs produced for Chapter 4 represent the approximate extent of farmland in the medieval Cornish landscape at the time of the climatic / demographic optimum of the thirteenth / fourteenth centuries (Preston-Jones & Rose 1986: 153; Johnson & Rose 1994: 114).

Finding the Medieval Landscape

The HLCs in this book present an approximation of the medieval landscape's

---

[3] Using ArcInfo and ArcView computer programmes published by the software company ESRI.
[4] For the causes and effects of field boundary loss in the South West over the last two hundred years see e.g. Dymond 1856; Williamson 2002.

structure when arable farming was at its greatest extent, probably in the thirteenth or fourteenth centuries. Nevertheless, this medieval land use pattern is inextricably linked to the historic landscape of the early middle ages. The close relationship between the two periods can be demonstrated by plotting evidence derived independently from other sources, such as place-names, against the HLC. Scholars have shown that Cornish habitative place-name elements (e.g. *tre* and **bod*) normally originated between the sixth and eleventh centuries and that they provide the best available indication of the location of early medieval settlements (Padel 1985). In **Figure 5**, *tre* place-names first recorded during the middle ages are plotted against HLCs of two parts of Cornwall. It is clear from these maps that settlements with names in *tre* occur exclusively within the 'medieval farmland' character type, reflecting its early medieval origins (see also below, Ch. 4, 83-98).

The major difference between the early and later medieval land use patterns appears to be that an expansion of farmland on to former rough ground occurred between the tenth and thirteenth centuries in Cornwall, Devon, Somerset and elsewhere (Johnson & Rose 1994: 114-15; Allan 1994; Rippon 1997: 186-205). In Cornwall this development is characterised by settlements with Cornish topographical names (although these had existed before), and in the east by settlements with English names (e.g. Colliford in St Neot; Austin et al. 1989). The main difference between the model of the medieval landscape presented in this book's HLC maps and the actual early medieval landscape is that *less* ground will have been under cultivation before the tenth century, and it seems very unlikely that any significant areas of early medieval arable are not included in the 'medieval farmland' depicted in them.

Herring has compared the evidence of Domesday Book with the Cornwall HLC results and calculated that approximately 30% of Cornwall was rough ground before the enclosure of heath and moorland that began in earnest in the eighteenth century (Herring 1999b: 20). Rackham has argued from the Domesday data that 33% of the county was rough ground in the eleventh century (Rackham 1986: 335). The HLCs prepared for this book show that 35% of the 300km^2 characterised was rough ground in the middle ages. This suggests the overall quantity of rough ground changed little over the course of the middle ages. The Nature Conservancy Council's survey of ancient woodland also suggested that the distribution of woodland in Domesday Book was broadly similar to that of today's landscape (Rose & Preston-Jones 1995: 52-3; Lister & Walker 1986).

In conclusion, HLC can provide a model for the structure of the historic landscape at different times in the past. It is a particularly effective tool for studying the landscapes of regions like south-west England where post-medieval changes have been relatively slight. The strength of HLC maps is that they describe the whole landscape, and present a relatively complete framework within which data from other sources can be analysed in greater depth. They are a valuable tool for archaeologists who want to analyse information about the landscape in its historical and geographical contexts.

Scales of Analysis

Spatial Scales

In common with much recent research in landscape history, the evidence used in

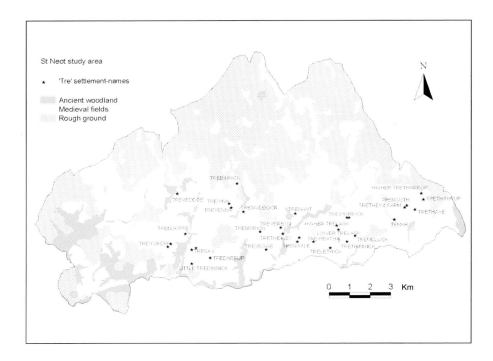

Fig. 5: 'Historic Landscape Characterisation' and *tre* place-names first recorded before AD 1550 in two Cornish study areas, around St Neot and the southern fringes of Bodmin Moor (top) and around Tintagel (bottom).

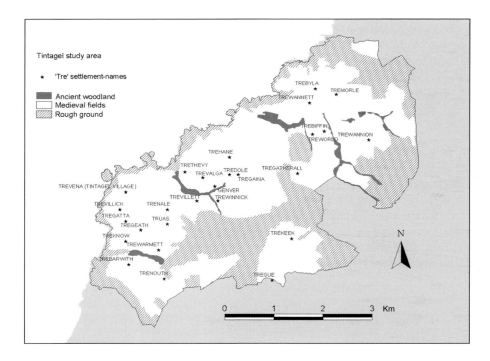

this book is drawn from a wide range of different sources. However, different sources can supply very different categories of evidence, which are not necessarily immediately comparable with each other at the same. Furthermore, by using evidence at only one scale, relationships which might have been apparent at another scale can be lost.

Archaeological evidence often comes in the form of point data. A south-western English example is provided by the sites of early medieval inscribed stones. The locations of these monuments have been plotted at a regional level by Thomas (1994) as part of his discussion of the putative settlement in the South West by incomers from Wales in the fifth and sixth centuries AD. Thomas develops an argument using linguistic evidence from the inscriptions and from his proposed typologies of the stones to suggest progressive immigrant settlement from the north coast southwards. Whilst this kind of 'cartographic' view is useful on a regional scale (Petts 1998: 81), it results in 'flat maps' which do not give much weight to local contexts. The relationships of the stones to local communications routes or local land use are not visible at the regional level and are therefore not discussed, even though the position of the stones in relation to their local context is likely to be crucial to their understanding. The distribution of settlements provides another example. Even though for certain research questions this could be combatted by the use of GIS (e.g. distance to nearest neighbour analysis), other important relationships between individual sites could remain unclear or hard to appreciate.

Investigating a small area in very great detail is an approach which can provide a very thorough understanding of the subtleties of landscape development in a particular area, and can be a powerful tool in pursuit of research questions. However, detailed local studies run the risk of only illuminating their own specific circumstances if no attempt is made to relate their results to wider patterns and interpretations. It can sometimes be difficult to relate detailed information won at the local level to wider patterns of land use or to regional and national research questions. Another difficulty, particularly in the case of excavations, is that sites of local significance can appear much more important than they really are in the absence of suitable comparanda at the regional level (Gwithian site GM/1 is perhaps an example: Thomas 1968a).

It is important to ensure that data are analysed at an appropriate scale so that that the perspectives which emerge from landscape research are not skewed either by heavily weighted discussion of individual sites or by under-appreciated local detail. There is no 'correct' scale of historical analysis, and the right scale depends on the research questions being addressed (Hodder 1986: 134; Thomas 1996: 95-8). In this book different sorts of data will be discussed at different scales according to the relationships under investigation.

Temporal Scales

Different types of evidence are not only suitable for analysis at different geographical scales, but also at different temporal scales. Information about some elements of the landscape may be available over very long periods of time, whereas other types of evidence may only be available over relatively short periods. Phenomena that develop over different time-scales may be linked by important relationships.

All these different phenomena may be relevant to the study of social and political structures, and they are also likely to have complicated interrelationships. On the one hand, it is possible to analyse phenomena such as Cornish medieval settlement patterns over relatively long periods of time: in this case it might be appropriate to consider changes over a thousand years or more (see Chapter 4). On the other hand, the tradition of early medieval stone crosses with distinctive 'Hiberno-Saxon' ornament had a much shorter period of development in the region—perhaps only from the ninth to the eleventh centuries (Preston-Jones & Okasha 1997). The landscape context of this sculpture can be studied over a relatively short period (see Chapter 7). Nevertheless, the role of these monuments in society is likely to have been related to their position in the landscape, and this was almost certainly related to contemporary patterns of settlement and land use. Comparing the distribution of stone crosses to settlements or ecclesiastical sites may help illuminate not only the role of stones (and settlements or churches) in society, but also the sculptors' society's relationship to past settlement and land use (see Darvill 1997: 78). Relatively short-lived phenomena can owe their forms and meanings to long-term developments.

The concepts of different time-scales that are particularly associated with the *Annales* tradition such as *longue durée, conjoncture* and *l'histoire événementielle* are clearly relevant to these considerations (Braudel 1972; Knapp 1992a; Morris 2000: 4). However, events at one temporal scale should not be used to explain processes which occurred at other scales in a deterministic way. Nor should this tripartite division of temporal scales be seen as *Annalisme's* most important contribution to a contextual methodology, as some archaeologists have implied (Bintliff 1991). Instead, it must be recognised that different aspects of the landscape and human intervention in the landscape will affect each other in different ways at different times according to context.

Making Use of the Data

This chapter has argued that landscape archaeologists should employ the greatest possible range of evidence in pursuit of their research questions, and that texts, artefacts, images and landscapes can be analysed within the same general framework (Moreland 1992, 1998). Approaches that use archaeology or history to fill in the gaps in the other sources are not suitable for landscape archaeology, since they risk ignoring the recursive nature of the data, privileging one source over another, or ignoring pieces of evidence from one discipline that do not fit conveniently into another discipline's gaps (see e.g. Small 1999: 122-3; Kepecs 1997a, 1997b). As Ian Morris has argued, in order to grasp the subtle relations between different sources, it is necessary to make the fullest investigation of detailed contexts: 'we must examine verbal and nonverbal languages together, comprehensively, in contextual detail, to identify cleavages which often have little to do with the medium through which people expressed them' (Morris 2000: 27).[5]

Comprehensively integrating information from different sources is certainly compatible with the traditions of *Annales* history and the needs of landscape archaeology, which base their interpretations on 'thick description' of detailed contexts. This is surely the most appropriate method for studying the structures

---

[5] Similar views are expressed by M. Johnson 1999: 32-3; Hall 1999: 202; Carver 2002a.

and patterns of social life in the early medieval South West. In addition, it provides a way for the new contexts developed through detailed case-studies of 'localised' data to be analysed in relation to broader historical themes. In this way the interplay between agriculture and production, elite centres and social control, and the religious ideology of ecclesiastical sites will be investigated in the following chapters through the spatial patterning of successive early medieval landscapes.

3

The location and form of early churches in south-west Britain

This chapter explores the location and form of early ecclesiastical sites, and investigates the spatial and administrative relationships between churches and royal centres. As in the following chapters, the emphasis falls on Cornwall and the four modern counties that now encompass the western parts of early medieval Wessex: Devon, Somerset, Dorset and Wiltshire.

The county of Cornwall provides a coherent area for study, both in terms of its physical geography and its cultural history. The analysis in this chapter uses a list of likely early medieval monastic sites based on evidence from tenth-century charter material and Domesday Book compiled by Lynette Olson (1989). The fourteen collegiate churches recorded in Domesday Book and the *Inquisitio Geldi* were distinctively different from other churches in Cornwall in the late eleventh century and form a highly unusual group in Domesday Book. Their privileges (geld-free estates) and continuing collegiate status set them apart from most of the old minster churches of Wessex and England and suggest that they had maintained their high status for much longer (Padel 2002: 328). Like St Kew, mentioned in the *Vita Prima Sancti Samsonis* (Fawtier 1912; Flobert 1997; Olson 1989), some of the churches must certainly have their origins in the seventh century or even earlier as monastic communities. Nevertheless, it is not certain that all did and there is little historical or archaeological evidence from any of these sites dating to before the ninth century.

Olson's identifications have generally been accepted in this book, with the possible exceptions of St Carroc, St Anthony-in-Roseland and Paul (which she regards as very uncertain cases; Olson 1989: 105). In addition, it is highly likely that there had been other similar churches that lost their superior status before the compilation of Domesday Book, and that the list of early monasteries in Cornwall remains incomplete. For example, Charles Thomas has suggested, on the basis of archaeological evidence for fifth/sixth-century activity, that Phillack was an early ecclesiastical centre (1973, 1994). Whilst the status of many churches may have varied over time, the continuing high status of Phillack in the later pre-Conquest period is also suggested by surviving sculpture and the large burial ground which extends well beyond the modern graveyard (Preston-Jones & Okasha 1997; Petts 2001). In the later middle ages it was also the mother church of nearby Gwithian, where a chapel of possible pre-Conquest date was recorded in the nineteenth century (Thomas 1958). There is no written evidence to suggest monastic status at late Saxon Phillack, but it seems likely that it had been a significant early foundation. Likewise, the churches of St Matheriana at Minster and Tintagel are not discussed by Olson, presumably because the former was probably not a particularly early foundation and neither have written evidence for an ecclesiastical community in the late Saxon period. However, both Susan Pearce (1978: 106-8) and Charles Thomas (1993: 109-13) have suggested Minster was a community founded in the ninth or tenth centuries. For the purposes of the current discussion, both Phillack and Minster (with Tintagel) have been added to the list of probable ecclesiastical communities in early medieval Cornwall **(Table 1; Fig. 6)**.

Compared to Cornwall, western Wessex is a rather more artificial choice of study area. Its political history as part of the same unit only began with the conquests of the Gewissan royal house from around the beginning of the seventh century (Yorke 1995: 6-7), and there are many differences in topography, geology and cultural history across the area. The region did not all come under Anglo-Saxon political control at the same time, and at the beginning of the period under consideration here (from the later fifth century onwards) only a small part of eastern Wiltshire and perhaps a little of Dorset were subject to significant Anglo-

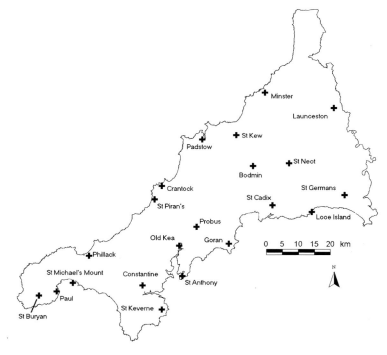

Fig 6: Possible early monasteries in Cornwall (based on Olson 1989, with additions).

Saxon cultural influence, and western Devon may not have been incorporated into the kingdom of Wessex until the eighth century (Finberg 1953a). Nevertheless, certain trends can be identified across the four counties of western Wessex. Many of the distinctive characteristics of the middle Saxon landscape were not formed until the seventh century and after, and as such they were profoundly influenced by ecclesiastical culture[1]. It will therefore be useful to characterise the religious landscape in this area and compare 'Anglo-Saxon' practice with neighbouring 'Celtic' Cornwall.

This book's aim is not to make 'new' discoveries of early minsters in Wessex, but to investigate the roles of churches in the landscape. The identifications of important churches therefore generally follow those of scholars who have recently worked on the individual counties. These include Nicholas Orme (1996a) for Devon **(Fig. 7)**, Teresa Hall (2000) for Dorset **(Fig. 8)**, Mick Aston (1986) and Michael Costen (1992b) for Somerset, and Jonathan Pitt (1999) for Wiltshire **(Fig. 9)**.

For the purposes of the following discussion, it has been assumed in all but a few

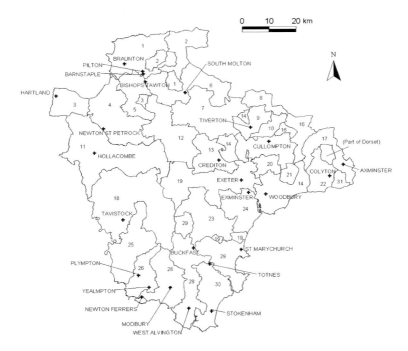

Fig. 7: Late Saxon hundreds and important early medieval churches in Devon (after Thorn & Thorn 1985).

Devon hundreds: *1. Braunton; 2. Shirwell; 3. Hartland; 4. Shebbear; 5. Fremington; 6. South Molton; 7. Witheridge; 8. Bampton; 9. Tiverton; 10. Halberton; 11. Black Torrington; 12. North Tawton; 13. Crediton; 14. Budleigh; 15. Hayridge; 16. Hemyock; 17. Axminster; 18. Lifton; 19. Wonford; 20. Cliston; 21. Ottery St Mary; 22. Colyton; 23. Teignbridge; 24. Exminster; 25. Roborough; 26. Plympton; 27. Ermington; 28. Stanborough; 29. Haytor; 30. Coleridge; 31. Axmouth.*

---

[1] This is discussed in Chapters 4 to 6.

Name	Likelihood of superior early medieval status	Grid ref. (NGR)	Location	Latest possible century of origin	Category of Evidence	Main reference
St Anthony	Certain	SW 85483203	Valley bottom	10th	Documentary	Olson 1989
Bodmin	Certain	SX 07306703	Valley bottom	10th	Documentary	Olson 1989
St Buryan	Certain	SW 40922572	Hilltop	10th	Documentary/extant	Olson 1989
St Cadix	Possible	SX 13465459	Valley bottom	11th	Documentary	Olson 1989
Constantine	Certain	SW 73112907	Hilltop	10th	Documentary	Olson 1989
Crantock	Certain	SW 79056056	Valley side	11th	Documentary	Olson 1989, Olson 1982
St Germans	Certain	SX 35935775	Valley side	10th	Documentary	Ralegh Radford 1973-6; Olson & Preston-Jones 1998/9
Goran	Probable	SW 99954231	Valley head	11th	Documentary	Olson 1989
Old Kea	Certain	SW 84434172	Valley bottom	11th	Documentary	Olson 1989
St Keverne	Certain	SW 79122130	Hill slope	10th	Documentary	Olson 1989
St Kew	Certain	SX 02167688	Valley bottom	10th	Documentary	Olson 1989
Launceston	Certain	SX 32488570	Hill slope	11th	Documentary	Olson 1989
Looe Island	Probable	SX 25055218	Island	10th	Documentary	Olson 1989
St Michael's Mount	Certain	SW 51452983	Island	10th	Documentary	Olson 1989
Minster	Certain	SX 11009050	Valley head	11th	Extant	Pearce 1978; Thomas 1993
St Neot	Certain	SX 18616786	Valley side	9th	Extant/documentary	Olson 1989
Padstow	Certain	SW 91577541	Valley bottom	10th	Documentary	Olson 1989
Paul	Possible	SW 46452708	Hillslope	11th	Documentary	Olson 1989
St Pirans	Certain	SW 76855639	Dunes	10th	Documentary/extant	Olson 1989
Phillack	Probable	SW 56533842	Dunes	(6th)/10th	(Excavated)/documentary	Thomas 1973; Pearce 1978
Probus	Certain	SW 89904772	Valley head	10th	Documentary	Olson 1989
Tintagel	Probable	SX 05058845	Plateau	(6th)/10th	(Excavated)/excavated	Nowakowski & Thomas 1992

Table 1: Likely major early medieval ecclesiastical communities in Cornwall.

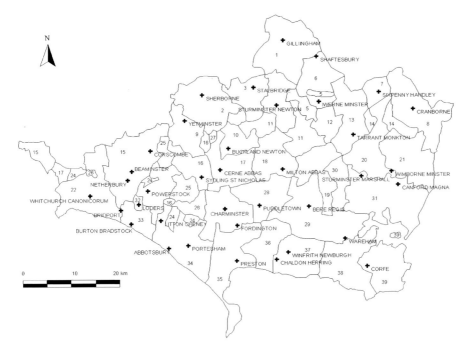

Fig. 8: Late Saxon hundreds and important early churches in Dorset (after
Hall 2000 and Thorn & Thorn 1983).

Dorset hundreds: *1. Gillingham; 2. Sherborne; 3. Brunsell; 4. Newton; 5. Farrington;
6. Sixpenny; 7. Handley; 8. Alvredesberge; 9. Yetminster; 10. Buckland; 11. Hundesburge;
12. Pimperne; 13. Langeburge; 14. Knowlton; 15. Beaminster; 16. Modbury; 17. Stana;
18. Hilton; 19. Combsditch; 20. Badbury; 21. Canendone; 22. Whitchurch; 23. Redhove;
24. Eggardon; 25. Tollerford; 26. Frampton; 27. Dorchester; 28. Puddletown; 29. Bere Regis;
30. Charborough; 31. Cogdean; 32. Loders; 33. Goderthorne; 34. Uggescombe;
35. Cullifordtree; 36. Chilbury; 37. Winfrith; 38. Hasler; 39. Ailwood.*

cases that the early medieval church stood on the same site as its later medieval
successor. In a few cases archaeological work has shown that earlier churches were
succeeded by later ones on different sites. At Shapwick (Somerset), for example, the
original church site some 650m east of the present village was not abandoned until
perhaps the fourteenth century (Aston & Gerrard 1999). At Keynsham (Somerset),
a substantial amount of Anglo-Saxon sculpture has come from the area of the later
medieval abbey, suggesting that the early medieval church was here rather than on
the site of the present parish church (Lowe 1987). It is therefore appropriate to
sound a note of caution, and there may be small errors in the exact geographical
identification of some of the church sites considered in this book. In general,
though, analysis of standing remains and excavations have shown that it was normal
for medieval churches to replace pre-Conquest minsters on the same sites.[2]

[2] e.g. Britford (Wiltshire: Taylor & Taylor 1965: 105-108) Glastonbury (Somerset: Rahtz 1993);
Wells (Somerset: Rodwell 1982; 2001); Exeter (Devon: Henderson & Bidwell 1982); Sherborne
(Dorset: Gibb 1975); Wareham (Dorset: Taylor & Taylor 1965); Buckfastleigh (Devon: Reynolds
& Turner 2003).

Fig. 9: Late Saxon hundreds and important early churches in Wiltshire
          (after Reynolds 1999 and Thorn & Thorn 1979b).
Wiltshire Hundreds: *1. Highworth; 2. Scipe; 3. Staple; 4. Cricklade; 5. Malmesbury;
5a. Chedglow; 5b. Startley; 6. Dunlow; 7. Thorngrove; 8. Chippenham; 9. Bradford;
10. Melksham; 11. Whorwellsdown; 12. Westbury; 13. Warminster; 14. Heytesbury; 15. Mere;
16. Dunworth; 17. Chalke; 18. Cawdon; 19. Cadworth; 20. Branch; 21. Dole;
22. Rowborough Regis; 23. Rowborough; 24. Cannings; 25. Calne; 26. Kingsbridge;
27. Blackgrove; 28. Thornhill; 29. Ramsbury; 30. Selkley; 31. Studfold; 32. Swanborough;
33. Elstub; 34. Kinwardstone; 35. Amesbury; 36. Underditch; 37. Alderbury; 38. Frustfield;
                    39. Downton; 40. Damerham.*

The Physical Locations of Early Churches

Cornwall

Cornwall is notable today for its coastline, much of which is dominated by
spectacular cliffs. On the south coast these are broken by the drowned estuaries of
rivers like the Fal, Fowey and Tamar; on the north coast, where the cliffs are most
dramatic, the wide sandy mouth of the Camel provides the only substantial
anchorage for boats between Newquay in Cornwall and Barnstaple in Devon. Also
characteristic of the coast south west of Padstow are the large areas of wind-blown
dunes that border the sea shore at Perran Bay and St Ives Bay, and now cover earlier
farms, fields and churches (e.g. Thomas 1958). Moving inland, the landscape of
Cornwall, and much of southern and western Devon, is dominated by rolling hills
and deeply incised valleys **(Plate 14b)**. The valleys cut through Devonian rocks
including sedimentary slates, siltstones, gritstones, sandstones and limestones

(Edmonds et al. 1975: 21-33). Valley bottoms are normally narrow, and lack the broad floodplains so common in central Wessex. Valley sides are mostly convex in section, so that valley bottoms cannot normally be seen from hilltops, and vice versa. The highest ground is in the eastern and northern part of the county, where Brown Willy on Bodmin Moor rises to 417m above sea level. Bodmin Moor and the other granite masses of Hensbarrow, Carnmenellis, Penwith and the Scilly Isles are roughly aligned in a row leading westwards which begins with Dartmoor in Devon (ibid. 43-51). In some areas variations in the local geology mean that there are less steeply incised plateaux and broader, shallower valleys, for example in north Cornwall around St Kew and above cliffs on the north coast around Newquay. In general, however, the county is rolling hill country.

The differences between the valley sides and the hilltops are heightened by varying historic land uses. Most commonly it is woodland, meadow and pasture that occur on the steeper, lower valley slopes, with arable land on gentler hill slopes above. Rough pasture is characteristic of the moors, ridges and sea-clifftops (Herring 1998). With the exception of parts of the dunes, the work of many generations has helped form Cornwall's soils. Even the acidic podsols of the uplands are a result of human action: they began to replace earlier brown soils around eight thousand years ago as a result of Mesolithic tree-clearance (Caseldine 1999: 29). Bronze Age and late medieval fields on the high moors show that virtually all areas can be farmed with sufficient effort, and it is possible that the relatively minor climatic variations of the last five thousand years have had little effect on people's ability to support themselves from the land anywhere in Cornwall (Caseldine 1999: 32; see also Caseldine & Hatton 1994: 44-45).

Nevertheless, there have been variations in the area exploited for cultivation over the last three thousand years, with some important changes occurring in the first millennium AD. The reasons for this are likely to have been complicated, and not to have resulted from one single factor, such as climatic change or disease among the human population. The newly introduced Christian religion made a major contribution to the way the early medieval landscape was restructured. These points are considered in greater detail in Chapter 4.

Cornwall has an extremely varied countryside, which can often seem intimate and secluded, particularly when viewed from within the steep narrow valleys. In this sense it is quite different to most regions of southern and eastern England, where broader valleys tend to create a more open countryside. In the popular imagination this sense of difference is linked to the 'Celtic' people who lived in the west, and certainly to their churchmen. Famous examples such as Skellig Michael (Co. Kerry, Ireland) have led to suggestions that isolated hilltop and island sites were the classic locations for monasteries in the 'Celtic' west (Thomas 1971b: 94-5; Aston 2000a: 31-41). Can such a pattern be detected in the Cornish evidence?

Of around twenty likely early medieval monasteries in Cornwall, two are located on hilltops or ridges and two on islands. The church at St Buryan, whose community was documented in the tenth century (S450) and almost certainly existed earlier (Thomas 1988), stands on top of a ridge at 123m above OD.[3] Whilst the site is prominent, it is not spectacular. Hills of similar height rise all

---

[3] OD stands for 'Ordnance Datum', i.e. mean sea level as defined by the Ordnance Survey of Great Britain. All the heights in this book are given in metres above OD.

Fig. 10: A nineteenth-century facsimile by G.F. Storm of an illustration from the late Saxon Lanalet Pontifical showing the consecration of a church. Although connected with St Germans in south-east Cornwall, the Pontifical was probably produced in western Wessex, perhaps at Wells (Gage 1834: facing p.251).

around, and just over 3km to the north there are several that rise much higher. These include the much steeper summits of Carn Brea (198m) and Bartiney Downs (224m), both of which are topped by prehistoric enclosures. The church at Constantine, a possible monastic site (Olson 1989: 90), also stands on a ridge (90m), although in this case the valley sides are steeper than at St Buryan. Nevertheless, higher hills rise within a short distance to the west and the north. As the ridge where the church is sited continues south it does not descend significantly for some 600m. If a dominant hilltop position had been the most important factor behind the location of the church, there are many more impressive sites in the vicinity that could have been selected.

The church at Bodmin may have become the seat of a Cornish bishop for a period in the early middle ages, and was the greatest Cornish ecclesiastical landholder at Domesday. It is possible that the ecclesiastical centre here originated on a hilltop site and moved down later into the neighbouring valley (ibid. 66-78). The most obvious comparison is with the probable pre-Saxon foundation at Glastonbury in Somerset. Here, post-Roman activity on Glastonbury Tor was indicated by the presence of imported Mediterranean pottery and associated features, and the site also appears to have functioned as a hermitage in the late Saxon period (Rahtz 1971, 1991). At Glastonbury, however, the occupation of the main Abbey site on lower ground c.1km to the west probably originated around the same time or shortly after that on the Tor **(Plates 9a, 9b)**. At Bodmin, Olson suggests the establishment in the valley was founded at some point after AD 800 as a successor to St Petroc's earlier centre at Padstow. If there was an earlier ecclesiastical settlement near Bodmin, it may have been some sort of minor centre (e.g. a hermitage) rather than a major monastic site (Olson 1989: 53-6). It has been suggested that the fifteenth-century Berry Tower may be the last vestige of such a complex. It stands on the ridge to the north of the medieval church, and was originally part of a chapel of the Holy Rood. However, archaeological evidence has not yet been recovered in support of early medieval occupation here (Adams 1959-61). At St Stephen's, Launceston, the church is sited in a prominent position just above the break of slope on the north side of the valley of the River Kensey. As at Bodmin, however, scholars have suggested Launceston may be a relatively late foundation, perhaps replacing an earlier community dedicated to St Padern at South Petherwin (Finberg 1964b: 178-9); its location may therefore not be typical of the earliest Cornish churches.

Early ecclesiastical sites on islands in the sea are also considered typical of the 'Celtic' west, although the evidence from Cornwall is ambiguous in this respect too. Sites at both Looe Island and St Michael's Mount have produced small quantities of imported Mediterranean pottery of the fifth to seventh centuries. At Looe Island, one sherd of B-ware suggests occupation in the post-Roman period (Thomas 1981a). There was a chapel of St Michael here in the later middle ages, but also a medieval chapel and associated buildings on the mainland opposite (Picken 1982-6; Todd 1983). These were excavated in the 1930s and seem to have produced no early medieval finds (Olson & O'Mahoney 1994). The documentary sources do not help clarify which site should be regarded as the earlier. Whilst it may have been the island chapel, it is important to note that at Tintagel, where substantial late Antique activity has been demonstrated by archaeology, the main early religious focus appears to have been on the mainland cliffs where the present parish church now stands, opposite the 'Island' promontory (see below, Ch. 3, pp. 54-6). Looe Island may have been either a secular or a religious centre in its earliest phases and more archaeological work is required to clarify its nature. The same is true of the other Cornish island monastery, St Michael's Mount **(Fig. 11)**. Here, an ecclesiastical community probably existed before the Norman conquest (Olson 1989: 89-90), and a charter (of doubtful authenticity) suggests it could have been granted to Mont St Michel in Normandy as early as the reign of Edward the Confessor (S1061). Like Looe Island, a limited amount of imported Mediterranean pottery has been recovered from the site (Thorpe 2000; Dark 2000: 167), and the nature of the earliest medieval occupation remains unclear. Many scholars presently favour an interpretation that sees the Mount as a secular stronghold which only became predominately ecclesiastical in the tenth or eleventh centuries (Herring 1993: 62-6; Herring 2000: 120-4).

So of about twenty likely early monasteries, only four or five had churches located on an island or hilltop. In these cases the nature of the earliest occupation, where any evidence of it survives, does not make it clear that they were originally ecclesiastical centres rather than secular ones.

The remaining sites occupy a variety of locations **(Table 2)**. Four are located on hillslopes, above the break of slope but below the ridge line (though the church at Paul is located quite low down in its valley). The other major churches all occupy positions on low ground or well within valleys. St Piran's now lies buried beneath the dunes of Penhale Sands, but before this inundation, it may have stood in an area of low-lying coastal fields, perhaps similar to those excavated at Gwithian (Fowler & Thomas 1962). St Germans, St Neot and Crantock stand a short distance above their valley bottoms, and Minster is secreted at the head of a side valley, now completely hidden from view by trees. St Kew, the church with the earliest reliable pre-Conquest documentary evidence (Olson 1989), is situated in a valley-bottom close to a small river, as is Bodmin. This shows that the early Cornish religious communities did not always locate their centres on remote hilltop or island sites, but instead chose a range of locations, most commonly in valleys. Such locations were common all over western Britain and Ireland, where it is possible that certain church names refer to valley-bottom land first settled by monks (Hurley 1982: 307). Far from being remote, the early Cornish monasteries were located at the heart of contemporary patterns of settlement and agriculture.[4]

Wessex

The four counties of western Wessex cover a much greater area than Cornwall and between them present a highly varied geology and topography. Some parts of the region, especially Devon west of the River Exe, are rather similar to much of east Cornwall, with rolling hills and narrow valleys in the lowlands and the great granite mass of Dartmoor dominating the centre. To the east, most of Somerset, Dorset and Wiltshire are quite different, and there are several distinctive sub-regions. Bordering the Bristol Channel, for instance, is the low-lying former marshland of the Somerset Levels. Here islands of solid ground such as those once occupied by the monks of Glastonbury, Muchelney and Athelney have provided the main foci for settlement since prehistory. In the east and south of the region, extensive chalk downlands dominate the countryside, cut by the occasional valleys of major rivers like the Wiltshire Avon. In contrast, the clay vales of north Wiltshire and Dorset are low-lying and topographically gentler landscapes crossed by many small streams, providing the 'cheese' country to the downlands' 'chalk'. Other areas like the

Hilltop/ island in sea	Hill slope	Valley side/head	Valley bottom/ dunes
St Buryan	St Keverne	St Neot	St Kew
Constantine	Launceston	St Germans	Padstow
St Michael's Mount	*Paul*	Minster	St Pirans
Looe Island	Probus	Crantock	*St Anthony*
			Bodmin
			Old Kea
			St Cadix
			Phillack

Table 2: Locations of the churches of Cornish ecclesiastical communities in the later pre-Conquest period (italics indicate sites of particularly doubtful status; Olson 1989: 105).

[4] This subject will be returned to in Chapter 4.

Fig 11: St Michael's Mount, Cornwall. [Photo: Steve Hartgroves/Historic Environment Service, Cornwall County Council.]

Blackdown Hills, the Dorset heaths, and the Mendips all comprise distinctive sub-regions. As in Cornwall, the history of land use in the different regions of Wessex is long and complex, and the area under cultivation in places such as the Levels or the Downs has varied greatly over the last three thousand years (Rippon 1997; McOmish *et al.* 2002). Unifying trends are hard to identify in such diverse physical landscapes. For the purposes of this discussion, the principal differences between the topographies of Wessex and Cornwall are perhaps that Wessex tends to have more open landscapes, with much broader, shallower valleys and more accessible valley bottoms.

The location of early churches in England has been considered by John Blair, who has argued that early religious communities in many parts of Western Europe shared similar locations:

> The summits or shoulders of low hills and promontories, islands in marshy floodplains and headlands in the bends of rivers or on the sea-coast...
>
> (Blair 1992: 227)

He notes that there was a monastic dimension to such locations which is perhaps to be related to a sense of separateness on the part of monastic communities (Blair 1996b: 10). It is true that many prominent early churches are in 'commanding locations' (Blair 2005: 194), including famous churches such as Breedon (Leicestershire), Brixworth (Northamptonshire) and Tynemouth (Northumberland).

Drawing on his analysis of Wessex churches, Patrick Hase has called for a kingdom-by-kingdom approach (1994: 54). He prefers an ecological explanation for church location to an ideological one, noting that the majority of Wessex minsters were sited close to watercourses:

The reason for this overwhelming preference for sites close to water is that these are, in a chalk country, the optimum sites for modern agriculture and settlement.

(Hase 1994: 58)

According to Hase, early religious communities in Wessex were located within the best agricultural land rather than in positions which gave them a physical prominence.

Analysis of the sites of all the important early medieval churches of Wessex shows that they were generally located close to the bottoms of valleys, including the vast majority of sites with evidence for early foundations **(Table 3)**. Numerous sites in Wessex are both very close to water and also occupy low islands or hillocks, even though they are surrounded by higher and steeper hills on either side of the river floodplain, making them clearly visible from many points in the surrounding landscape.[5]

Valley bottom or island in marsh	Valley head	Hill slope	Hill top or spur
Padstow	Doulting	Glastonbury	Exeter
St Kew			Shaftesbury
Axminster			Malmesbury
Crediton			(Glastonbury)
Plympton			
Beaminster			
Cranborne			
Gillingham			
Iwerne Minster			
Sherborne			
Sturminster Marshall			
Wareham			
Whitchurch Canonicorum			
Wimborne			
Muchelney			
Bath			
Athelney			
Taunton			
Wells			
Banwell			
Cheddar			
Congresbury			
Damerham			
Bradford on Avon			
Britford			
Tisbury			
Ramsbury			

Table 3: Locations of major churches with reliable evidence for foundation in the ninth century or earlier.

[5] e.g. Britford (Wilts); Chippenham (Wilts); Wareham (Dorset); Puddletown (Dorset); Sturminster Newton (Dorset); Crewkerne (Somerset); Cullompton (Devon); Exminster (Devon); for numerous further examples from the Thames valley see Blair 1996b.

Study of church sites by county shows that valley-bottom locations are most common in Wiltshire and central Wessex, and that they become increasingly less common further west **(Table 4)**. In the Wessex heartlands, ecclesiastical centres are characteristically on the banks of rivers, or on the edges of their floodplains. In very many cases, the valley sides rise up above the churches, making their valley-bottom locations quite marked **(see Fig. 12)**. Even at sites in this region where churches stand on the valley sides, they are not often far from the valley floor and are usually not more than a short way up the hillside (e.g. Buckland Newton (Dorset); Sydling St Nicholas (Dorset); Axminster (Devon)). This suggests that physical domination of the surrounding landscape through an elevated position was not the general rule in Wessex, and only a small minority of churches in the region occupy such sites (see Corcos 2001). Instead, churches occupied central positions in valleys, commonly raised just above the level of the floodplain, and visible to people travelling along routeways such as rivers or ridge lines.

Locations on hilltops or ridges are rather more common in the far south-west than in the Wessex heartlands of Wiltshire and Dorset. As already discussed, however, the physical topography of the western part of the Cornubian peninsula is different to that of south-central England: the steep, narrow valleys common in Cornwall and western Devon contrast with the more open landscapes found in much of Wessex. Nevertheless, there are still more early churches in valley bottoms and other low-lying places than any other kind of location, even in Cornwall.

In this sense, the location of churches in both Cornwall and Wessex was different to that of many of the high-status centres of the preceding post-Roman centuries, when prehistoric hillforts had been reoccupied in many parts of the South West.[6] The foundation of churches in the valleys suggests they were part of a new pattern of landscape organisation which is also typified by many middle

	Valley bottom	**Valley side/ valley head**	**Hill slope**	**Hilltop/ridge/ promontory**
(of all sites)	(59%)	(15%)	(10%)	(17%)
Wiltshire	79%	6%	6%	9%
Somerset	63%[1]	17%	8%	11%
Dorset	60%	24%	8%	8%
Devon	45%	15%	11%	29%
Cornwall	36%[2]	23%	18%	23%[3]

[1] Includes sites on low islands in marshland
[2] Includes sites amid sand dunes
[3] Includes sites on islands in the sea
(Figures are approximate since identifications of minster churches remain provisional)

Table 4: Physical locations of ecclesiastical centres.

[6] e.g. Chûn Castle (Cornwall: Thomas 1956); Cadbury Congresbury and South Cadbury (Somerset: Rahtz et al. 1992; Alcock 1995); High Peak and perhaps Raddon (Devon: Pollard 1966; Gent & Quinnell 1999a).

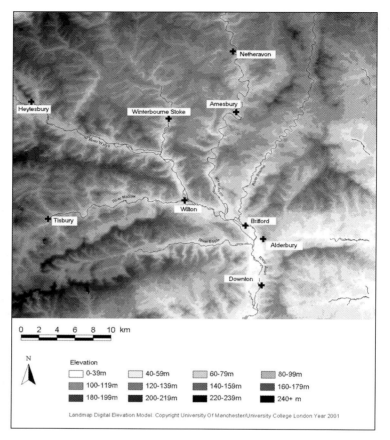

Fig 12: The valley-bottom locations of important early medieval churches
in south-east Wiltshire.

Saxon settlement sites in Wessex. Various factors might have affected the location
of churches and these observations on physical geography need to be considered
alongside churches' relationships to other elements of the landscape including
secular settlements of all kinds and contemporary estates and administrative
structures.[7] Evidence considered in the following sections and chapters suggests
that churches and Christian ideologies were at the very heart of the restructuring
that took place in the early medieval landscape.

The Form of Early Ecclesiastical Centres

Cornwall

Little is presently known about the physical layout of Cornwall's early medieval
ecclesiastical communities, either from survey or excavation. Documentary
sources suggest that more than one saint was probably venerated at many sites,
indicating that more than one church or altar may have existed at each centre. For
example, the original dedication of St Kew was to Docco, as recorded in the *First*

---

[7] On the value of integrating so-called 'mental' and 'material' landscapes, see Bradley 2000b.

Life of St Samson (Olson 1989), but Kew (earlier Cywa) was co-patron by the mid-tenth century (S810; **Plate 14a**). Kew may originally have been patron of a subsidiary chapel within the monastery that was later moved into the parish church (Hooke 1994a: 37). At St Neot, an otherwise unknown St Gueriir may have been venerated in the ninth century and before (Orme 1996a; Keynes & Lapidge 1983: 254-5). St Guron may have been at Bodmin before being joined by St Petroc's cult, and the twelfth-century *Life of St Petroc* maintains a tradition that Padstow was home of St Gwethenek before St Petroc (perhaps also indicated by the Domesday Book name-form *Lanwenehoc*: Thorn & Thorn 1979a: 4,4; Orme 1996a: 109; Olson 1989: 58). However, whilst dedications indicate the name(s) of the saint(s) venerated, they do not necessarily date to the time when the church was first founded.

It is possible that there was more than one church at important ecclesiastical centres in the early middle ages. Though there is little hard evidence outside Ireland, this seems to have been a common arrangement at monasteries in Wales, Scotland and other parts of the British Isles (Petts & Turner, forthcoming). Early chapel sites or possibly hermitages in the South West with multiple churches include St Helen's, Scilly and perhaps St Levan; they may have been modelled on larger-scale complexes at monastic sites (O'Neil 1964; Ratcliffe 1994; Cornwall SMR). In the later medieval period several of the earlier monasteries had subsidiary chapels within their graveyards which could have perpetuated the sites of earlier structures. These include Crantock **(Fig. 13)**, Probus, and St Kew (Olson 1982; Cornwall SMR). The excavators of a probable late pre-Conquest building discovered in the graveyard at Tintagel have claimed that it is the earlier incarnation of the parish church (Nowakowski & Thomas 1992). However, churches were most commonly rebuilt on the same site as their predecessors (Blair 1996a: 13-18), and the standing Norman structure at Tintagel may have succeeded a pre-Conquest building. If so, the foundations excavated by Nowakowski and Thomas may relate to a subsidiary chapel, or another building that was part of the ecclesiastical complex.

None of the churches belonging to the earliest monasteries have been excavated or identified as standing fabric. Examples from the later pre-Conquest period include St Piran's Oratory, a small rectangular structure now buried beneath the sands of Perran Bay, which perhaps belongs to the tenth century (Todd 1987: 293). Charles Thomas has suggested that the chancel of St Matheriana's church at Minster preserves the fabric of a small church dating to AD *c*.1000. It is of similar dimensions to the structure excavated nearby at St Matheriana's other church, Tintagel (Thomas 1993: 109).

Although there is presently little evidence that field cemeteries were normally enclosed before the eighth or ninth centuries (**Ch. 1, pp. 6-7**, above), monasteries may have been bounded with simple enclosures from an earlier date. At St Buryan in Cornwall (Olson 1989), excavation of part of the churchyard boundary suggested that the site's founders had reused an existing Romano-British settlement as an ecclesiastical enclosure (Preston-Jones 1987: 156-7). Such enclosures are paralleled at some other important early ecclesiastical sites in western Britain, and the space within these boundaries seems to have been divided up in increasingly complicated ways from the eighth century onwards (Petts 2002a: 30-2). Crosses were used to mark boundaries within monastic sites in various parts of the insular world including Ireland (Bitel 1990: 63-4) and Anglo-

Fig 13: Crantock, north Cornwall viewed from the north-west. The church is surrounded by extensive burial grounds probably dating from the Iron Age to the later medieval period. A second chapel once stood in the small field to the north of the church. [Photo: Steve Hartgroves/Historic Environment Service, Cornwall County Council.]

Saxon Wessex. In Ireland, both surviving monuments and documentary sources suggest crosses played an important role in defining different zones (Aitchison 1994: 231-3). In Cornwall, the presence of crosses from the ninth century onwards (e.g. St Neot, **Plate 6c**) may have been linked to increasingly complex division of space within the communities' enclosures, although it is possible that earlier monuments were carved in wood and so have not been preserved, as may have been the case at Iona (Sharpe 1995: 373) and Clonmacnoise (King 1994)).

Early ecclesiastical centres also provided a focus for burial. Whilst they did not receive all burials in any given area, they may at least have catered for the social elite. Material recovered from a ground surface cut by early burials at Tintagel churchyard suggests ritual feasting at the graveside, a practice that Thomas argues may have been derived directly from Mediterranean models (Thomas 1994: 206). Nevertheless, the modern graveyards around the sites of several early ecclesiastical centres seem considerably smaller than their early medieval predecessors. Large numbers of burials have been unearthed outside the burial grounds at Tintagel, Crantock, St Piran's and Phillack (Petts 2001), implying that the wider community gained access to burial at these ecclesiastical sites. Crantock, St Piran's and Phillack may also perpetuate the sites of pre-Christian burial grounds which could already have been important in the spiritual life of the district when the churches were founded (Olson 1982).

Wessex

Excavations at Wells and Winchester have shown early medieval archaeology can survive at some of the greatest churches, but lower-ranking minsters are little known. Relatively few have been subject to recent investigation in Wessex, so the evidence is partial. Comparisons with a few examples from other regions suggest what Wessex sites may have been like.

At the heart of each ecclesiastical centre was a church or group of churches (see Blair 1992: 246-51). The plans of a number of churches in western Wessex are at least partially known. Examples where excavation in modern times has taken place include Sherborne (Dorset; Gibb 1975), Exeter (Devon; Henderson & Bidwell 1982), Wells (Somerset; Rodwell 2001; Plate 2a) and Winchester (Hampshire; Kjølbye-Biddle 1986). Others are known from post-medieval records or from early or still unpublished excavations; these cases are inevitably less well understood, e.g. St Mary's, Wareham (Dorset; Taylor & Taylor 1965); Muchelney (Somerset; Reynolds 1950); Glastonbury (Somerset; Rahtz 1993). Most of the buildings that have been excavated in the four western counties of Wessex date to the later part of the Saxon period, although parts of the complex at Wells may date to middle Saxon times.

In a number of cases there was more than one church or chapel on the site. Excavated examples include Wells and Glastonbury, and perhaps Sherborne. Topographical evidence suggests that there may have been similar arrangements on other sites like Exeter and Buckfastleigh (Devon; Blair & Orme 1995; Reynolds & Turner 2003). Church groups were common at important ecclesiastical sites throughout Christian Europe and the Mediterranean. Like many examples in north-east Gaul, Anglo-Saxon groups often exhibit strongly linear plans, as at Canterbury, Northampton, Lindisfarne and Jarrow (Blair 1992).

Churches were at the heart of ecclesiastical complexes, but also within their precincts were other buildings and areas which fulfilled various functions; some of these are discussed briefly below. In addition there were commonly boundaries surrounding those elements of the site that made up the most densely occupied nucleus. Some case-studies of post-medieval town plans have suggested areas that could have been defined by a boundary (e.g. Sherborne: Barker 1980), but elsewhere archaeological and topographical studies have shown how ecclesiastical sites were marked off from the rest of the landscape. Perhaps the most obvious examples are sites that reused Roman walled places for churches (Blair 1992: 236). Examples in the area under consideration include Exeter and Bath, both of which may have been in continuous occupation from the post-Roman period onwards as Christian foci (Allan et al. 1984; Bell 1996). In some cases substantial boundary ditches have been excavated which could have surrounded sites and may date to the middle Saxon period (e.g. Glastonbury: Leach & Ellis 1993; Bath: Bell 1996). Elsewhere, the topographical position of sites could have set them apart from other places, particularly in the case of monasteries such as those on low islands in the marshes like Muchelney and Athelney (Somerset). Helen Gittos has recently questioned the significance of boundaries around ecclesiastical sites as signifiers of sacred space on the grounds that consecrated areas for burial do not seem to have developed until the late Saxon period in England (Gittos 2002: 207). However, her argument does not preclude the likelihood that ecclesiastical space other than cemeteries had a special status. In some ecclesiastical foundations, internal boundaries may have divided up different parts of the site (e.g. Wimborne (Dorset); Blair 1983). The existence of crosses within precincts from at least the ninth century onwards in southern England (and earlier in the north of the country) is suggestive of religious space marked out physically. The great majority of Anglo-Saxon crosses in western Wessex come from ecclesiastical centres such as Glastonbury, Bath and Keynsham (Somerset; Foster 1987; Lowe 1987; **Fig. 14**). The sacred ground within the ecclesiastical settlement in Wessex was differentiated from the rest of the countryside through the device of constructed or marked boundaries as it was in Ireland and elsewhere (Mytum 1992; Ó Carragáin 2003; Turner 2003c).

From an early date, there was more to many ecclesiastical centres than just the church or churches. Waste products and manufactured items of middle Saxon date have been recovered from a number of sites indicating industrial activity. At Glastonbury, excavated evidence suggests ninth-century glass-making within the ecclesiastical precinct and activity of various periods including iron-working in the tenth century at the Mound site, just to the west (Rahtz 1993; Carr 1985). Iron-working of middle Saxon date has been identified at Gillingham (Dorset; Heaton 1992), Carhampton (Somerset: Hollinrake & Hollinrake 1997), Romsey (Hampshire; Scott 1999) and Ramsbury (Wiltshire), where other finds included quantities of animal bone, pottery and quern stones imported from overseas (Haslam 1980). The fact that industrial activities were undertaken near church sites shows that they were places with more than one function. Whilst it is possible

Fig. 14: Fragment of a probable tenth-century cross from Glastonbury Abbey (Foster 1987, No. 14). The fragment, now in Glastonbury Abbey visitor centre, is cut from Bath limestone and is decorated on three sides. (Dimensions: height 0.27m; width 0.26m; depth 0.27m. [Photograph courtesy of the Trustees of Glastonbury Abbey. © Glastonbury Abbey.]

that the items produced were only for 'internal' consumption, ecclesiastical sites would still have acted as focal points for craftsmen and those who supplied raw materials.

Ecclesiastical centres were also settlement sites, and John Blair has suggested that the combination of central-place functions they maintained may have promoted the development of towns around them in the later Saxon period (Blair 1988a: 47-50). At Avebury (Wiltshire), domestic structures and boundary ditches dating to the middle Saxon period have been excavated close to the site of the church which itself dates in part to the late Saxon period (Pollard & Reynolds 2002: 197-202). At Carhampton (Somerset), imported sixth- and seventh-century pottery (B- and E-ware), metal-working debris and occupation levels dated by radiocarbon to the middle Saxon period are suggestive of a settlement complex which may have focused on a church there (Hollinrake & Hollinrake 1997). Ceramic material suggesting settlement has also been recovered close to the church at Romsey in Hampshire (Scott 1999). Such evidence hints that ecclesiastical centres in much of Wessex may have been similar to those identified elsewhere in England where relatively dense settlement, a range of craft activities, and long-term, stable settlement distinguished ecclesiastical sites from ordinary settlements (e.g. Whitby (North Yorkshire; Rahtz 1976); Hartlepool (Co. Durham; Daniels 1988); Blair 2005: 196-204).

Important early church sites were significantly different from many contemporary settlements in both Cornwall and Wessex (see Chapter 4). Not only were they intended to be permanent, but they were surrounded by boundaries which meant that access could have been controlled by the ecclesiastical elite (Turner 2003c). They were foci for settlement and had industrial areas, both of which may have been more intensively used than their equivalent sites elsewhere in the landscape (Blair 1992: 258). As estate centres, important church sites seem to have been the focus of industrial and agricultural production and places where goods were consumed; this would have made them central places in economic terms. As discussed below and in Chapter 4, this centrality was also apparent in their administrative functions and their relationships to royal centres, not to mention their roles in spiritual life.

Churches and Royal Centres

The Christian church and the social elite were closely linked in early medieval Britain, and the church often drew its most prominent members from the ranks of royal and noble families (see Higham 1997). However, the evidence discussed below hints that the churches of Cornwall may have been less dependent upon royal power than their equivalents in western Wessex.

The limited evidence of sixth- to eighth-century written sources suggests both the existence of kings and that the social elite of Cornwall were responsible for establishing the earliest churches and granting them estates. Gildas' *De Excidio Britanniae* famously describes how the south-western ruler Constantine (the 'tyrant whelp of the filthy lioness of Dumnonia' (Winterbottom 1978: 29)) killed two royal youths in front of an altar, probably in a monastery church. This episode apparently occurred at the time Gildas was writing, probably in the sixth century (Olson 1989: 8; Thomas 1994: 212). A *comes* named Guedianus, perhaps a lower-ranking member of the royal elite, appears in an episode in the *First Life of St*

Samson, which may date to as early as the seventh century (Olson 1989: 16).
Around the end of the seventh century, Aldhelm wrote a letter concerning
ecclesiastical affairs to Gereint, then king of Dumnonia, admonishing him to
ensure regularity according to the Roman tradition in the ecclesiastical affairs of
his kingdom (Lapidge & Herren 1979: 155-60). Not only did Aldhelm write
concerning bishops in Dumnonia, but he also appears to have visited Devon and
Cornwall and spent some time in churches in the region (Aldhelm, *Carmen
Rhythmicum* (trans. Lapidge & Rosier 1985: 177)). Wendy Davies has argued that
there was a British charter tradition which allowed estates to be granted from the
king to the church in the west, just as there was in the Anglo-Saxon east (Davies
1982). The practice is suggested at this time in Cornwall by the record of King
Gereint's early eighth-century grant of land at Maker to the church of Sherborne,
where Aldhelm was bishop (Finberg 1953b: 16).[8]

Constantine, Guedianus and Gereint were clearly members of a hierarchical
social elite and were also closely involved in the religious affairs of the region.
There can be little doubt that Cornwall had kings in the post-Roman and early
medieval periods, and that they would have provided some or all of the region's
churches with estates by grants. However, the archaeological and topographical
evidence suggests that the relationships between royal elite and churches may
have gone through a number of changes during the period from the fifth to the
eleventh centuries.

Identifying Royal Centres in Cornwall: Archaeological Evidence

The archaeological evidence for early medieval royal centres in Cornwall is
limited to a very few sites. Among them is the most spectacular of all post-Roman
or early medieval royal centres in the west of Britain, the cliff top peninsula
fortress of Tintagel.

The greatest volume of archaeological evidence relates to settlements of the
earliest post-Roman phase, those of the third to sixth centuries AD.[9] The
excavated sites likely to have been high-status centres in post-Roman Cornwall
were also occupied in the late Roman period, which strongly suggests that like
other contemporary settlements they continue a pattern established during the
third century AD. Quantities of imported post-Roman goods have been recovered
from the strongly fortified site at Chûn Castle in Penwith and from St Michael's
Mount, hinting that they may have been elite residences at this time (Thomas
1956; Herring 1993: 60-1; Herring 2000; although the interpretation of the latter
site remains uncertain, it may have had a dual secular and sacred role). Chûn and
the Mount are significant sites, but if volume of imported goods and density of
occupation can be considered to reflect status, then neither came close to the
importance of Tintagel.

Thomas (1993: 82-5) and Morris et al. (1999) have summarised the evidence
for the use of Tintagel Island in the late Roman period, including a small coin
hoard and a large amount of pottery which probably dates to the third and fourth

---

[8] In addition, some tenth-century Cornish charters apparently maintain distinctive 'Celtic'
elements, and there are references to possible Cornish kings in a few later pre-Conquest sources
(Olsen 1989: 78-84; James 2001: 245).
[9] The different phases of early medieval settlement in Cornwall are discussed fully in Chapter 4,
pp. 71-82.

centuries. Thomas speculates that Tintagel Island may have been the *Purocornavis* of the Ravenna Cosmography (a Byzantine collection of itineraries compiled from earlier sources), and that its occupation (though of uncertain nature) may have been linked to the tin industry (Thomas 1993: 83-4). The presence of official imperial agents is implied by the presence of two late Roman 'milestones' in the area, one at Trethevy and one now in Tintagel parish church (of uncertain original location).

The main phase of occupation at the site in the first millennium is dated by a very large amount of pottery and other goods imported from the Mediterranean region, and by radiocarbon dating (Thomas 1981a; Fulford 1989; Morris & Harry 1997). The forms of pottery and other artefacts present indicate that the active trade with the Mediterranean lasted from the later fifth century to the mid-sixth century, reaching a peak around AD 500, and radiocarbon dating suggests that occupation on the site may well have continued into the seventh century (Morris & Harry 1997: 120). As the excavators have argued, a site such as Tintagel requires a special explanation:

> In the social context of post-Roman Britain, it would...seem perverse not to accord sites such as Cadbury [Somerset] and Tintagel 'royal' status, with a descending hierarchy of other royal sites identified as *urbs* or *villa regis*...
>
> (Morris & Harry 1997: 124)

Tintagel was at the peak of the post-Roman settlement hierarchy, and it was a centre for trade or exchange controlled at the highest level. The most likely commodity to have been traded from Cornwall over such long distances in the early medieval period is tin. In order to be in a position to trade the elite must have had effective mechanisms for collecting produce and storing it prior to trading. Strictly speaking this is speculation—no tin ingots, for example, have been discovered so far at Tintagel. However, the remains of other produce such as cereals (particularly barley and oats) have been recognised in the recent excavations, and it is likely that these were the result of organised production in the local area (ibid. 118).

The form of the settlement at Tintagel Island is quite unlike anything else known from Cornwall in the first millennium AD. The main difference lies in the number and density of buildings. A field survey undertaken in 1985 by the RCHME recorded the earthwork remains of well over a hundred structures on the Island's plateau and terraces, and excavations on both the terraces and on the landward part of the site beneath the Lower Ward of the thirteenth-century castle have revealed the remains of further structures (colour plate 4 in Thomas 1993; Morris et al. 1999; **Plates 4a, 4b and 5**). Whilst the insubstantial nature of some of the excavated buildings suggests that many would not have been permanently occupied (Thomas 1993: 88-92), many of the less substantial buildings could have had a storage function and others might have been used for industrial processes as shown by finds of probable metal-working debris (Morris et al 1999: 210; Morris & Harry 1997: 72-3). The possibility that the settlement at Tintagel was divided up into different zones for different activities, the evidence for industry and extensive trading activity, and the form of the buildings at the site has led Dark to argue that Tintagel was 'very much a "Late Antique" settlement'

(Dark 2000: 156). He has suggested that there may have been a Byzantine mercantile element in the community at Tintagel by analogy with sites in continental Europe (Dark 2001: 91), and there are certainly morphological parallels between Tintagel and some contemporary newly founded Byzantine trading places in the Mediterranean like Monemvasia (Laconia) (Kalligas 1990: 29-30). The ideological and political implications of these likely links are important when considering the relationships between Tintagel and early Christian institutions in Cornwall.

Few other early medieval high-status sites have been investigated, and the only one to have produced a substantial volume of material is Winnianton (also called Winnington) on the west coast of the Lizard peninsula. This is much later than Tintagel, and belongs to a period of strong Anglo-Saxon influence in Cornwall. 'Winnianton' is an isolated English *tun* place-name in the far west, and in Domesday Book was King William's principal manor in Cornwall and the head manor of the hundred which took its name (though this was later known by its Cornish name, Kerrier) (Thorn & Thorn 1979a: 1,1; Padel 1987: 13). A large quantity of late Saxon pottery has been recovered from the eroding cliff-section at Winnianton, although the size and layout of the settlement are not known (Jope & Threlfall 1956; Thomas 1963).

Identifying Royal Centres in Cornwall: Documentary Evidence and Place-Names

There are no documentary sources that cast light on the location of high-status sites of the earliest phase of settlement in Cornwall discussed here, the post-Roman or late Antique period. As Ann Preston-Jones and Peter Rose have noted, some sites traditionally associated with (semi-)mythical kings were excavated earlier in the twentieth century, but none apart from Tintagel have produced any evidence for post-Roman occupation (e.g. Castle-an-Dinas and Castle Dore; Ralegh Radford 1951; Quinnell & Harris 1985; Preston-Jones & Rose 1986: 138). Between the sixth and ninth centuries, the most useful source for identifying possible royal settlements is place-name evidence. The Cornish place-name element *lys ('court') is believed to indicate the likely sites of royal centres (Padel 1985: 150-1; as its equivalent *llys* did in medieval Wales: see e.g. Longley 1997, 2001). A cautious approach is necessary since the limited amount of archaeological work has not yet shown that place-names in *lys will reveal archaeological evidence of early medieval activity. For example, excavations at Arrallas did not produce any early medieval material (although the site investigated was a cropmark near to the hamlet, rather than the later medieval settlement of Arrallas itself: Preston-Jones & Rose 1986: 138). There were almost certainly other royal centres in this period which have not yet been identified through place-name or archaeological evidence. Nevertheless, a number of sites with *lys names were important manorial centres at the time of Domesday including Liskeard (probably *lys + personal name (Padel 1988: 110), Helstone and Helston (both *hen-*lys* 'ancient court' with later English *tun* 'estate centre' (ibid. 1988: 96)). The Domesday manor of Lesnewth (*lys + *nowyth* 'new': ibid. 109) was the administrative centre of the medieval hundred of the same name. These examples may show continuity of function between Cornish and English secular centres, and hint that places with *lys names may indeed represent high-status settlements of the pre-English period. The identifications of possible secular centres of the sixth to ninth centuries here follows Preston-Jones and Rose (1986: 137-9), with the addition of Helsett in Lesnewth parish. Like Helstone and Helston, this place-name may incorporate the Cornish elements *hen* and **lys*, 'the old court' (plus an unidentified suffix: *ICS Index*; Gover 1948: 71). It seems likely that Helsett was the earlier administrative centre of the area, and was replaced at some time by Lesnewth (rather than Padel's suggestion of Helstone, which is some distance from both; Padel 1988: 96, Fig. 15).

There appears to have been a significant shift of royal centres between the late-/post-Roman periods (AD *c.*250-600) and the following centuries. Judging by the archaeological evidence, first-millennium occupation at Tintagel and Chûn Castle came to an end some time in the seventh century at the latest (Morris & Harry 1997; Thomas 1956). The **lys*-named settlements appear to be part of the early medieval pattern like settlements with *tre* names, rather than part of the late-/post-Roman settlement pattern (see below, Ch. 4, 71-82).

Any continuity between Cornish royal or secular administrative centres of the sixth to ninth centuries and later ones of the Anglo-Saxon period was only partial. This is shown by Domesday Book, which is the main source for the location of the ninth- to eleventh-century high-status settlements. Whilst some of the Cornish sites with **lys* names continued to be larger than average manors held by important people, they did not necessarily maintain any wider administrative functions. A good example can be seen in West hundred. Whilst Liskeard remained an important manor in the hands of the major Anglo-Saxon landowner Merleswein in 1066 (Thorn & Thorn 1979a: 5,2), the head manor of the Domesday Book hundred was Fawton (ibid. 5,1). This had also been held by Merleswein, but its English name (the *tun* by the Faw stream: *ICS Index*) and topographical position on the edge of rough ground suggest it was a new centre established in the tenth or eleventh centuries. This appears to be an example of an earlier Cornish centre being replaced by a new administrative centre after the area came under direct Anglo-Saxon political control. Similar examples come from west Cornwall, where Connerton and Winnianton were the administrative capitals of their respective hundreds at the time of Domesday. Both have at least partially English place-names which are otherwise very rare in this part of Cornwall in the middle ages (Padel 1999).

Cornish high-status centres can therefore be seen to have had three main periods of development in the early middle ages. First, there were those centres of which Tintagel is the best example which continued a pattern established in the third century and which lasted until the seventh century (these can be labelled 'Phase 1' settlements). Secondly, there are the probable **lys* centres of the early medieval Cornish elite (Phase 2) which appear to have developed after Tintagel and its contemporaries were deserted; some of these continued through into the high middle ages, but some lost their importance **(Fig. 15)**. Finally, there are the royal and noble manorial centres of Domesday Book (Phase 3), many of which developed when the Anglo-Saxon kingdom of Wessex took control of the region in the ninth and tenth centuries.

Secular and Ecclesiastical Centres in Cornwall

Any discussion of the relationships between religious and secular centres in early medieval Cornwall must begin with Tintagel. The work of the last three decades has cast significant doubt on the theory that the Island at Tintagel was an early monastic centre, and it is clear that Ralegh Radford's initial interpretation of the site as an ascetic Celtic monastery must be seriously questioned (Thomas 1993; *cf.* Ralegh Radford 1935, 1962). This 'deconstruction' of the monastic interpretation is based partly on the wealth demonstrated by the exotic finds from the site, which have been thought inappropriate to a monastic setting. However, work on monasteries elsewhere in the early Christian world has shown clearly that ideal and reality did not always match up in this respect: the consumption of luxurious foodstuffs on monastic sites in Egypt was not uncommon, yet it was far from the monastic ideal (Harlow & Smith 2001). An abundance of high-status goods is not necessarily enough to define a site as 'secular' rather than 'sacred'. At Tintagel, scholars seeking to re-evaluate the theory that the site was a monastery have perhaps been over-zealous in removing all ecclesiastical elements from the history of the site. The recently excavated inscription from the Island hints at a close connection between the secular elite and the literate culture of the church (see Morris et al. 1999: 213-14), and it is possible that the settlement on the Island would have comprised both ecclesiastical and secular elements. The Island settlement at Tintagel may owe its form to models derived from continental

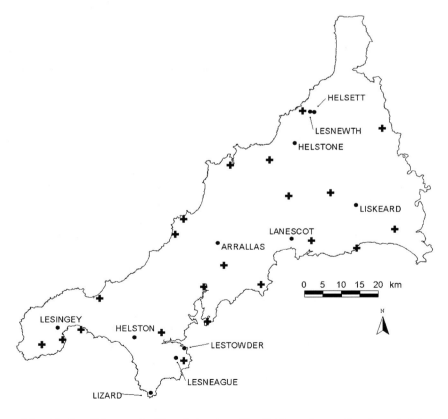

Fig. 15: Possible royal vills of the (pre-English) early medieval period in Cornwall (circles), and likely early medieval monasteries (crosses).

Europe and the Mediterranean world, and it would hardly be an exaggeration to describe the dense settlement here as proto-urban (particularly compared to other places in western Britain). In many parts of the late Roman world, the church was closely linked to urban centres (Brogiolo 1999: 120-5; Gauthier 1999: 205). In many regions these had changed in late Antiquity almost beyond recognition from their form in the Classical period to be little more than small fortified areas incorporating churches and administrative centres (Haldon 1999). Christian centres were normally in towns (or their remnants), and the idea of the town had become closely linked to the ideology of the church (see Chapter 8). The rich range of imports at the kingly settlement at Tintagel suggest it may have developed under Mediterranean or continental European influence. It may also have been a centre for significant Christian ideological influence coming from the same regions.

This interpretation seems reasonable in the light of the excavations at Tintagel churchyard. At this site, which stands on the clifftop around 500m south of the Island, evidence for early Christian funerary activity was revealed in the early 1990s **(Fig. 16)**. Graves in the earliest levels were surrounded by spreads of burnt clay containing sherds of imported pottery as well as foodstuffs; the excavators have suggested this could reflect the influence of Mediterranean practice in funerary rituals at the site (Nowakowski & Thomas 1992; Thomas 1994: 197-209). As at the contemporary Christian burial site at Phillack (Thomas 1994: 197-201; Okasha 1993: 205-07), the burial ground at Tintagel is known to extend some way beyond the confines of the modern graveyard from chance finds of cist graves in the adjoining fields (Canner 1982). It seems likely that here at St Matheriana's church is a 'sacred' site which was closely linked to the early royal site on the Island (Thomas 1993: 99). In summary, there appears to have been an intimate relationship between the royal elite and the new Christian church at Tintagel at this time. Although further archaeological research is needed before proper interpretations can be made, it is likely that similar sites may have existed around the same time at Looe Island and St Michael's Mount.

Judging by the limited evidence which is presently available for the location of royal centres in the succeeding period (Phase 2, sixth to ninth centuries), this close physical relationship between royal and ecclesiastical sites did not continue. Although it seems likely that Cornish kings were involved in endowing monastic centres, they do not appear to have founded them at or adjacent to royal administrative centres. The closest physical relationships belonging to this period are between the church at Minster and Lesnewth, and the church at St Keverne and Lesneage. Nevertheless, both of these are probably exceptional cases. Minster may not have been founded until the ninth century or later, and Lesnewth (the 'new *lys*') may also have been established late; the relationship between them is more typical of the tenth and eleventh centuries than earlier. On the Lizard, Lesneage may have been an agricultural centre for the church of St Keverne rather than a secular estate. The name, first recorded in 967 (S755) as *Lesmanaoc* probably means either 'the monks' court' or 'the court of the Meneage', which may originally have been the area over which St Keverne had some sort of ecclesiastical jurisdiction (Padel 1985: 156; Olson 1989: 108). The *lys* of Lesneage may have functioned like the barton-farms which Rosamond Faith has noted in Anglo-Saxon England (Faith 1997: 37). The places most likely to have

Fig. 16: Aerial view of Tintagel and St Matheriana's church. [Photo: Steve Hartgroves/Historic Environment Service, Cornwall County Council.]

been Cornish royal courts on the Lizard peninsula both lie over 12km to the south west at Predannack and/or Lizard itself (Padel 1987).

This distance between noble and religious centres seems more typical of Phase 2. The closest *lys centre to St Kew was Helstone, around 8km away; St Buryan was 6km from Lesingey, Bodmin 12km from Lanescot, and St Germans 12km from Liskeard. This was also the closest *lys to the community at St Neot, some 7.5km to the north-west **(see Table 5)**. Although this discussion is extremely unlikely to be based on identifications of all the royal sites that existed during this period, the distance between churches and *lys estate centres does suggest that churches in early medieval Cornwall were not immediately dependent on royal power (unlike many in Wessex; see below). This is also suggested by the nature of the Cornish churches' estates, which are discussed in Chapter 5 (123-9).

The establishment of Anglo-Saxon political control and cultural supremacy in the ninth and tenth centuries appears to have led to a substantial restructuring in the relationship between ecclesiastical centres and royal power in Cornwall. Whilst some royal centres of the previous period appear to have continued into Phase 3 (e.g. Liskeard, Helston and Helstone), in other cases new royal and elite manorial centres were established. Several of these were established to act as administrative centres for their wider regions, and their names became the English names of the hundreds used in Domesday Book (Thorn & Thorn 1979a). In terms of their relationships with important ecclesiastical sites, these new centres appear to have represented another sort of change. Several of them were located much closer to collegiate churches than their Cornish predecessors had been, for example the hundredal centres of Connerton, around 3.5km from Phillack, and Tybesta, about 4.5km from the church of St Probus. The new hundredal centre at Fawton was established only 1.5km from the church of St Neot, and also provides a likely example of a new royal centre encroaching on to the estates of an established collegiate church. In several cases this encroachment appears to have been even more extreme. The manor of St Kew, the earliest Cornish monastery attested in the documentary sources (Olson 1989: 16-20), was in the possession of King Harold in 1066 even though at least part of the estate had been granted (or confirmed) to the church in the tenth century (S810). A similar history seems likely at both Probus and Launceston where kings Edward and Harold (respectively) had held the manors before the Norman Conquest. Neither estate paid geld in 1086, suggesting they had formerly been ecclesiastical. This appears to represent a process of secularisation similar to the one that took place at many monastic settlements in Ireland around the same time (Graham 1993: 41; e.g. Killaloe: Bradley 1994).

Identifying Royal Vills in Wessex: Documentary Sources

In the Middle and Later Saxon period the landscape of Wessex was divided into estates that were held by a variety of owners. These estates were administered from places which commonly took their names from areas or topographical features with which they were associated (Aston 1986; thus Cannington in Somerset is the 'Quantocks *tun*' (*tun* = 'farmstead, estate' (Padel 1999: 91)) ; Bruton (Somerset) is the '*tun* on the River Brue'; Wilton (Wiltshire) is the '*tun* on the River Wylye'; and Colyton (Devon) is the '*tun* on the River Coly'). Such places were commonly held by kings and their families, and these are known as *regiae villae* or 'royal vills'.

Church	Distance (to nearest 0.5 km)	Royal centre	Status (certainty that site was a Phase 2 royal centre):
St Petroc, Bodmin	12 km	Lanescot	Probable
Constantine	7.5 km	Helston	Very probable
Crantock	11.5km	Arralas	Possible
Lammana	12 km	Liskeard	Very probable
Launceston	20 km	Lesnewth	Probable
Minster	2 km	Lesnewth	Probable
Old Kea	13 km	Arralas	Possible
Padstow	18.5 km	Helstone	Very probable
Paul	3.5 km	Lesingey	Possible
Phillack	14 km	Lesingey	Possible
Probus	6.5 km	Arralas	Possible
St Anthony	9.5 km	Lestowder	Possible
St Buryan	6 km	Lesingey	Possible
St Cadix	5.5 km	Lanescot	Probable
St Germans	12.5 km	Liskeard	Very probable
St Gorans	15 km	Lanescot	Probable
St Keverne	2 km	Lesneague	Possible
St Kew	8 km	Helstone	Very probable
St Michael's Mount	6 km	Lesingey	Possible
St Neot	7.5 km	Liskeard	Very probable
St Piran's Oratory Perranzabuloe	11.5 km	Arralas	Possible

Table 5: Distance from important churches to possible royal centres of the sixth to ninth centuries AD in Cornwall (italics indicate churches of particularly doubtful status: Olson 1989: 105)

Royal vills can be identified from various documentary and archaeological sources. Sawyer (1983) has discussed their identification using pre-Conquest documents, and compiled a list of sites in England based on this evidence. Literary sources such as Bede and annals like the *Anglo-Saxon Chronicle* contain explicit references to a few sites, and charters indicate the locations of nineteen more (although five of these remain unidentified). Other royal vills are suggested by records of events whch took place at or close to them such as the deaths or burials of kings. The wills of Alfred (S1507) and Eadred (S1515) each record land which these kings left to their relatives, and the estates in question are mainly referred to using the name of the royal vill which acted as the estate centre. However, even these documents are not believed to be complete catalogues of all the land held by either king. Sawyer argues that royal land fell into two categories: first, core estates which were essentially inalienable from the crown, and second personal property which could be left to people other than the next king (although changes in status of estates, particularly from personal property to 'core' land, did take place: see Sawyer 1983: 279; and Wormald 2001). Whilst the wills refer to land in the second category, it is uncertain how many estates fell into the first.

Domesday Book provides one possible way to fill in the gaps in our knowledge. Sawyer has argued that the royal estates of Domesday probably reflect ancient arrangements, so that most of the eleventh-century royal estates would also have been royal three or four hundred years before (and especially those which were not assessed for tax, or which paid by an archaic method such as the *feorm* or food-render; Sawyer 1983: 285). This theory is supported by the evidence from western Wessex, as shown by **Table 6**. Of the forty-three sites listed where reliable evidence indicates royal vills before AD 1000, Domesday Book records that twenty were in the hands of King Edward in 1066 and another two were royal boroughs. Eight were held by members of the family of Earl Godwin of Wessex (including King Edward's wife Eadgyth/Edith and her brother Earl (briefly King) Harold). Eight had passed into the hands of monasteries or bishops, but only four were held by thegns. This clearly suggests that royal land tended to remain with the crown or in the immediate circle of the royal family.

Identifying Royal Vills in Wessex: Archaeological Evidence

In the majority of cases it is a guess that the royal centre was close to the surviving parish church (Blair 1988a); relatively few early medieval royal estate centres have been excavated in England. Those that have suggest such sites comprised a common range of buildings, in particular large timber halls such as those found at Yeavering and Cheddar (Hope-Taylor 1977; Rahtz 1979).[10] In central and western Wessex, only Cheddar has been excavated on a large scale. The archaeological sequence from the site appears to have begun in the late ninth or early tenth century, and occupation continued into the later middle ages. Occupation may not have been continuous, and it is possible that a royal reeve was the only resident for extended periods. Royal visits would have been occasional, such as those attested in itineraries and in charters, one of which records that a grant was made whilst the king was at Cheddar *in palatio regis* (Sawyer 1983: 292; Hill 1981: 88-90). Indeed, this may have been one of the most significant differences between royal centres and contemporary monasteries or minsters: whilst the former were sporadically used by an itinerant royal family and staffed by a few officials, the latter were bases for permanent communities.

The difficulties involved in distinguishing royal vills from minsters or monasteries have led to much recent debate. Sites such as Northampton and Brandon in Suffolk have been interpreted as either monastic or royal centres (e.g. Williams et al. 1988; Blair 1995a; Carr et al. 1988). Flixborough in Lincolnshire epitomises some of the problems; differences over time in assemblages that could have been associated with one class of site or the other (e.g. certain types of animal bones or *styli* for writing) have led the excavator there to suggest that the site itself fluctuated between royal and ecclesiastical functions (Loveluck 1998).

Blair has called for the re-interpretation of a number of sites as minsters based on a combination of certain excavated characteristics and associated historical or

---

[10] see Rahtz 1999 for a recent distribution map of sites, and papers in Frodsham and O'Brien 2005 for recent perspectives on Yeavering.

Royal vill	First recorded	Domesday name	County	Holder in 1066
Axminster	757	*Alseminstre*	Devon	King Edward
Axmouth	Alfred's Will	*Alsemude*	Devon	King Edward
Branscombe	Alfred's Will	*Branchescome*	Devon	Bishop Leofric of Exeter
Braunton	973	*Brantone*	Devon	King Edward
Colyton	939x946	*Culitone*	Devon	King Edward
Cullompton	Afred's Will	*Colitone*	Devon	Thorbert
Exminster	Alfred's Will	*Axeminstre*	Devon	King Edward
Hartland	Alfred's Will	*Hertitone*	Devon	Countess Gytha
Lifton	Alfred's Will	*Listone*	Devon	Queen Edith
Tiverton	Alfred's Will	*Tovretone*	Devon	Countess Gytha
Damerham	Alfred's Will	*Dobreham*	Dorset	King Edward
Dorchester	833	*Dorecestre*	Dorset	King Edward
Puddletown	976	*Piretone*	Dorset	Earl (King) Harold
Sturminster Marshall	Alfred's Will	*Sturminstre*	Dorset	Archbishop Stigand
Sutton Poyntz	891	*Sutone*	Dorset	King Edward
Wareham	786	*Warham*	Dorset	(Town)
Whitchurch Canicorum	Alfred's Will	*Witcerce*	Dorset	*St Wandrilles (1086)*
Bath	796	*Bade*	Somerset	Queen Edith
Burnham	Alfred's Will	*Burneham*	Somerset	Brictsi
Cannington	Alfred's Will	*Candetone*	Somerset	King Edward
Carhampton	Alfred's Will	*Carentone*	Somerset	King Edward
Cheddar	956	*Cedre*	Somerset	King Edward
Chewton Mendip	Alfred's Will	*Ciwetune*	Somerset	Queen Edith
Congresbury	Alfred's Will	*Cungresberie*	Somerset	Earl (King) Harold
Crewkerne	Alfred's Will	*Cruche*	Somerset	Queen Edith
Frome	955	*Frome*	Somerset	King Edward
Kilton	Alfred's Will	*Chiluetune*	Somerset	Alfward and Leofric
Somerton	733	*Sumertone*	Somerset	King Edward
Taunton	722	*Tantone*	Somerset	Archbishop Stigand
Wedmore	Alfred's Will	*Wetmore*	Somerset	King Edward
Wimborne	718	*Winborne*	Somerset	King Edward
Yeovil	Alfred's Will	*Ivle*	Somerset	Thegns
Amesbury	858	*Amblesberie*	Wiltshire	King Edward
Bedwyn	968	*Beduinde*	Wiltshire	King Edward
Calne	977	*Cauna*	Wiltshire	King Edward
Chippenham	853	*Chepenham*	Wiltshire	King Edward
Chisledon	Alfred's Will	*Chiseldene*	Wiltshire	St Peter's, Winchester
Downton	Eadred's Will	*Duntone*	Wiltshire	Bishop of Winchester
Edington	878	*Edendone*	Wiltshire	St Mary's, Romsey
Pewsey	Alfred's Will	*Peuesei*	Wiltshire	St Peter's, Winchester
Wardour	899	*Werdore*	Wiltshire	St Mary's, Wilton
Warminster	899	*Guerminstre*	Wiltshire	King Edward
Wilton	838	*Wiltunie*	Wiltshire	(Town)

Table 6: Royal vills with pre-AD 1000 evidence in Devon, Dorset, Somerset and Wiltshire and their Domesday Book holders *TRE* (after Sawyer 1983, with additions; see also Wormald 2001: 272-3). King Alfred's will probably dates to between 872 and 888 (Keynes & Lapidge 1983).

literary evidence (Blair 1995a, 1997). His case is most persuasive for Northampton, where buildings which lay in a roughly axial alignment between two later churches had initially been interpreted as royal palaces, but are perhaps more plausibly seen as components of an ecclesiastical complex.

The relationship between 'secular' and 'sacred' was a crucial dynamic in early medieval culture, and neither can be understood properly without reference to the other (Markus 1997: 85-7; Fletcher 1997: 160-92). In non-Christian northern Europe, the aristocratic hall acted not only as a central settlement, but also as a sacred centre in the early middle ages (Herschend 1993; Fabech 1999b). Aspects of this sort of link may have been maintained through the conversion period in Wessex. Ecclesiastical and royal centres of the Middle Saxon period certainly appear to have shared very similar settlement forms, and this probably reflects the deliberate expression of a common Christian ideology (Blair 2005: 211-12).

In the period before the emergence of Christian Anglo-Saxon kingdoms, many settlements in England were typified by a certain impermanence. Buildings seem to have been demolished after short periods of use, and entire settlements seem to have 'shifted' across the fifth- and sixth-century landscape (e.g. Mucking (Essex); West Stow (Suffolk): Hamerow 1991). However, around the end of the sixth century there were significant changes in elite settlement sites which led to increased internal division within settlements and more regular layouts, combined with much more stability in the landscape (e.g. Cowdery's Down (Hampshire), Chalton (Hampshire), Wicken Bonhunt (Essex) (Millett & James 1983; Champion 1977; Wade 1980)). These enclosed sites seem to be associated with the social elite, a conclusion which is supported by the documentary sources: the early eighth-century law code of King Ine of Wessex implies that only the settlements of the nobility were fortified (Hamerow 1991: 7; Ine Cap. 45: Attenborough 1922: 51). Some traditional models of village formation suggest the essential form of the English landscape was a product of the tenth and eleventh centuries (Lewis et al. 1997: 191-204; Jones & Page 2003: 57-9). However, archaeologists are now realising that in several regions middle Saxon settlements exhibit a high degree of stability and longevity, and that middle Saxon landscapes have helped structure the detail of the countryside through to the present day (Reynolds 2003: 130-2).

Of various important social and political changes that occurred around this time (e.g. Carver 1989), the conversion to Christianity was surely one of the most significant. One reason for the relatively rapid adoption of Christianity across Anglo-Saxon England may have been that the sophisticated, literate culture of the Christian church was able to offer any royal family that converted opportunities to enhance its own authority. For example, the church probably introduced new kinds of property rights and new concepts of land ownership (Kelly 1990: 40-5). The 'closure' of elite settlements may have been a way of expressing this re-ordered ideology in relation to property (Turner 2003c). The morphological similarity between permanent, bounded ecclesiastical centres and the new high-status secular sites is striking (Pestell 2004: 48-64). With secular elite sites which were similar in form to ecclesiastical settlements, the elite could justify its expanding powers over property and land with reference to the church and the new 'Christian' form of settlement. The church in turn benefited from royal patronage and protection for its ecclesiastical settlements. 'Secular' and 'sacred'

elite settlements of the conversion period reflected a shared ideology: a new kind
of permanence, a certain centrality and the power to control land. The close
relationship between secular and religious elements of the elite continued and
developed into the later Saxon period. This may account for some of the problems
archaeologists have faced in telling them apart. Both are forms of elite settlement,
and their shared ideology is reflected in their close physical similarities.

Royal Vills and Churches: Spatial Relationships

The spatial relationships between royal centres and churches could provide clues
to other links between them. Close proximity could suggest a high level of
dependence or inter-dependence. In Iceland, for example, Jesse Byock has argued
that the early church was 'vulnerable to secular interference because of its inability
to exercise control over its property' (Byock 2001: 305). In Britain the Anglo-
Saxon kings were instrumental in the conversion and adaptation of their kingdoms
to Christianity (Yorke 1999, 2003; Higham 1997), and Patrick Hase has argued
that ecclesiastical centres in Wessex were nearly always directly dependent on royal
vills (Hase 1988: 45-8; 1994: 53). On the other hand, a significant degree of spatial
separation could hint that churches enjoyed a greater degree of independence from
secular (or even religious) elites after their initial foundation, as suggested above
for the early Cornish monasteries. John Blair has argued that it was common for
English minsters to begin life as relatively autonomous institutions which were
gradually 'secularised' (Blair 1988a, 1995a, 1997).

Some of the major monasteries of Wessex such as Malmesbury, Muchelney and
Glastonbury have no known close link to a royal estate centre, and they themselves
controlled large estates; these tend to be some distance from the nearest known
royal vill **(see Table 7)**. There were also smaller monasteries which had often come
into the possession of more important houses by the later Saxon period that were
distant from royal centres. For example, Tisbury (Wiltshire), whose existence is
first attested in the eighth century, had become a possession of Shaftesbury Abbey
by the time of Domesday Book (S1256; Talbot 1954: 34; Darlington 1955);
Bradford on Avon (Wiltshire), perhaps founded by Aldhelm, was also held by
Shaftesbury in 1066 (for the grant of AD 1001 see S899; **Plate 3a**); and
Beaminster (Dorset) seems to have been the possession of St Peter's, Gloucester
and subsequently Sherborne (S1782; Hall 2000; for discussion of these church
estates, see Ch. 5, 119-23, below).

On the other hand, there were also major land-holding monasteries of the later
Saxon period that were located immediately next to royal vills and were themselves
the centres of extensive estates. Prominent Wessex examples include Amesbury
(Wiltshire), Wilton (Wiltshire), Bath (Somerset) and Winchester (Hampshire).

Blair (1988a: 37-8) and Hase (1994: 61) have suggested that the earliest
churches were founded as part of a deliberate policy by the west Saxon kings to
ensure a network of churches, and there are close connections between many
royal centres and 'minsters'. Of the royal vills known to have existed before AD
1000 in western Wessex, a clear majority (*c.*70%) were probably within 1km of the
nearest certain or likely monastery or minster church **(Table 8)**. Only thirteen of
the vills listed are further than this from a church, though of these four sites were
themselves in ecclesiastical ownership in 1066 (although there is no indication
that they were ever major minsters: Branscombe (Devon); Chisledon; Edington;

Wardour (Wiltshire)). Of the remainder, Hartland (Devon), was associated with an important land-holding ecclesiastical community 2.5km away at Stoke St Nectan. Four of the rest are estates known to have royal associations from King Alfred's will, and may therefore not always have been 'core' estates of the crown holdings (Kilton, Burnham, Axmouth and Lifton). Otherwise, the consistent coincidence between early royal vills and minster churches supports the idea that minsters and royal vills were often deliberately sited close together.

In Wiltshire the site at Cowage Farm, Foxley provides a good example (**Fig. 17**; Hinchcliffe 1986). After being identified through air photography, geophysical survey and trial trenching has revealed a seventh- or eighth-century settlement

Church	County	Closest royal vill	Distance (to km)	Ownership
Axminster	Devon	*Axminster*	<1km	Royal
Crediton	Devon	*Exeter (burh)*	11km	Ecclesiastical
Exeter	Devon	*Exeter (burh)*	<1km	Royal/ecclesiastical
Plympton	Devon	*Plympton*	<1km	Ecclesiastical/royal
Beaminster	Dorset	Kingland	4km	Ecclesiastical
Cranborne	Dorset	Knowlton	4km	Ecclesiastical
Gillingham	Dorset	Gillingham	1km	Royal
Iwerne Minster	Dorset	Child Okeford	4km	Ecclesiastical
Shaftesbury	Dorset	*Shaftesbury (burh)*	<1km	Royal/ecclesiastical
Sherborne	Dorset	Milborne Port	4km	Ecclesiastical
Sturminster Marshall	Dorset	*Sturminster Marshall*	<1km	Royal
Wareham	Dorset	*Wareham*	<1km	Ecclesiatical/royal
Whitchurch Canonicorum	Dorset	*Whitchurch Canonicorum*	<1km	Royal
Wimborne	Dorset	*Wimborne*	<1km	Royal/ecclesiastical
Athelney	Somerset	*Athelney (burh)*	<1km	Royal/ecclesiastical
Banwell	Somerset	*Congresbury*	6km	Royal/ecclesiastical
Bath	Somerset	*Bath*	<1km	Royal/ecclesiastical
Cheddar	Somerset	*Cheddar*	<1km	Royal/ecclesiastical
Congresbury	Somerset	*Congresbury*	<1km	Royal/ecclesiastical
Doulting	Somerset	Bruton	9km	Ecclesiastical
Glastonbury	Somerset	*Somerton*	10km	Ecclesiatical
Muchelney	Somerset	Curry Rivel	4km	Ecclesiastical
Taunton	Somerset	*(Taunton)*	(<1km)	Royal/ecclesiastical
Wells	Somerset	*Chewton Mendip*	9km	Ecclesiastical
Bradford on Avon	Wiltshire	*Bath*	8km	Ecclesiastical
Britford	Wiltshire	Britford	<1km	Royal
Damerham	Wiltshire	*Damerham*	<1km	Royal/ecclesiastical
Malmesbury	Wiltshire	*Chippenham*	14km	Ecclesiastical
Ramsbury	Wiltshire	Aldbourne	4km	Ecclesiastical
Tisbury	Wiltshire	*Wardour*	3km	Ecclesiastical

Table 7: Major early churches (pre-AD 900 evidence) and nearest known royal vill (italics indicate reliable pre-AD 1000 evidence for royal vill or *burh*). ('Ownership' indicates earliest known owner of the estate where the church stood. 'Ecclesiastical' includes both episcopal and monastic owners. 'Ecclesiastical/royal' indicates uncertainty or cases where both large royal and ecclesiastical estates were centred on the same location).

Royal vill	Date first recorded	County	Nearest minster church or monastery	Distance
Axminster	757	Devon	*Axminster*	<1 km
Axmouth	Alfred's will	Devon	Colyton	3 km
Branscombe	Alfred's will	Devon	Colyton	7 km
Braunton	973	Devon	Braunton	<1 km
Colyton	939x946	Devon	Colyton	<1 km
Cullompton	Alfred's will	Devon	Cullompton	<1 km
Exminster	Alfred's will	Devon	Exminster	<1 km
Hartland	Alfred's will	Devon	Stoke St Nectan	2.5 km
Lifton	Alfred's will	Devon	Launceston	6 km
Tiverton	Alfred's will	Devon	Tiverton	<1 km
Dorchester	833	Dorset	Fordington	<1 km
Puddletown	976	Dorset	Puddletown	<1 km
Sturminster Marshall	Alfred's will	Dorset	*Sturminster Marshall*	<1 km
Sutton Poyntz	891	Dorset	Preston	<1 km
Wareham	786	Dorset	*Wareham*	<1 km
Whitchurch Canicorum	Alfred's will	Dorset	*Whitchurch*	<1 km
Wimborne	718	Dorset	*Wimborne*	<1 km
Bath	796	Somerset	*Bath*	<1 km
Burnham	Alfred's will	Somerset	Cannington	11 km
Cannington	Alfred's will	Somerset	Cannington	<1 km
Carhampton	Alfred's will	Somerset	Carhampton	<1 km
Cheddar	956	Somerset	*Cheddar*	<1 km
Chewton Mendip	Alfred's will	Somerset	Chewton Mendip	<1 km
Congresbury	Alfred's will	Somerset	*Congresbury*	<1 km
Crewkerne	Alfred's will	Somerset	Crewkerne	<1 km
Frome	955	Somerset	Frome	<1 km
Kilton	Alfred's will	Somerset	Stogumber	9 km
Somerton	733	Somerset	Northover	6 km
Taunton	722	Somerset	*Taunton*	<1 km
Wedmore	Alfred's will	Somerset	Wedmore	<1 km
Yeovil	Alfred's will	Somerset	Yetminster	6 km
Amesbury	858	Wiltshire	Amesbury	<1 km
Bedwyn	968	Wiltshire	Bedwyn	<1 km
Calne	977	Wiltshire	Calne	<1 km
Chippenham	853	Wiltshire	Chippenham	<1 km
Chisledon	Alfred's will	Wiltshire	Aldbourne	9 km
Damerham	Alfred's will	Wiltshire	*Damerham*	<1 km
Downton	Eadred's will	Wiltshire	Downton	<1 km
Edington	878	Wiltshire	Westbury	5 km
Pewsey	Alfred's will	Wiltshire	Pewsey	<1 km
Wardour	899	Wiltshire	*Tisbury*	3 km
Warminster	899	Wiltshire	Warminster	<1 km
Wilton	838	Wiltshire	Wilton	<1 km

Table 8: Royal vills (reliable pre-AD 1000 evidence) and nearest minster churches (italics indicate reliable pre-AD 900 evidence). King Alfred's will probably dates to between 872 and 888 (Keynes & Lapidge 1983).

comprising a group of timber halls within an enclosure. The morphology of this part of the site is very similar to excavated high-status examples of the same period at Cowdery's Down and Chalton (both Hampshire: Millett & James 1983; Champion 1977). Outside the main focus lay an apsidal-ended rectangular building in its own regular enclosure. A 2m-wide trench was excavated across the west end of this structure and through the northern enclosure boundary. Though no definite graves were encountered, human bone was identified. The building is very similar in size and form to the early church at St Paul-in-the-Bail, Lincoln, and an ecclesiastical explanation seems most convincing (Hinchcliffe 1986: 251-3; Gilmour 1979). The position of this likely church in relation to the complex of halls suggests it was a secondary element of the settlement rather than the original focus. It is possible that the site at Cowage Farm provides a model for understanding the establishment of many other churches in middle Saxon Wessex, in valley-bottom locations adjacent to existing royal or aristocratic centres.

Of the pre-AD 1000 royal vills, a large majority (nearly 80%) seem to have been on sites with valley-bottom locations similar to those most common for Wessex minsters. This suggests that ecclesiastical centres and royal vills were topographically located according to similar principles. Six of the ten sites which are in other positions (on hill slopes or valley sides) are first noted as royal centres in Alfred's will, suggesting once again that the places mentioned in the will were rather different from the sites which formed the core of the ancient royal estates (Sawyer 1983: 279).

Early ecclesiastical centres and royal vills in Wessex were commonly located in close proximity to one another and normally shared similar valley-bottom locations. Although some of the churches at royal estate centres held extensive estates, many others only held a small amount of land at Domesday, suggesting they were not very wealthy and were perhaps more dependent on the royal vills. As suggested by Hase (1988, 1994) and Blair (1988a), this suggests a high degree of royal involvement in

Fig. 17: Part of the middle Saxon site at Cowage Farm, Foxley (Wiltshire). The probable church lies in a separate enclosure to the east of the main settlement. (After Hinchcliffe 1986 fig. 1.)

ecclesiastical affairs. There were also some early church sites which are not close to royal vills, but which were on ecclesiastical land that was either their own endowment or part of a major ecclesiastical landholder's estate in the later Saxon period (see Table 7). Many of these sites share similar types of locations to royal vills, and the form of the few excavated sites is very similar to contemporary secular elite centres. These could represent the first foundations by the secular elite of quasi-autonomous monastic communities. As suggested above, ecclesiastical and royal centres were part of a common tradition of settlement. Both were a kind of elite centre, commonly founded and staffed by members of royal and comital families. Royal and ecclesiastical centres had a similar role in the landscape, and it seem likely that the majority of West Saxons would have regarded them as very similar kinds of places.

Conclusion

The evidence considered in this chapter shows how a common religious tradition of important monastic sites was established in two different parts of early medieval Britain. There were many important similarities between the early churches of Wessex and Cornwall, but also some interesting differences.

In Wessex, churches were most commonly sited close to the bottoms of broad valleys, just above the level of the river floodplain. In Cornwall too, despite the fact that the physical topography is much steeper than in most of Wessex, major churches were normally established in low-lying positions in valleys or near the coast, and only rarely occupied islands or dominating hilltops. In both areas this probably resulted from a need for the church to occupy a central position in the everyday life of the district. The major churches themselves are likely to have acted as spiritual centres for both religious communities and ordinary people living in their territories. In Cornwall, for example, some major churches were established at pre-existing (and thus originally non-Christian) burial grounds. In Wessex, there is evidence to suggest they were also economically important as foci for industrial activity and subsidiary settlements. The next chapter returns to these themes.

The earliest medieval churches of both regions were closely linked to centres of royal power. In Wessex, this pattern seems to have remained the norm for most minster churches throughout the early middle ages. However, the situation in Cornwall may have been rather different. There is no sign of a close physical relationship between monasteries and royal settlements after the demise of the 'late Antique' centres like Tintagel around the beginning of the seventh century. This suggests that Cornwall's monasteries may have been relatively autonomous in the early middle ages, at least until the time political control was established by the English kingdom. These regional differences in the relationships between royal centres and churches will be developed further with reference to the evidence of church estates and administrative structures in Chapter 5.

4

Ecclesiastical centres and changing settlement patterns

Introduction

This chapter investigates the relationships between important early ecclesiastical sites and changing settlement patterns, and makes suggestions about how the foundation of major churches influenced the development of the early medieval landscape. It begins with a review of settlement patterns in early medieval Cornwall which provides important background information and shows how sites of different periods have been identified and mapped in the subsequent discussion. Then follow three case studies from Cornwall which analyse how newly founded churches related to changing patterns of farmsteads and agricultural resources, becoming central to core zones of settlement between the seventh and ninth centuries. The final part looks at the evidence from Wessex where settlement patterns are harder to investigate than in Cornwall. Nevertheless, the general picture derived from archaeological work and historic landscape studies suggests similar patterns developed here to those detected in Cornwall.

The Settlements of Cornwall, AD *c.*300–1300

Many of the questions with which this book is concerned relate to the organisation of the landscape and how this may have changed in the early middle ages. Shifts in settlement pattern may reflect social and cultural changes, and it is therefore important to identify them (Alcock 1993: 55-72). To compare the settlement patterns in two different periods, it is necessary to have information about both. Any patterns detected can then be compared with other data, such as information about sites with religious significance, or similar analysis of settlement patterns from other regions.

This sort of approach is commonly used when analysing settlement patterns based on pottery scatters and other finds recovered during field survey, particularly in the Mediterranean (e.g. Barker 1995). When thinking of south-western England, it is important to remember that the data for different periods may be derived from a range of different sources. This section discusses the example of settlement patterns in Cornwall from the Iron Age to the late medieval

71

period, where four main phases can be distinguished between AD *c.*300–1300. It shows how models of early landscapes can be derived from the different kinds of data available. A similar approach has been used later in the chapter to study the developing medieval settlement pattern in Wessex.

Phase 1: Cornish Settlements from the Iron Age to the Sixth Century AD

Modern scholars count Cornwall amongst the least 'Romanised' parts of Britain (Todd 1987). This lack of 'Romanisation' is reflected in the region's Roman-period sites and artefacts, particularly in the west. Whilst highlighting the occurrence of small amounts of imported material in Cornwall, Henrietta Quinnell has pointed out that around 95% of all pottery from Roman-period sites in the county was locally produced on the Lizard peninsula. This echoes the situation during the Iron Age, when almost all the pottery in Cornwall derived from the county's southernmost peninsula, which suggests that distribution channels may have remained relatively undisrupted by any political changes (Quinnell 1986).

Evidence from excavated settlements reflects strong continuities between the Iron and the Roman period (Quinnell 2004: 216). The most commonly recognised type of Late Iron Age settlement in the South West was not the hillfort, but the 'round'.[1] Rounds were normally enclosed by a bank and ditch. They were often roughly round, though rectangular, square and even triangular examples are also known (Johnson & Rose 1982). Many hundreds of sites are known in west Devon and Cornwall **(see Figs 2 and 18)**. Examples like Trevisker (ApSimon & Greenfield 1972) and Castle Gotha (Saunders & Harris 1982) show that rounds date mainly from the second century BC onwards, and that occupation continued into the first centuries of the Roman period with few changes. Only one excavated round was abandoned before the beginning of the Roman period, Threemilestone near Truro (Schweiso 1976).

A few excavated rounds were occupied from prehistory through to the fourth century AD or later (e.g. Penhale: Johnson et al. 1998/9), but significant changes to the prehistoric settlement pattern took place during the second and third centuries AD. Whilst some old rounds went out of use in the second century AD, many new rounds were established at around the same time. These include Grambla (Saunders 1972), Shortlanesend (Harris 1980), Kilhallon (Carlyon 1982), Reawla (Appleton-Fox 1992), and Trethurgy (Quinnell 2004: 212). The reasons for changes in settlement locations between the earlier and later Roman periods are unclear, although Quinnell has suggested a link to population growth (ibid. 216).

The rounds occupied in the Iron Age and early Roman period cannot be distinguished morphologically from those of the later Roman and post-Roman periods. It is therefore not possible to plot two distribution maps of the two periods on this basis, and the only certain way to differentiate between rounds of different periods is by dating excavation assemblages.

Whilst Cornwall seems to have been less 'Romanised' than other parts of Britain, it also appears to have been less severely affected than other areas by the

---

[1] For the abandonment of Cornish hillforts in later prehistory see Quinnell & Harris 1985: 129.

Fig. 18: Newberry Round, St Teath, Cornwall (the circular feature cut by the double hedge-bank in the centre of the photograph); behind it to the left is Castle Goff (Lanteglos by Camelford), once thought to be a round but now considered a possible medieval fortification (Creighton & Freeman 2006). [Photo: Steve Hartgroves/Historic Environment Service, Cornwall County Council.]

'ending' of Roman Britain (Turner 2004b). As far as settlements are concerned, this is demonstrated by the excavated rounds at Trethurgy and Grambla, both of which have yielded imported Mediterranean pottery of the fifth and sixth centuries (Quinnell 2004). Rounds at Halligye (St Mawgan-in-Meneage), Tremough and Mullion may be other examples (Dark 2000: 168; Lawson Jones 2002: 22; Thorpe 2003: 27-8). It seems likely that other rounds would also have been occupied in these centuries, but may not have been supplied with pottery imports. Quinnell has demonstrated that much Roman-period pottery at Trethurgy was not deposited in the archaeological contexts where it was found for up to two hundred years after manufacture (Quinnell 2004: 176-7). Furthermore, recent research has shown that local pottery production in west Cornwall continued into the fifth and sixth centuries (ibid. 110-11; C. Thomas, pers. comm.). Saunders' interim publication on Grambla also states that the 'usual coarse ware' (i.e. Cornish 'Roman' pottery) was excavated from contexts stratigraphically shown to post-date those containing post-Roman pottery imported from the Mediterranean (Saunders 1972: 52). Recent work at Tintagel has established a sequence of radiocarbon dates which clearly imply local pottery production continued into the fifth century (Morris et al. 1999: 212). Finally, large quantities of imported Mediterranean pottery have recently been found in association with gabbroic forms from the Lizard at the post-Roman beachmarket site of Bantham Ham in Devon (Horner 2001: 8). Quinnell's research shows that several rounds have probable post-Roman occupation, and suggests that there is considerable potential for re-dating assemblages from others based on an increasingly good understanding of locally produced pottery.

The majority of known Roman sites in Cornwall are rounds, but other places also remained in use beyond the end of the fourth century AD. In parts of Penwith and the Isles of Scilly, so-called 'courtyard houses' have been recognised in substantial numbers. These settlements comprise buildings set closely around a yard to form houses which occur both singly and in small groups. The excavated sites at Goldherring and Porthmeor, both groups of courtyard houses set within rounds, have produced possible evidence for their continuing use in the fifth and sixth centuries (Hirst 1936; Guthrie 1969). A courtyard house at Halangay Down on St Mary's, Scilly may have been occupied as late as the seventh or eighth centuries (Ashbee 1996).

Although not widespread until recently, the increasing use of radiocarbon dating on large-scale developer-funded excavations is beginning to yield important results relating to this period. Two possible unenclosed settlements were identified on the route of the Bear's Down to Ruthvoes pipeline in central Cornwall, including features dated to the fifth or sixth centuries that have been interpreted as gullies around roundhouses at Lanhainsworth near St Colum Major (Lawson Jones 2001). At Stencoose (St Agnes) a small structure of fifth- or sixth-century date appears to have gone out of use around the beginning of the seventh century. When a medieval strip-field system was established in the area some time in the middle ages it was on a completely different alignment to the underlying Roman field system (ibid. 85-90). Other examples of marked differences between the alignments of Romano-British fields and medieval strip-fields have been identified at Trenithan Bennett, Trenowah and Tremough (Rose & Preston-Jones 1995; CAU 1998a; Lawson Jones 2002).

It also seems likely that patterns of trade and exchange continued into the post-Roman centuries, and may even have developed over longer distances than formerly. Cornwall is well known for its tin, and scholars have argued that tin production increased sharply in Cornwall during the third and fourth centuries to feed an increasing demand for pewter objects in Britain, and to compensate for the increasing difficulties faced by the Roman administration in exploiting the Iberian tin supplies (Quinnell 1986: 129-30; Todd 1987: 231-2). Tin ingots have been found in several late- and post-Roman contexts in Cornwall and the South West (S. Gerrard 2000: 21-24). These include Par Beach, St Martin's, Scilly, where an ingot was excavated within a late Roman building, and Trethurgy, where an ingot was found in a fourth-century midden (Quinnell 1986: 130). The find of four ingots at Praa Sands, Breage suggests strongly that the extraction and exchange of tin continued into the post-Roman period, since they were found in probable association with timbers radiocarbon dated to 600–790 cal AD (Penhallurick 1986; Biek 1994). At the mouth of the Erme in south Devon a large group of ingots was found just offshore, presumably coming from a ship wrecked on the rocks in the estuary. Although it was not possible to date the ingots from associated contexts, they are mostly similar in size and shape to the Praa Sands examples. The wreck site is also adjacent to the possible post-Roman beachmarket at Mothecombe, where sherds of imported Mediterranean pottery were retrieved from an eroding cliff face (Turner & Gerrard 2004), and a post-Roman context is a strong possibility for the Mothecombe ingots (Fox 1995).

Significantly, several of the best-known post-Roman sites were also occupied in the late Roman period. The most important is Tintagel; here occupation commenced in the third or fourth century, when the site received a range of goods similar to that of important rounds like Trethurgy and Reawla (Thorpe 1997: 82). Smaller, but still significant, quantities of both late and post-Roman material have been recovered from the small hillfort of Chûn Castle in Penwith (Thomas 1956; Preston-Jones & Rose 1986: 138), and also more recently at St Michael's Mount (Herring 1993: 60-1; CAU 1998b: 18; Herring 2000: 119-22). This evidence strongly suggests that the major post-Roman centres of Cornwall were in fact established (or re-established, as some are on sites originally dating to the Iron Age) as part of a late Roman settlement pattern (see also Dark 2000: 164-70).

Based on the material from the settlements which have been excavated so far, there is good evidence for continuities between the settlement patterns of the Iron Age and earlier Roman period (c. 200 BC–c. AD 200) and later Roman period and post-Roman period (c. AD 200–c. AD 600). There is also little to suggest that the Roman presence had a substantial effect on local settlement practice, indeed it seems more likely that 'native' social, political and economic factors had most influence on these aspects of life. With reference to the material culture of the Cornish late Roman period, Quinnell has argued that:

> Close fostering of local traditions may have produced a community which was successful for far longer than those in regions of Roman Britain usually appraised as comparatively civilised both in classical and modern terminology.
>
> (Quinnell 1993: 40)

It seems likely that the same local cultural resilience is detectable in Cornish settlement practice both in and around the 'Roman' centuries.

Phase 2: Early Medieval Settlement Patterns from the Sixth to Ninth Centuries AD

There were significant changes in the form of Cornish settlements AD c. 500–900. Settlements ceased to be defined by large banks and ditches, and the most common settlement form became the 'unenclosed' farmstead. The evidence for these unenclosed early medieval farmsteads comes from two sources, archaeology and place-names; the latter are presently the most informative.

The archaeological evidence for unenclosed early medieval settlement sites in Cornwall is rather slight. One site has been confidently ascribed to this period by its excavator, Charles Thomas: GM/1 near Gwithian in west Cornwall (the original place-name is lost; Thomas 1958). The site is now being prepared for publication, but preliminary reports noted that the stratigraphy had been much disturbed by animal action and other factors (Thomas 1968a: 314). Despite this, Thomas was able to suggest a typology of pottery for early medieval Cornwall from the fifth to the eleventh centuries. This has provoked some debate, in particular relating to the date of so-called 'grass-marked' sherds (Hutchinson 1979; Preston-Jones & Rose 1986: 175-6). This material has been found at a number of occupation sites in Cornwall and Scilly (mainly in unstratified contexts), but the uncertainties mean these sites cannot presently be assigned to the sixth to eighth centuries. The current research on Gwithian being undertaken by Charles Thomas and the Cornwall Archaeological Unit should clarify this issue somewhat, but the site does appear to have seen a lengthy period of early medieval occupation.

Certain types of place-names help fill the present gaps in the archaeological data. The place-name evidence for early medieval settlement has been considered by Preston-Jones, Rose and Herring (Preston-Jones & Rose 1986; Rose & Preston-Jones 1995; Herring 1999b, 1999c). Padel has provided the foundation for this work through his collection and analysis of medieval Cornish place-names (Padel 1985, 1988). He argues on linguistic grounds that habitative place-name elements (i.e. those denoting a settlement) such as *tre* and **bod* were used to coin names principally between the fifth and eleventh centuries. Many such names must have been coined in the seventh century and before, since names with both elements occur in Devon in areas of otherwise strongly Anglicised nomenclature. He also notes that the formation Trenowyth ('new *tre*') is found in a tenth-century charter indicating that even names of this type will date to the early middle ages (Padel 1985: 223-5; Padel 1999: 88-90). Preston-Jones and Rose have plotted the distributions of *tre* settlements and other place-names to analyse the early medieval settlement patterns in five different parts of Cornwall (Preston-Jones & Rose 1986; Rose & Preston-Jones 1995). They state that there is little reason to doubt that the locations of medieval (and modern) *tre* settlements represent the locations of their early medieval predecessors (1995: 52). Unfortunately, this hypothesis remains archaeologically untested. Nevertheless, there is documentary evidence from the tenth and eleventh centuries which suggests that *tre* settlements can have moved little since that time. Several Anglo-Saxon charter boundary clauses describe very small estates with the same names as the medieval and modern settlements. In these cases it is physically impossible for the settlement to have moved more than a couple of hundred metres since the time of the charter (the settlement must have been within the charter bounds), and even this seems unlikely (e.g. Trethewey, St Keverne (S832); Trerice, St Dennis (S1019); Hooke 1994a).

It is probable that many settlements with topographical name-elements were occupied during this period, although it is not yet possible to demonstrate conclusively which were established at what stage before the Norman Conquest. Preston-Jones and Rose have shown that early medieval settlement in the upland parish of Davidstow occurred in at least two phases (1986: 143). They noted that places with Cornish topographical names generally occur on higher ground than sites with *tre* names, and that the former do not 'fit' into the relatively regular pattern of *tre* settlements in the valley. This suggests the topographical place-names are part of a later episode of settlement. However, Preston-Jones and Rose also found that in the Padstow area some places with topographical names do form part of a pattern otherwise made up of *tre* settlements. They concluded that whilst 'some topographical names must be later [than *tre* settlements], not all are' (ibid. 143-4). This argument implies that in early medieval Cornwall there were 'core' areas of settlement typified by settlements with *tre* names, and that these areas were subject to some kind of organisation (ibid. 141-4; Rose & Preston-Jones 1995: 52-6; Padel 1985: 127). It is therefore possible to be fairly confident on both linguistic and topographical grounds that many settlements with habitative name-elements (e.g. *tre*, **bod*) existed in the seventh, eighth and ninth centuries on or very close to their later medieval sites. However, it is not possible to be certain using either sort of evidence how many topographical name-elements were applied to settlements until the centuries immediately before the Norman Conquest (when they are first recorded in documents).

The distribution of *tre* names probably reflects the 'core' areas of settlement in Cornwall during the seventh, eighth and ninth centuries **(Fig. 19)**. Exceptions to this are the two easternmost areas of Cornwall where very few *tre* place-names occur in Stratton hundred and around Callington in East hundred. Here most Cornish place-names were replaced by English place-names, as also happened in Devon during the early middle ages (Svensson 1987).

The exact nature of the relationship between the rounds and the *tre* settlements is important for settlement history but as yet unresolved. The latest occupation in rounds or other settlements which had been in use during the Roman period appears to have been in the late sixth or early seventh century at sites such as Tintagel or Trethurgy, or exceptionally in the seventh or eighth centuries, as at Halangay Down, Scilly, and possibly Chûn Castle, Penwith (Ashbee 1996; Thomas 1956). Unless there was total desertion of the landscape when the rounds ceased to

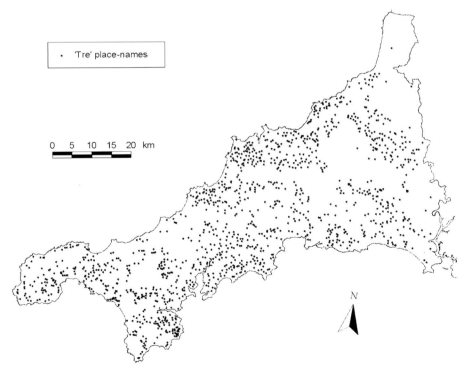

Fig. 19: Medieval settlements with *tre* place-names in Cornwall
(data: Oliver Padel/*ICS Index*).

be occupied, unenclosed early medieval settlements such as those with *tre* place-names must have originated at this time or before. Several possible scenarios for their development have been discussed by Rose and Preston-Jones (1995). First, it is possible that unenclosed settlements apart from the courtyard houses of Penwith had existed in Roman Cornwall, and that the *tre* settlements have their origins in these. No firm evidence for such Roman-period settlements has been discovered, but Rose and Preston-Jones note that some of the Penwith courtyard houses 'appear to be part of [the] medieval pattern' of settlement (1995: 64). The implication is that medieval settlements are on the site of earlier unenclosed settlements, and perhaps have their origins in the third century AD. Secondly, and similarly, it is possible that while some rounds were abandoned, others became *tre* settlements and that their defences have been obliterated by later use. Those rounds close to later settlements may have been preserved as a result of slight settlement shifts (ibid. 56-60). However, no firm evidence has yet been recovered for Romano-Cornish settlements on the site of early medieval settlements, and few rounds appear to have been reoccupied as settlement sites at any time in the middle ages (Thomas 1966: 97). A third possibility is that the rounds were completely abandoned and that the unenclosed settlements represent a break with the earlier tradition. This seems to be suggested by the settlement pattern of the Padstow area, where Rose and Preston-Jones comment that the relationship between rounds and medieval settlements 'appears random and could indeed be so' (1995: 61-2). They also note that in some areas there appears to be a retraction from higher ground at the end of the Roman period which is reflected by abandoned rounds situated at higher altitudes than early medieval settlements (ibid. 57-60). If such a shift can be equated with a decline in the size of the population, this may also help explain why no new rounds seem to have been built in the fourth century or later.

In their paper's conclusion, Rose and Preston-Jones propose a model which sees retraction in the area settled during the Roman and post-Roman periods, 'with many [sites] deserted but most continuing or shifting only slightly, to become the *trefs* etc. of the early medieval period' (ibid. 66). They consider the early medieval settlement pattern to be a continuation and development of the Romano-British pattern (ibid. 67). However, they also argue that the end of 'defended' settlements implies an important political and social dislocation (ibid. 62). Herring has argued that the desertion of the rounds shows that major social and economic changes took place in or around the sixth century which led to a complete reorganisation of the countryside, resulting in an early medieval landscape of strip fields and unenclosed settlements (1999b, 1999c).

Cornwall is a relatively small county, and Roman-period settlement extended over a very great part of it (as shown by the distribution of rounds, **Fig. 2**). Any subsequent settlement pattern was bound to include some of the area occupied during the Roman period, unless it had concentrated solely on the uplands such as Bodmin Moor. In the absence of evidence for any direct continuity from Roman to medieval settlements, a model emphasising the difference between Roman and early medieval settlements rather than continuity is arguably more acceptable at present. The apparent contraction of the settled area in the early middle ages was noted above. Rose and Preston Jones (1995: 57-60) and Rose and Johnson (1983) have shown that the fields surrounding some rounds were completely abandoned, only to be reoccupied later in the middle ages when new fields and farms were established on different alignments. There are also significant political and social differences between enclosed and unenclosed settlements, and changes in settlement form may imply important changes and developments in social relations (Rose and Preston-Jones 1995: 66). Some scholars have suggested that it may reflect the development of a more egalitarian social structure (Herring 1999b, 1999c). At a local level, there seem to be differences between the locations of rounds and the locations of *tre* settlements. Whilst the latter tend to be about half way up valley sides, commonly in sheltered positions near the break of slope (Preston-Jones & Rose 1986: 143), rounds tend to occupy more exposed spurs and the upper edges of valleys (Thomas 1966: 87).

In conclusion, the post-Roman period witnessed a retraction in the area settled, and radical changes in the form of most settlements. Rose and Preston-Jones place these changes in the fifth century and link them to the decline of the Roman administration (1995: 66). However, as the settlement evidence discussed above shows, late Roman administrative structures in Cornwall may have endured into the sixth or early seventh centuries (see also Dark 2000: 168-70). The change from rounds to *tre* settlements may be associated with the changes in local power structures shown in the rapid decline of late and post-Roman sites such as Tintagel and Trethurgy in the later sixth or early seventh centuries. The evidence from settlement studies suggests that this period may have witnessed political turbulence that was at least as important as the changes of the fifth century.

By comparing **Figs 2 and 19** it can be seen that while rounds and *tre* place-names occur together in many areas, there are some distinct differences between their distributions. Noticeable areas where *tre* place-names are absent but rounds are present include the parish of Cardinham south-west of Bodmin Moor, the hills east of Crowan and west of Stithians in the northern part of Kerrier hundred, Helston Downs, and St Agnes Downs. However, these maps are full of detail and hard to interpret at such a small scale: the detailed case studies presented below present further evidence in support of these arguments.

Phase 3: Settlement Patterns of the Ninth to Eleventh Centuries AD

There is a greater variety of evidence for settlement patterns from the second half of the early middle ages in Cornwall, and it further confirms the idea of 'core' areas of settlement (identified above through *tre* and other habitative place-names). The evidence comes from three sources, archaeology, historical documents and place-names.

The settlement at Mawgan Porth is still the region's most completely excavated and best-understood site of this period (Bruce-Mitford 1997). It comprised at least three houses set around small 'courtyards' and a cist-grave cemetery which was assumed to have been associated with the settlement. The site is particularly notable for the large quantity of 'bar-lug' pottery (over 2,000 sherds), as well as several other forms of bowls and platters, and for the form of the dwellings there, which seem to be longhouses similar to those of later medieval Cornwall. The excavator has estimated the life-time of the site to have been AD *c*.850–*c*.1050 on the basis of the excavated pottery and a coin of Æthelred II minted at Lydford in Devon AD 990 x 995. Mawgan Porth is located between two dense distributions of *tre* settlements in the areas around Padstow and Crantock which are broken by the St Breock Downs (Padel 1999: 89). In addition to the excavated material, the site's marginal location suggests it is a relatively late addition to the settlement pattern. It was abandoned after encroachment by blown sand from the adjacent beach probably in the mid-eleventh century. Mawgan Porth thus suffered a similar fate to Gwithian site GM/1, whose final phases also appear to date to the later pre-Conquest period (Thomas 1968a).

At least thirty other sites have produced pottery similar to that from Mawgan Porth (Hutchinson 1979, amended in Bruce-Mitford 1997). A few of these date to the period after the Norman Conquest (e.g. Launceston Castle: Saunders 1977), but many seem to be pre-Conquest sites. Perhaps the most notable example is Winnianton, site of the head manor of the hundred of Winnianton (Kerrier) at Domesday, where large quantities of grass-marked and bar-lug pottery have been recovered from the eroding cliff-section (Jope & Threlfall 1956; Thomas 1963). However, in common with most of the other settlement sites believed to date to this period, no excavation has been undertaken to modern standards. The majority of finds of grass-marked and bar-lug pottery are therefore from uncertain or unstratified contexts (e.g. Hellesvean: Guthrie 1954, 1960; Phillack Towans: Somerscales 1957) or have not been adequately recorded or published (e.g. Perran Sands: Penna 1968). However, it is important to note that when associated with medieval settlements, the pottery is found in places with a variety of types of Cornish place-names, not just those with habitative name elements. This suggests a range of Cornish place-names were in use for settlements by the later pre-Conquest period.

Two main sources of documentary evidence cast light on the nature of later early medieval settlement in Cornwall, charters and Domesday Book. The Anglo-Saxon charters record the names of estates and also often document the estate bounds. As noted above, charter bounds can be useful as they demonstrate that a number of settlements can have moved only slightly (if at all) since the tenth or eleventh centuries. They also show that in addition to *tre* place-names, Cornish topographical names were definitely in use as settlement names by the tenth century (e.g. Grugwith: S832; Pennare: S755).

Domesday Book is a rich source of pre-Conquest settlement names. It records around 350 names in Cornwall, 93 of which are *tre* place-names (Padel 1985: 224). The other 250 names include those with other habitative elements as well as a variety of topographical place-names. Nevertheless, a distribution map of the settlements recorded in Domesday Book for Cornwall is far from a representation of the full settlement pattern in 1086, since many hamlets are not mentioned separately from head manors.[2] Pre-Conquest charters and Domesday Book therefore both provide partial reflections of the pattern of settlement.

Place-name evidence can help to fill in the picture provided by the other sources, but once again it must be used with caution. Many Cornish topographical names are likely to date from the ninth, tenth and eleventh centuries, although some may only have been applied to settlements in the later middle ages. The location of individual settlements may suggest which among them form part of the early medieval settlement pattern: by analogy with

---

[2] This includes some estates mentioned earlier in Anglo-Saxon charters, e.g. Traboe in St Keverne: S832. For maps and discussions of the Cornwall Domesday evidence see Ravenhill 1967; Thorn and Thorn 1979a; Thorn 1986; Thorn 1999.

settlements with English place-names in similar locations, those on high moorland or in other 'marginal' positions may be late medieval (see below; Austin et al. 1989: 28-31; Preston-Jones & Rose 1986: 143-5). Many Cornish topographical names make reference to flora, locations or land-use which clearly suggest the colonisation of previously marginal areas. Examples that show this process began in the early middle ages include Draynes in St Neot parish (first recorded in 1086; *dreyn* = 'thorns' or 'thorn bushes'), Penharget in St Ive (1086; *pen* 'top' + **hyr-yarth* 'long-ridge'), and Hammett in Quethiock (1086; **havos* 'summer shieling'; the latter is particularly significant as it indicates that a once seasonally occupied settlement had become a permanent estate centre by the time of the Domesday survey: see Herring 1996 on transhumance; other data from Thorn & Thorn 1979a; Padel 1985).

Padel has noted that English place-names were first given to settlements in Cornwall in significant numbers in this period. He suggests that names with the generic *tun* are likely to date to the centuries immediately before the Norman Conquest (Padel 1999: 91), although it is uncertain when the other English place-names of Cornwall were coined. In the eastern areas of the county between the Lynher and Tamar and in Stratton hundred (where Cornish names are virtually absent), it seems likely that the English toponymy has a similar history to that in neighbouring parts of Devon (Svensson 1987). However, in the rest of Cornwall many English place-names may derive from the later medieval and post-medieval periods (Austin et al. 1989: 30-1). Except in the areas around Stratton and Callington, very few English place-names are recorded in the Domesday survey or in Anglo-Saxon charters (Thorn & Thorn 1979a; Hooke 1994a).

The archaeological information, historical documents and place-names provide a range of sources on which to build an understanding of the developing settlement pattern in the pre-Norman period. The process of 'colonisation' of heath, moorland and other 'marginal' areas which began at this time was to carry on into the later middle ages. Nevertheless, the pattern was still focused on the core lowland areas where the earlier *tre* settlements had been located, and it was therefore a development based on the earlier medieval pattern rather than a break with it (Preston-Jones & Rose 1986).

Phase 4: Later Medieval Settlement

The fourth and final phase of Cornish settlement considered in this book is the continuing medieval expansion on to the heaths, downs and moors of Cornwall in the period after the Norman Conquest. This led to the greatest extent of land being cultivated in the area since the late Roman period. Although a reasonable number of medieval settlements in Cornwall have been excavated, as Preston-Jones and Rose point out (1986: 150), the vast majority have been found to date only to the later medieval, post-Conquest period. This appears to be because these are typically the settlements which were founded latest and abandoned earliest, and now provide recognisable earthwork sites for study. Misleadingly, some archaeological sites have come to be known by reference to the closest inhabited farmstead. For example, archaeologists refer to the excavated site in Lesnewth parish at SX 12369016 as 'Treworld', although in fact it is around 600m uphill from the medieval hamlet of that name (Dudley & Minter 1965). Medieval documents show that the first element of the place-name of another example,

Tresmorn, is *ros 'promontory, moor' rather than tre. The lack of excavated evidence for pre-Conquest settlement in part reflects a lack of excavation projects at lowland sites in Cornwall (Preston-Jones & Rose 1986: 150).

The sites which have been excavated suggest that in common with other parts of the South West medieval colonisation of Cornwall's moors and heaths accelerated after the Norman Conquest, and that settlement density in 'marginal' areas reached a peak in the fourteenth century (see Preston-Jones & Rose 1986: 146-53; Allan 1994).

Medieval documents such as manorial surveys begin to provide a very rich source of settlement names in the later medieval period. Certain place-names are also indicative of later medieval settlements. In west Cornwall, where English did not become the common vernacular until the late- or post-medieval period (Payton 1999), settlements with the generic chy 'house, cottage' (as opposed to ti, the earlier form of the same word) are likely to date to the later thirteenth or fourteenth centuries, and seem to refer to minor dwellings and low-status tenements (Padel 1985). In more easterly parts of the county, English place-names became increasingly common in the centuries after the Norman Conquest. This is reflected in the relatively dense distributions of English place-names on upland parts of Bodmin Moor compared to neighbouring lowland areas (Austin et al. 1989; Johnson & Rose 1994).

Summary

The evidence outlined above suggests four main phases of development in the medieval Cornish settlement pattern. The first is the late (and post-) Roman phase, typified by rounds. The second is the earliest medieval pattern, reflected by habitative place-names including those with the generic element tre. The third phase is reflected in the later pre-Conquest pattern. This still has tre settlements at its core, but around its edges and in the spaces many settlements with Cornish topographical names have been established (and in the east some with English names). The final phase is represented by the later medieval settlements which commonly occur on higher moorland and in other 'marginal' areas.

This quick overview of the development of Cornish medieval settlement is a simple model with which more detailed information from case studies can be compared. It also serves to illustrate the method that has been used to locate various types of monuments and compare patterns relating to different stages in the development of the landscape.

In the following pages the three main early medieval settlement phases in Cornwall will be investigated at a detailed local level, using HLCs to place the settlements in a wider context, and to relate these sites and patterns of agriculture to ecclesiastical centres. It will be argued that major early churches provided central foci in the early medieval Cornish landscape.

Using the Historic Landscape Characterisation

The Historic Landscape Characterisation (HLC) technique was introduced in Chapter 2. The characterisations in this book show the approximate extent of late medieval cultivation and enclosure at its peak (in the thirteenth to fourteenth centuries). In Cornwall they provide a background or context against which data about settlement patterns can be plotted for selected case studies. As described in

Fig. 20: Aerial view of St Neot church from the south-east. The course of the little St Neot River is marked by the sinuous line of trees (flowing from top-centre to bottom-left corner of the photograph). [Photo: Steve Hartgroves/Historic Environment Service, Cornwall County Council.]

the following section, the results show clearly that places with *tre* names are at the core of the medieval settlement pattern. This analysis also illustrates the extent of landscape change in many areas between the late Roman period and the medieval period. Even though the HLC depicts the maximum extent of medieval farmland, many rounds still lie outside this area, in land that was rough ground during the later middle ages **(Figs 28 on p.88 and 33 on p.92)**. The nature of the settlement evidence in much of Wessex means it is harder to compare early medieval patterns with the HLC. Nevertheless, the archaeological and historical studies considered in the final section of this chapter suggest that the early medieval landscape of Wessex developed in a comparable way to that of Cornwall. HLCs show that important early ecclesiastical sites in Wessex were at the heart of core medieval agricultural zones, just as they were in Cornwall **(Figs 41, 42, 43 on pp.103, 104, 105)**.

Three Cornish Case Studies

The three case-study areas focus on three early medieval churches. The boundaries of the case studies are provided by the early modern parish boundaries, which are likely to match the medieval parishes closely (Orme 1999). The three case studies all form roughly coherent topographical units. The first focuses on the early medieval monastery of St Neot **(Fig 20, Plate 6c)**. It comprises the four medieval parishes of Cardinham, Warleggan, St Neot and St

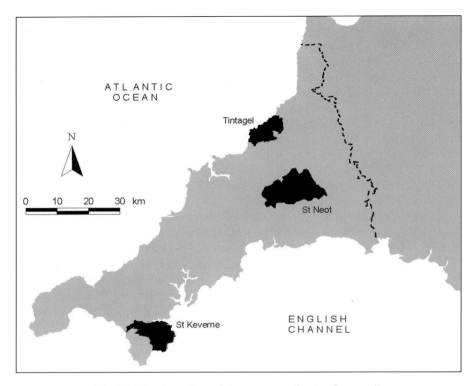

Fig. 21: The location of the case studies in Cornwall.

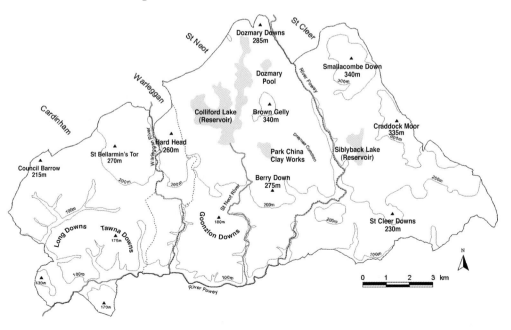

Fig. 22: The topography and tithe map parish boundaries of the St Neot
case-study area.

Cleer. It is bounded to the north by Bodmin Moor and to the south by the River Fowey **(Fig. 22)**. The Tintagel case study includes the medieval parishes of Tintagel, Minster, Forrabury, Trevalga, Lesnewth and St Juliot **(Figs 23 & 51)**. It is bounded by the sea to the west and north and Tresparret, Otterham and Waterpit Downs to the east. The St Keverne study encompasses the medieval parishes of St Keverne, St Anthony-in-Meneage, Manaccan, St Martin-in-Meneage and St Mawgan-in-Meneage. It is bounded to the north, east and south by the sea and Helford estuary, and to the west mainly by the Goonhilly Downs **(Figs 24 & 27)**. Each of these areas includes land at different altitudes and a range of different geologies and soils (Edmonds et al. 1975).

In all three case studies, the medieval farmland and rough ground identified in the HLCs covered the greater part of the medieval landscape **(Figs 25, 26 & 27)**. Together the case studies cover 296km² (8.2% of Cornwall), of which 35% was rough ground, 59% medieval farmland, and 6% woodland. This accords well with Rackham's estimate for the county of 33% rough ground in the eleventh century (Rackham 1986: 335) and Herring's of 30% (Herring 1999b: 20) **(Table 9)**. Both fields and rough ground provided important economic resources. The medieval farmland zone was the principal area for arable, although some crops were occasionally grown on land that was normally rough ground. The medieval farmland also provided most year-round grazing land, and was the area where permanent early medieval settlements were located.

The rough ground also had an economic value, and probably provided resources such as turf, furze, and summer grazing (Herring 1986: vol. 1, 98-113; 1999b: 20). The rough ground often occurred on the higher hills and downs, but there were significant areas at lower altitudes too. The clifftops around Tintagel were used extensively as rough ground, and in St Neot areas of rough ground occurred below the 200m contour at Goonzion Downs, Treslea Downs and Cardinham Downs, and below the 150m contour at Tawna Downs and Holtroad Downs. Environmental or climatic determinism is not adequate to explain the distribution of these different resources. Only the gley soils common on the Lizard peninsula may have retained so much moisture throughout the year that agriculture would have been difficult (Caseldine 1999), so helping to explain why the relatively low-lying downs of St Keverne parish were not farmed for arable in the medieval period. Even so, the distribution of Romano-British settlements suggests that there were attempts to use this land for agriculture in the pre-medieval period. Finally, woodland provided grazing, fuel and building materials; in medieval Cornwall this was mainly located in the steep lower slopes of the river valleys.

	Total area	Woodland	Medieval farmland	Rough ground
St Neot	150 km²	11 km²	77 km²	62 km²
Tintagel	60 km²	1.5 km²	37.5 km²	21 km²
St Keverne	86 km²	4 km²	61 km²	21 km²
Total	296 km²	17 km²	175 km²	104 km²

Table 9: The quantity of the three different medieval landscape resources in the Historic Landscape Characterisations of each study area (to nearest 0.5 km²).

Fig. 23: The landscape of the Tintagel case-study area. The view looking east from St Matheriana's church on Glebe Cliff (about 95m above sea level) towards Condolen Barrow (308m) and the ridge of Waterpit Down. The windswept coutryside of the north Cornish coast is scattered with farmsteads and small hamlets, many of which have early medieval origins.

St Neot

No early medieval settlements in the St Neot area have been excavated, but analogy with other parts of Cornwall suggests this was the time when enclosed Romano-British settlements (rounds) were replaced by unenclosed early medieval settlements. There are fifty-three likely or possible rounds in the St Neot area, and they are distributed fairly evenly across it. The HLC shows that rounds frequently occur on the extreme edge of the area of medieval farmland or just within the zone of rough ground **(Fig. 28)**. Of the seven certain rounds, five are in such positions. As the medieval farmland appears to have been expanded considerably

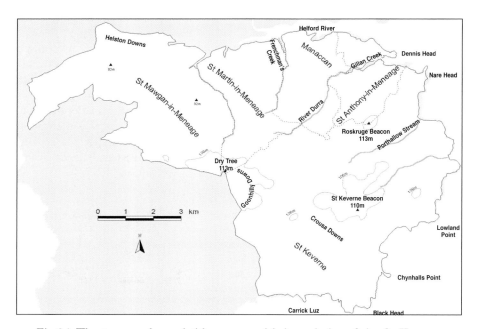

Fig 24: The topography and tithe map parish boundaries of the St Keverne study area.

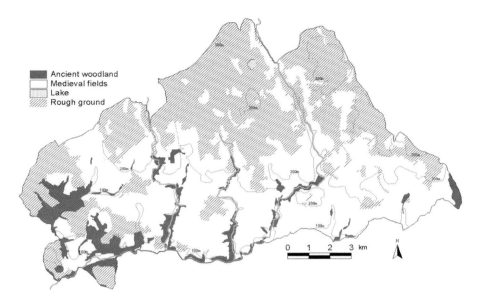

Fig. 25: The Historic Landscape Characterisation of the St Neot study area.

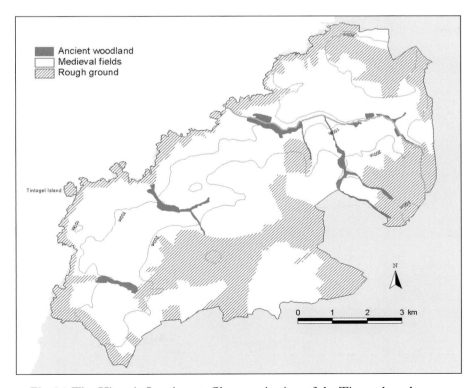

Fig. 26: The Historic Landscape Characterisation of the Tintagel study area.

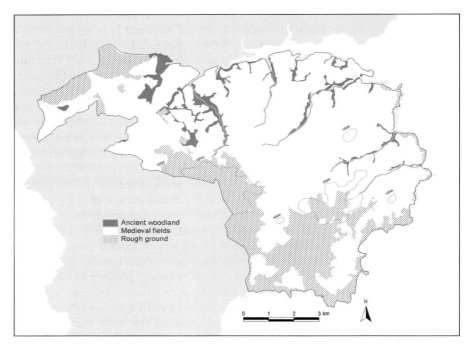

Fig 27: The Historic Landscape Characterisation of the St Keverne
study area.

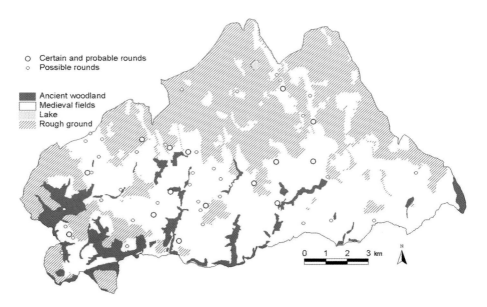

Fig. 28: Rounds in the St Neot study area, and the HLC.

into this area in the late pre-Conquest and later medieval periods, it is likely that most of these rounds (e.g. Higher Langdon, Berry Castle and Lestow) would have been well within the rough grazing zone in the earlier middle ages. This indicates a likely contraction in the area under cultivation between the end of the Romano-British period and the early middle ages, since rounds are most likely to have been surrounded by their fields, as has been demonstrated elsewhere in Cornwall (Johnson & Rose 1982: 173-5; Rose & Preston-Jones 1995: 60). The distribution of rounds also shows some variations. Although rounds are fairly evenly distributed in the south and west, there are few known examples in the south-eastern part of the study area. There are scattered examples in the northern sector and several cases in the valley of the River Fowey.

Settlements in the study area with the *tre* place-name element occur exclusively in the zone of medieval farmland **(Fig. 29)**. This distribution exhibits a number of important differences compared to that of the Romano-British rounds. Particularly striking is the area of medieval Cardinham parish. Here there are two certain and two likely examples of rounds, and twelve further possible cases. There is also one example of a large round or small hillfort at the multivallate enclosure of Bury Castle in Cardinham, perhaps a central place in the Iron Age. However, there are no examples of *tre* settlements at all, and only very few Cornish place-names with habitative elements (one *tyr* at Trezance and one *hendre* at Hendre (see Padel 1985)). In the northern part of the study area there is a complete lack of habitative Cornish place-names north of Trebinnick, although there are a number of rounds. This strongly suggests that settlement in these zones was considerably more dense in the Iron Age and Romano-British periods than in the early medieval period.

Places with names in *tre* and other habitative elements tend to cluster in the

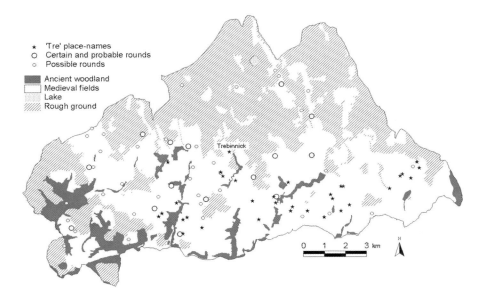

Fig. 29: Rounds, settlements with *tre* place-names (first recorded before 1550) and the HLC in the St Neot study area.

southern portions of the medieval parishes of Warleggan, St Neot and St Cleer. It is likely that this area formed the 'core' of the zone of early medieval settlement. Within this zone the church of St Neot appears to act as a focus for early medieval settlements **(Fig. 30)**. There are virtually no *tre* settlements outside a 3km radius of the church to the north, west or south, the zone beyond this being characterised by a belt of rough grazing and woodland several kilometres wide. It is only to the east in the southern part of St Cleer parish that they continue to occur. This distribution is likely to depend upon the location of Liskeard, some 7.5km to the south-east of St Neot. Liskeard was almost certainly a major secular administrative centre in the early middle ages, and it is possible that it acted as a focus for early medieval settlement in a similar way to the church at St Neot.

In contrast to the early foundation at St Neot, there seems to be little correlation between the location of the other medieval parish churches in the area and the distribution of early medieval settlements with habitative name-elements. This suggests they did not act as focal points when the early medieval settlement pattern was being established, and probably that they were founded later. Cardinham is completely outside the distribution of *tre* settlements, and Warleggan lies on its western edge. The chapel at St Luke's, which may have had semi-parochial status in the fourteenth and fifteenth centuries, is at the northern extremity of St Neot parish far distant from the main areas of medieval farmland (Rose 1994: 79). Other than St Neot, only St Cleer lies within the main zone occupied by settlements with *tre* names **(Fig. 31)**.

The 'core' of early medieval farmland was probably expanded into the woodlands and on to the moors and downs from the late pre-Norman period onwards, continuing with greater momentum in the twelfth and thirteenth centuries (settlement phases 3 & 4; Austin et al. 1989: 17-38; Johnson & Rose

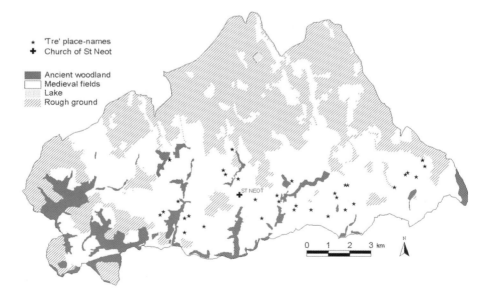

Fig. 30: The church of St Neot and settlements with *tre* place-names in the
St Neot study area, and the HLC.

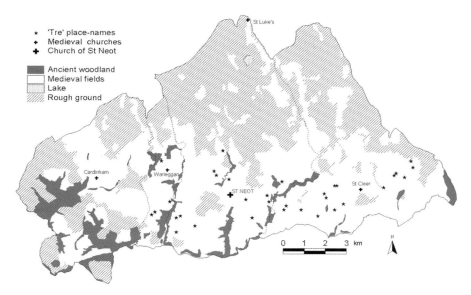

Fig. 31: Late medieval parish churches, tithe map parish boundaries, and settlements with *tre* place-names (first recorded before 1550) in the St Neot study area, and the HLC.

1994: 77-87). Post-conquest documents which give a rough indication of the limit of cultivated ground also suggest that expansion was a relatively late phenomenon (see Austin et al. 1989: 23-38; Rose 1994: 79-80). The main distribution of settlements with English place-names is on the edge of the woodland and rough ground, and it is likely that many of them were established during this expansion of the settled area. Parish churches like Cardinham and Warleggan stand in areas with many such place-names, and it is possible that they were established around this time to serve newly-independent estates in these areas of 'secondary' settlement **(Fig. 32)**.

Tintagel

The major post-Roman centre at Tintagel Island is the only settlement in the Tintagel area with excavated occupation evidence from the early medieval period. Of eight certain or probable rounds in the study area, the HLC shows that three are located in the zone of medieval rough ground, and two further examples are immediately adjacent to it. This contrasts with the pattern of settlements with *tre* place-names, which are focused in the area of medieval farmland above the coastal rough grazing on the clifftops **(Fig. 33)**.

Both rounds and settlements with *tre* place-names are quite densely distributed in the (later medieval) parish of Tintagel. This illustrates the fact that there were also some significant continuities between the Roman and medieval periods: the re-adjustment of the sixth to seventh centuries was a re-focusing and retraction of the farmed area, not a complete shift to previously unused land. This area had been the immediate hinterland of the elite centre at Tintagel Island, and it is likely to have been the core of the estate which provided an agricultural surplus for the Island's rulers. The farmers who lived in the settlements with *tre* names which

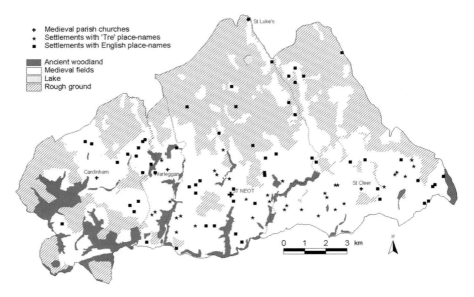

Fig. 32: Late medieval parish churches, tithe map parish boundaries, settlements with *tre* place-names, and settlements with English place-names (first recorded before 1550) in the St Neot study area, and the HLC.

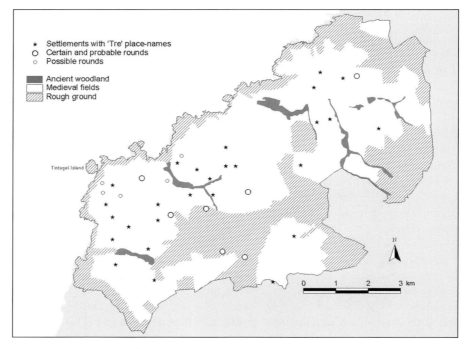

Fig. 33: Rounds and settlements with *tre* place-names (first recorded before 1550) in the Tintagel study area, and the HLC.

cluster around Tintagel were the successors to this estate. Tintagel churchyard may have remained active as a religious centre throughout the early middle ages, despite the desertion of the neighbouring high-status centre in the late-sixth or seventh centuries. It is possible that the early Christian site here took on some of the central-place attributes of Tintagel Island after its demise; it certainly appears to have acted as a focal point for the surrounding agrarian landscape.

As in the St Neot case study, settlements with English place-names are largely peripheral to the pattern of Cornish names, and probably represent later pre-Conquest or even post-Conquest expansion from the earlier medieval 'core' **(Fig. 34)**. The HLC reveals that many of these settlements are on the very edge of the medieval rough ground (e.g. Treven, Treway, Ringford, Trela, Vendown and Downrow). Some have names that indicate their relationship to rough grazing land such as Anderton ('under-the-down'), Vendown ('marsh on the down') and both the Trevens (that in Tintagel was atte Fenn in 1317; the St Juliot example was la Fenne in 1314: *ICS Index*). Nearby Newton stands isolated high (*c.*230m) amid Tresparret Downs; Oliver Padel has suggested that 'Newtons' in Cornwall may date to the twelfth to fifteenth centuries (this example was first recorded in 1317: *ICS Index*; Padel 1999: 92).

St Keverne

Rounds are distributed fairly evenly in the area around St Keverne. Sixty-three examples have been identified, of which sixteen are certain instances and a further

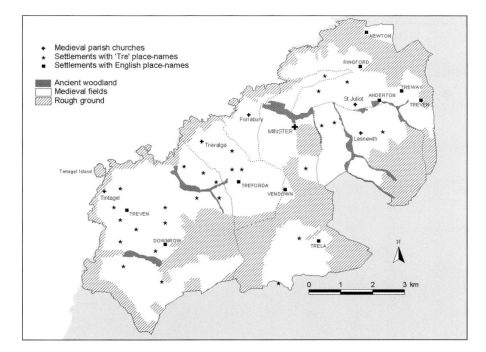

Fig. 34: Settlements with *tre* place-names, and settlements with English place-names (first recorded before 1550) in the Tintagel study area, and the HLC.

twelve are considered probable examples. The remainder have been identified through field- and place-names or through preliminary field or air survey. Compared to the other two Cornish study areas, rounds are relatively infrequent in the zone of rough ground identified by the HLC, with only four possible examples in rough ground, one probable example in woodland, and another at Gweek that stands in fields probably cut from woodland only a few hundred years ago **(Figs 35 and 36)**. This may suggest that the directly cultivated area in the Meneage remained more constant throughout prehistory and up to the late or post-medieval period than elsewhere. The terminal reave of the Trebarveth Bronze Age field system may be the boundary which still defines the edge of the area of rough grazing known as Main Dale, although in the past it probably extended further to the east than today (Johns & Herring 1996: 79). In addition, several prehistoric standing stones stand near the division between the rough ground and the anciently farmed land (e.g. Crousa, Tremenheere and Trelanvean). In neighbouring West Penwith, where standing stones are much more common than on the Lizard, it has been argued that marking this division was originally one of their principal roles (Peters 1990). As noted above, the downs of the Lizard are one of few areas in Cornwall where poor soil conditions may have prevented effective agriculture, and this may have constrained farming activity in the past (Caseldine 1999).

While the general extent of cultivated land in the St Keverne area may have remained more or less constant, it is nonetheless possible to identify areas with different concentrations of rounds. In particular, the area around St Keverne churchtown seems not to have been densely settled in the Iron Age or Roman period. It is possible that this is an area in which more rounds were destroyed owing

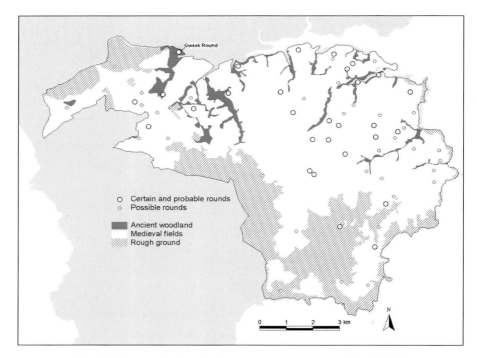

Fig. 35: Rounds in the St Keverne study area, and the HLC.

Fig. 36: Gweek Round, Gweek (formerly in the parish of Mawgan-in-Meneage). [Photo: Steve Hartgroves/Historic Environment Service, Cornwall County Council.]

to more intensive medieval exploitation. Nevertheless, sites like Gear (a major round or small hillfort now in St Martin-in-Meneage parish) and the many rounds which have been identified close to it suggest that the foci of the settlement pattern in the Iron Age and Romano-British periods differed to those of later times.

This area, and St Keverne parish in particular, has the densest distribution of *tre* settlements in the whole of Cornwall, and the early medieval landscape of settlement can be mapped here with some confidence (Johns & Herring 1996: 56-8). As in the other study areas, *tre* settlements occur exclusively in the zone of medieval farmland. Particularly notable is the area around St Keverne itself, which has been identified as a probable monastic centre from early medieval documentary sources (Olson 1989; **Fig. 37**). There is a particularly marked concentration of settlements with *tre* names here, which strongly suggests that the church acted as a central focus when the early medieval settlement pattern was being established between the sixth and ninth centuries. The area with the densest distribution of *tre* settlements also seems likely to have been the core of the estate of St Keverne's monastery, which was held in the later medieval period by Beaulieu Abbey.

Fig. 37: The church and village of St Keverne and its landscape. St Keverne lies at the centre of a landscape that is thick with settlements. [Photo: Steve Hartgroves/Historic Environment Service, Cornwall County Council.]

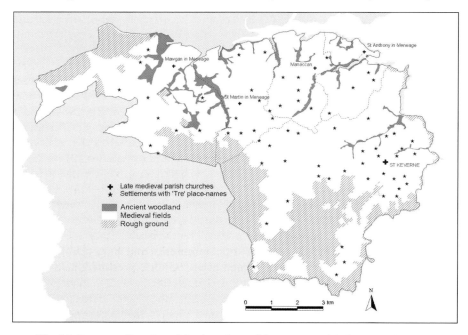

Fig. 38: Late medieval parish churches, tithe map parish boundaries, and settlements with *tre* place-names (first recorded before 1550) in the St Keverne study area, and the HLC.

Early medieval settlements do not appear to cluster in the same way around the other nearby sites that later became medieval parish churches (St Mawgan-in-Meneage, St Anthony-in-Meneage and Manaccan; Fig. 38). It has been suggested that St Mawgan-in-Meneage could have been an early medieval monastic centre, and *Scanct Mawan* is recorded as a dependency of the royal manor at Winnianton in Domesday Book (Orme 2000; Thorn & Thorn 1979a: 1,1). However, if St Mawgan was a monastery it does not seem to have influenced local landscape in the same way as St Keverne, which may suggest it was a later foundation or a less important site. An interesting comparison can be made with St Petroc's at Bodmin. This site was traditionally not founded until some time after AD *c.*800, when St Petroc's main house was supposed to have moved to Bodmin from Padstow (Olson 1989: 53-6). Oliver Padel's maps of Cornish place-names reveal that the area around the new foundation is largely devoid of early medieval *tre* place-names, like the neighbouring parish of Cardinham (Padel 1999: 89-91).

Important Churches and Early Medieval Settlements in Cornwall

The evidence discussed above strongly suggests that the early medieval settlement pattern was based around 'core' areas of settlements and their farmland which were surrounded by outer zones of rough moorland and woodland. It has previously been suggested that Cornwall's early churches were located in isolated positions, but this does not seem consistent with the evidence from settlement studies (e.g. Todd 1987: 244; Aston 2000a: 41). As shown above, early ecclesiastical centres at St Keverne, St Neot and Tintagel are surrounded by dense concentrations of early medieval settlements. In addition, the settlement pattern established during the early medieval centuries was substantially different to that of the preceding period. Although much land remained under cultivation, there was a general retraction and re-focusing of medieval farmland on to the new core settlement areas. Important ecclesiastical centres commonly lay at the heart of these zones.

Padel's maps of Cornish habitative place-name elements suggest that similar concentrations surround many other likely early ecclesiastical communities including Padstow, St Kew, Crantock, Probus, St Germans and St Buryan (Padel 1999: 89). In some cases, these settlements may represent the dwellings of members of the religious community. It is possible that the *domus* of Wrmonoc's ninth-century Life of St Paul Aurelian represent settlements held by individual members of religious communities rather than separate monasteries (Olson 1989: 23). The tenth-century charter for St Buryan (S450) grants land divided into seven places (*in septem loca divisam*). Five of the six places whose names survive in the charter have habitative place-name elements in either *tre* or **bod* (Hooke 1994a: 22-7), and the charter shows that the religious community directly held settlements in the surrounding area **(Fig. 39)**. The Domesday Book entries for St Neot also hint that individual members of communities may have held particular farms from their churches, since a named priest (Godric presbiter) held part of the community's estate (Thorn & Thorn 1979a; 4, 28; 5, 14, 2).[3] It is therefore possible that the ecclesiastical centres did not have extensive living accommodation—perhaps just churches or chapels where members of the community could congregate for meetings at certain times.

---

[3] See also Pearce's discussion of the estates of Hartland in Devon (Pearce 1985).

Fig. 39: Aerial view of St Buryan looking north-west. The church and modern village are surrounded by fields; the higher hills and rough grazing ground of Tredinney Common and Bartinney Downs can be seen on the horizon. [Photo: Steve Hartgroves/Historic Environment Service, Cornwall County Council.]

The early Cornish ecclesiastical centres appear to have been at the centre of the re-ordered landscape of early medieval settlements and landscape resources, and to have provided focal points in landscapes of highly dispersed settlement. Rather than being determined by pre-existing practices or patterns of secular endowment, much of the emerging medieval landscape of settlement and agriculture appears to have been organised around the newly established churches.

Changing Settlement Patterns in Wessex, AD *c.*400-900

The development of settlement patterns in central and western Wessex during the early middle ages is not thoroughly understood, and so it can be hard to relate ecclesiastical sites to local developments. In general, the relationship between Roman and early medieval settlements is unclear because of a lack of evidence regarding the latter. Although the Roman-period settlement pattern is fairly well known in many areas of Wessex, the settlements of the sixth to ninth centuries have proved rather more difficult to locate. In Cornwall, it was possible to use place-names to get an impression of the settlement pattern in this period. Unfortunately the chronology of English place-name development in the South West is uncertain and it is very hard to reconstruct settlement patterns based on the distribution of particular elements (but see Padel 1999). For these reasons it is not yet possible to present the same kind of detailed case studies for Wessex as undertaken above for Cornwall. Despite this, the archaeological work that has been undertaken on early medieval settlements in Wessex strongly suggests that the settlement pattern overall developed in a broadly similar way to Cornwall: agricultural settlement seems to have focused on core lowland zones during the middle Saxon period. As in

Cornwall, plotting the location of early churches in Wessex against HLCs reveals their centrality in the medieval agricultural landscape.

Some recent archaeological work has begun to address problems such as a lack of distinctive artefacts on sites of this period by making use of radiocarbon dating techniques. In Devon three sites have come to light in recent years which may reflect similarities between Devon and Cornwall in the fifth and sixth centuries. At Hayes Farm (Clyst Honiton) part of a large cropmark enclosure was shown to post-date a Roman settlement (Simpson et al. 1989: 12-13). At Raddon (Stockleigh Pomeroy; c.6.5km north-east of Crediton), recent excavations have shown that a Neolithic and Iron Age hilltop enclosure was re-used in the post-Roman centuries (Gent & Quinnell 1999a). Finds of charred grain suggest settlement activity at the site, where a late prehistoric ditch was also re-cut and where there may have been episodes of burial in the post-Roman period. At Haldon Belvedere (Dunchideock), a Neolithic settlement c.7.5km south-west of Exeter, the nature of the post-Roman activity is uncertain since only one pit was scientifically dated to the period (Gent & Quinnell 1999b). Somewhat better understood is the site at High Peak, 5km west of Sidmouth, where excavations in the late nineteenth and twentieth centuries produced finds of imported Mediterranean pottery (Pollard 1966). Although this is a small sample of sites, it is notable that all reuse prehistoric settlements and that three of the four are located on prominent hilltops. These are quite different to most later medieval settlements in Devon, which tend to be located away from exposed ridges in or on the edges of more sheltered valleys, as in Cornwall. This hints that at some point between the late or post-Roman period and the time when the medieval settlement pattern was established, there was a significant change in ideas about what sites were most suitable for settlements. As shown in Chapter 3, important early churches in Wessex tended to be located in prominent sites close to valley bottoms, rather than on exposed hilltops. This was probably an important factor that guided the changing structure of the landscape: the sites which acted as 'central places' in the seventh and eighth centuries (churches and royal vills) were no longer located in hilltop positions as those of the post-Roman period had been (typically reused hillforts and other prehistoric enclosures).

In Ireland a move into lower-lying areas during the early centuries of Christianity was perceived by a martyrologist around the beginning of the ninth century. Though the pagan citadels he mentions may have been very ancient, his stanzas emphasise the spiritual power of the new churches in the valleys (Charles-Edwards 2000: 469-71):

> *The fortress of Cruachain has*
> *vanished with Ailill, victory's child;*
> *a fair dignity greater than kingdoms*
> *is in the city of Clonmacnoise...*

> *The fort of Emain Machae has melted*
> *away, all but its stones;*
> *thronged Glendalough is the*
> *sanctuary of the western world...*

The great hills of evil have been
cut down with spear-points,
while the glens have been made
into hills.

(from *Félire Óengusso*, trans. Greene & O'Connor 1967: 61-5)

Like the martyrologist, modern archaeologists have also detected a general change in the landscape of Ireland, where the settlement pattern of ring-forts and crannogs appears to focus increasingly on low-lying areas in the early medieval period (Fredengren 2002: 261-30).

A similar shift in 'central place' location probably occurred in Somerset between the late and post-Roman period and the early middle ages. Here, the hillforts of South Cadbury and Cadbury Congresbury are well known and have produced considerable evidence for fifth- and sixth- century activity (Rahtz et al. 1992; Alcock 1995). Many other Somerset hillforts have also produced Roman material, which may hint at similar activity on a broader scale (Burrow 1981: 172-84). Cadbury Congresbury is a particularly interesting example. Here, a hillfort with late Roman occupation continued in use and was partly re-fortified in the post-Roman period. On the slopes of the hill below the fort, a late Roman temple was used at the same time for burials, and an extensive cemetery developed around the site (Watts & Leach 1996). However, at some time in the early middle ages, the ecclesiastical centre of Congresbury was founded *c.*1km south of the hillfort on the banks of the River Yeo, close to the point where it flows out into the North Somerset Levels.[4] The focal point of the area had moved, and settlement in the medieval parish developed predominately in the lower ground between the Levels and the upland grazing of the Mendip Hills (see Aston 1994a: 224).

When this shift took place is an important question. Another poet's lines present an interesting perspective on late Roman attitudes to life in the fifth-century countryside:

An ancestral home needs our presence and our tears;
labour which grief has urged is often best.
It is sinful to neglect a ruin already
compounded by neglect: now is the time,
after the fires have cooled, to rebuild, even if
we are rebuilding only shepherds' huts

Rutilius Claudius Namatianus,
De reditu suo (trans. Isbell 1971: 221-2)

Rutilius Namatianus is referring here to his return to southern Gaul from Rome in 416, when the Visigoths were beginning to establish control over the region. Though this is far from southern England, archaeologists have begun to identify a pattern of changed but continuing occupation at Roman rural

---

[4] This had happened by the ninth century at the latest, since Congresbury was granted by King Alfred to Asser along with Banwell, c.6km to the south west; Asser's Life of King Alfred describes them as '...two monasteries so well provided with goods of all sorts...' (Keynes & Lapidge 1983: 97).

settlements all over western Europe during the fifth and sixth centuries (Lewit 2003; Chavarría & Lewit 2004: 30-7). In Wiltshire, several late Roman settlements have produced evidence for continuing occupation in the fifth and sixth centuries, including Coombe Down on Salisbury Plain (Entwistle et al. 1994), Overton Down (Fowler 2000: 228-9), Castle Copse, Great Bedwyn (Hostetter & Howe 1997: 374), Cleveland Farm in Ashton Keynes, and perhaps Market Lavington (Eagles 2001). Some scholars choose to see the occupation of such settlement sites on the downs as the tail-end of a Romano-British agricultural boom (Faulkner 2000: 137-49), whereas others regard it as evidence for a thriving but modified 'late-antique' economy in central southern Britain (Dark 2000: 113-17). Whatever the social status of these sites in post-Roman Britain, a number seem to have been used as settlements until at least the early sixth century.

Some such places are located in areas that continued to support fairly concentrated populations from the Roman period through to the late medieval period. It is axiomatic for landscape archaeology that earlier patterns of land use and settlement will influence later ones; however, it is important to distinguish between real and apparent continuities. Peter Fowler has argued that the medieval landscape of settlement is essentially a 'British' one, established years before the Romans ever arrived (Fowler 2000: 257-60). In some ways this is true: similar areas were almost certainly cultivated in the parishes of West Overton and Fyfield (the focus of Fowler's study) during the Iron Age and in the late medieval period. However, it is also important to account for some of the shorter-scale fluctuations in land-use patterns which could be crucial to understanding the relationships between different periods. Fowler's plan of the extent of arable land in his study area during prehistoric and Roman times as opposed to the later middle ages clearly illustrates that a much greater area was under the plough in the earlier periods (**Fig. 40**; Fowler 2000: 233; see also McOmish et al. 2002: 100-15). Since the early medieval landscape probably witnessed significant expansion in the farmed area from the later ninth century onwards (Chapter 7), it could be suggested that the contrast between the late Roman and middle Saxon patterns would have been even more marked.

Whilst much of the Roman-period agricultural landscape probably remained under cultivation, it seems likely that certain areas may have been given over to rough pasture as settlement increasingly concentrated on sites in the lower valley sides as late Roman settlements on the higher ground were abandoned. This might have been in imitation of high-status sites such as royal vills and ecclesiastical centres, and if so it would have occurred from the time they began to be systematically established in the seventh and eighth centuries.

Unfortunately, there are relatively few excavated settlement sites in central or western Wessex which illustrate the nature of rural settlement and its relationship to church sites during this crucial period. Examples like Collingbourne Ducis (Pine 2001), Trowbridge (Graham & Davies 1993) and Abbot's Worthy (Fasham & Whinney 1991), and likely cases such as Tidworth (Godden et al. 2002), Bathampton and Salisbury (Nenk et al. 1995), suggest that settlements of middle Saxon date are indeed to be found mainly on the lower slopes of valleys close to river floodplains. However, since the number of excavated sites is limited, it is hard to establish their relationship to major ecclesiastical centres. Extensive

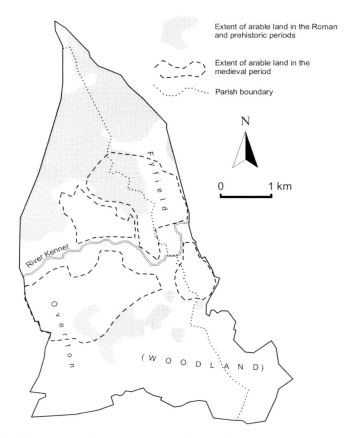

Extent of arable land in the Roman
and prehistoric periods

Extent of arable land in the
medieval period

Parish boundary

N

0   1 km

Fig. 40: The extent of arable land in the prehistoric period and the later
middle ages in West Overton and Fyfield, north Wiltshire (redrawn after
Fowler 2000: 233, Fig.16.1).

fieldwalking surveys, which can provide good evidence for the distribution of rural
Roman and later medieval settlements, have also proved rather ineffective at
identifying early medieval settlements. The East Hampshire Survey, the East
Berkshire Survey and the Kennet Valley Survey (Berkshire) all failed to locate
significant quantities of pre-Conquest pottery, probably because it is fragile and
decays quickly when subjected to ploughing (Oake & Shennan 1985; Ford 1987;
Lobb & Rose 1996). Despite these problems, some of this work has produced
hints that the landscape was re-orientated in the early medieval period (compare
Lobb & Rose 1996: figs 17 & 18).

    One fieldwalking survey in central Wessex has identified a small but significant
amount of early/middle Anglo-Saxon pottery. The Middle Avon Valley Survey,
undertaken between 1979 and 1986, surveyed fields several kilometres to either
side of the River Avon in Hampshire just south of the Wiltshire border, a stretch
of river with two probable late Saxon minster churches at Breamore and
Fordingbridge (Light et al. 1994). Sherds of early medieval chaff-tempered
pottery were recovered, but the dating of this material remains uncertain (perhaps
ranging from the fifth to the ninth or tenth centuries; Hinton 1994: 35; Timby

2001). Without other artefactual or scientific dating evidence, it can be hard to disentangle early Saxon occupation sites from middle Saxon sites because of the difficulties of understanding the pottery. Even so, the Middle Avon Survey has show that settlement persisted in the region from the Roman period through to the early middle ages, and that it probably clustered in certain areas throughout this time (e.g. around Breamore). Unfortunately, the survey results do not show clearly what changes there were in the settlement pattern of the wider area, largely because the work focused on the lower valley sides.

At Shapwick (Somerset), a ten-year research project has applied a battery of techniques including intensive fieldwalking, place-name analysis and regressive map analysis to a single parish, and has begun to show the value of an interdisciplinary approach (Aston & Gerrard 1999). The aim of the project was to investigate the establishment of the present nucleated village and its fields. This

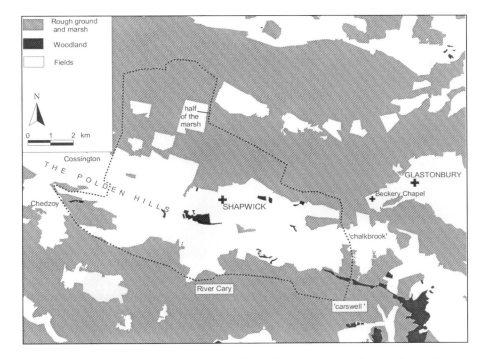

Fig. 41: Shapwick and the Polden Hills, Somerset. The figure shows the possible extent of Glastonbury's *Pouholt* estate (S253; after Aston 1994a: 232) and the extent of different types of land use. The medieval fields are confined to the drier ridge of the Poldens. The mapping of different land uses in this figure is based on the Historic Landscape Characterisation of Somerset undertaken by Somerset County Council and English Heritage (Aldred 2001). The methodology used in the Somerset project was somewhat different to the one presented in this book, but nevertheless the characterisation reflects fairly accurately the approximate extent of different land-uses in the middle ages. [Characterisation © English Heritage/Somerset County Council. © Crown Copyright. All rights reserved. Licence number 100042056.]

has resulted in the identification of around ten Roman settlements and the possible locations of at least four of their early medieval successors (C. Gerrard 2000). The possible early medieval settlements tend to cluster in the agricultural land below the ridge of the Poldens and above the marshland in the area that later became medieval open field; they also appear to focus around the site of the former church, which could have been established as early as the eighth century (Aston & Gerrard 1999: Fig.10).[5] This contrasts with the Roman period when settlements seem to have been rather more evenly spread across the parish, and concentrations of Roman material have been found in areas that were probably marsh and woodland in the early middle ages. It is therefore likely that the cultivated area had contracted in the first part of the early medieval period. In or

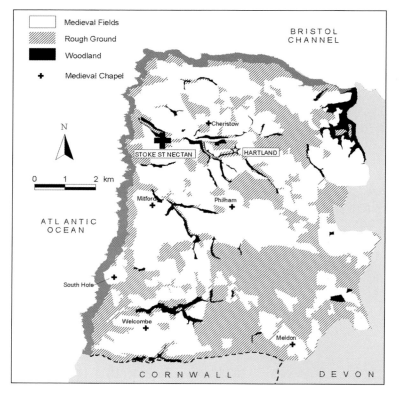

Fig. 42: Hartland hundred (Devon) and the medieval chapels of Hartland (after Pearce 1985). The Historic Landscape Characterisation in this figure is derived from the Devon County Council/English Heritage characterisation of Devon. This was undertaken using the same methods as the Cornish characterisations presented in this book, with the exception that the earliest source routinely consulted was the first edition of the late nineteenth-century large-scale Ordnance Survey mapping (see Turner 2005). [Characterisation © English Heritage/Devon County Council. © Crown Copyright. All rights reserved. Licence number 100042056.]

[5] It was probably during the eighth century that the estate on the Polden Hills (including Shapwick) was granted to Glastonbury Abbey

around the tenth century the settlement pattern of the area was reorganised once again when a nucleated village was created and the dispersed settlements were abandoned (Aston & Gerrard 1999; **Plate 8a & Fig 41**).

Plotting the location of major early churches in Wessex against Historic Landscape Characterisations reveals that ecclesiastical centres were at the heart of medieval agricultural landscapes in this region just as they were in Cornwall. The churches at Shapwick, Hartland (Devon) and Ottery St Mary (Devon) provide good examples of sites that are central to extensive areas of agricultural land **(Figs 41, 42 & 43)**. At Shapwick and Ottery, the low-lying marshes and hilltop rough ground that lay at the margins of the settled core are first recorded in the boundary clauses of Anglo-Saxon charters (see below, Ch. 7, 161-5).[6] In the Cornish case studies described earlier in this chapter it was possible to relate this pattern to changing distributions of early medieval settlements. Unfortunately this is not yet possible for Wessex, largely because the chronology

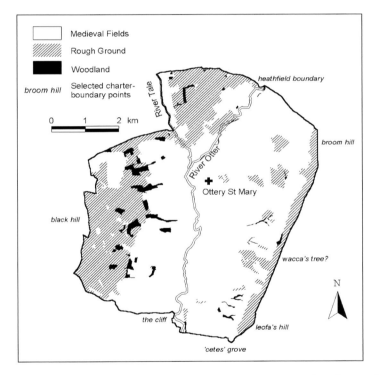

Fig. 43: Ottery St Mary (Devon) and selected boundary points from a late Saxon charter boundary clause (S1033; after Hooke 1994a). The HLC is again derived from the Devon County Council/English Heritage characterisation of Devon (Turner 2005). [Characterisation © English Heritage/Devon County Council. © Crown Copyright. All rights reserved. Licence number 100042056.]

[6] For translations and discussions of charter-bounds, see Grundy on Wiltshire (Grundy 1919, 1920), Somerset (Grundy 1935a), Dorset (Grundy 1933, 1934, 1935b, 1936, 1937, 1938, 1939); for Devon, see Hooke 1994a.

of early medieval place-names is less well understood for this region than in Cornwall. However, the archaeological and place-name studies from Wessex discussed in this chapter suggest that the gravitation of settlement and agriculture to core areas in this region was analogous to the situation in Cornwall.

Conclusion

In general terms, it seems highly likely that there was a re-focusing of the settled landscape in the centuries after the conversion to Christianity, and that the process was intimately related to the establishment of new kinds of high-status sites, in particular ecclesiastical centres. This seems to have occurred not only in Cornwall, but also in central Wessex where Anglo-Saxon culture appears to have been dominant from as early as the fifth century, and in areas like Devon which may not have come under Anglo-Saxon political control until the later seventh or eighth century. The evidence from Shapwick and elsewhere in Wessex suggests that like contemporary ecclesiastical centres, most secular settlements from this time onwards were set within arable land on the lower hillsides and valley bottoms. This conclusion is also supported by the evidence from early medieval administrative structures in Wessex presented in the following chapter.

5

Ecclesiastical centres and early medieval administrative structures

By the middle of the eleventh century, the counties of south-west England were divided into medium-sized administrative units called 'hundreds'. In turn each hundred typically contained many estates. Churches and ecclesiastical communities could hold estates of their own, and the nature of these holdings could be an important factor in both the development of the landscape and the religious institution. Ecclesiastical estates are considered in the second part of this chapter, but the first section concentrates on the nature of secular and ecclesiastical administrative units.

In central Wessex the origins of the hundreds should probably be sought in the middle Saxon period, though in Cornwall their histories are rather more obscure. Late Saxon hundreds were administered from central royal settlements; historians have suggested that each major church may similarly have had a dependent *parochia*[1] within which it exercised spiritual power.

Hundreds, *Parochiae* and Minsters in Wessex

Patrick Hase has suggested that there was a close relationships between minster churches and royal vills, based in part on the apparent regularity of ecclesiastical provision in each Anglo-Saxon administrative area: 'in Wessex it looks as if there was a conscious policy to ensure that every *regio* had a church, a royal church' (Hase 1994: 53). In general this argument has to be based on the distribution of churches in Domesday hundreds, since these are the earliest units whose boundaries can be reliably reconstructed on a wide scale that may have developed from a system of early administrative *regiones*.

Some scholars have objected to the idea that hundreds have early roots on the grounds that they are not referred to in historical texts before the tenth century. The first specific reference to a 'hundred' in Anglo-Saxon England occurs in the Hundred Ordinance, a document that was probably composed some time in the

---

[1] *Parochia* has become the conventional historical term for the (hypothetical) large Anglo-Saxon forerunners of later medieval parishes.

reign of King Edgar (AD 939-961; Whitelock 1979: 429). Indeed, in the earlier twentieth century Reichel argued that a 'hundred' was not a geographical unit at all, but rather that it referred to a group of landowners who held estates around a royal manor (Reichel 1939: 336-7). He therefore believed that the early territorial organisation of the Christian church could not have been related to the hundreds (*contra* Page 1915).

However, there is other evidence that suggests the origins of the hundred should be sought in an earlier period. One of the most important functions of the hundred was to act as a unit of local government, and to this end monthly assemblies known as hundred courts were held at locally well-known meeting-places. The earliest reference to public assemblies of this sort is in a charter of Coenwulf of Mercia from well over one hundred years before the Hundred Ordinance (Stenton 1971: 298-9; ES1186a (endorsement to S106)). The Hundred Ordinance itself does not deal with how a hundred should be laid out, but rather refers to a system that was clearly already in place and well-established (Reynolds 1999: 75-6).

Place-name evidence provides a useful source of information on the hundreds. The names of many of the medieval hundreds derive from the names of their pre-Conquest meeting places. Some hundreds are named after royal vills where the hundred courts met from the tenth or eleventh centuries, and it is possible that some of these represent territories that were newly organised at this time (Loyn 1984: 142). However, many other hundreds are named after meeting-places that were some distance from royal centres. There is some evidence to suggest that meeting-places at royal vills or other estate centres replaced others elsewhere in the land unit whose names were subsequently lost. This process is shown by some exceptions to the rule from Devon, where two different hundred names occur for the same hundred in documents associated with the Domesday survey which were bound into the Exeter Book. Thus *Aleriga* hundred in the second Exeter Domesday list of hundreds (*Exon* list II) is *Hernintona* (Ermington) in *Exon* list I; *Rueberga* (Roborough) in *Exon* list II is *Walchentona* (Walkhampton) in *Exon* list I and the Devonshire Tax Returns; and *Tainebruga* (Teignbridge) in *Exon* list II is *Taintona* (Kingsteignton) in *Exon* list I and the Devonshire Tax Returns (Thorn & Thorn 1985 *Appendix*; Anderson 1939: 92-3). In some regions it has been argued that these earlier meeting-places may represent the assembly sites of early social groups, as suggested by names such as Armingford (the *ford* of the *Earningas* (Cambridgeshire)) and Hurstingstone (the stone (*-stan*) of the people of (*-ingas*) the wooded hill (*hyrst-*) (Huntingdonshire); Meaney 1993: 70; 1997: 236). Occasionally, hundred names appear to represent simply the name of the social group itself, such as Braughing (the people of *Breahha* (Hertfordshire)) and Hitchen (the *Hicce* (Hertfordshire); Meaney 1993: 80). The occurrence of meeting-places close to sites of pagan English religious activity could also suggest that traditional meeting-places were established early and persisted (e.g. Meaney 1993: 90; 1997: 211; Pantos 2004: 172-3). In the Danelaw, the occurrence of large numbers of Anglo-Saxon hundred and wapentake names (as opposed to Scandinavian names) referring to sites away from manorial centres suggests that administrative units in the mould of hundreds were in existence before the Scandinavian settlement and that they (or at least their meeting-places) endured through it (Turner 2000).

Charters are another source of evidence for early Anglo-Saxon *regiones* or folk-groups and their territories. Some early charters granting land to the church mention names believed to be those of early folk-groups in whose territory a church had been founded. Lands administered by the church often seem to have maintained the same territorial extent for long periods of time, and to have reflected earlier secular land divisions (as for example by the correspondence in the extents of early bishoprics and kingdoms (Costen 1994: 97)). There are a number of examples where the names of folk-regions may be recorded, including S94 (the *Stoppingas*) and S89 (the *Husmerae*; Hooke 1986; 1998: 46-51). Although the land granted in such a charter should not be assumed to be co-extensive with the early folk *regio* (since the church is not likely to have been granted an entire *regio* as a new estate), these grants show that such territorial divisions did exist.

This evidence strongly suggests that units fulfilling a similar range of functions to the later hundreds existed in England before the tenth century. It seems that the system of administrative units developed throughout the early medieval period and may have had its roots in the earliest stable Anglo-Saxon social groups. The hundreds that were regularised by the tenth-century kings and re-organised through the exchange of land at various times were probably based on administrative units of considerable antiquity (Stenton 1971: 299-301; Yorke 1995: 125-6; Reynolds 1999: 76).

Minsters and Hundreds

Just as evidence for social groups below the level of the kingdom is important, so are records of their association with church foundation. Proponents of the 'minster hypothesis' for the territorial organisation of the early church have argued that ecclesiastical centres were founded within such regions in order to minister to their inhabitants. There is some evidence from topography and administrative history which supports an early origin for *parochiae* based on putative *regiones* (e.g. at Gloucester and Worcester; Bassett 1992). In the case of central Wessex, Hase has argued that churches were established regularly at royal administrative centres to serve 'archaic' hundreds such as those suggested for Hampshire by Klingelhofer (Hase 1988, 1994; Klingelhofer 1992).

The evidence from Wessex provides some support for these theories. A comparison of the location of certain and likely high-status churches with late Saxon hundred boundaries shows that there was only one major church in the majority of central Wessex hundreds **(Table 10)**.

Recent studies by Jonathan Pitt (1999) and Teresa Hall (2000) have recognised this regularity, although they attribute it to different causes. Pitt argues that the high number of Wiltshire hundreds with one church must result from the foundation of new 'hundred' minsters in the late Saxon period. He considers the hundreds to have been re-organised and re-structured to such an extent in the late pre-Conquest period that this regularity would not have been evident if an earlier pattern of ecclesiastical provision had simply been maintained (Pitt 1999: 180-2; see also Blair 1985: 118). On the other hand, Hall suggests that the relative *lack* of correspondence between Dorset hundreds and minsters should be seen as the result of changes in estate organisation and hundredal membership in the late pre-Conquest period (Hinton 1987; Hall 2000: 41-5).

	Hundreds with no superior church identified	Hundreds with **1** superior church	Hundreds with **2** superior churches	Hundreds with **3** superior churches
Wiltshire (40 hundreds)	20%	50%	30%	0%
Dorset (39 hundreds)	31%	53%	13%	3%
Somerset (36 hundreds)	22%	61%	14%	3%
Devon (32 hundreds)	41%	28%	28%	3%

Table 10: Certain and likely high-status churches and hundreds in central and western Wessex. Figures are approximate since identifications of minsters remain provisional (extent of hundreds based on Thorn & Thorn 1979b (Wiltshire); 1980 (Somerset); 1983 (Dorset); 1985 (Devon); see also Figs 8, 9 & 10).

Both Pitt and Hall reach these conclusions whilst attempting to investigate the same problem: whether early medieval ecclesiastical *parochiae* can be reconstructed from hundred boundaries. In this respect they are following the work of Hase (1988) and Blair (1991) who have detected, in Hampshire and Surrey respectively, a correspondence between probable *parochiae* and hundred boundaries. Pitt and Hall are disappointed by the complexity revealed in their studies; both recognise that the boundaries of hundreds could have changed fairly often in the pre-Conquest period as a result of estates changing ownership, and that high-status churches were not all founded at the same time or in the same ways. They acknowledge that it is frequently difficult to date such developments, and conclude that no simple correlation can be made between the extent of hundreds and early minster *parochiae*. Neither hundreds nor the churches in them were necessarily very ancient at the time of Domesday Book. It is certain that in many cases the boundaries of middle Saxon administrative units would not have been the same as late Saxon hundred boundaries. Case-studies such as Yorke's discussion of the Worthy estates in Hampshire reveal the processes which could lead to change (Yorke 1995: 126-30). Crediton in Devon provides another likely example: the Domesday hundred (most of which was in ecclesiastical ownership in 1086) appears to encompass a smaller area than an earlier grant to the church of Crediton (although the boundary clause is a later addition to the eighth-century charter; S255; Hooke 1994b: 84).

Irregularities in any possible 'system' of regular church provision by hundreds are shown both by instances where there are no recognisable superior churches within a hundred, and cases where there are more than one. In-depth studies have not been able to 'discover' new high-status churches for many of the late Saxon hundreds where they had not previously been identified, and it seems likely that this reflects to some extent genuine irregularities in ecclesiastical provision (Pitt 1999; Hall 2000). As Pitt points out, late Saxon churches of superior status had diverse origins, and it is hard to demonstrate that a 'system' of minsters was planned at any given time (1999: 182). The many irregularities suggest that the network of churches grew in rather a piecemeal fashion even if a general model existed whereby each hundred would have a minster church.

However, these discussions also serve to illustrate a very important point. In some cases, churches known to have been founded early are associated with administrative units which are also thought to have maintained a degree of stability into the late Saxon period (e.g. Bradford-on-Avon & Malmesbury (Wiltshire): Pitt 1999: 110-57; Sherborne (Dorset): Hall 2000: 41). Early churches were therefore probably associated with early administrative units. It has often been suggested that the *regiones* out of which hundreds may have developed were administered from central royal vills (Yorke 1995: 125-7; Hase 1994); the close relationship between many superior churches and royal vills has already been discussed in Chapter 3. In other cases, where the hundredal system was rearranged, it seems possible that new churches could have been established or existing *parochiae* rearranged to maintain a regular system (Pitt 1999: 180). Both examples of early churches established in putative early *regiones* (Blair 1991; Hase 1994; Hall 2000) and later re-organisations of ecclesiastical and hundredal systems (Pitt 1999) show that the relationship between churches and administrative units was one of central importance throughout the early Christian period in southern England.

This association between Christian ideology and late Saxon administrative geography has also recently been emphasised by Reynolds (1997, 2002). He has argued that criminals subject to judicial killings were buried with increasing regularity in execution cemeteries on territorial boundaries during the middle and later Saxon period. The custom appears to have begun developing from the seventh or eighth century and to have become virtually universal in central southern England by the tenth century (including central Wessex; see Reynolds 2002: figs 1-3). Reynolds argues that the exclusion of executed criminals from communal burial grounds would have been regarded as a further form of punishment – instead of burial in consecrated ground at the heart of the Christian community, they were banished to the unproductive boundaries of the land where assorted malevolent beings were believed to lurk (Semple 1998; Reynolds 2002). This shows not only that the boundaries of hundreds became increasingly formalised and closely identifiable in the late Saxon period, but also that Christian ideology played an important role in their definition.

Hundreds and parochiae

In Dorset, the hundred of Sherborne matches almost exactly the likely *parochia* of that church, with only one additional parish included in the hundred (Hall 2000: 41). As Hall comments, in this case it seems quite likely that this is the result of the loss of evidence for a connection, rather than the result of there never having been a relationship between the two churches (ibid. 44). Other close correlations occur between the boundaries of hundred and reconstructed *parochia* in the cases of Whitchurch Canonicorum, Gillingham, Cranborne and Puddletown. In both Dorset and Wiltshire, likely or probable minsters rarely had dependencies outside the hundred in which they stood, and the reconstructed *parochiae* are almost always smaller than the hundred (Hall 2000: 42; Pitt 1999: 97). The same appears to be true of Somerset (relationships between churches identified by Aston (1986); Domesday hundreds defined by Thorn & Thorn (1980)).

Further examples are evident in Devon. Pearce has shown that Hartland Abbey held chapelries at Cheristow, Welcombe and Harton in the later middle ages, along with several others in the parish of Stoke St Nectan (Pearce 1985: 265-9); these all lie within Hartland hundred and it is possible that they formed part of a *parochia* originally focused on the church of Stoke St Nectan itself **(Fig. 42)**. Reichel noted that West Alvington had chapelries at South Milton, Malborough, Salcombe and South Huish, which all lie in the southern part of Stanborough hundred in south Devon (1939: 338). Plympton church had chapelries in the later middle ages at Brixton, Wembury, Plymstock and Shaugh, all in Plympton hundred (though Sampford Spiney, a moorland-edge estate with a dependent chapel, lay in Roborough; Reichel 1939: 337; see Bearman 1994: 64).

The Geographical Location of Major Churches within Hundreds

The idea that important churches were central to hundreds is also supported to a great extent by their geographical locations within hundreds. Many Wessex minsters are geographically close to the centre of their hundreds, as shown by maps comparing hundred boundaries with the locations of the superior churches **(Fig. 7 (Devon), Fig. 8 (Dorset) and Fig 9 (Wiltshire))**.

Specific cases show that within the hundred, the church was often also central in terms of agricultural resources. For example, Faith (1997: 18-22; S895) has discussed how Sherborne (Dorset) was sited amid arable fields at the heart of its hundred. Topographically, the probable site of the mid-Saxon cathedral stands a few metres above the River Yeo, whose valley sides rise up to over 100m above the valley floor within a few kilometres on either side.

The ecclesiastical estate of Ottery St Mary in east Devon formed a single hundred at the time of Domesday. The form of the medieval and post-medieval landscape, and the boundary clauses of two late Saxon charters relating to the estate (S721; S1033) all suggest that the early medieval landscape here was also arranged with the meadow in the valley bottom, the arable land on the gentle slopes of the valley sides, and the pasture on the steeper upper slopes of the valley and the ridges along which the boundaries ran **(Fig. 43)**. The boundary clause of AD 1061 (S1033) names various points such as *bromdune* ('broom hill'), *leofan dune* (Leofa's hill), and *heth feld mere* (perhaps 'the heathfield boundary') which show the boundaries using these ridges and running across heathland (Hooke 1994a: 207-12). The location of the church of Ottery is directly comparable to its much earlier exemplar at Sherborne. In both cases, the churches are at the centre of the rich agricultural landscape, far from the heaths which lie at the margins of the land unit.

The distribution maps in **Figs 7, 8 and 9** show that there are some churches that are close to the boundaries of hundreds. In many cases, however, a certain kind of 'centrality' can still be suggested. The south-east Wiltshire churches of Britford (Cawdon hundred) and Alderbury (Alderbury hundred) provide good examples. The two sites are barely 2.5km apart, and yet they appear to have been the most important churches in their respective hundreds (Pitt 1999: 26-9, 40-3). The hundreds of Cawdon and Alderbury lie immediately to the west and east (respectively) of the River Avon. Although the small River Ebble also flows through the heart of Cawdon and the Bourne through Alderbury hundred, the Avon is by far the most important river in the area, being a major route of communication and transport. The Avon's course was punctuated by late Saxon times with a regular distribution of important churches and royal estate centres: the probable minsters of Britford, Alderbury, Downton (Wiltshire), Breamore and Fordingbridge (Hampshire) all lie on one 15km stretch of the river south of Salisbury. Hooke has shown how agricultural resources in this part of Wiltshire were structured in the landscape using the evidence of Anglo-Saxon charter bounds (Hooke 1988, 1998). In the valley bottoms, the most valuable and productive land was probably the zone of watermeadows lying next to the rivers. Adjacent to the watermeadows on the hillsides lay the arable land, typically indicated in charter bounds by reference to 'furlongs' and 'acres'; beyond this zone was the grazing and woodland of the hilltops and ridges, characterised by references to features such as woodland clearings and heathy fields (Hooke 1998: 125-7). At the heart of this system lay the riverside meadowland, and the minster churches were generally sited so that they lay within or on the edge of this meadow. In cases such as Alderbury, Britford and many other examples in Wiltshire and Dorset, the apparent liminality of the church in relation to the hundred boundaries belies a centrality in terms of the landscapes of agriculture and communications.

It thus seems likely that there were close relationships between administrative units and major churches throughout the Christian Saxon period. Changes in administrative and estate structures seem to have been reflected by changes in ecclesiastical structure, as shown for example by churches which were founded within new *burhs* like Shaftesbury and Bridport (Hall 2000: 35), and in cases where new churches were founded after hundred boundaries were re-organised (Pitt 1999: 181). Within administrative units, churches were often geographically central; if they were not, this was commonly where other key elements of the landscape such as agricultural resources and communication routes were situated away from the geographical centre of the hundred. Such relationships illustrate that churches were at the *ideological* centre of hundreds: they were central to ideas about how the landscape ought to be organised and administered. Similar relationships can be observed between churches and their estates, a subject discussed below (119-29).

Cornish Hundreds and Early Churches

The Cornish hundreds are understood less well than those of Wessex. Whilst Picken argued that they were established after Anglo-Saxon control over Cornwall was secured, Thomas preferred an earlier origin (Thomas 1964a, 1994; Picken 1965-7; 1994: 216-17). The earliest list of Cornish hundred names occurs in the folios of the Geld Inquest of *c.*1084-1086, which are bound into the Exeter Domesday Book (Picken 1965-7; Thorn & Thorn 1979a). The names recorded here are not Cornish, but the English names of the manors which acted as their administrative centres around the time of Domesday. However, this does not necessarily mean that the hundreds themselves were English innovations. Elsewhere in England the late Saxon kings were undertaking administrative reorganisations which often involved focusing administrative functions at central manors. This process led to hundreds losing their earlier names and taking on those of administrative centres (Turner 2000).

In most cases, the earliest mention of the Cornish names of the hundreds occurs in the twelfth or thirteenth centuries (Picken 1965-7). However, the name of one hundred, Trigg, is recorded in two pre-Conquest documents. The first is King Alfred's will, which records that Alfred left to Edward his eldest son the estate of Stratton in Triggshire (*æt Strætneat on Triconscire*; S1507, composed AD *c.*872 x 888; Keynes & Lapidge 1983). The earliest reference to Trigg is in the *First Life of St Sampson*, in a discussion of the saint's journey through Cornwall ('when he was walking through the district they call Trigg' (*pagum quem Tircurium vocant*; Olson 1989: 16). Thomas has discussed the name and suggests it may be derived from two words meaning 'three' and 'armies / tribes' (Thomas 1994: 216). The later medieval hundred of Trigg or Stratton was sub-divided into three smaller hundreds (Stratton, Lesnewth and Trigg), and Thomas suggests that this division may have its origins in the early medieval period **(Fig. 44)**.

The hundreds recorded in the eleventh century may have been subject to some

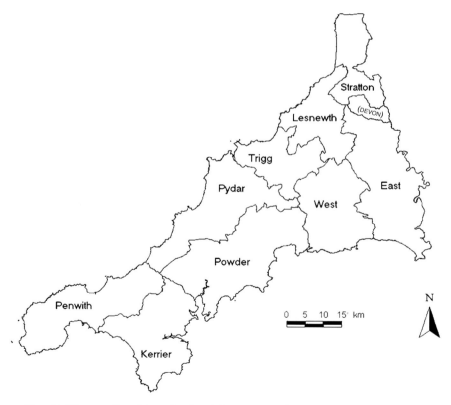

Fig. 44: The medieval hundreds of Cornwall (after Thorn & Thorn 1979a and Ravenhill & Padel 1991).

reorganisation in the late Saxon period. In particular, there are hints that several had once been subdivided. These subdivisions may have been analogous to Welsh 'commotes', of which there were commonly two or three to each *cantref* (Jones 1998). Besides Trigg, a number of other Cornish hundreds were also partitioned. In south-east Cornwall, the names of East and West Wivelshire suggest that a larger region had been split (the name is Anglo-Saxon *twy-feald-scir*, 'two-fold shire'; Picken 1965-7). In the Geld Inquest, Rielton and Pawton hundreds appear to represent the area of medieval Pydar hundred. In addition, the hundreds of Trigg and Lesnewth each contain approximately one hundred settlements with *tre* place-name elements (Padel 1985: 216). Although the hundred of Stratton contains very few place-names with *tre*, it seems likely that these were replaced by English names (e.g. those with the suffix *-tun*) in or before the tenth century (Padel 1999: 88-94). Padel notes that Kerrier has approximately 228 settlements whose names contain *tre* as the first element, and he suggests that this may be because it was a 'double hundred' (*cf.* Welsh *cantref*, 'one hundred trefs': Padel 1985: 227). The evidence relating to the hundreds therefore suggests that there could have been a fairly complex administrative system in development in Cornwall during the early middle ages, but that it may have gone through changes and reorganisations that cannot now be easily understood and are not clearly reflected in the earliest source, Exeter Domesday Book.

In Wales a similar system of *cantrefi* was probably established between the seventh and ninth centuries to act as a basis for the extraction of dues and for public administration (Charles-Edwards 1970-2; Jenkins 1988; in some parts of Wales this process may have begun at a later date: Jones 1998: 174-7). Here, the *cantrefi* were closely linked both to royal power and to ecclesiastical organisation (Longley 1997). For example, in Glamorgan there appear to have been 'twin' sites of royal and ecclesiastical centres a couple of miles apart (Jenkins 1988: 44-5), and in Dyfed the seven hundreds each had an important monastery (Charles-Edwards 1970-2).

In Cornwall it is less clear than in Wessex and Wales that there was a close link between ecclesiastical and hundredal administration. The map of medieval hundreds and likely early monasteries shows that in each hundred there were several high-status churches. If the hundreds had previously been sub-divided into smaller units, it is possible that there could have been a regular distribution of churches, perhaps one per administrative unit. For example, it is possible that in Kerrier hundred the division might have occurred along the boundary provided by the Helford River. The church of St Keverne might then have served the land to the south of the river and the church of Constantine the area to the north. However, because the dates of any administrative reorganisation remain unknown and the foundation dates of the various churches are uncertain, any such arrangement is purely hypothetical.

The evidence for pastoral provision in early medieval Cornwall and the *parochiae* through which it might have been administered also seems relatively slim. In a few cases there is clear evidence for large numbers of dependent chapels, which may suggest the area was formerly dependent on a church for pastoral care (see Hall 2000). John Blair has suggested that the advent of Anglo-Saxon political control in Cornwall coincided with the establishment of a system of minster churches like those found in Wessex, and that relationships between minsters and dependent chapels in Cornwall belong to this period (Blair 2005: 304-6). On first inspection, the example of Launceston appears to support this argument. Launceston Priory had at least twelve dependent chapels in the later middle ages (Hull 1987: xxi). Rights over these appear to have been granted to the church at various times, and did not necessarily represent the area it administered since its foundation. Other scholars have also suggested that Launceston was a relatively late foundation and that it may have encroached on the territory of an earlier monastery of St Padern at either North or South Petherwin (Hull 1987: xxii-xxiii; but *cf.* Finberg 1953a). However, despite the likelihood that this network of dependencies was a relatively late development, there seems to be no clear relationship between the secular administrative units and Launceston's possible *parochia* such as that commonly found in western and central Wessex. Launceston's hypothetical *parochia* appears to cross both hundred and county boundaries in an area with a complex administrative history.

Launceston is also the only church in Cornwall for which large numbers of dependent chapels can be easily identified. If a new system of ecclesiastical organisation had been created in the late Saxon period (Blair 2005: 304-5), we might expect to find much clearer traces of it (as in Dorset (Hall 2000), Wiltshire (Pitt 1999) or Somerset (Aston 1986)). Instead, it seems much more likely that the rather scrappy vestiges of Cornish *parochiae* that can be discerned represent a system that began to be modified early, probably as a result of the foundation of local churches (Olson 1989: 95-6). The evidence for ecclesiastical estates in Cornwall (below, 123-9) also suggests that rather than active patronage, the majority of the ancient Cornish monasteries would have suffered considerable losses under Anglo-Saxon rule (*cf.* Blair 2005: 305).

There are quite a lot of churches with signs of superior status in Cornwall, including some with one or two dependent chapels. Many of these are also churches identified by Olson as pre-Conquest clerical communities. For example, the medieval parish of St Kew contained a chapel dedicated to St Aldhelm (Adams 1957; Orme 2000) whilst St Buryan had chapelries at Sennan and St Levan (Thomas 1988). In St Neot there was a chapel at St Luke's which had a kind of semi-official parochial status in the later middle ages, and although it eventually won burial rights the dead were originally buried at the mother church (Hull 1987: 36-7). Nicholas Roscarrock's sixteenth-century catalogue of south-western saints and customs associated with them records that Crantock church:

> had of old seaven churchyards belonging vnto it, And seaven parishes did vse to com yerelie vnto it from there seaven severall churches, bringing with them Relick*es* & placing them on seaven severall stoanes like Aulters designed for it, as an old Preist, an eye witness, hath informed mee.
>
> (Orme 1992: 66)

It is possible that such customs may be all that remained of earlier, more formal relationships between the former monastery at Crantock and dependent chapelries in its territory (Olson 1988: 27).

Thomas has suggested that Minster church near Tintagel once provided pastoral care for an area comprising several later parishes (Thomas 1993: 109). The extent of Minster's influence is hinted at by the *Life of St Nectan*, a twelfth-century document which Orme has shown to have as much relevance to the ecclesiastical politics of north-east Cornwall as to hagiography (Orme 1992: 45-50). The *Life* seems to record an attempt by the important church of Hartland (Devon) to extend its influence over the other churches of north-west Devon and north-east Cornwall. However, it avoids claims over those churches in the area whose saints were well-known cult figures (such as St David and St Petroc), or those saints whose churches are of superior status (and their dependencies). In the area around Tintagel, the churches of Minster, Tintagel, Trevalga and Lesnewth appear to fall into one or other of these categories since they are omitted from the document (ibid. 50). This suggests there was an established ecclesiastical territory in the area. In addition, a close link between Minster and Tintagel churches is suggested by their shared dedication to St Matheriana, found nowhere else in Britain.

The medieval church of St Keverne was paid a pension by Helston, which suggests that there may have been a dependent relationship between the two (Hockey 1976: 223). Helston was the head manor of the hundred of Kerrier at the time of Domesday and any such relationship could suggest St Keverne formerly had a larger *parochia* than its later medieval parish, which was nevertheless the biggest in the Lizard peninsula. Historically, St Keverne parish is the heart of the region known as the 'Meneage'. This name is derived from the Cornish *manach* 'monk', and may mean 'monkish (land)' (Padel 1985: 156; Olson 1989: 108-9). It is related to the Cornish *meneghy* 'sanctuary' (Padel 1985: 163). The Meneage is today considered to be the parishes of St Keverne, St Anthony-in-Meneage, Manaccan, and St Martin-in-Meneage, with the eastern half of St Mawgan-in-Meneage (Henderson 1958: 262). The earliest recorded use of the element *manach* is in a place-name recorded in a charter of 967 when King Edgar granted the estate of *lesmanaoc* (**lys* + *manach*, i.e. Lesneage) to his 'faithful *minister*' Wulfnoth Rumuncant, a man bearing both English and Cornish names (S755; Hooke 1994a: 37-40). The earliest recorded use of the 'Meneage' to describe the region is in a charter dated *c*.1070 (Hull 1962: 1-2). Olson notes that the 'monkish land' of the Meneage 'corresponds to no known civil or ecclesiastical unit' (Olson 1989: 108). In her analysis she tries to identify the name with estates of land or another recorded unit of property, rather than in terms of the ownership of ecclesiastical or other administrative rights. However, it seems likely that this regional name could refer to the area of land over which a major land-holding monastery exercised such powers, rather than to property it held. Olson identifies St Keverne as the major monastery in question. The 'Meneage' also forms a coherent geographical unit bounded by the sea to the east (with rough grazing on many of the clifftops), the Helford River to the north (with woodland near the shore along most of its length), and the upland rough grazing of Goonhilly Downs and Helston Downs to the west **(Figs 24 & 27)**. The small parishes of Manaccan and St Anthony to the north of St Keverne look likely on topographical grounds to have been later divisions of a pre-existing ecclesiastical administrative unit. However, there is no historical evidence from later medieval institutional links or other sources to suggest St Keverne had rights over the whole area. By the end of the Anglo-Saxon period it must have shared its ecclesiastical rights in the area with the church of St Mawgan-in-Meneage, which is mentioned (by place-name) in Domesday Book, and which had a dependent chapel with pre-

Conquest origins at St Martin-in-Meneage. The suggestion that the Meneage formed a large *parochia* of St Keverne must therefore remain tentative. Other large parishes in Cornwall may also indicate the partial extent of pre-Conquest *parochiae*, and some churches such as Perranzabuloe and (Old) Kea had very large medieval parishes (Orme 1999: 212-13).

The evidence of post-Conquest dependencies and large medieval parishes suggest that in Cornwall high-status churches had once had rights for the provision of pastoral care over fairly extensive areas. However, in contrast to the hundreds of Dorset and elsewhere in Wessex, it is hard to see hundreds and hypothetical *parochiae* in Cornwall which share the same boundaries. In part this may be because more minor churches were founded earlier in Cornwall than in Wessex, so eroding the traces of *parochiae* which survived in other areas (see Chapter 7). Administrative reorganisations may also have obscured any relationships, but it seems likely that unlike much of Wales and Anglo-Saxon England, there was not a very close correlation between ecclesiastical and secular administrative units in early medieval Cornwall.

Early Medieval Ecclesiastical Estates

The development of the early medieval landscape has often been discussed in terms of the so-called 'multiple estate' model developed by G.R.J. Jones (1976, 1985). The model pictured royal centres that drew support from a range of smaller outlying agrarian units. Each unit within the 'multiple estate' would have had access to basic necessities such as arable land and grazing for flocks, but particular units would have been responsible for the production of particular items, such as dairy products or wool (Hooke 1998: 52). The system of multiple estates is thought to have been formalised out of the early folk *regiones* during the middle Saxon period, the time when Christianity was becoming established in Britain. As discussed below, the foundation of churches is likely to have had a fundamental impact on the way these landscapes developed.

Various different theories have been offered to explain how churches were established and maintained in early medieval Britain. Central to them all is the nature of the relationship between churches and land, either their own estates or those of secular authorities. Martin Carver has argued that in the conversion phase different models of Christianity can be identified, in part through the ways ecclesiastical institutions were supported (Carver 1998a, 2001, 2003). He has proposed three models for economic infrastructure which he argues can imply different forms of wider political organisation. These models of ecclesiastical organisation are firstly 'episcopal', a system dependent on the collection of tithes, and therefore associated with a Roman-style, tax-extracting system and closely allied to royal power; secondly, 'monastic', where land was endowed and the estate was self-supporting, and generally excluded from the tax system; and finally 'secular', where the church was dependent on the direct patronage of local secular elite families for survival, and therefore controlled to a greater extent by local elites than the churches of the other two 'options'. Carver has argued that these three different types of Christianity were adopted preferentially in accordance with what a community would tolerate and in alignment with its political thinking; a community might change from one option to another as its political system changed (Carver 1998a: 20-6; 2001: 12-20).

Early Ecclesiastical Estates in the Wessex Landscape

In early medieval southern Britain, a number of scholars have identified systems of ecclesiastical organisation similar to those discussed by Carver. Steven Bassett has suggested that the earliest tier of churches in what became southern Mercia were founded according to a monastic model; these churches stood at the heart of districts within which they held sizeable estates (Bassett 1998: 1-4). On the other hand, Patrick Hase thinks most minster churches in early central Wessex were staffed by communities of clerics and established by kings at royal vills with only very small endowments of land: 'These small churches thus formed part of the network of royal social, economic and political control apparatus' (Hase 1994: 61-2). Taken on their own, these models do not appear to explain adequately the situation in early Wessex.

In the late pre-Conquest period, a number of Benedictine monasteries and nunneries existed in central and western Wessex controlling their own estates, which were often very large. These included Tavistock and Buckfast (Devon), Athelney, Muchelney, Bath and Glastonbury (Somerset), Abbotsbury, Cranborne, Cerne, Horton, Sherborne, Milton and Shaftesbury (Dorset), and Wilton, Amesbury and Malmesbury (Wiltshire) (Blair 1985: 105-12). All these houses had been 'reformed' during the Benedictine revival in the period after *c*.940 (Yorke 1995: 210-25). However, the often extensive and dispersed estates which these houses held at the time of Domesday had not always been associated with them in the period before the Reform, and they were often the result of this new phase of monastic refoundation. Michael Costen has discussed the case of Glastonbury, the most famous and best endowed of these monasteries, and shown how its estate developed largely in the tenth century (Costen 1992a). Other reformed houses probably had similar histories, and even those which held extensive estates before the mid-tenth century had not necessarily held them since the seventh century. Asser records that Shaftesbury was granted a great deal of land when Alfred founded it for his daughter Æthelgifu, even though it seems possible that no church at all existed at Shaftesbury before this event (Keynes & Lapidge 1983: 105; Hall 2000: 100). These examples show that the extent of ecclesiastical estates could fluctuate over time, and that this could be related to changes in the nature of the establishments themselves.

Despite the changes brought about by the Benedictine reforms, it is certain that some seventh- and eighth-century churches in Wessex held large estates. Glastonbury itself is one example (e.g. S253; Costen 1992a: 26); others, with examples of charters which granted them estates, include Crediton (S255), Bath (S51), Malmesbury (S231, S243), Muchelney (S249, S261) and Wells (S262). Although some of these grants refer to areas immediately around the churches in question (e.g. S255), others give control over land that was some distance from the owners' establishments. There were other early monasteries in Wessex which are not easily recognisable as such in their later Saxon forms, either because records from earlier times have been lost or because the nature of the establishments themselves changed. At Tisbury (Wiltshire) no church is recorded in the late Saxon period when the estate was held by Shaftesbury Abbey, yet earlier evidence suggests an important monastery existed in the eighth century (Kelly 1996: 3-10; S1256 (AD 759) Pitt 1999: 55). At Bradford-on-Avon (Wiltshire) a monastery may have been founded by Aldhelm (as reported by

William of Malmesbury in the twelfth century). A charter of AD 1001 records the grant of a *cenobium* at Bradford to Shaftesbury Abbey (S899; Pitt 1999: 145-57), which probably included the 38 hides held here by the abbey at Domesday (Thorn & Thorn 1979b: 12,4; Pitt 1999: 150-7; **Plate 3a**). The loss of ecclesiastical land to royal and lay hands, particularly in the ninth century, has been discussed by Fleming (1985), and it seems likely that other small monasteries suffered a similar fate but were less well recorded than Tisbury or Bradford. Iwerne Minster (Dorset) is another example associated with Shaftesbury. The abbey held an estate of 18 hides here at Domesday, but later medieval parochial rights suggest an extensive *parochia* had been focused on Iwerne Minster in the pre-Conquest period (Hall 2000: 17).

The evidence therefore suggests that some of the early ecclesiastical centres in Wessex were monasteries in Carver's sense: religious communities supported by their own land (Carver 2001: 13-14). However, as Blair has argued (1985: 115), it would be a mistake to assume that the evidence for the existence and diminution of monastic centres and their estates shows that all the earliest churches of Wessex were significant landholders; if this had been the case there would have been little space for *royal* estates around the royal vills which were so often located immediately next to superior churches (Hall 2000: 41). Other evidence suggests that many early ecclesiastical settlements were communities with little land of their own (Blair 1985: 114-25).

Perhaps the most well-known source of the early Christian period in England which is likely to relate to these minor monastic communities is Bede's famous letter to Bishop Egbert of York. It denounces both aristocratic and royal foundations which did not follow exacting monastic rules (Farmer 1990: 345-6). Early communities of this sort are hard to detect in Wessex, though Ine's law on the payment of church-scot suggests that churches dependent to some extent on ecclesiastical taxation (rather than large estates) were widespread by the early eighth century (Attenborough 1922: 36-7; Wormald 1999: 368-9). Many of the Wessex churches recorded in Domesday Book with small endowments of a few hides may well reflect clerical communities which held land that was geographically within that of a royal or secular elite estate (Blair 1985: 114-16; Hase 1994; Hall 2000: 41). Notable examples include the churches of Wiltshire listed in Domesday Book at the end of the king's holdings, but held in 1066 or 1086 by various priests or monastic houses (Thorn & Thorn 1979b: 1,23a-j). Not many of these churches are recorded prior to Domesday, which also hints that they were considered part of the royal estate: few of the royal vills on the 'core' of royal land are mentioned in early medieval sources (Sawyer 1983: 285). Wessex churches appearing in Domesday Book with around 4 hides or less in 1066 seem to have been mentioned only incidentally before the eleventh century in sources like King Alfred's will (S1507), which was dealing with the transfer of the royal estates where they were situated (e.g. Damerham; Keynes & Lapidge 1983: 178). Some such estates were granted by kings to bishops or monasteries, but any churches on them were not mentioned separately in the relevant charters; examples include Downton (Wiltshire; S891), Great Bedwyn (Wiltshire; S756) and Pewsey (Wiltshire; S740). It seems likely that where the estates of the church in question were small and linked closely to those of the main estate centre, the church was not counted separately for the purposes of the grant.

There are forty examples of probable and likely superior churches in the counties of Dorset, Somerset and Wiltshire where some record survives of the size of their estate in pre-Conquest sources or Domesday Book, but which were never recorded as holding more than 4 hides. Only three of these were sited further than 1km or so from the nearest royal vill or *burh* (Northover and Stogumber (both in Somerset) and Brixton Deverell (Wiltshire)). This strongly suggests that these churches had a close relationship with royal authority, and may suggest a high level of dependence on royal resources.

Where important churches held only a small amount of land it seems likely that it would have been intermixed within the lands of the royal vill or aristocratic estate where they were located. In Domesday Book small ecclesiastical estates often occur in Wiltshire and Devon in the form 'the church of this manor has *n* hides of the land' of the main estate. In these entries, the land of the royal estate in question has just been noted in the preceding Domesday entry (e.g. Wootton Rivers, Westbury, Winterbourne Stoke, Netheravon and Collingbourne Ducis (Thorn & Thorn 1979b: 1,15-19)). In this sense minor church estates may originally have been like the other specialised elements of the royal estate which were designated to produce various components of the royal *feorm* (see Faith 1997: 38-53).

The surviving sources do not allow clear interpretations or distinctions to be made between the vast majority of individual early medieval churches. This is because the communal Rules followed, the make-up of the communities within particular churches, and the size of ecclesiastical estates are known to have changed in various cases at various times (Blair 1985). Spatial relationship between churches and royal centres and evidence for the size of estates may provide some useful clues, though the example of Tisbury shows that the latter cannot necessarily be projected back or forward in time.

Despite these uncertainties, the evidence suggests that both royal estates with dependent churches and more independent monastic estates followed the same 'grammar' in terms of their organisation in the landscape; the church was central to both in physical and ideological terms. Major land-holding churches most commonly lay at the heart of a 'core' area of their estates. This core appears to have been analogous to the area dependent on a royal vill. It was commonly tax-exempt, and has been labelled 'inland' by Faith (1997: 16-28, 48-53). At Sherborne, for instance, the bishop of Salisbury and the monks of Sherborne held a substantial area of tax-exempt land at the time of Domesday Book (Thorn & Thorn 1983: 2,6; 3,1). As Faith argues, this area probably formed the core 'inland' of the early ecclesiastical community. It may have been identical with the *praedium* which was apparently enclosed by Bishop Wulfsige in the late tenth century when he refounded the monastery under the Benedictine Rule (S895). Faith has argued that this area could even be reflected by a long sinuous boundary, now made up of roadways and field boundaries, which roughly surrounds the site of the monastery at a distance of *c*.2.5km (Faith 1997: 20-2; Barker 1984; **Fig. 45**). It may be significant that this boundary appears to run roughly parallel to the parish boundary, but a few hundred metres within it (especially in its northern portion). Wulfsige's charter appears to indicate that the hedges and ditches of the boundary were made around the *praedium* in response to increasing pressure of disputes and encroachments on to the ecclesiastical estate (Faith 1997: 21). The boundary

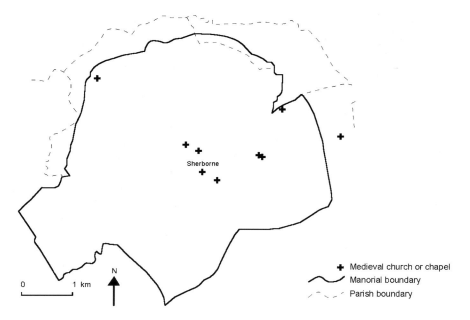

Fig. 45: The post-medieval manorial boundary of Sherborne (after Barker 1984 and Faith 1997: 20). The boundary possibly reflects Sherborne's early medieval *praedium* (or 'inland') (Faith 1997); two medieval chapels lay close to the manorial boundary.

noted by Faith and others may therefore reflect the limits of the community's agricultural land, at the heart of which was the church itself; outside the boundary probably lay unenclosed heath used as pasture.

Few of the core estates of churches with the largest and most ancient endowments have charters with detailed boundary clauses. Nevertheless, this arrangement of church, agricultural land and peripheral rough ground is detectable in the bounds of charters granting land units which may either already have had churches within them, or where churches belonging to a subsequent phase of ecclesiastical foundations (effectively acting as 'sub-minsters') were established following the grant. An example is provided by Shapwick in Somerset. Here, the 20-hide estate of *Pouholt* was granted to Glastonbury Abbey in the first half of the eighth century by King Ine (S248; S253). Attached to one of these grants is a simple boundary clause in Latin which mentions features and areas bordering the estate in the cardinal directions: to the east lies Chalkbrook; to the south, the River Cary from the point where the Carswell stream flows into it as far as Chedzoy; to the west is the territory of Cossington; and to the north is 'half of the marsh' (S253; Abrams 1994; **Fig. 41**). The majority of these boundaries lie in the marshland, which until its drainage in the post-medieval period formed a wet hinterland to the dry fields of the Polden ridge. It was here, in the heart of the arable land, that Glastonbury's estate church (or 'sub-minster') was situated (Gerrard 1995; Aston & Gerrard 1999).

Boundary clauses may have become more complicated with the passage of time and perhaps increasing pressure from secular landholders, but there is some evidence to suggest that in western Wessex this way of ordering ecclesiastical estates

—a church at the core of intensively farmed land with rough pasture and wasteland beyond—persisted into the later part of the period, and indeed that it was understood as the way the landscape ought to be organised. S255 is a charter granting land for the foundation of a monastery at Crediton in Devon, issued in 739 by King Æthelheard to Bishop Forthere. Although the charter itself is believed to be authentic, the boundary clause appears to be a later addition, probably composed in the late tenth or early eleventh century by the community at Crediton (Hooke 1999: 98; Finberg 1969b: 44-69). As such, it may represent a rather idealised version of the bounds of an early medieval ecclesiastical estate. The boundary clause describes a large area centred on the ecclesiastical community and the fertile fields of the Creedy and Yeo valleys. The boundary of the estate was apparently rather more dangerous territory according to some of the boundary markers: a precipitous drop, a wolf-pit and a wolf's valley, and probably a number of prehistoric barrows (Hooke 1994a: 86-99; Finberg 1969b). The latter, as Sarah Semple has argued, seem to have been particularly associated with monsters and evil spirits in the late Saxon period (Semple 1998). Two further boundary markers from the charter are perhaps indicative of the learned context of the boundary clause's composition, *grendeles pyt* ('Grendel's pit') and *caines aecer* ('Cain's acre'), both of which reinforce the idea that this was a dangerous margin. The Grendel of the boundary clause probably relates to the fearful monster slain by the hero of the Anglo-Saxon epic *Beowulf*; as Semple has discussed, the Grendel of the epic was considered to be a creature that lurked on the boundaries of the land (Semple 1998: 113-14). As his brother's murderer, Cain was blighted in the Christian tradition, and it seems likely that the land described as his 'acre' was rough heathland when the boundary clause was composed (Hooke 1994a: 95). The occurrence of both Grendel and Cain in the same boundary clause seems more likely to be a literary construct than a mere coincidence, since in *Beowulf* Grendel himself is described as a descendant of Cain (lines 99-114; Klaeber 1950; I am grateful to Victoria Thompson for discussion of this point). The land concerned was probably heath or moor, like the nearby 'heathfield' mentioned in the boundary clause of the neighbouring estate of Down St Mary (S795). The 'dragon's lair' (*wurmstealle*) of Sandford's woodland boundary is also evocative of the supernatural dangers lurking in the woods and heaths at the margins of the Crediton estates (S890; Hooke 1994a: 184).

Ecclesiastical Estates in Cornwall

Evidence for early medieval ecclesiastical estates in Cornwall comes mainly from the folios of Domesday Book, although there are a small number of pre-Conquest charters containing valuable information about certain churches. In Domesday Book the Cornish church with the largest estate was St Petroc's at Bodmin, although it is important to note that the bishop of Exeter's estates in the county were considerably larger (these partly perpetuated lands granted earlier to the bishops of Sherborne, and to the bishop of Cornwall whose see was combined with Devon in 1050; S1296; Orme 1991: 22).

In the later eleventh century Bodmin's estates did not form one contiguous block, but were dispersed over a wide area.[2] To a lesser extent the churches of St

---

[2] Even including some land in Devon at Hollacombe and Newton St Petrock: S388; Thorn and Thorn 1985: 51,15-16.

Piran's and perhaps St Kew also held estates dispersed along the north coast of Cornwall in the later pre-Conquest period (Olson 1989: 90; Thorn & Thorn: 1979a, *Notes* E 1,4)). As a result there were blocks of detached ecclesiastical land, for example those in the area around Tintagel. St Petroc's held land at Treknow and Bossiney (Thorn & Thorn 1979a: 4,20; 4,13), and St Piran's probably held the estate of *Tregrebi*, centred on Genver in Tintagel parish (ibid. 5,8,10). However, comparing these estates with those of the other Cornish clerical communities recorded in Domesday Book suggests that they are not typical. Analogy with the late Saxon growth of dispersed estates held by some major Wessex monasteries like Glastonbury suggests that rather than being ancient endowments some of these Cornish estates may have been the result of land grants to favoured houses in the tenth and eleventh centuries.

The fourth chapter of the Exeter Domesday Book for Cornwall (and in modified form, of Exchequer Domesday) records the land of various churches. Most of the entries note that the canons of a particular church hold a particular estate; for example 'the canons of St Achebrans hold St Keverne' (ibid. 4,23). Apart from the dispersed estates noted above, all the other ecclesiastical estates appear to comprise the immediate areas around the land-holding church. One of the most notable features of the Domesday Book entries for these estates is that without exception they are described as never having paid tax before the Norman Conquest. Olson argues that this geld-free status reflects an arrangement that had persisted since before the Anglo-Saxon political take-over of Cornwall, and points out that the Cornish estates of English ecclesiastical land-holders (the bishop of Exeter and Tavistock Abbey) did not hold the same privilege (Olson 1989: 91-3).

The case of St Germans suggests that previously exempt land had tax levied upon it when it passed out of the hands of its original owner. Here, a 24-hide estate had been split into two parts, with one half held by the canons of St Germans and the other by the bishop of Exeter (and previously the bishop of Cornwall; Hooke 1994a: 18; Thorn & Thorn 1979a: 2,6). The canons' 12 hides remained exempt in 1066, whereas the bishop's paid tax for 2 hides. The exemption from geld may indeed represent a pre-Anglo-Saxon arrangement.

These Cornish ecclesiastical estates and their workers did not pay geld to the king, but only dues to their churches. Such exempt 'inlands' are not unique to Cornwall in Domesday Book, and can be found all over England (Faith 1997: 16-38). Nevertheless, the concentration of them in Cornwall is highly significant, and indicates an unusually large body of churches with freedom from secular dues (including Launceston (St Stephens), St Neot, St Piran's, Crantock, St Buryan, Probus, Constantine, St Germans, St Michael's Mount and St Petroc's, Bodmin: Thorn & Thorn 1979a: 4,1-29). This evidence is complementary to previous discussion which showed how Cornish religious communities were generally distant from Cornish royal vills and were not closely tied to secular administrative organisation. It suggests once again that major Cornish churches of the pre-Anglo-Saxon period had been relatively free from secular interference.

Information about Cornish churches' estates also suggests that this independence was eroded in the later pre-Conquest period. Several Anglo-Saxon charters record grants of land to Cornish churches. At St Buryan, King Athelstan granted the church one *mansa* 'divided in seven places' (*septem loca divisam*), which can probably be equated with the single hide the church held in Domesday

(S450; Thorn & Thorn 1979a: 4,27). King Edgar granted the estate at Lanow in St Kew to the monastery of SS Docco and Kew, whose site is most likely that of the present parish church (Olson 1989: 81-4; Hooke 1994a: 33-7; **Plate 14a**). The estate at St Kew later passed into secular hands, since in Domesday Book it is recorded as having been a manor of King Harold in 1066 (though part of the manor became ecclesiastical again in the twelfth century; Olson 1989: 82-3). These Anglo-Saxon charters probably represent refoundation grants, and there is some evidence to suggest that during the late Saxon period there was serious secular encroachment on to formerly ecclesiastical estates. The fate of St Kew's lands provides one example, and King Harold had also taken land from St Petroc's (Thorn & Thorn 1979a: 4,21). Another charter records how a large estate at Tywarnhayle was granted into secular hands in the tenth century, probably at the expense of St Piran's, in whose later medieval parish (Perranzabuloe) all this territory lay (S684; Olson 1989: 95).

A more detailed examination of pre- and post-Conquest material from two case-studies suggests that the estates of other Cornish collegiate churches suffered similar depletions after successive Anglo-Saxon and Norman control had been established in the region.

St Keverne

St Keverne was the only land-holding religious house recorded in Domesday Book in the Lizard peninsula. This is how the estate is recorded in 1086:

> The Canons of St Achebran's hold *Lannachebran* [St Keverne], and held it before 1066. 11 acres of land. Land for 7 ploughs; 1 plough there. Pasture, 20 acres. 8 cattle; 30 sheep. When the ´count received it, value 40s; value now 5s.
>
> (Thorn and Thorn 1979a: 4, 23).

The size of the estate in 1066 is not recorded, but somewhat confusingly Domesday states that it paid 40s when it was received by the count (of Mortain), as opposed to 5s in 1086. This suggests that much of the estate may have been acquired and reduced in value and perhaps size by the count between 1066 and 1086 (discussed further below). The land recorded in Domesday probably represents the core of the clerical community's estates. It is almost certain that this was the same land which later formed Beaulieu Abbey's manor of Lanheverne. Beaulieu was granted the church of St Keverne in 1235 by Earl Richard of Cornwall, who had in turn been granted the land by his brother Henry III. The main centre of Beaulieu's lands in St Keverne was at the barton of Tregonning, just north of the churchtown (Henderson 1931: 51-3; Johns & Herring 1996: 85, 210-13). In the mid-thirteenth century the Abbey's estates in the parish also included the properties of Rosenithon, Trelean Veor, Treleage Vean, Treskewes, Gwenter and Carnpessack (Henderson 1958: 264-8). The majority of these are in the immediate vicinity of the churchtown, and this is the area where *tre* settlements cluster most densely. None of the places just listed are recorded as separate estates in Domesday Book. It is therefore likely that the land where these settlements are located had been attached to St Keverne before the Norman Conquest, and had probably formed the core of the estate of St Keverne's community since its foundation.

Nevertheless, the estate granted to Beaulieu may well have been smaller than St Keverne's original early medieval estate. Some evidence to suggest the extent of this comes from another eleventh-century document. The earliest use of the term 'Meneage' to describe the region is in a charter dated *c.*1070 in which Earl Robert, count of Mortain and the greatest post-Conquest landholder in Cornwall, conveyed to Mont St Michel three estates in *Amaneth* or *Manaek*, one of which had its centre at the same *Lismanoch* or *Lesmanaek* (Lesneage) that had been granted to Wulfnoth Rumuncant in an Anglo-Saxon charter of AD 967 (S 755; Henderson 1958: 270; Hull 1962: 1-2; Hooke 1994: 37-40).

Henderson argued that it is likely to have been as a result of its monastic history that Earl Robert granted the land at Traboe and Lesneage to Mont St Michel in *c.*1070 (ibid. 270). Henderson also suggested that all pre-Conquest grants by Anglo-Saxon kings in Cornwall should be regarded as the appropriation of Celtic monasteries' lands (Henderson 1958: 270). In the specific case of St Keverne, Hooke has followed this argument by suggesting that the three Anglo-Saxon charters from the Meneage show St Keverne's estates being broken up and put into secular hands in the tenth century (Hooke 1994b: 83-4). It may be more accurate to say that the estates were being granted into private hands, since the grant to Æthelweard (S832) is not certainly authentic, and estates defined by the same boundary clauses (S1027) were granted in 1059 to Bishop Ealdred of Worcester (formerly abbot of Tavistock, and subsequently archbishop of York).

The Anglo-Saxon charters do not state who was in possession of the lands concerned before they were granted, so it is not possible to be certain that it was the community of St Keverne in the case of the Meneage documents. However, the *c.*1070 grant by the count of Mortain to Mont St Michel suggests that this was indeed the case, since it deals with much of the same area. The estates granted in this document were Traboe and Lesneage (in St Keverne) and Trevegris and Carvallack (in St Martin-in-Meneage). Henderson mapped the area he believed to have been encompassed by the *c.*1070 grant, and it includes almost all of the lands also involved in the major Anglo-Saxon grants of Traboe and Lesneage. In addition, it takes in further land in an area reaching down to the Helford River in the north of St Martin-in-Meneage (Henderson 1958: 272; Hull 1962: xxiii; **Fig. 46**).

The grant of *c.*1070 appears to cover a large area of land in the Meneage, but according to Henderson's reckoning of its extent it only included one estate which was recorded in Domesday Book (out of sixteen in the Meneage recorded in the survey). Domesday Book records neither of the important estates of Traboe or Lesneage, even though they had been the subject of tenth- and eleventh-century Anglo-Saxon charters. This strongly suggests that the area of the *c.*1070 grant had been part of another estate at the time of Domesday. As noted above, Domesday Book states that the count received *Lannachebran* some time after 1066 and shows that the estate decreased significantly in value between this event and 1086. As noted above, the count also granted a substantial estate to Mont St Michel in *c.*1070. It seems most likely that either a part or the whole of the area of the *c.*1070 grant had been deducted from *Lannachebran* in the interim by the count and granted to the monastery of Mont St Michel. If only a part of the *c.*1070 grant was taken out of *Lannachebran*, it is possible that before conveying it to the Normandy house the count had reunited an area of formerly monastic land which

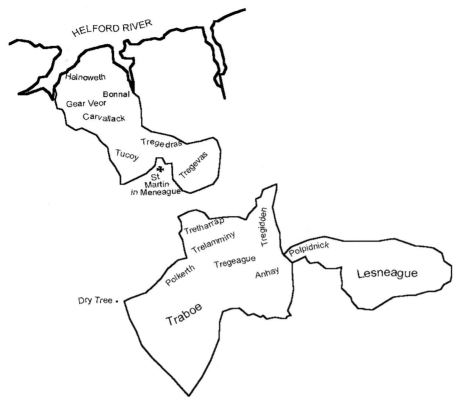

Fig. 46: Sketch-plan showing the land granted in Meneage by the Count of Mortain to Mont St Michel in Normandy, *c.*1070 (based on Charles Henderson's map: Henderson *Calendar 5*, 205).

had been broken up by the Anglo-Saxon grants to Wulfnoth Rumuncant and Ealdred. Whether all or part of the land came from St Keverne's estate, it seems likely that the monastery had once held extensive lands in the Meneage, including the nuclear area around the churchtown, and probably the estates in the centre and north of the region mentioned in the Anglo-Saxon charters and Earl Robert's grant to Mont St Michel.

St Neot

In 1066 the church of St Neot and Godric *presbiter* together held the two manors of St Neot, a total of 3 hides of land which had never paid tax. These estates probably lay in the valley of the St Neot River (also called the Loveny), south of the moorland edge and north of the River Fowey. The population of the two estates is enumerated in Domesday Book as 3 *servi* (slaves), 3 *villani* (villans), and 10 *bordarii* (bordars).[3] Such a high proportion of bordars is just what Faith has argued should be expected of the 'inland' of a monastic estate (Faith 1997: 70-4).

By the later middle ages, St Neot had become an ordinary parish church and

[3] Villans and bordars were peasants with different rights. See Faith 1997: 59-75.

had lost the collegiate status recorded in Domesday Book. The road from land-owning community to parish church is documented in Domesday Book and later sources, and other evidence suggests it was a journey that had begun well before the Norman Conquest. Although 3 hides had been held by Neot's community in 1066, by 1086 all but 1 Cornish acre had passed into the hands of a certain Odo, who held the estates from the count of Mortain. Between 1086 and 1095, William of Mortain probably acquired the rest of the church's property. Around that year the priory of Montacute in Somerset (a foundation of the count) acquired St Neot church together with its remaining estates and the demesne tithes (Henderson 1929: 40-1). Thus the whole of the estate of St Neot had passed into secular hands and subsequently been granted to a newly founded church by the end of the eleventh century, a similar history to that described above for the estates of St Keverne.

It seems likely, however, that the area from which St Neot drew revenue had once been greater than that recorded in Domesday Book. Fawton, which was the head manor of the hundred and administrative centre of the count of Mortain at Domesday, was probably first established in the late Anglo-Saxon period. The exact extent of its estates is unclear: at 2 hides, the area of agricultural land attached to Fawton in Domesday Book seems relatively small (particularly in comparison to nearby Liskeard's 12 hides). However, the Domesday entry also records that Fawton had land for 30 ploughs, with 20 *servi*, 30 *villani* and 20 *bordarii*, suggesting that the hidation recorded may not reflect the actual size of the estate. Perhaps Fawton's most significant attribute was the massive area of pasture it controlled (described in Domesday Book as 7 leagues long and 4 leagues wide). This mainly represents the rough grazing land on the moors north of the manorial centre.

Topographical considerations and later documentary sources encourage the tentative suggestion that this area would once have been attached to St Neot's church. This was the only known major high-status centre between the moor and the River Fowey before the foundation of Fawton, and on purely geographical grounds is the most likely place to have controlled this territory. In the later medieval period, several grants were made of estates north of Fawton to the priories of Launceston and Montacute (Austin et al. 1989: 26-30). This hints that the land had been ecclesiastical in the pre-Anglo-Saxon past, like the estates in the Lizard that were granted by Robert of Mortain to Mont St Michel (Henderson 1958: 270).

The general historical context and the specific local conditions also suggest this reconstruction is correct. As discussed by Austin et al. (1989) and Gerrard (S. Gerrard 2000), the moors in the northern part of the area contain rich tin deposits which were probably exploited on a more-or-less continuous basis from prehistory to the nineteenth century. Maddicott has argued that the Anglo-Saxon kings of the late ninth and tenth centuries relied increasingly on south-western resources such as tin for the prosperity of their kingdom, and that they (re)established centres such as Lydford and Exeter in Devon to control trade and distribution (Maddicott 1989: 35-6). It is known from Alfred the Great's will that the kings of Wessex owned land in Cornwall, and it is fairly certain that Alfred himself was active in the area south of Bodmin Moor (e.g. his visit to the shrine of St Gueriir, probably at St Neot; Keynes & Lapidge 1983: 173-78, 89). Many ecclesiastical centres in England saw their estates reduced by royal powers at about this time for specific political and economic reasons (see e.g. Nelson 1983; Fleming 1985). It is reasonable to suggest that much of the land over which St Neot had exercised control was appropriated by the crown when Fawton was established, at least partly in order to supervise trade and distribution of the resources of the moorland, including tin.

Thus the church of St Neot may have controlled an extensive area of land around the southern edge of Bodmin Moor in the later part of the ninth century, comprising its Domesday estates, and probably those of Fawton as well. As a pilgrimage centre it was famous enough to attract kings of Wessex such as Alfred the Great. However, in the late ninth or tenth century, the same kings established the manorial centre of Fawton to bring the resources of the moorland more firmly under their control and to act as the centre of the hundred. This meant that the resources on which St Neot drew were reduced. The community's impoverishment continued in the eleventh century when first the estate held by Godric in 1066 and later all but 1 acre of the rest of its land was seized by the count of Mortain, who had also gained control of Fawton. Finally, the church lost its independence and its remaining land when it was taken by Earl Robert of Mortain and granted to his foundation at Montacute at the end of the eleventh century.

The tradition of granting land to churches had probably developed in Cornwall from an early date, certainly before Anglo-Saxon control over the region was established. Domesday Book records at least some of these ecclesiastical estates before most of them were completely secularised or granted to distant monasteries during the later middle ages. Various sources suggest that in their heyday the estates of communities like those at St Keverne and St Neot had comprised fairly large, contiguous areas. In contrast to the lands of many west Saxon minsters, Cornish monastic estates were not closely tied to royal centres. By the late eleventh century many Cornish estates had suffered extensive secular encroachment, as reflected both in Domesday Book and in other documentary sources. However, they were still free from secular dues, and Domesday Book makes it clear that it was the saints for whom the communities and estates were named who were the sole beneficiaries of their own lands. The clustering of ordinary settlements around major Cornish churches reflects the fact that the saint and his or her church were at the heart of the ecclesiastical estate, and acted as the central focus for life in the region.

Conclusion

In Cornwall, ecclesiastical communities were endowed with fairly extensive estates by early medieval kings, and they appear to have enjoyed freedom from taxation on their lands. These estates normally comprised a contiguous block of land in the environs of the monastery's central church. Along with their distance from royal centres and the lack of congruity between possible *parochiae* and secular administrative structures, such endowments imply the major churches of the seventh to ninth centuries were relatively independent of the secular elite.

In Wessex some churches were founded as semi-independent monasteries and endowed with substantial grants of land but, in contrast to Cornwall, the majority of early churches were probably established by the elite adjacent to royal administrative centres. Important churches in Wessex were commonly central to the estates and administrative units that became increasingly formalised from the conversion period onwards, and even if churches were not physically in the middle of such units they were often central to patterns of agricultural resources within estates.

6

The changing ritual landscape
of the conversion period

In both Anglo-Saxon Wessex and British Cornwall, the period from the fifth to eighth centuries witnessed the change from traditional 'pagan' to Christian religious observance.[1] Evidence of cult sites in both areas in the fifth and sixth centuries is relatively slim. It is possible that some Roman temples continued to be used for 'pagan' worship up to the seventh century, although Brean Down and Lamyatt Beacon had burials and buildings which may have been Christian (Rahtz 1991: 7-8; Yorke 1995: 166). Place-name evidence suggests there could have been sacred groves and other similar sites which existed in a dispersed landscape of cult sites (e.g. the *nemet* ('sacred grove') place-names of Devon). In both Anglo-Saxon England and the Brittonic regions the 'pagan' societies of the Iron Age, Roman period and immediate post-Roman periods maintained networks of sacred foci (Cunliffe 1997: 190-208); many of these could have had continuing religious significance during the conversion period.

There is little evidence for pagan Anglo-Saxon temple-building. Blair has argued that in parts of Anglo-Saxon England constructed cult sites emerged just before the conversion to Christianity under the influence of Christian practice (Blair 1995b), though place-name evidence suggests that in southern England pagan Anglo-Saxon cult sites were without substantial structures and were sited at places like clearings in the woods and on hilltops until the conversion period (e.g. Yorke 1995: 167-; Meaney 1999). Blair has discussed the way sites like trees and wells could themselves have perpetuated ancient cult sites, or else the modes of traditional belief that had formerly been attached to other places (Blair 2005: 475-8). Examples in western Wessex include the ash tree 'which the ignorant call sacred' in the charter bounds of Taunton (Somerset; S311), and the ash trees of St Nectan's grove in Devon (reported in the twelfth-century *Life of St Nectan*: Doble 1970: 74-5). Stone pillars are another possible type of pagan Anglo-Saxon site that may have acquired a new Christian significance (Blair 1994: 64). In view of the various early medieval law codes, penitentials and church councils

---

[1] For a comprehensive recent discussion, see Pearce 2004: 77-133.

which prohibited pagan activity during the early middle ages, it seems likely that 'undercurrents of heathen belief' survived in the countryside, gradually dwindling to hints and superstitions in the later middle ages (Morris 1989: 62).

In west Cornwall 'fogous' are commonly associated with rounds, and normally take the form of long, thin underground chambers, (e.g. Halligye fogou, St Mawgan-in-Meneage; Startin 1982). Their function is uncertain: although they have been thought to be ritual structures, it seems more likely that they were stores (Todd 1987: 173-5). Whatever the case, no examples are known to have been in use later than the fourth century (ibid. 173-5). A small D-shaped building belonging to the late Roman period and after was excavated at Trethurgy; the excavator's favoured interpretation is that it was a shrine, though use as a store has not been ruled out (Quinnell 2004: 208-9). Other classes of pre-Christian sacred sites may have been incorporated into the new Christian landscape. Various Cornish place-names may allude to pagan sacred loci, such as the element 'nemet' in 'Lanivet', meaning a sacred grove (Padel 1985). The early hagiographical sources set incidents at caves, standing stones and paths. In one incident in his *Vita Prima* St Samson convinces some apostates he finds worshipping at a standing stone to return to the Christian faith (and is supposed to have Christianised the monument in question with his mark); in another, a fearful cave-dwelling serpent or dragon is killed by the saint who then lives temporarily as a hermit in the cave whilst his followers build a monastery nearby (Olson 1989: 14-28). While these may be commonplaces of the hagiographical genre, it seems likely that such sites were venerated in pre-Christian times, as they were elsewhere in Britain and Europe. Archaeological evidence cannot often demonstrate clearly the way such sites were used, or even the period of use. However, it does show that monuments such as standing stones were common in the Cornish landscape (e.g. the Longstone at Tremenheere, St Keverne; i.e. 'the estate' (*tre*) 'at the menhir' (*men hir*), whose medieval place-name is first recorded in 1312 (*ICS Index*)).

Holy wells were part of medieval Christian and probably pre-Christian religious practice throughout the South West, occurring widely in all five south-western counties. Like the burial sites discussed below, wells occur both at places that later became major Christian foci (e.g. Wells, Somerset), and also dispersed through the landscape, for instance the *halgan well* ('holy well') in the charter bounds of Ruishton, Somerset (S310; S352; S1819), *halgan wyl* at Portisham, Dorset (S961); and *halgan weies lake* or 'holy way stream' at Fontmell Magna, Dorset (S419; see Rattue 1995: 63-4). Blair has suggested that cult sites like these represent a kind of vernacular religion which co-existed with 'official' (normally high-status) Christian sites. Like the cemeteries discussed below (133-140), these appear to have existed throughout the early middle ages and may have perpetuated minor pre-Christian cult foci within the Christian landscape; examples may include those documented cases whose boundary-clause names refer to non-Christian supernatural creatures such as the *pucan wylle*, 'puck's well' at Weston, Somerset (S508; Semple 2002; Blair 2005: 472-3). Holy wells in Cornwall are commonly regarded as the quintessential 'pagan' Celtic survivals (Rattue 1995: 46), and some may indeed perpetuate the sites of pre-Christian sacred springs. The well-chapels at Madron, St Levan and Constantine (St Merryn) may be amongst the earliest standing medieval buildings in Cornwall, and potentially provide evidence for the elaboration of sites with earlier sacred significance in the late Saxon period (**Plate 6a**; Todd 1987: 293; Blair 2005: 375).

Nevertheless, holy wells were also a fundamental element of the later medieval Christian landscape, providing water for baptisms and other purposes. Although there were times when worship at wells and other traditional sites was attacked by the Anglo-Saxon church hierarchy (e.g. by Ælfric and Wulfstan), they were ubiquitous in the later middle ages and sometimes elaborately constructed (Rattue 1995: 89-100). It is likely that their number multiplied significantly in the later Saxon period and after the Norman Conquest. James Rattue lists eight late medieval or modern holy wells which may first be recorded in Anglo-Saxon charters as springs without religious associations, including four examples in Devon and Somerset (Rattue 1995: 64-5). Whilst all the likely early Cornish monasteries had holy wells nearby, so did many ordinary parish churches. The geographical positions of many such wells, which tend to stand very close to later medieval chapels or churches and within their glebe land, probably suggest that they acquired their holy status by association with the church in question after it was founded. The dedication of the holy well of St Keverne hints at this. The well is first recorded in the thirteenth century as *funten kiran* (Henderson 1958: 277). The patron saint of St Keverne only seems to have been identified with St Ciaran of Saighir and commonly referred to as *Kieranus* in the Latin sources from the thirteenth century onwards (Orme 2000: 160). The fact that the well was associated with Kieran rather than a saint with the earlier name form *Achebrannus* (as recorded in Domesday Book) may suggest that it post-dated this change and was therefore of late medieval origin.

Without reliable archaeological evidence for continuity of use, it is impossible to identify which wells are very ancient and which only gained their sacred associations in the middle ages: not all are 'ancient' cult places. The relatively ephemeral nature of sites like wells and holy trees means that activity is normally hard to date by archaeological methods, and also that there are commonly few references to them in historical sources. For these reasons, the discussion in the following pages concentrates on other types of sites. Besides an unknown number of existing pre-Christian monuments, a range of small new religious foci were created in the early medieval period including burial sites, crosses and chapels. Crosses, chapels and minor churches will be returned to in Chapter 7; the remainder of this chapter will assess evidence for isolated burial sites and the roles they played in the developing Christian landscape.

Field Cemeteries in Western Wessex

For burial sites as well as settlements, the ending of Roman Britain did not necessarily mean the abandonment of established locations in the South West. Although few sites which date to this period are presently known in Devon (e.g. the cemetery at Kenn; Weddell 2000), there are numerous examples of early medieval burial sites in Somerset, Dorset and Wiltshire.

Excavations have shown that some burial sites in Somerset and Dorset have periods of use spanning the late Roman, post-Roman and middle Saxon periods, as recently discussed by Petts (2001). One of the most important examples is Cannington (Somerset), where a cemetery which may originally have accommodated as many as 2,000 individuals was in use between the fourth and the late seventh or eighth century (Rahtz et al. 2000), but Camerton (Somerset) is another case (Wedlake 1958) and there are possible smaller examples from Portland (Dorset) and Wells (Somerset) (Petts 2001).

Other cases such as Ilchester/Northover and Bradley Hill (Somerset) show that some Roman period cemeteries continued in use into the post-Roman centuries, but were disused before the period of West Saxon cultural dominance (Leech 1981; Leach 1994). Burials and cemeteries at former Roman temples illustrate that although certain places may have remained focal sites for ritual practice in the very late and post-Roman periods, the nature of that use could change. Roman temples were not normally used as funerary sites during the Roman period, but between the fifth and seventh centuries burials occurred at a number of them including Henley Wood, Brean Down, Lamyatt Beacon (Somerset), probably Nettleton (Wiltshire), and perhaps Maiden Castle (Dorset) (Watts & Leach 1996; Leech 1986; Wedlake 1982; Wheeler 1943; Petts 2001). The Henley Wood example is particularly important as it demonstrates a very close spatial relationship between the cemetery and the contemporary high-status settlement at Cadbury Congresbury, only c.130m to the south. Such a relationship may also be reflected at Cannington (Somerset) and possibly at Raddon (Devon; Gent & Quinnell 1999a).

These centuries witnessed the conversion of the greater part of the region to Christianity under British and subsequently Saxon leaders. However, there does not appear to have been a clear break in burial tradition at any point between the fourth or fifth and eighth centuries, as might have been expected with the conversion. Present evidence tends to suggest that in most of Somerset and Dorset, and in a large part of western Wiltshire, burial practice changed relatively little during this period. Some early burial sites remained active in the eighth century and later, whereas others went out of use in the sixth or seventh centuries. Some sites which appear to have been used specifically as Christian cemeteries in the early post-Roman period failed to remain active into later times, including examples like Lamyatt Beacon and Brean Down where there may have been small churches on site (Wedlake 1982; Leech 1986).

Some cemeteries that did persist from post-Roman times into the middle Saxon period were associated with sites that became important elite centres later in the early middle ages, whether predominantly ecclesiastical or secular. Examples include Carhampton (Hollinrake & Hollinrake 1997) and probably Wells in Somerset (Rodwell 1982), and Wareham in Dorset (Hinton 1992; Petts 2001). However, other cemeteries that were not located at the sites of important churches seem to have remained active or come into use in the seventh century. Field cemeteries like Cannington continued to provide important venues for burial well into the Christian period.

In Dorset, examples from the Isle of Purbeck show how cemeteries separate from churches could exist in the early middle ages. At Ulwell in the parish of Swanage, a cemetery of around sixty dug graves and cist burials has been shown by radiocarbon dating to have been used throughout the seventh and eighth centuries, and perhaps later (Cox 1988). There are a number of other burial sites in the same area that could belong to the early middle ages, although they have not been scientifically dated. At Ballard Down and at Durlston Cliff small cemeteries with both dug graves and cist burials were uncovered, and a further cist burial was found nearby at Langton Matravers (RCHM 1970; Petts 2001). None of these four sites has any obvious relationship to a church or chapel, and it seems likely that they functioned as Christian field cemeteries in the early middle ages.

A limited number of references in Anglo-Saxon charter bounds probably refer to such field cemeteries, for example at Stanton St Bernard (S368) and East Overton (S449) in Wiltshire (Reynolds 2002). Early antiquarian references hint that such sites have been disturbed in the past, for instance at the Sanctuary, near Avebury in Wiltshire (Pollard & Reynolds 2002: 233-4). John Blair has shown that burial grounds of this sort existed in late Anglo-Saxon Oxfordshire, and notes that it was possible for them (and the burial rites conducted at them) to be under the control of ecclesiastical centres some distance away, for example Chimney, controlled by the minster at Bampton (Blair 1994: 73). Until at least the ninth or tenth centuries rural burial sites away from churches probably continued to function in Wessex and more widely in Anglo-Saxon England; the stimulus for change and more centralised control of burial appears to have been the development of increasing numbers of local churches and the resulting loss of income for longer-established ecclesiastical centres (Lucy & Reynolds 2002: 20-1; Gittos 2002: 202-4). This suggests that even those burials that took place some distance from important churches had by this time come under their control. Although burials continued in long-established cemeteries based perhaps on family or other social groups, by the ninth and tenth centuries these burial sites had clearly been incorporated into a broadly 'Christian' landscape.

'Anglo-Saxon' Burials in Central Wessex

Anglo-Saxon cultural influence in central Wessex from the fifth century onwards has been inferred from the presence of distinctively Anglo-Saxon material culture, mainly in the form of grave goods, but also as some settlement-related finds (Eagles 2001). There is a particularly marked concentration of burial evidence from the Avon valley and its tributaries around Salisbury in Wiltshire. Fifth-century cemeteries have been identified at Petersfinger, Winterbourne Gunner, Harnham and Charlton, and burial continued at all these sites into the sixth century (Meaney 1964; Eagles 2001: 206). Finds such as pottery and building remains have been recovered close to several of these cemeteries, as at Collingbourne Ducis in the Bourne valley (Eagles 2001; Pine 2001). It seems most likely that settlements and their cemeteries in this part of Wessex were sited very close to one another during the fifth and early sixth centuries, and burial sites, like settlements, occur in a wide range of topographical positions (e.g. Overton Hill and Bassett Down: Semple 2003). Sarah Semple has also discussed the possibility that early Anglo-Saxon cemeteries may have acted as foci for a wider range of ritual activities than just burial (Semple 2004). Several of the sites she considers comprise multi-centred ritual landscapes dispersed over fairly extensive areas. In some ways this decentralised 'late pagan' landscape in England is analogous to pre-conversion landscapes in Scandinavia, where ritual sites (including settlements and burials) were scattered across areas of the landscape rather than being focused on a single elite site (Welinder 2003: 510-12); Charlotte Fabech, discussing southern Sweden, has highlighted the contrast between the 'decentral and horizontal cosmos' of pre-Christian Nordic ideology and the 'centrality and verticality' of Christian ideology (Fabech 1999a: 469).

In late sixth- and seventh-century Wessex, however, a different pattern begins to emerge. Cemeteries and burial sites appear to become increasingly distant from settlement sites, with a growing tendency for them to occupy locations on hilltops or plateaux (Semple 2003). There is also a corresponding increase in 'isolated' burials of one or two individuals, typically in barrows. In the sixth and earlier seventh centuries these are normally the burials of male individuals, but by the later seventh century, when they dominate what is known of the burial record of the area, females are in the majority (Eagles 2001). Both Eagles and Semple note the distinctive topographical positions of the majority of these burials, which tend to be on downland away from the main areas of settlement.

However, whilst some are on escarpment edges with wide views across territory, such as the primary barrow-burial of a male on Roundway Down (Semple 2003) and the Swallowcliffe Down female (Speake 1989), others such as Yatesbury 1 (Semple 2003) and the secondary barrow-burial of a female on Roundway Down (Semple & Williams 2001) are in less topographically prominent locations. Eagles and Semple also note that these burials tend to occur close to routes of communication, in some cases by a Roman road, in others by a routeway identified in later Anglo-Saxon charters as a herepath. They suggest that the prime motivation behind the location of these monuments was the desire for prominence in the landscape of communications, with the implication that these 'conspicuous' burials were marking territories of some kind, perhaps relating to fluctuating frontiers between developing kingdoms (Eagles 2001: 212-3, 219; Semple 2003). However, it does not seem easy to explain others in this way, for example those located squarely in what had become the West Saxon heartlands around Salisbury (e.g. Ford Down and Salisbury Racecourse; Musty 1969; Yorke 1995: 59-60; Eagles 2001: 225).

If these monuments *are* to be seen as territorial markers, it may be that instead of marking the boundaries of kingdoms they stood on the edges of more localised territorial units centred on newly established elite centres (i.e. royal vills and churches). Since such units would have formed the geographical 'building blocks' of kingdoms, it is possible that at times their boundaries would also have been the boundaries of larger political units. This interpretation does not conflict with the observation that these 'conspicuous' burials were commonly adjacent to major routes: to have fulfilled a role as a boundary marker a monument would need to have been visible to people moving through the landscape, no matter what size the geographical unit it marked.

Some of these seventh-century burials (though by no means all) stand on or close to modern or post-medieval administrative boundaries, and a few can be shown to have stood on boundaries in the late Saxon period. These examples hint at the kind of land divisions such burials may have been used to mark. A barrow at Swallowcliffe Down (Wiltshire), which contained a richly furnished intrusive female burial, may be that mentioned in a tenth-century charter boundary-clause (Speake 1989). The barrow stands close to the point where the parishes of Ansty, Swallowcliffe and Alvediston meet, and therefore close to the boundary between the hundreds of Dunworth and Chalke. In addition, this boundary probably represents the dividing line between two areas dependent on different ecclesiastical centres. To the north, a land-owning church at Tisbury is known to have existed by the early eighth century, and it may have controlled a *parochia* including Swallowcliffe and Ansty (Pitt 1999: 54). To the south, Alvediston was later a chapelry of Broad Chalke, where a fragment of ninth-century sculpture probably indicates the presence of an important early church (ibid.: 45). A primary seventh-century barrow burial nearby in Alvediston may also mark the same boundary (Eagles 2001: 219).

The intrusive barrow burial at Ford Down lies near the Roman road leading from Old Sarum to Winchester, and close to the parish boundaries between Clarendon Park and Laverstock to the south and the Winterbournes to the north (Musty 1969). Although this is not a hundred boundary, Pitt has suggested that two ecclesiastical *parochiae* may have bordered here, focused on Alderbury to the south and Idmiston to the north (Pitt 1999: 28-9).

In north Wiltshire, the female burial at Roundway Down stands close to the meeting point of the parishes of Roundway, Bromham and Rowde, and therefore close to the hundred boundaries of Cannings, Calne and Rowborough (**Fig. 47**; see Semple & Williams 2001). It is likely that different royal and ecclesiastical centres controlled the antecedents of these units, and the woman at Roundway

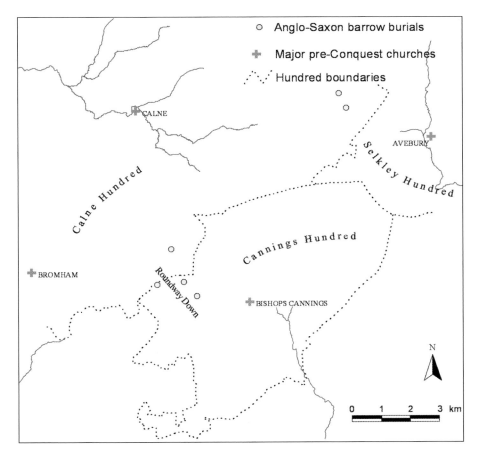

Fig. 47: Anglo-Saxon barrow burials, important early medieval churches and late Saxon hundred boundaries in part of north Wiltshire.

may have been buried in her barrow when these regions were beginning to crystallise. However, for this argument to be upheld, the middle-Saxon idea of a boundary needs to be defined as a boundary 'zone' rather than a narrow or imaginary line like that of later medieval and modern times. This is because several other burials of approximately the same date exist on and around Roundway Down, but all are further away from the modern parish boundaries. These burials probably represent not only an extensive burial 'zone' (Semple 2003), but also a boundary zone.

In early medieval Ireland, boundary zones of wilderness acted as 'buffers' between neighbouring polities (Ó Carragáin 2003), and there is other evidence to suggest that boundaries may have been more fuzzy in the middle Saxon period than in later times. Some of the earliest Anglo-Saxon charter boundaries record only a few landmarks which are often not clearly defined, particularly when crossing rough upland or marshy areas. Glastonbury's *Pouholt* charter, mentioned above, is an example: here, the northern boundary of the estate is simply defined as 'half of the marsh' (S253; Abrams 1994; **Fig. 41**). An eighth-century Mercian charter granting 8 hides at Evenlode in Gloucestershire notes only six boundary points, including an area of marshland (*cenepes moor*) and a possible burial mound (*mules hlæwe*; S109; Hooke 1998: 87). Another eighth-century Mercian charter grants 10 hides for the construction of a *cænubium* in the territory of the *Husmerae* (S89). Two of the three landmarks given in its boundary are tracts of woodland: in the northern zone or region (*plaga*) the wood named *cynibre*, and to the west, Morfe forest. Not all early charter boundary clauses are this vague, and some have fairly detailed descriptions (e.g. S264, Little Bedwyn, Wiltshire). However, it seems likely that boundaries in areas of rough ground could have remained relatively ill-defined in the middle Saxon period and in many cases later. It may only have been the expansion of settlement into marginal areas, which began in earnest in the tenth century, that necessitated clearer definitions of many boundaries. Hooke has discussed how areas of rough ground could be subject to ownership disputes as a result of poorly defined boundaries throughout the middle ages and into the early modern period (Hooke 1998: 78-80).

Many of the 'conspicuous' burials of western Wessex were taking place within the 'Christian' period; burials furnished with grave goods in both field cemeteries and barrows in Hampshire and Wiltshire continued after burials at nearby churches had begun (Geake 2002). Although the religious agenda of the people buried in middle Saxon barrows are the subject of enduring interest (Blair 2005: 53-4), a number of recent discussions have downplayed religious affiliation, preferring to concentrate on social and political explanations for barrow burial. Semple has suggested the significant confrontation reflected by barrow burial is not between pagans and Christians, but between different polities (Semple 2003). Howard Williams has pointed out that monument reuse (including barrow burial) continued from the fifth to the seventh centuries and overlapped the conversion period, and that it cannot necessarily be interpreted as either pagan or Christian. He too prefers an interpretation which stresses the power of burial monuments to emphasise claims over territory (Williams 1997: 25). Based on the evidence considered above, a geographical relationship between the new Christian centres and the location of many 'conspicuous' burials can be suggested: the monumental burials would be on the margins of areas of settlement whose centres were marked by churches and royal vills. Their location may have been linked to a 'Christianised' way of ordering the landscape which put the royal vill and/or church at the centre of an area of settled fields, surrounded by a boundary zone of wilder uncultivated land. The monumental burials were thus placed at visible points in this margin.

Burials and Cemeteries in Cornwall

Some elite burials may have acquired a new social and political significance in the early medieval period connected to the emergence of an independent polity and the establishment of a Christian ideology. Some may have been used to show power over the land, like those marked by inscribed stones discussed below. Others expressed the ability of the deceased to access the spiritual power of the church through burial in the cemeteries of major ecclesiastical centres like Phillack, Crantock or Tintagel. They may also have provided opportunities to enact new rituals such as the funeral *cenae* which may have taken place in Tintagel graveyard in the sixth century (Nowakowski & Thomas 1992).

However, the historical and archaeological evidence suggests that most burials continued to take place in cemeteries that were not directly associated with churches or chapels until at least the eighth century and perhaps later. In Cornwall, the burial customs of the early medieval period developed and continued traditions that had existed since the Iron Age (Pearce 2004: 102). There were certain modifications, such as the development of oriented burial and the elongation of cists, but the kind of locations employed for burial remained substantially the same (Petts 2001). Indeed, some cemeteries—such as Trevone and Trethillick near Padstow, both sites of medieval chapels (Preston-Jones 1984: 176; Petts 2001)—were probably used more or less continuously for burial from the Romano-British period until the later middle ages.

Most burials of the early medieval period took place in stone-built cists or dug graves. Grave goods are virtually unknown, and without good stratigraphic evidence or radiocarbon dating it is very hard to date the burials accurately because of the similarity to pre-Christian and later medieval practice. Cemeteries away from religious centres could exist as late as the tenth century. At Mawgan Porth, a cist cemetery was found in probable association with a settlement that was not deserted until the tenth or eleventh century (Bruce-Mitford 1997). Other probable early medieval cist cemeteries in the same parish include Carnanton and Lanvean (Preston-Jones 1984: 168). In the parish of St Kew, the earliest documented Cornish monastery, two cist-burial grounds have been excavated at St Endellion and Treharrock (Trudgian 1987; Johns 1995). At St Endellion the medieval parish church was close to the cemetery, although the latter appears to be much more extensive than the parish graveyard. The parish boundary also divides the early cemetery in two. This suggests the cemetery probably pre-dates the burial ground and the foundation of the church. Like Treharrock and Mawgan Porth, a burial ground at Treath on the Lizard was not associated with a medieval chapel; Henderson observed at least four stone-built graves being disturbed in the garden of a house here (Henderson 1958: 328).

These sites illustrate that burial places, like settlements, were dispersed across the early medieval landscape. Petts has argued that they were not commonly enclosed until the eighth century, and many were probably still unbounded considerably later (Petts 2001).

Inscribed Stones

Inscribed stones are found all over western Britain and Ireland. Those of south-west Britain occur mainly in Cornwall, where there are around thirty-five surviving examples, with others in Devon and west Somerset **(Plate 6b & 7)**.[2] Although Thomas has argued against significant continental European input (Thomas 1994: 278), the monuments of the South West seem to show an absorption and fusion of two streams of influence, from both Irish-influenced south Wales and from continental Europe (Knight 1996). It has recently been argued that some of the compositions demonstrate considerable literary sophistication (e.g. Howlett 1998; Thomas 1998), and the inscribed stones of the post-Roman centuries represent the work of an elite consciously identifying themselves as such, and in some cases also as Christians (Knight 1992).

The dating of these monuments is a contentious topic (Okasha 1993; Thomas 1994: 69; *cf.* Thomas 1998). Whilst Okasha and Thomas concur that the inscriptions show the majority to have been produced between the fifth and seventh centuries, some monuments continued to be erected after this. The Lanteglos-by-Camelford stone bears a vertical inscription (in the manner of the earlier Latin- or ogam-inscribed stones) written in old English, proving that similar monuments continued to be commissioned well into the early middle ages (Okasha 1993: 141-5). The use of inscribed stones in Cornwall probably spans the transition from settlement predominantly in rounds to settlement in unenclosed farmsteads.

Although relatively few of them bear obviously Christian iconography or formulae, about half of the thirty-five monuments in Cornwall come from churchyards. It has been argued that the presence of an inscribed stone and a *lann* place-name or enclosure strongly suggests an early Christian site (e.g. Preston-Jones 1992: 112; Thomas 1994: 312). Not surprisingly though, excavation has yet to show that any inscribed stone is contemporary with a south-western *lann*-type enclosing boundary. It is likely that stones now in churchyards probably have one of three origins. Firstly, they may have originated at unenclosed burial sites which were elaborated with churches in the eighth century or later. Secondly, they may have been set up at the sites of early monasteries, likely examples including the stones from St Kew and Phillack, and possibly the Lundy stones (Okasha 1993: Nos. 52, 39, 25, 26, 27 & 28; Thomas 1994: 163-82). Finally, many were probably transported to churches from other places. The known history of many inscribed stones proves that they can easily be moved about for a variety of purposes, and it is possible that they may have been recognised in the later middle ages as 'Christian' monuments and transported to churches for incorporation in the fabric of a building or churchyard. In Cornwall, the Carnsew stone may have stood next to a burial excavated in the nineteenth century (Okasha 1993: No. 16; Thomas 1994: 183-96), and inscribed stones are known from unenclosed field cemeteries in Wales at Arfyn (Angelsey) and Pentrefoelas (Denbighshire) (Knight 1999: 140; Petts 2002a).

---

[2] See Thomas 1994 and Okasha 1993 for a catalogue, photographs and the known history of each monument.

Around half the Cornish inscribed stones are not located at churches, chapels or former religious sites. Whilst many were probably funerary monuments, they may also have acted as boundary markers. Handley has suggested that the meanings of inscribed stones changed over time, and has argued that stones associated with land ownership tend to be later in date than those whose role was solely memorial (Handley 1998: 353-4). The use of inscribed stones in Cornwall may be relatively late compared to that in Wales and Ireland, where the tradition probably developed earlier (Thomas 1994). Handley's interpretation suggests that many stones in Cornwall were erected at a time when the early medieval landscape was being reorganised, in the sixth or seventh centuries. There are a number of relevant examples. The stone at Boslow in West Penwith is located on the parish boundary between the medieval parishes of St Just and Sancreed, and close to the boundary between rough grazing land and ancient enclosed land depicted by modern and early Ordnance Survey maps. It stands on a low hump which may be a small barrow (Thomas 1994: 293). The nearby stone at Madron occupies a similar position between the parishes of Morvah and Madron (Okasha 1993: Nos. 3 and 31). The Worthyvale stone stands on the parish boundary between Minster and Lanteglos-by-Camelford, and was first seen in this position by Carew around 1602 (ibid.: No. 72). Four inscribed stones lie on the south-western fringes of Bodmin Moor. One is now at Cardinham parish church, though the medieval and later history of this monument is uncertain. It was first recorded by Iago in 1877 leaning against the outside wall of the church, but was subsequently modified to act as a cross-shaft, a function it still performs today (**Plate 7**; Okasha 1993: 88). It is possible that it was extracted from the chancel wall during restoration work in 1872 along with the Cardinham Cross (ibid.: 1993: 85-90), but the churchyard was not necessarily its original site. Two other stones at nearby Welltown were both recognised in the earlier twentieth century doing service as gate-posts (Okasha 1993). In view of the area's plentiful supply of suitable stone it seems unlikely they would have been moved far from their original locations for this purpose. All three of these stones are in Cardinham parish, an area with a relatively dense distribution of rounds, but little evidence for early medieval settlements **(Fig. 48)**. A fourth monument at Lancarffe is located just across the western boundary of Cardinham parish, which was also an early medieval boundary zone between the hundreds of Trigg, Pydar and West (Thorn & Thorn 1979a, Appendix). The earliest known locations of all these monuments are adjacent to tracks which provide access from the south and south-west up towards the higher ground of Bodmin Moor. The concentration of English place-names in the Welltown area suggest that it may have been rough grazing in the early medieval period rather than 'core' medieval farmland (as suggested by Rose 1994: 79-80). All the stones are today close to areas of moorland and trackways, and they may originally have acted as markers for both travellers and people who lived in the area.

Some prehistoric standing stones are believed to mark the division between prehistoric arable and rough grazing (Peters 1990). David Petts has compared the distribution of standing stones and early medieval inscribed stones. He convincingly argued that standing stones were rarely reused as inscribed stones, but also suggested that this means inscribed stones were not normally used as boundary markers between arable and rough grazing in the early middle ages

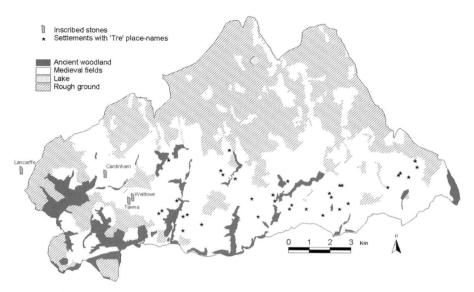

Fig. 48: Inscribed stones (names) and settlements with *tre* place-names (first recorded before 1550) in the St Neot study area, and the HLC.

(Petts 2002b: 204-5). This is not necessarily the case, since inscribed stones could have been used to mark the edge of *medieval* rather than prehistoric farmland. As discussed above, there were areas of rough ground at all altitudes in early middle Cornwall, not just on hilltops. Indeed, there are many examples of the use of stones (not necessarily inscribed) as markers in early medieval boundaries. Examples include the stone rows at Trerice (the *stanraewe* of the charter boundary clause (S1019)), and Culbone in Somerset, which was Christianised with the addition of an incised cross to one of the stones; a nearby standing stone, the Culbone Stone, also had a cross added at some time in the early medieval period (Riley & Wilson-North 2001: 89). In Cornwall stones appear as markers in the charter boundary clauses of St Buryan (S450), Tywarnhayle (S684), Lamorran (S770; *men ber*, the 'short stone'), Traboe and Trevallack (S832), Landrake (S951), and Illand (S1005; *mæggean stane*, the 'great stone'; Hooke 1994a). In the Lizard peninsula the parishes of St Keverne, St Mawgan-in-Meneage, St Martin-in-Meneage, Graderuan and Cury meet at a group of barrows on Goonhilly Downs which are probably those referred to by the name *cruc drænoc* in AD 977 (S832; Hooke 1994a). A standing stone was found and re-erected here in the twentieth century, though it presumably stood in the early eighteenth century when it was mentioned by its modern name of 'Dry Tree' in the bounds of the manor of Traboe (*Henderson Calendar 5:* 208). In Wales, there are also numerous references to boundary stones in the charter boundaries of the *Book of Llandaff* (Handley 1998: 341).

Jeremy Knight has argued that inscribed stones in Wales may have had more to do with showing personal power than with Christian ideology (Knight 1999: 140). This may also have been the case in Cornwall, but if so, this power was being exercised in a landscape that was fast becoming a 'Christian' one. Those buried next to inscribed stones could have been pagans or Christians, although the evidence from the inscriptions suggests that increasingly they were the latter (Thomas 1998). Whichever was the case, burials and/or inscribed stones like the Welltown and Worthyvale examples were located in boundary zones close to the edges of areas of rough grazing, and as such may have been intended to emphasise the power of the elite over the settled land. These zones were themselves increasingly defined by a Christian ideology: the relationship between the ecclesiastical centres, the settlements clustering around them, and the rough ground at the margins was fundamental. Although the dates and original contexts of the inscribed stones are often very hard to establish, it seems plausible that many of them could have played a part in defining the boundaries of the developing early Christian landscape.

Conclusion

The major ecclesiastical centres were not the only sacred sites in the Cornish landscape. Sacred sites also encompassed both those that had been sacred before the conversion and newly established minor sites. Amongst pre-existing sites, it seems burial grounds and perhaps holy wells continued to be used or venerated. Minor foci created in the Christian period include sites that were like these pre-existing ones, and other new kinds of sacred places like burial grounds and holy wells (sites that normally appeared later including crosses, chapels and minor churches are considered in Chapter 7). Rather than being established all at once, these sites appeared at different times over a long period. Monuments like inscribed stones played crucial roles in different phases of this development, but all contributed to defining the landscape as a Christian one. The 'Christianisation' of the wider landscape was not a short-term project completed in an early 'Age of Saints', but one that developed over several centuries.

In Wessex, patterns of minor ritual foci were also changed by the development of the Christian landscape. New patterns of burial during the seventh and early eighth centuries may result in part from the creation of new administrative geographies associated with changing religious and political structures; many of the middle Saxon burials in barrows could have marked the edges of territories centred on newly founded churches and royal vills.

After the English conquest of Cornwall in the ninth and tenth centuries, the new elite built manorial centres close to or at the sites of several important early churches, whose estates they often appropriated or granted away. Probably from the eighth century in Cornwall and the ninth or tenth century in Wessex, the estates and religious rights of the major centres began to be eroded severely by secular landowners and minor churches. These changes are discussed in Chapter 7.

7

Developing medieval landscapes
The multiplication of churches
and other Christian monuments

An important church like Glastonbury was a key point in the early medieval landscape. It controlled extensive estates in the Somerset Levels and beyond, and acted as a centre for religious devotion and economic activities. However, by the eighth or ninth centuries major sites like Glastonbury were not the only type of church in the south-western landscape. Even from the limited evidence available for Cornwall it is possible to see that there were churches of various kinds, both in terms of status and period of origin. The preceding chapters investigated the way the landscape changed in the first centuries after the conversion to Christianity. This chapter will consider the evidence for types of churches other than the important early foundations, and the role of Christian monuments like sculpted stone crosses. Though some of the churches have earlier roots, these sites and monuments became increasingly common in the later Saxon period.

Both early medieval and modern observers have identified several categories of churches in later pre-Conquest England, including 'sub-minsters', chapels, estate churches and sites with specialised functions like hermitages. Teresa Hall has suggested there was a secondary tier of minster foundations in Wessex belonging to the period after the foundation of the earliest monasteries and minster churches (Hall 2000: 28-9). Some such churches, which must have acted as religious foci for surrounding areas, would have been dependent on major foundations even if they were some distance away. Estates like Brent (Somerset) may have been provided with a 'sub-minster' from a relatively early date (S238). The area had been the property of Glastonbury since perhaps the seventh century, and archaeological evidence suggests occupation here dating from as early as the seventh or eighth centuries onwards (Gaimster & Bradley 2001: 314). At Shapwick on Glastonbury's *Pouholt* estate there could have been a church as early as the eighth century (**Fig. 41**; Gerrard 1995). These 'sub-minsters' may have been relatively common in the later Saxon landscape, particularly on the land of major ecclesiastical institutions. In Devon possible Anglo-Saxon fabric has been noted in the churches of Branscombe (Devon SMR) and South Brent (Gerrard 1997), which in 1066 were part of the estates of Exeter Cathedral and Buckfast Abbey respectively. The church at Sidbury, east Devon, was also held by the bishop of Exeter at Domesday, and here a fragment of Anglo-Saxon sculpture and part of a possible pre-Conquest church may represent the remains of a late Saxon 'sub-minster' (Taylor & Taylor 1965; Thorn & Thorn 1985). A probable example has been excavated at Potterne (Wiltshire), which was on the estate of the Bishop of Ramsbury in 1066, showing that such churches were sometimes built in wood and later replaced with stone churches (Davey 1964, 1990).

Other kinds of church or chapel may have co-existed with major establishments from an early date. There were minor Christian foci within the territory of Glastonbury, and their geographical proximity suggests they must have been dependent on the monastery. The site at Beckery lies at the western edge of the same island in the marshes as the abbey. In the middle Saxon period a chapel appears to have been constructed on the site of an earlier burial ground (Rahtz & Hirst 1974). It is possible that this site represents a 'traditional' burial ground that was brought into the Christian landscape by the addition of the chapel after acquisition by the abbey; a charter of spurious authenticity claims this happened in AD 725 (S250).

The same document mentions a number of the abbey's other properties in the Somerset marshes, and Aston has suggested that several of them could have supported hermitages in the early middle ages (e.g. Nyland, Marchey and Godney: Aston 2000a: 58; 2000b: 100-1). These examples all comprise small islands in the Somerset Levels, which could have been attractive as places for an eremitic lifestyle. The eighth-century *Life of St Guthlac* (Colgrave 1956) describes how the eponymous saint choose a similar site for his hermitage; his island in the Lincolnshire fens was home to a fearful burial mound and its wicked supernatural inhabitants (Semple 1998: 112).

Perhaps the most likely place to have been a hermitage in the area around Glastonbury is the Tor **(Plate 9a)**. Here, Rahtz excavated both Anglo-Saxon and earlier, post-Roman occupation (Rahtz 1971, 1991). Monastic settlement is suggested by the discovery of fragments from a late Saxon stone cross close to buildings with rock-cut foundations. Whilst exposed and relatively isolated, the site is only just over a kilometre from the abbey church **(Plate 9b)**. In this sense it is reminiscent of the earlier hermitage of St Cuthbert on Inner Farne: suitable for relatively ascetic contemplation, but not too distant from the monastery at Lindisfarne or the Northumbrian royal centre at Bamburgh if urgent business should beckon. Very few likely hermitage sites have been excavated in southern England, although occasional documentary references suggest possible locations, as at Badgworthy on Exmoor. This site, now a deserted settlement with substantial earthwork remains, is first mentioned in a twelfth-century charter as *terram heremitarum*, hinting that it could have been a hermitage in the pre-Conquest period (Weaver 1909: 121; Riley & Wilson-North 2001: 100-2).

A final type of small church that occurred within ecclesiastical territories may have acted as a marker for estate or territorial boundaries: for instance, at the point at which travellers entered the agricultural land associated with the mother church. Beckery is one possible example, at the western edge of Glastonbury's island. An ecclesiastical estate at Dawlish in Devon had a church of St Michael as one of its boundary markers in the 1040s (S1003; Thorn & Thorn 1985: 2,4; Hooke 1994a: 204-207). At Sherborne, chapels of St Cuthbert and St Peter stood close to the manorial boundary of the later middle ages, which did not always coincide with the parish boundary, but was separated from it by an area of rough ground (**Fig. 45**; Barker 1984: 9; Faith 1997: 20). This may support the idea that the boundaries of estates were sometimes considered to be the edges of their cultivated land; it may have been this that was sometimes marked by chapels or crosses rather than the outer boundary line (beyond the rough ground) defined in the late or post-medieval period.

Wessex

The late Saxon period witnessed the increasing fragmentation of large estates and a growth in the number of minor landowners. At the same time there was a large increase in churches attached to individual landowners' estates, which went on to form the basis for the later medieval network of parish churches. It is possible that middle and late Saxon chapels like Beckery and 'sub-minsters' like Shapwick, Sidbury or Tisbury provided the models for these local churches.

The rise of small estates

Ecclesiastical provision certainly expanded in the late Saxon period, and in some places settlement patterns seem to have changed almost beyond recognition. The character of estates altered in important ways, most commonly through the process of fragmentation. Whilst these changes were without doubt important, their significance should not be exaggerated: changes both in society and its spatial structure must be regarded as strongly rooted in middle Saxon forms of organisation.

Minor estates below the level of kings and ealdormen had probably always been a feature of the Anglo-Saxon landscape of Wessex. For example, Ine's laws refer to estates of between 3 and 20 hides held by a class of minor nobles, the *gesithcund* (noble-born) men, whose *wergeld* was notably higher than their contemporaries (Ine cap. 63-6: Attenborough 1922: 56-9; Faith 1997: 156). From the ninth century onwards, their place in the social hierarchy was taken by the class called thegns.[1] These were men who received land in return for service in the royal household and in war (Faith 1997: 155). The temporal attributes of the thegn are reported, perhaps in rather idealised form, in the early eleventh-century text known as *Geþincðo* (Whitelock 1979).[2] It describes how a *ceorl* who acquired 5 hides of land, a bell, and a *burh-geat* (probably a manorial enclosure) and who owed certain types of service at the king's hall, was entitled to thegnly rank. A later version also added a church and kitchen to this list of requirements (Reynolds 1999: 60). The attainment of rank was thus related to the possession of a certain kind of property.

In the later Saxon period, increasing numbers of small estates were brought into existence, and they are probably linked to the growth of the thegnly class. The land given to thegns acted as a kind of permanent salary, and ensured their continued service in either a military or some other capacity (Faith 1997: 156-7).

---

[1] Thegns are first recorded in sources such as the *Laws of Alfred and Guthrum*: Attenborough 1922: 98-9.
[2] For regional variations from the standard of *Geþincðo*, see Faith 1997: 156-7.

In Norfolk by the time of Domesday many hundreds of estates were in the hands of small landowners (Williamson 1993: 114-26). In Yorkshire, a proliferation of tenth- and eleventh-century sculpture has been interpreted as the work of a new class of local landlords eager to express their identity (Carver 1998a: 26). These changes in eastern England have sometimes been interpreted as the result of the Scandinavian settlements and the distribution of land by the elite amongst their followers (Morris 1984: 5; Richards 1991: 30). However, it is not clear that settlement structure in the Danelaw was based on contemporary practice in Denmark (see e.g. Lund 1976: 479-80; Brink 1998: 34-7). The economic and social changes of the ninth century affected the whole of England, and if the Vikings had some responsibility for the increasing number of small estates, it was probably as a result of their creation of an environment where a thegnly class with greater power over its own land was both desirable and necessary (Williamson 1993: 124-5).

The increase in small estates in Wessex is partly recorded in the Anglo-Saxon charters. In the tenth century there was not only a surge in the number of estates being granted, but also a tendency for them to be smaller and have much more detailed boundary clauses (Hill 1981: 26; Hooke 1998: 86-7). Unlike the relatively vague descriptions appended to seventh- and eighth-century charters, the documents of the later Saxon period often describe estates in considerable detail (see e.g. Hooke 1994a *passim*). The reason for this increasing definition may have been that landscape was being more and more intensely exploited by immediately neighbouring estates.[3]

The need for the kings of Wessex to endow thegns with estates led to significant alterations in the structure of the countryside (Faith 1997: 157). These are reflected both in the fragmentation of large estates and the expansion of the settled area into formerly marginal land. Estate fragmentation affected both royal and ecclesiastical land in the ninth and tenth centuries. Large ecclesiastical estates were acquired by kings in the ninth century both to reward thegns and to add to the royal holdings, sometimes perhaps for defensive purposes.[4] Costen has suggested that minor estates created by fragmentation around the edges of major royal or ecclesiastical landholdings may be reflected by *-ington* place-names in Somerset, citing concentrations of them around Frome and Ilminster as possible examples (Costen 1992b: 115-17). Even major churches like Winchester sometimes appear to have resorted to pleading in an attempt to protect their territory from land-hungry Anglo-Saxon kings like Edward the Elder:

> Furthermore, the bishop and the community at Winchester beg that in charity for the love of God and for the holy church you desire no more of the community's land, for it seems to them an uncalled for demand, so that God need blame neither you nor us for the diminution [of the endowment] in our day; for there was a very great injunction of God about that when those estates were given to the holy place.
>
> (S1444; cited & trans. Rumble 2001: 236-7)

---

[3] For example, those of the Wiltshire chalklands; see Hooke 1988; Costen 1994: 100-2.
[4] See the discussion by Fleming (1985: 250-5), who cites examples from Somerset, Wiltshire and Devon.

Tom Williamson has argued that another way in which new estates were created in the later Saxon period was by extension of the settled area into former marginal land (Williamson 1993: 126). In Wessex, the result of this process was expansion into areas that were formerly rough grazing or marshland, such as the Somerset Levels (Rippon 1994). At estates like Puxton in Somerset, archaeological evidence suggests a growing amount of marshland was brought into cultivation from the tenth century onwards (Rippon et al. 2001). Puxton lies in the Levels c.4km north of Banwell and c.3km west of Congresbury, both high-status churches whose estates bordered the marshes. Although they were in ecclesiastical hands by the ninth century, in the tenth and eleventh centuries they appear to have been in royal ownership.[5] It seems likely that Puxton was a minor estate established on the edge of a former ecclesiastical one in the tenth century, perhaps on royal initiative.

Michael Costen and Steven Rippon have argued that such economic expansion is detectable in the Domesday record for Somerset through a comparison of the hidage and ploughlands (Costen 1992b: 123; Rippon 1994: 242). Late Saxon reclamation may be implied by a comparison of the hidage assessment of an estate, perhaps not altered since the earlier tenth century, and the number of ploughlands, which may have been assessed just prior to 1086. It is possible that areas with a significantly higher number of ploughlands than hides represent areas where there was expansion of the farmed area in the late Saxon period; Rippon notes a particular increase in the area around Brent Knoll (Rippon 1994: 242), and Costen argues that estates bordering the uplands in west Somerset like Carhampton and others in neighbourng regions of Devon witnessed dramatic increases in the settled area (Costen 1992b: 124-5). In east Devon it is possible that different patterns of fields visible in the modern landscape owe their ultimate origins to the late Saxon period. For example, in Axminster hundred (Devon) there are strong differences in the patterns of fields around the minster church and royal vill of Axminster (founded by the early eighth century) and the outlying parishes of the Blackdown Hills. Around Axminster the patterns of strip fields recorded by post-medieval maps (and medieval documents; Fox 1972) are regularly organised across the valley floor, whereas in outlying parishes the steep-sided valleys are generally covered with much more irregular fields **(Plate 8b)**. These may have been created by the holders of the numerous small estates which Domesday Book records as owing dues at the royal vill (e.g. Smallridge, Membury, Weycroft, Undercleave and Deneworthy; **Fig. 49**; Thorn & Thorn 1985: 1,11). It is possible that recently recognised settlement sites belonging to this period like Cleave Hill (Membury) are related to an expansion of agriculture into the marginal land at around this time (Exeter Archaeology, forthcoming).

As *Geþincðo* suggests, at the heart of the landed estates belonging to the thegns were the bell (and presumably its bell-tower) and the *burh-geat*. As defining attributes for thegnly status these estate centres were of great importance (Williams 1992; Faith 1997: 163). The *burh-geat* may refer to a kind of settlement enclosure within which the bell, the kitchen and other elements of the lordly residence such as a hall would have been located. Settlements of this kind are

---

[5] Until they were granted to Duduc, the future bishop of Wells, perhaps in the reign of Cnut: S373; S806; S1042; Keynes and Lapdige 1983: 264.

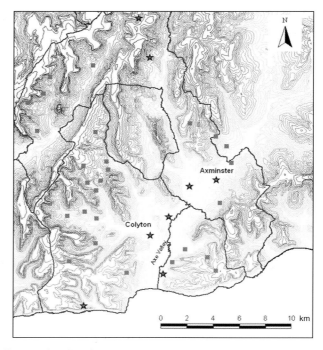

Fig. 49: Domesday Book royal estate centres (stars) and manors with less than five hides (squares) in east Devon. The map shows clearly how the royal centres are located in the broader valley bottoms, with smaller manors located in the hills around (the darker the contours, the higher the elevation). There were important early medieval churches at Colyton and Axminster, the latter first recorded in the *Anglo-Saxon Chronicle* in the 750s, and a string of royal manors in the prime agricultural land along the bottom of the Axe Valley. The boundaries are those of medieval hundreds (after Thorn & Thorn 1985). [© Crown Copyright. All rights reserved. Licence number 100042056.]

referred to in 'Burgate' place-names which are scattered across southern England, and a probable example at Yatesbury (Wiltshire) has been partly excavated (Reynolds 1999: 63). Despite extensive archaeological investigation in the modern village, no evidence of middle Saxon settlement has been recovered from this site, which lies towards the western edge of the Marlborough Downs (Reynolds et al. forthcoming), suggesting the settlement may have been newly established on marginal land in the late Saxon period. Trowbridge is another excavated example of a probable thegnly settlement in Wiltshire, although here a middle Saxon settlement existed earlier on the site which lies close to the banks of the River Biss (Graham & Davies 1993). In Hampshire, the enclosed sites at Faccombe Netherton and Portchester, which reused an ancient Roman fort, have been interpreted as the estate centres of late Saxon thegns (Cunliffe 1975; Fairbrother 1990). Documentary evidence suggests that though Portchester was probably held at the time of the Norman Conquest by a thegn, it had once been in the hands of the church of Winchester (S372; Cunliffe 1975: 1-3; Munby 1982: 35,4).

Thegns could be dependent on other thegns, or owe their allegiance to insitutions other than the king. Major ecclesiastical landowners often tried to take advantage of this to limit damage to their estates. Leases provided a way for military service to be provided by thegns on church land. The lease was designed to ensure that the estate returned to the church after a specified period (Faith 1997: 161-3). However, it often proved hard even for major churches to reclaim the land and as a result large amounts of territory could be permanently alienated into the hands of minor landowners (ibid. 1997).

The establishment of thegnly estates led to various reorganisations of the landscape. Domesday Book shows that Glastonbury's Polden estate, centred on Shapwick, had been divided by the eleventh century into the units perpetuated in the later medieval parishes. Before 1066 these units had been held by dependent thegns (who 'could not be separated from the church'; Thorn & Thorn 1980: 8,5). It seems likely that here administrative replanning of the estate was accompanied by the establishment of nucleated villages with open fields in each unit, and archaeological evidence suggests this probably occurred some time in the tenth century (Corcos 1984; Aston & Gerrard 1999: 28-9). Mick Aston and Chris Gerrard suggest that this settlement nucleation may have been instigated by the church in order to increase revenues after the Benedictine reform of the mid-tenth century, though Michael Costen has pointed out that nucleated villages also developed on non-ecclesiastical estates (Costen 1992a). One possibility is that the thegns who held the newly fragmented estates from the church were responsible for nucleation and the establishment of regular fields. Nevertheless, thegnly estates also existed in areas dominated by dispersed settlement patterns, for example around Crediton and Axminster in Devon; so although the rise of nucleated settlements and thegnly estates may be contemporary in some places, social change cannot necessarily be expected to have resulted in settlement pattern reorganisation everywhere (Yorke 1995: 269-74; Lewis et al. 1997).

Estate Churches

Well after the initial period of the growth of power of the thegn, the twelfth-century version of *Geþincðo* adds ownership of a church to the attributes required for thegnly status (Yorke 1995: 251), and Blair has suggested that:

> The urge to have private churches was deep-rooted in early medieval aristocratic culture, so there was a natural tendency for units of landlordship, of whatever size, to acquire them.
>
> (Blair 1994: 136)

The late Saxon period appears to have been a time of considerable expansion in ecclesiastical provision in Wessex and all over England (Morris 1989: 140-64; Yorke 1995). Evidence for this change comes principally from archaeological and documentary sources. Unfortunately, the dates of most churches' foundations are unclear, since relatively few have been excavated and documents do not often mention them before the twelfth century (Blair 1994: 137). Rushton's study of Sussex suggests that the majority of churches in that part of southern England existed by the end of the eleventh century and that the process of parochialisation was well underway. This may suggest that many churches had been established for some time by then (Rushton 1997). Where archaeological excavation has taken place, the results often suggest estate churches were founded in the tenth century, as at Trowbridge (Wiltshire; Graham & Davies 1993) and Portchester (Hampshire: Cunliffe 1975). Architectural sculpture and standing fabric suggest further examples at Knook, Alton Barnes and Limpley Stoke (Wiltshire: Taylor 1968; Taylor & Taylor 1965; Darlington 1955), Winterbourne Steepleton (Dorset: Hinton 1998: 67), East Coker, and perhaps Wilton (Somerset: Gittos & Gittos 1991; Foster 1987: 66) **(Fig. 50)**.

Such minor churches took a variety of different forms. The base of a tower surrounded by burials which was excavated at Portchester (Hampshire) may be the remains of a turriform nave of the kind known from Earls Barton (Northamptonshire; **Plate 2b**) and Jevington (Sussex). These seem to have been multi-purpose structures with a chapel on the ground floor and living accommodation above (Auduy *et al* 1995). Small churches of more familiar form with either a one- or two-cell plan include the examples at Alton Barnes and Trowbridge (Wiltshire).

Richard Morris and Rosamund Faith have both suggested that the estate church was generally planned as part of the lordly residence from the outset, and medieval manor houses and churches are very commonly found side-by-side (Morris 1989: 249; Faith 1997: 165). There are hints of late Saxon occupation adjacent to present-day churches from archaeological evaluations at Bawdrip and East Stoke (Somerset), Yatesbury (Wiltshire), and Shapwick (Dorset) (Gaimster & Bradley 2001: 314; Nenk et al. 1995: 239, 260; Cox 1999). However, Reynolds argues that such churches are normally secondary elements in thegnly complexes, as shown by excavated examples like Trowbridge, Portchester Castle and Raunds (Northamptonshire; Boddington 1996). Topographical evidence commonly supports the idea that the church was an addition to the site, as at Faccombe

Fig. 50: The late Saxon church at Alton Barnes, Wiltshire.

Netherton (Hampshire; Reynolds 1999: 130-4; Lucy & Reynolds 2002: 20-1). It seems likely that churches may have been established by thegns as part of a process by which they secured increasing power over their estates.

Blair has noted that initially there may have been no contention between the old established churches and new estate churches, since the latter would not necessarily have infringed the established rights of the former (Blair 1987: 269). From around the beginning of the tenth century onwards, however, local churches began to acquire rights at the expense of older foundations, and this would ultimately lead to them becoming parish churches in the later middle ages. In King Edgar's second law code, for example, it is stated that if a thegn has a church with a graveyard on his bookland,[6] one-third of his tithes could go to it (Morris 1989: 128-9; Whitelock et al. 1981: 97-9).

By initiating burial at their churches, local lords may have been actively seeking to elevate their own status. In the early eleventh century, one of King Æthelred's law codes divided churches into four types: *heafodmynstres* (head minsters), *medemran mynstres* (middle-rank minsters), *laessan* (lesser [ones]), and *feldcircan* (field-churches) (8 Æthelred 5; Whitelock et al. 1981: 389-90). This appears to have perpetuated and developed the tenth-century ranking in Edgar's law code of the 960s, which had a three-fold division of old minsters (*eald mynstru*), churches with graveyards on thegns' bookland, and churches without graveyards, clearly suggesting higher status was assigned to sites with burial rights (2 Edgar 1-3; Whitelock et al. 1981: 97-9).

The commencement of burial could have brought estate churches into conflict with older ecclesiastical institutions if it meant burial taxes were diverted from them. Such well-established churches had probably been the beneficiaries of these taxes since at least the ninth century, even if the burials they controlled had taken place on other sites (e.g. Chimney, Oxfordshire: Blair 1994: 73; Gittos 2002: 201). Ecclesiastical taxes are first recorded in Ine's laws (Ine cap. 4: Attenborough 1922: 36-7), which makes it seem likely that jurisdictions of some sort had been established in Wessex by the beginning of the eighth century. Athelstan's laws suggest that at the beginning of the tenth century burial payments were customarily made to ecclesiastical centres that provided pastoral care, and the most likely explanation is that these were the superior minsters of the later laws (1 Athelstan 4; Whitelock et al. 1981: 46; Pitt 1999: 6). Gittos has recently linked an increasing concern to delimit the sanctified area where burial could take place to the ability to derive revenue from it. Thus consecrated enclosed cemeteries around Saxon churches may only have developed from the tenth century onwards as a result of an increasing need to define the burial area; those churches without burial rights may never have been enclosed (Gittos 2002). Some old minsters maintained their rights over revenues such as burial fees and tithes during the late Saxon period and well into the middle ages, even when numerous estate churches had been founded within the areas under their control (e.g. Taunton: Costen 1992b: 154). However, the majority seem to have lost power in the face of encroachment by new churches on manorial estates, a process which accelerated after the Norman Conquest (Blair 1985: 137). Faith has argued that these processes reflect the increasing ability of secular lords to exercise social control over the population of their new estates (Faith 1997: 167).

---

[6] 'Bookland' was land granted by charter (Faith 1997: 159-61).

One further type of church was sited on what Lucy and Reynolds have termed 'adaptive' cemeteries (2002: 20). These churches appear to have been founded on existing cemeteries and to have perpetuated such burial grounds into the later middle ages. As a class of site these are ill-defined in Wessex, but examples elsewhere in England probably include Cherry Hinton (Cambridgeshire: O'Brien 2002) and Barton-on-Humber (Lincolnshire: Rodwell & Rodwell 1982). Blair has suggested that churches perpetuating burial grounds of this sort may be more common in western England than elsewhere (Blair 1996a: 12). It is possible that in areas dominated by dispersed settlement patterns, the location of a church may have been more easily influenced by the position of pre-existing ritual sites than in areas where well-defined nucleated settlements were forming, although this remains to be demonstrated archaeologically. As noted above, some such churches were established as secondary foci within the *parochiae* of existing high-status churches, such as Beckery (Rahtz & Hirst 1974). Nevertheless, these may have provided the model for others established by the new thegnly class to serve their own estates.

In some ways, the thegnly estate churches of the later Saxon period represent a major change, one that led to the disintegration of earlier patterns of ecclesiastical organisation (Blair 1988b). Helen Gittos discusses innovations in churchyard consecration for burial that seem to have little in common with earlier arrangements (Gittos 2002). In other ways, however, estate churches seem to have been modelled on earlier churches and to have reused the old symbolic language in the newly emerging late Saxon landscape. Perhaps most obviously, the association between estate churches and thegnly settlement strongly echoes the earlier association between royal vills and high-status churches which was clearly maintained into the later Saxon period. The presence of chapels on royal sites like Cheddar in the tenth century may also have provided a model for the intimate association between religious buildings and elite living accommodation that could be represented by the turriform naves of Portchester and Earls Barton (Cunliffe 1975; Rahtz 1979; Auduy et al. 1995). The analogy between high-status churches and estate chapels goes further, however; both provided foci for a range of activities by the inhabitants of dependent areas, who by the tenth and eleventh centuries may have been coming to define their identity in relation to their local church as well as to their local lord (Blair 2005: 501-4). The position of most local churches at the heart of local settlement patterns and communication networks also echoes the location of earlier ecclesiastical centres. Even in relation to the provision of pastoral functions the new churches were acting in a similar way to the old ones; for example, the control of burial rights seems to have been a concern of the older churches by the tenth century; new estate churches were simply acting like their better-established counterparts when they sought to provide cemeteries, even if this led to competition and ultimately to innovative ritual practices (see Gittos 2002).

With this in mind, it is tempting to think of the ranking of churches in Æthelred's law code as representing a continuum rather than as four distinct and well-defined classes. At the top of the scale were the cathedrals and old, well-established ecclesiastical communities like Glastonbury; at the bottom were lowly field-churches without burial grounds. Between them lay the mass of minsters, 'sub-minsters' and estate churches. All had their place within the system and many may have owed various dues to other establishments, just as in the secular world thegns could owe service to other thegns who in turn served kings or other nobles. The 'lesser' minsters of 8 Æthelred 5 are widely interpreted as representing the majority of estate churches (e.g. Morris 1989: 129). It may be that contemporaries did not think in terms of a well-defined line distinguishing the new from the older established churches. Instead, as the terminology suggests, they may have regarded 'lesser' churches as just another type of minster, but one with fewer rights, less land and less individual power. Nevertheless, they do reflect a new development: the growing power of local lords to influence aspects of life at a local level.

Cornwall

The Vatican codex Reginensis Latinus 191 contains a list of forty-eight Brittonic names dated by palaeographic and linguistic evidence to the tenth century. The text has been plausibly interpreted by Olson and Padel as a list of the names of Cornish saints (Olson & Padel 1986). They consider the main significance of the list is to show

> the later pattern of parish church dedications, and thus by implication the spheres of influence of those churches, as being already in existence not long after the year 900.
>
> (Olson & Padel 1986: 69)

This interpretation has been followed by subsequent authors (e.g. Hooke 1999: 98). It implies that the parochial organisation of the later middle ages was fixed from an early date. However, this is not exactly what the document shows. Whilst it certainly seems to be a list of the names of saints associated with churches and chapels in early tenth-century Cornwall, this does not necessarily mean all the medieval *parishes* were already established. In fact, later medieval documents reveal dependent relationships between several of the saints' churches in the list. Such relationships show differences of status between sites, and perhaps different periods of origin. For example, both *Berion* and *Salamun* appear in the list, patrons of the churches of St Buryan and St Levan respectively. St Buryan is identified by Olson (1989) as an early monastery, and throughout the middle ages St Levan was one of its chapelries (Orme 1999). Likewise, Phillack (the list's *Felec*) was the medieval mother church of Gwithian (the list's *Guidian*) (*Lake* 3: 155-6). Another saint named on the list, *Congar*, only has a non-parochial dedication in Cornwall, at St Ingungar in Lanivet parish (Olson & Padel 1986: 44). In addition, at least fifteen of the names on the list have not been identified with dedications to any Cornish saints, leaving open the possibility that earlier dedications have disappeared. Dedications to saints were certainly lost in Cornwall over the course of the middle ages, as happened at St Martin-in-Meneage (discussed below). The list shows that many local churches had been founded by the early tenth century, and it suggests they had begun to develop patterns of ecclesiastical rights which later became parishes. However, it cannot be accepted as showing a fully developed parochial network which was not subject to further change.

Differences in status are sometimes reflected by relationships between various sites. Perhaps most striking is the community at Launceston with its many dependent chapelries (above, Ch. 5, 116). But other important churches also had chapelries within their territories that did not become independent parishes until later, for example Probus with chapels at Cornelly and Merther (*Lake* 1: 248-51; *Lake* 3: 323-8).

There are probably two main reasons why these differences (and others described below) have not always been emphasised in studies of the Cornish church. Firstly, as Padel and Olson suggest (1986: 68-9), the establishment of significant numbers of local churches may have begun in Cornwall relatively early, possibly in the later eighth or early ninth century (perhaps comparable with Wales: Davies 2002: 393-4). Although there is presently little archaeological or historical evidence to support this claim, such a date would fit with the burial evidence from minor sites in Cornwall and from elsewhere in western Britain (Petts 2002a; see below). Any such churches may have begun to share the rights and privileges of pre-existing ecclesiastical communities from an early date, with the result that written evidence for relationships never existed; this may explain why there is somewhat less material of this sort in Cornwall compared to some other south-western counties, such as Dorset (Hall 2000: 7).

The second reason may be that deliberate imitation of existing sites during the early middle ages has obscured the differences. As Harvey and Jones have shown, later developments were often rooted in the practices of the past; they have argued that hagiographies in medieval Cornwall explained and legitimised contemporary developments with reference to existing social structures (Harvey & Jones 1999: 227-9). As in Wessex, a kind of deliberate imitation is also identifiable in the ecclesiastical foundations themselves: the place-names, physical form and rights of minor establishments in the county often seem to have been modelled on the major pre-existing churches.

In Domesday Book for Cornwall many of the estates of major landholding ecclesiastical communities have names with the generic element **lann* (e.g. *Lanscauetone* (Launceston), *Lannachebran* (St Keverne), *Lanbrebois* (Probus), *Langoroch* (Crantock), and *Lanpiran* (Perranzabuloe); Thorn and Thorn 1979a: 4). As discussed in Chapter 1, however, the only **lann* name known to have existed before the tenth century was *Landwithan*. This was believed by Finberg to represent a large estate around Launceston granted by Egbert to Sherborne, and therefore to be referring to a major church (Finberg 1953a: 112). St Kew, Domesday Book's *Lanehoc* (Thorn & Thorn 1979a: 1,4), was just *Docco* in the seventh-century *Vita Prima Sancti Samsonis*. Including these examples, around fifty medieval parish churches had **lann* place-names. However, as Padel has pointed out, very few Christian religious sites that did not gain full parochial status in the later middle ages (e.g. chapels or minor burial grounds) had names incorporating the **lann* element (Padel 1985: 144; see also Petts 2002a). This suggests that **lann* names were specific to churches with a certain status at the time the parish system was forming. It seems likely that they could have been given their names in imitation of the major ecclesiastical communities.

An example from southern Cornwall may illustrate this process and also suggests the kind of people who may have been responsible for it. During the reign of Athelstan, 'Count' Maenchi granted the small estate of *Lanlouern* to St Heldenus (S1207; Hooke 1994a: 18). The grant has been identified by Padel as 'our only true "Cornish charter"' (Padel 1978: 26), and belongs to the distinctively western British charter tradition described by Wendy Davies (1982). Padel identifies the estate concerned as Lanlawren (Lanteglos-by-Fowey) and the beneficiary as the church of

St Ildierna at Lansallos, *c.*1.5km to the south (Padel 1978). It has been tentatively suggested that Lansallos may have been a small monastery, but there is little other evidence to suggest that this was the case (Olson 1989: 84; Hooke 1994a: 18). The name 'Lansallos' may be **lann* + a personal name (Padel 1988; Orme 1996a), perhaps even that of a secular founder rather than a saint (Thomas 1988: 24), and in 1066 the manor was held by a thegn (Thorn & Thorn 1979a: 5,3,7). Instead of a monastery, a local lord with a Cornish background (Maenchi) may have been endowing a minor church with land in order to support it, rather like later medieval glebe. Combined with the evidence in the tenth-century list of Cornish saints' names, this document shows that the foundation of local churches cannot be attributed solely to changes associated with the establishment of Anglo-Saxon political control in Cornwall. Members of a Cornish aristocracy were already founding minor churches dedicated to Cornish saints when Wessex became politically dominant in the region.

Local churches could also mimic the physical form of major ecclesiastical communities. It was not uncommon in western Britain for minor sites to have at least two churches or chapels, a characteristic shared with many monasteries (Petts & Turner, forthcoming). Examples from the late Saxon period in Cornwall probably include Constantine (St Merryn) and Porth Chapel in St Levan **(Plate 10a)**. Whilst major ecclesiastical sites appear to have been enclosed from an early date, few local churches or burial grounds seem to have been enclosed until the later pre-Conquest period (Petts 2002a). Some of these later churches reused existing prehistoric enclosures. The place-name of Cardinham (*ker* 'round' + *dinan* 'fortlet': Padel 1988: 65) suggests that the site's curvilinear graveyard enclosure is a reused Iron Age or Romano-British settlement. The church lies in an area largely devoid of early medieval habitative place-name elements. The church may have been founded during a phase of settlement expansion that led to the establishment of numerous settlements with English place-names in the vicinity, and the HLC revealed significant areas of rough ground here in the later middle ages **(Fig. 32)**. Cardinham may have been founded in imitation of its more illustrious neighbours at Bodmin and St Neot. According to William Worcester the local saint Meubred lay in the church there as did the saints of Bodmin and St Neot in the neighbouring monasteries (although he remained unmentioned in the sources until the fifteenth century; Orme 2000: 190). Furthermore, in 1613 the church glebe was equipped with four marker crosses, at least two of which remain today at Poundstock Cross and Wydeyeat Cross ((Henderson *EC*: 75-83; Langdon 1996: 26-7). These are post-Conquest in date, although the latter could be twelfth-century (see Langdon 1896: 174). This arrangement, with crosses marking the boundaries of the church land, may have been intended to imitate the pre-Conquest crosses around St Neot and Bodmin (see below, 161-5). Other crosses that were sometimes set up at local churches both before and after the Norman Conquest (e.g. at St Cleer or St Dennis) may also have been intended to imitate earlier examples at major churches such as St Neot and St Buryan (Preston-Jones & Okasha 1997).

Categories of Churches

Given that later pre-Conquest developments were rooted in earlier practice; it is sometimes hard to establish the status of Cornish churches and the relationships between them; nevertheless, it is possible to suggest some of the different categories of church that may have existed.

Firstly, there were small chapels which provided minor religious foci within the territories of important churches. As discussed above, the patron of St Levan near St Buryan is mentioned in the tenth-century list of Cornish saints' names (Olson & Padel 1986), and Thomas has suggested that the remains at Porth Chapel could date to as early as the seventh century (**Plate 10a**; Thomas 1988: 25). Likewise *Guidian* appears in the same list, a saint who should probably be identified with the patron of St Gothian's chapel at Gwithian near Phillack. Here a sequence of ecclesiastical buildings and burials that is likely to reach back well into the early medieval period lies submerged beneath wind-blown sand (Thomas 1958). On the Isles of Scilly, Charles Thomas has reinterpreted the early buildings once thought to be hermits' chapels as churches for the islanders. The buildings on Tean, St Helen's and possibly Samson appear to have been preceded by early cemeteries, though the churches themselves probably date to the eighth to tenth centuries at the earliest (Thomas 1980, 1985: 180-7). There is a chance that these structures had wooden predecessors. However, the dwellings in the contemporary settlement at Halangay Down on St Mary's seem to have been stone-built: their last phase was in the seventh or eighth century, and it might be expected that churches of the same period on the islands would have been built of stone too (Thomas 1985: 184-5; Ashbee 1996: 28-9).

In eastern Cornwall, it is possible that there was a chapel in the pre-Conquest period at St Luke's in the far north of St Neot parish (Rose 1994: 79). The place-name Carneglos (*carn* 'rock-pile, tor' + *eglos* 'church, chapel'), on the other side of the valley in Altarnun parish, suggests that the chapel was present early enough to give rise to a Cornish topographic name. Most of the place-names in this part of the moor are English and probably date from the eleventh century or later. St Luke's chapel was distant from the main areas of early medieval settlement, and from any later medieval manorial centre. It was probably built by St Neot's community to mark the edge of their territory and to provide for the spiritual needs of travellers and those working the rough ground of the uplands.

It seems likely that some early small church or chapel complexes could have been the settlements of hermits (Blair 2005: 216-17). Written sources such as the *First Life of St Samson* record possible sites, such as the cave where the eponymous saint lived for a while in Cornwall. The ninth-century *Life of St Paul Aurelian* notes that Paul had once lived alone in Brittany in a *monasterium*, and that St Sitofolla lived in a *domus* (perhaps a small coenobitic community) somewhere on the shores of the English Channel (Olson 1989: 14-28). Little archaeological evidence has so far come to light for such hermitages, however, and bearing in mind Thomas' reinterpretation of the Scilly sites, most of the known examples seem likely to be small chapels.

A second class of churches seems to have been rather like the 'sub-minsters' of Wessex. These are churches that show some signs of superior status, but now lack enough evidence for us to be confident that they were ever major communities of monks or clerks. Some have dependent chapels that are demonstrably early, suggesting even more ancient origins for the mother church. For example, St Merryn had within its medieval parish the chapels at Constantine, where a cist-grave cemetery and unusual well chapel may indicate a significant early medieval religious site (Henderson 1958; Todd 1987).

Examples like Old Kea and Goran in the Cornwall geld accounts show that some such churches had once held estates that they lost to secular landholders before 1086, a history typical of higher-status Cornish religious centres (Olson 1989: 90-1; above, Ch. 5). Domesday Book incidentally records the names of several such churches as the names of estate centres, for example St Mawgan-in-Meneage (Thorn & Thorn 1979a: 1,1). *Maucan*, the saint of St Mawgan, is first referred to in the tenth-century list of saints' names where he occurs (in geographical order) before *Achobran* (i.e. St Keverne) (Olson & Padel 1986). In the later middle ages St Mawgan's parish was the second largest on the Lizard (after St Keverne). This hints that St Mawgan was a foundation of some importance, and Orme suggests it may have been the main cult centre for Maugan in all the Brittonic lands (Orme 2000: 183).

The history of saints' cults at St Mawgan's chapelry of St Martin-in-Meneage shows that even minor dependent centres within the territory of such 'sub-minsters' could be old and complex sites (ibid. 184). Up to four different saints were associated with the site in the middle ages. Two estates adjacent to the churchtown were called Nance-with-Mathiana and Barrimaylor. The medieval name-forms show that the former is Cornish *nans* ('valley') with *merther-anowe*, and the latter *merther-meglar* (Henderson 1958: 330; *ICS Index*). They both incorporate the Cornish element *merther*, which Padel explains as 'saint's grave' (Padel 1985), plus a personal name. It is possible that there had been shrines here to saints Anowe (known as Anou in Brittany) and Meglar (perhaps identifiable with one or other of the Breton saints with similar names: Orme 2000: 184). The earliest reference to the place is in AD 977 and connects it with Meglar: in the Anglo-Saxon charter boundary clause of Trethewey the marsh below Barrimaylor is referred to as *pennhal meglar* 'the head of Meylor's marsh' (S 832: Hooke 1994a: 51).

In the fourteenth century two further saints were connected with the chapelry. In 1334 it was recorded as *parochia dedynini* (despite the fact it was not yet really a parish), although Dedymin had become inferior to Martin by 1385 (Orme 1996a: 101). Like some of the more important churches, there is clear evidence here for more than one saint's cult. This all reflects the complexity which can be found in Cornwall even in so minor a cult-centre, and one without burial rights in the earlier middle ages. The changing dedications provide a clear illustration of the difficulty inherent in using saints' names and dedications to write the early history of Cornish churches: it is now impossible to tell which of the three local cults was the first to be maintained at the site, or to say when any of them began. Even after St Martin superseded the others, the church only won burial rights from St Mawgan after petitioning the Pope in 1385, until which time the parishioners had to take their dead to the mother church for burial (Henderson 1958: 329).

Where new royal vills were not built adjacent to the sites of existing ecclesiastical communities, new churches were sometimes founded to serve their estates. Physically these may have imitated the fittings of existing ecclesiastical centres, as shown by the magnificent cross with crucifixion which probably comes from a chapel on the royal estate at Roseworthy (Okasha 1993: 133-7). Likewise, notable monuments of probable eleventh-century date exist on the bishop of Exeter's Domesday estates at Gulval and St Erth (Preston-Jones & Okasha 1997: 16).

Finally, minor lords with more modest estates were probably also establishing chapels at this time. The example of Lansallos, mentioned earlier in this section, suggests that the Cornish elite were able to endow churches just as the English

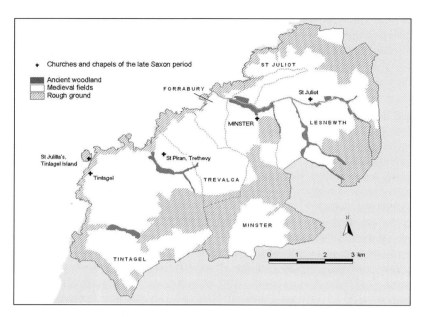

Fig. 51: Late Saxon churches in the Tintagel study area, tithe map parish boundaries and the HLC.

thegns of Wessex were doing at around the same time. Some such churches may have been associated with the establishment of new settlements and manors that were pushing into previously uninhabited land during this period, like St Neot's neighbour Warleggan, where manorial centre and church are apparently located together. Warleggan is a strip-parish, similar to those of the Wessex chalk valleys, which runs from the high moor down to the valley of the Fowey. The dedication of the church to Bartholomew (rather than to a 'Celtic' saint) has also prompted the suggestion that it was a late pre-Conquest or early Norman foundation (Orme 2000: 69).

The archaeological evidence, though presently limited to a few sites, suggests that even minor Christian religious sites of the late pre-Conquest period were elaborated with sculpture and buildings. The well-chapel of possible pre-Conquest date at Fenton Ia near Camborne may have elaborated an existing holy well (Thomas 1967). It may also have been the source of a carved altar slab of tenth- or eleventh-century date (Okasha 1993: 82-4), and an eleventh-century cross formerly stood nearby (Preston-Jones & Okasha 1997: 17). The chapel of St Dennis was a dependency of St Stephen in Brannel until the very end of the middle ages (*Lake* 1: 294; Orme 1999: 214). Limited excavation here in the 1960s and subsequently has shown that the chapel site reused a small hillfort around the time of the Norman Conquest; a cross from the site probably dates to the late eleventh or twelfth centuries and the whole complex may have been established by a prominent local landholder (Thomas 1965; Langdon 1896: 293-6; Preston-Jones 1992: 114; Preston-Jones 1999). Thomas has described the use of prehistoric enclosures for Christian burial in this period as simply a good way to make use of land that was unsuitable for agriculture (1988: 21), but it should instead be regarded as part of a significant change in burial practice. As Petts has shown, unenclosed burial was normal in western Britain until around the beginning of the ninth century (Petts 2002a). From this time onwards, burial sites were more and more commonly enclosed. In this respect they were not only imitating the burial grounds of the major ecclesiastical centres, but also reflecting the increasing desire of the church to control burial practices (ibid. 2002a). At Merther Uny in Wendron, Thomas has defined a sequence of burials and a chapel that were established around the end of the first millennium (Thomas 1968b). Perhaps at some point in the eleventh century, this site was also elaborated with a cross (Preston-Jones & Okasha 1997).

The archaeological and historical evidence shows that by the eve of the Norman Conquest there were numerous churches in Cornwall of different ages and with differing status. In addition to the major landholding collegiate churches, there were also a range of chapels perpetuating ancient cult sites, important cult centres like St Mawgan that may have supported small communities, and chapels founded by a variety of major and minor secular and ecclesiastical lords. In the area around Tintagel, for example, there were at least four churches in 1066 and maybe more, all with widely varying origins **(Fig. 51, Plate 10b)**. The late Saxon church with the highest status here was probably at Minster, where a tenth- or eleventh-century building may be incorporated into the later medieval fabric (Thomas 1993: 109). Archaeological excavation has revealed part of an ecclesiastical complex in Tintagel churchyard that probably perpetuated the site of one of the earliest Christian cemeteries in Cornwall, which in 1066 stood on St Petroc's manor of Bossiney (Nowakowski & Thomas 1992; Thorn & Thorn 1979a: 4,13). St Juliot, across the valley from Minster, was probably a later foundation associated with the small manor of the same name recorded in Domesday Book (Thorn & Thorn 1979a: 5,4,6). At St Jullita's on Tintagel Island a chapel with rights of burial and baptism was perhaps established around the end of the eleventh century, built on the remains of a post-Roman structure (Thomas 1993: 110-13). Finally, medieval records of a chapel dedicated to St Piran at Trethevy suggest that the canons of St Piran's may have founded a chapel here to minister to their estate of Genver, which they held in the pre-Conquest period (Thorn & Thorn 1979a: 5,8,10). The foundation of a number of chapels in the late Saxon period may reflect the growing power of landowners, both lay and ecclesiastical, to found their own churches on their own estates. If Minster once had ecclesiastical rights over this area as Thomas has suggested (1993: 109), they were severely eroded by these local churches and others founded before the end of the twelfth century at the manorial centres of Trevalga and Lesnewth. Even Forrabury, with its tiny parish at Boscastle, had probably escaped Minster's parochial control by 1291 (see Hingeston-Randolph 1889: 472-3).

Crosses in the Early Christian Landscape of Cornwall

Medieval crosses are a defining characteristic of the Cornish landscape. Around 700 examples survive, of which perhaps as many as fifty bear distinctive early medieval decoration (Preston-Jones 1999). The exact number of pre-Conquest monuments is uncertain because a number of crosses and fragments carry decoration that is hard to date exactly and some of them may have been produced after the Norman Conquest. The problem is compounded by complex patterns of influence in Cornwall's early sculpture, which came from both England and the Irish Sea region (current research is addressing these questions: Preston-Jones & Okasha 1997: 3-4).

The first crosses to appear on monuments in the region are probably the *chi-rho* stones of the early Christian period. These occur both as individual sculptures (probably architectural, e.g. Phillack and St Just) and as motifs cut on to inscribed stones (e.g. St Endellion, St Just & South Hill **(Plate 6b)**; Okasha 1993). The earliest free-standing sculpture seems to belong to the ninth century, and crosses and other monuments were produced in increasing numbers up to the end of the eleventh century. After this time, there is an explosion of much simpler medieval crosses which resulted in the large numbers visible in the Cornish landscape today (e.g. Turner 2002-3).

There are probably two main reasons for Cornwall's richness in this respect. The conquest of Cornwall by Wessex in the ninth and early tenth century, like the Norman Conquest a century or so later, probably involved a certain amount of redistribution of estates from the Cornish elite to English thegns and other landlords. The charters attest to a certain degree of acculturation, with Cornishmen adopting English names,[7] but thegns from elsewhere in Wessex were probably able to acquire new estates in the region, not least by expanding the settled area into marginal land. Crosses and other monuments like hogback stones may have been used to express their social aspirations (e.g. Lanivet: **Plate 11a & 11c**; Langdon 1896: 295-7, 412-14). Secondly, much of Cornwall's pre-Conquest sculpture is associated with major ecclesiastical sites like St Buryan, Phillack, St Piran's, Padstow, and St Neot, and such churches probably had a strong interest in clearly marking their territory. In the late pre-Conquest landscape, erecting crosses may have provided a way make claims on land and local power (Turner 2006).

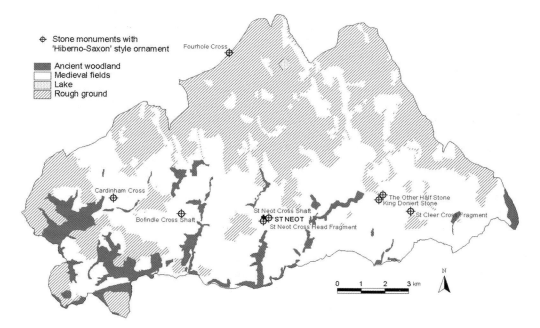

Fig. 52: 'Hiberno-Saxon' sculpture in the St Neot study area; and the HLC

[7] e.g. Wulfnoth Rumuncant: S755; Ælfeah Geraint: S770.

Crosses were certainly used to mark boundaries in pre-Conquest Cornwall. Four Hole Cross (St Neot; **Plate 15a**), Three Hole Cross (St Kew; **Plate 15b**) and Carminow Cross (Bodmin) still stand near to parish boundaries and a cross at St Piran's is recorded in a charter boundary clause (S684; Hooke 1994a: 31; Langdon 1896: 180-2). Another at St Keverne mentioned in two charter boundary clauses is discussed below. In northern England and other parts of Britain (Davies 1996: 5) special areas of 'protected space' may have developed around churches in the later pre-Conquest period. Wendy Davies suggests this 'protected space' may have developed as 'a defensive reaction against ruler aggression' (Davies 1996: 11). Crosses were used to mark ecclesiastical territories in Ireland and probably Wales (Ó Carragáin 2003: 137-41; N. Edwards 1999: 14). The evidence from Cornwall suggests similar developments took place here too. It seems likely that the context for this change in Cornwall was the increasing power of the secular elite to take land in the late pre-Conquest period, often at the expense of long-established and independent ecclesiastical communities. Just as churches may have used charters to 'defend' their estates in the late Saxon period (W. Davies 1998), they may also have set up crosses to counter the encroachments of the secular elite.

Around St Neot there are eight monuments with distinctively pre-Conquest decoration **(Fig. 52)**. The earliest examples are probably the St Neot cross shaft and cross head fragment **(Plate 6c)**, the Other Half Stone and the King Doniert Stone **(Plate 11b)**, which are probably later ninth-century in date (Preston-Jones 1999). Only four of the eight monuments were first reported at medieval parish churches, and the rest were distributed in a rough ring around the church of St Neot. They are all close to areas of ancient rough ground identified by the HLC, and astride important routeways. The Bofindle fragment and the King Doniert and Other Half Stones also mark the western and north-eastern limits of the distribution of *tre* settlement names. It seems likely that they could also have served for boundary markers around St Neot (Turner 2006).

Near Tintagel there are two pre-Conquest monuments, one from Waterpit Down and one originally from the vicinity of the farm at Trevillet. They probably date from the later tenth or eleventh centuries (Okasha 1993: Nos. 74 and 64; Preston-Jones 1999). Both have inscriptions which seem to incorporate English personal names, showing that they were probably set up after the time when English cultural influence was well-established. The earliest recorded location of the first cross shaft was on Waterpit Down some 2km south of Minster, and it seems this was the original site, since the cross base was also here (Okasha 1993: 318). The site lies in Minster parish on rough ground close to the southern edge of the Domesday estate of *Talcar*, which was almost certainly the core estate of the church at Minster.[8] It is visible to travellers following any of the long-distance routeways over the Down. Although the original location of the Trevillet cross is less certain, it may originally have marked the southern boundary of the cultivated land of Bossiney, held in 1066 by St Petroc's, Bodmin, and the location of Minster's sister church of Tintagel.

---

[8] The two names were virtually synonymous in the later middle ages, e.g. in the 1291 *Taxation of Pope Nicholas IV*, where the parish church is *ecclesia de Talkarn, alias Ministre* (Hingeston-Randolph 1889: 471).

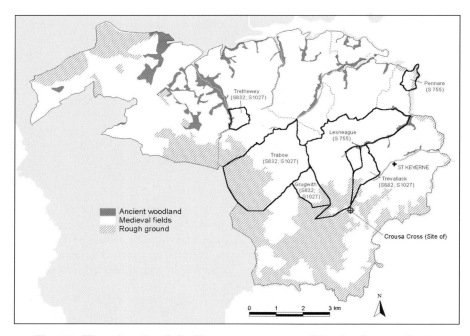

Fig. 53: The church of St Keverne, *crousgrua* ('the hag's cross'), the approximate course of the Anglo-Saxon charter boundaries in the Meneage area (after Hooke 1994a), and the HLC.

It seems likely that these pre-Conquest religious monuments marked territories associated with churches. These might have been early medieval *parochiae*, the churches' estates, or some other territorial units, such as a special zone of sanctuary. Analogy with other places suggests this area may have been both the core of the church's estate and a zone of protected space. In a recent paper, Ann Preston-Jones and Andrew Langdon have considered the medieval crosses in the parish of St Buryan, a likely pre-Conquest monastery that was probably refounded by a grant of Athelstan (2001; S450). They note that although the only pre-Conquest monument in the parish is located at the church, up to seven later medieval crosses may mark a zone of extended sanctuary depicted on a sixteenth-century plan approximately half way between the church and the medieval parish boundary (2001: 114-15). If so, at least part of the estate granted to the church by Athelstan at seven places in the medieval parish would have been within the sanctuary zone.

Other churches with zones of privileged sanctuary in medieval Cornwall included Probus, Padstow and St Keverne (Preston-Jones 1992; Preston-Jones & Langdon 2001). At St Keverne the sanctuary zone continued to be recognised into the late medieval period. John Leland wrote in his 1538 *Itinerary* that:

> Within the land of Meneke or Menegland is a paroch chirch of St Keveryn otherwis Piranus; and ther is a Sanctuary with x or xii dwelling howses and thereby was a sel of monks but now goon home to ther hed hows. The ruines of the monastery yet remenith.
>
> (cited in Henderson 1958: 256-7)

The original extent of the sanctuary is unknown, but in Henderson's view in the later middle ages it is likely to have encompassed the churchtown and the monastic lands of Tregonning and Lanheverne, which were the centre of Beaulieu Abbey's estates in the parish. The existence and survival of the sanctuary is an indicator of the superior status of St Keverne's community, and shows its continuing ability to control aspects of social life and legal custom in the landscape around it.

Unlike the St Neot and Tintagel study areas, there are no surviving examples of late pre-Conquest crosses from the Meneage. However, there is evidence that one cross formerly existed in the Anglo-Saxon boundary clauses of the estates of Trevallack and Lesneage: *crousgrua* is a boundary point in both documents (Cornish *crous* 'cross' + *gruah* 'hag, witch'; S832; S755; Hooke 1994a). The cross was located towards the edge of Crousa Common (which takes its name from the monument), and was about 2km west of St Keverne churchtown (**Fig. 53**). As such, it may have marked the edge of St Keverne's zone of privileged sanctuary. The cross stood close to the place where travellers across Goonzion Downs entered the cultivated land around the monastery, and marks the edge of the area which is distinguished by a dense concentration of *tre* settlements.

It is unclear why pre-Conquest sculpture is absent in the Lizard. It cannot be argued that the influence of Hiberno-Saxon art and sculpture was less strong in the far west of Cornwall, since monuments with characteristic pre-Conquest decoration are plentiful in the neighbouring region of Penwith (Preston-Jones & Okasha 1997). It is possible that the local stone was less suitable than that elsewhere; there are only three surviving medieval crosses in the St Keverne area which compares poorly with other parts of the county. Nevertheless, some stones were transported considerable distances to serve as crosses in the late Saxon period, including the Copplestone in Devon, which stood some 13km from its source on Dartmoor, and Roseworthy in Cornwall, around 40km from its source near St Austell (ibid. 18-19).

An alternative explanation could be that St Keverne itself was not under the same pressure as other churches to mark out the extent of its estates in the pre-Conquest period. Most of its land does not seem to have been lost until the second half of the eleventh century (see Ch. 5, 125-7). This contrasts with the situation around St Neot, where a great deal of sculpture survives; St Neot's community had notably land-hungry neighbours from perhaps the ninth century onwards, not only in the form of a new secular elite from Wessex, but also a new ecclesiastical one at St Petroc's, Bodmin.

All those coming into Minster's territory from the south would have seen the Waterpit Down cross, and must have realised they were crossing from the rough ground into the community's cultivated land. Likewise, several of the crosses around St Neot probably mark the edges of marginal land around the early medieval 'core' of settled land. *Crousgrua* probably marked the borders of St Keverne's sanctuary and was subsequently used as the boundary marker of successor estates to the church. These were bold attempts to defend long-established territories, but ultimately they were unsuccessful. Not only were aspects of this new iconography appropriated by the established churches' rivals in the form of churchyard crosses and gravestones, but both their estates and parochial rights were also diminished by the local churches and chapels that were being established in ever-increasing numbers.

Christian Monuments and Unchristian Margins in Wessex

Most early medieval sculpture from western Wessex is associated with the sites of monasteries or other churches. Of forty-two Somerset pieces considered by Foster to be of Anglo-Saxon date, thirty-three are from the sites of major churches (Foster 1987). These include examples from excavations, as at Glastonbury and Keynsham, as well as those which had been incorporated into later medieval walling as building stone. Documentary evidence suggests other examples from Somerset: writing in the twelfth century, William of Malmesbury described several monuments at Glastonbury which could have been Anglo-Saxon sculpture, but which have not survived.

There are also crosses from elsewhere in the landscape. The varied evidence from Wessex including documentary sources, place-names and surviving sculpture suggests such crosses had a range of functions. Some marked routes, like the memorials which may have been erected at Doulting, Frome and Bath to mark the passage of Aldhelm's body to Malmesbury after his death in 709 (Foster 1987; Blair 2005: 480). An early documentary source, the *Life of St Willibald*, implies that Anglo-Saxon noblemen sometimes erected crosses in prominent places on their estates (Talbot 1954: 154-5). There are several examples in Wessex of monuments that may pre-date the earliest incarnation of the churches where they stand today, for example at Codford St Peter (Wiltshire), Rowberrow (Somerset), West Camel (Somerset; **Plate 3b**) and Dolton (Devon) (**Plate 12**; Cramp 1975; Tweddle 1983). They may have been brought from elsewhere, but it seems likely that they represent a preliminary step on the way to founding an estate church.

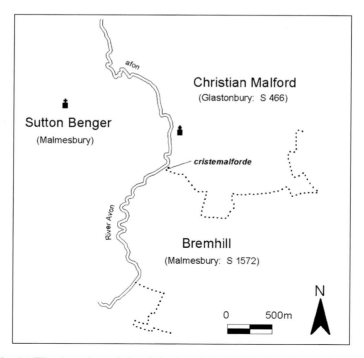

Fig. 54: The location of the *Cristel mæl ford*, Wiltshire (S466; S1575).

Fig. 55: The Copplestone cross-shaft, Devon. [Photo: Mick Sharp.]

Tentatively, it can be suggested that another role of crosses in later Saxon Wessex, as in Cornwall, was to act as boundary markers. Although not particularly common, references to crosses in charter boundary clauses provide a valuable source of evidence. Numerous boundary points called *rood* occur, such as the *rodestan* of the Ashton charter in Wiltshire (S727), delimiting land that was held with the neighbouring estate of Edington by Romsey Abbey in 1066. A *rood*, however, is not necessarily a stone cross: besides the potential for confusion with other name elements, Reynolds has made it clear that *wearg rood* refers to a set of gallows (Reynolds 1997). There are also various ambiguous references in the charters to boundary markers called *stan, stapol* or *cros,* some of which could refer to crosses. A less ambiguous reference is to *cristelmæl,* which translates literally 'Christ-image', meaning 'crucifix'. There are four charters with references to a *cristelmæl* from the South West, and ten from elsewhere in England (Blair 2005: 479).

Of the four south-western examples, the boundary clause of Christian Malford (S466) and the 'loose' boundary clause of Bremhill (S1575) both seem to refer to the same marker, at the *Cristel mæl ford* (from which the parish of Christian Malford in Wiltshire is named). This boundary mark appears to be at the south-west corner of Christian Malford, at the meeting point of this medieval parish with those of Bremhill and Sutton Benger (S305), and also at the boundary of the hundreds of Chippenham and Startley (Fig. 54). The cross stood at the boundary of a Malmesbury estate, since the monastery held both Bremhill and Sutton Benger in at least the ninth and tenth centuries. Christian Malford itself was granted to Glastonbury in the mid-tenth century, although the cristel mæl in question must have been erected some time before this (S466).

The charter of Buckland Newton in Dorset is a grant of 15 hides by King Edmund to Ælflæd, whom the grant describes as a nun. The boundary includes a marker at cristemæleighe, 'the clearing of the cross'. Although this is unlocated, it clearly represents a cross on the boundary of an ecclesiastical estate which may have been in Glastonbury's hands earlier in the pre-Conquest period (S303) and certainly was in the mid-eleventh century (Thorn & Thorn 1983: 8,3).

Two important boundary clauses probably referring to crosses which are still in their original locations come from Devon and Cornwall. The first is the final cristelmæl, mentioned in the charter of Tywarnhayle (Hooke 1994a). The second is the copelstan of the Nymed charter in Devon (S795). There is little doubt that this refers to the Copplestone from which the medieval and post-medieval settlement takes its name (Hooke 1994a), a large and elaborately decorated granite cross shaft probably of the earlier tenth century (Fig. 55). The Copplestone stands at the border of the estates of Nymed and Crediton, which was a major land-holding monastery from at least the early eighth century (S255) and seat of a bishop from AD 909. The place-name Nymed suggests an area of marginal country on the borders of Crediton's estates; although taken from the old name for the River Yeo, the word ultimately derives from the British nemeton, meaning a sacred wood. It perhaps refers to the same forest as the name of Morchard Bishop (i.e. 'great wood'), which is a few miles to the north-east. Down St Mary, just to the north, appears in Domesday as two estates both named done, meaning 'hill' or 'downland' (Thorn & Thorn 1985: 1,72; 6,4).

In his recent discussion of the crosses, John Blair has argued that the significant question is 'whether they were vehicles for new conceptions of articulating the landscape, or perpetuated old ones' (Blair 2005: 478-81). He suggests that the location of crosses should be seen in relation to their position on routeways, and regards them as marking significant points such as crossroads and fords, arguing that this seems similar to the pattern of pre-Christian sacred sites. As Blair says, some crosses may have perpetuated 'traditional' religious sites such as wells and holy trees. It is also very likely that a location on a routeway was significant: a cross was a monument whose impact would have been maximised when viewed by as many passers-by as possible. Like the burial mounds discussed above, it seems likely that a number of factors determined the location of crosses in the landscape, including the need for a roadside location. Blair may be correct to argue that crosses used the same 'vocabulary' as prehistoric, pre-Christian and 'traditional' ritual sites, but if so, they were using it to describe a new kind of landscape: this was not the old pagan landscape, but instead the new Christian landscape of estates with central sanctuaries and dangerous margins.

There are certain parallels between some of the 'landscape' crosses and the mid-Saxon 'conspicuous' burials considered in Chapter 6. Both are commonly located by routeways, and both were sometimes markers at the edges of marginal zones. They may therefore represent successive ways to mark out the borders of the settled land.

As time progressed, the monuments employed to do this became less ambiguous in their meaning, and more thoroughly 'Christian' in their iconography (the cross as opposed to the barrow). The 'conversion' of the landscape was an ongoing process that took several centuries to spread convincingly through the countryside.

The gradual nature of this process is exemplified by the late Saxon execution cemeteries discussed by Reynolds (1998, 2002). In the early Saxon period, 'deviant burials' (individuals who had suffered violent deaths, or unusual burial rites, e.g. beheadings, prone burials or hands tied behind the back) were normally buried in the same cemeteries as the rest of the community (Reynolds 1997: 35). However, from perhaps as early as the seventh century, such bodies began to be separated from communal burial places so that by the tenth century, executed criminals were buried exclusively in separate cemeteries (Reynolds 2002: 187). This practice seems to have been universal in the counties of central southern England, including Dorset and Wiltshire. Execution cemeteries are almost all located on hundred boundaries (Reynolds 1999: 105-10), suggesting that criminals were banished in death to the margins of the administrative land-unit. This would most commonly have meant a location in the 'waste' beyond the cultivated land.

The establishment of separate execution cemeteries is clearly related to the developing administrative system, but was also strongly imbued with a Christian ideology (Reynolds 1997: 38-9). By their actions, criminals had put themselves outside the community of Christian people; in death, that separation was maintained. As burial of the Christian community was increasingly controlled by the church in the late Saxon period (Gittos 2002: 201), the appropriate place for those outside the community was outside Christian burial grounds, and indeed beyond the community's settled land altogether. In the marginal pasture grounds and wastes, execution cemeteries were commonly associated with barrows and other prehistoric monuments, in particular linear earthworks (Reynolds 1999: 108). It is likely that the association of the burial of criminals with barrows is far from accidental. Sarah Semple has demonstrated that whilst the ideological position of barrows may have been somewhat ambiguous in the middle Saxon period, barrows were strongly associated with malevolent spirits in the minds of the later Anglo-Saxons. Execution cemeteries were located on them so that the souls of the departed were not only separated from the Christian dead, but actively tormented by the barrow's existing monstrous occupants (Semple 1998). In some cases, perhaps most notably Sutton Hoo in Suffolk, the same barrows used to commemorate people of the highest rank were later used as the focus of execution cemeteries (Carver 1998b: 137-43). This, and the general late Saxon association of barrows with evil creatures, suggests that the meaning of barrows had changed significantly between the seventh and the tenth centuries.

Conclusion

By the late pre-Conquest period, the influence of Christian ideology had reached out to the edges of the cultivated land and into the rough ground beyond. All minor ritual sites were encompassed within it and imbued with Christian significance, either as part of that ideology, or as physically and metaphorically 'beyond' its rule, and thus at the feared margins of society.

8

From south-west Britain to the wider world

There were considerable similarities between the early Christian landscapes of Cornwall and Wessex, and changes proceeded along broadly analogous 'trajectories' in both areas. Despite this, there were also some important differences. As Peter Brown has stressed a vibrant diversity is characteristic of the 'Micro-Christendoms' of northern Europe during the early middle ages (Brown 2003: 355-79). Local interpretations and adaptations of wider traditions were fundamental in the conversion of Britain and Ireland and the establishment of Christian sites and monuments across the countryside. This final chapter compares the development of Christian landscapes across the South West by considering the similarities and differences between Cornwall and western Wessex, and discusses some explanations. By way of conclusion, it outlines a general model for understanding how changes in the landscape might have resulted from the adoption of Christianity.

Similarities and Differences

The Location and Form of Important Early Churches

The significance of primary churches in both Cornwall and Wessex was emphasised by their topographical locations. The most important early medieval churches of Cornwall are not located on remote islands or spectacular hilltops, but chiefly in low-lying positions, often close to rivers and areas of valley-bottom watermeadow. None of the major early churches of Cornwall stand on particularly high or spectacular hilltops, which suggests that visual domination or physical remoteness was not a prime consideration in their locations. Although there was an increasing trend moving westwards from Wiltshire to Cornwall for important churches to be located on valley sides and hill slopes rather than on valley bottoms, this may reflect differences in the physical topography as much as anything else. Until the post-medieval period, few settlements (apart from mills) were sited in the valley bottoms of Cornwall and west Devon. It therefore seems likely that the locations of churches were guided by similar

171

concerns in both Wessex and Cornwall. Most early Cornish churches are in similar positions to the majority of high-status churches in central Wessex, where ecclesiastical centres are characteristically sited on the banks of rivers or on the edges of their floodplains. In particular, the vast majority of early church sites whose presence is indicated by reliable evidence of the ninth century or earlier are sited in valley-bottom locations.

In Wessex, early churches may have acted as the nuclei of relatively dense settlements from an early date, as perhaps at Avebury (Wiltshire), Romsey (Hampshire) and Bath (Somerset). In Cornwall, there is little or no evidence for the nucleation of settlement at early churches. Whilst this may be just a reflection of the lack of excavations, the historical evidence from saints' lives, charters and Domesday Book suggests that individual clerics held individual farms dispersed within the churches' immediate estates rather than living together next to the church.

In other ways, though, early church sites in the two areas were similar; they often had more than one church or altar, they were probably bounded or enclosed in some way, and they were intended to be permanent centres used continuously throughout the year. Although few church buildings have been excavated, known examples suggest that they were larger, more elaborate, and more permanent structures than almost any others in the contemporary landscape throughout the early medieval period. As well as ritual activities, major ecclesiastical sites were centres for industrial activities such as metal-working and for the processing and consumption of agricultural products. By contrast, many secular settlements seem to have been rather less stable, in particular the lower-status ones. Even at royal vills occupation was generally low-level except during the irregular visits of itinerant rulers and their entourages.

Early Churches, Settlements and Fields

Settlements may be mundane aspects of life, but their location and form is commonly affected or even directed by ideological factors (Carver 1993). Changes in ideology may therefore have meant changes in settlement patterns in the past. In Cornwall, a settlement pattern based on enclosed settlements known as 'rounds' persisted from the later Iron Age throughout the Romano British centuries and on into the fifth and sixth centuries. This pattern appears to have been affected little by the ending of Roman power in Britain, perhaps because cultural life remained relatively stable in the region throughout this period (Quinnell 1993). However, settlement studies reveal that major changes occurred in subsequent centuries. The archaeological evidence shows that rounds generally ceased to be occupied during the sixth century, and were replaced by the 'unenclosed' farmsteads which formed the basis of the medieval settlement pattern. These are generally recognised through their distinctive place-names (Padel 1985). Comparison of the distribution of rounds and early medieval settlements shows that the settlement pattern went through major changes, with significant areas of abandonment in the sixth and seventh centuries. New 'core' areas of settlement were created with relatively dense distributions of dispersed settlements. At the heart of many of these 'core' settlement areas stood important early medieval churches.

Patterns of agricultural resources changed along with the settlement pattern. The rounds of the Romano-British period were commonly surrounded by their field systems, as shown by air photography and field survey (Rose & Preston-Jones 1995: 58). However, the Historic Landscape Characterisations (HLC) clearly show that in the later middle ages many rounds stood in areas of rough grazing ground that was not normally sown with arable crops. Since the later medieval cultivated area is likely to have been considerably greater than that of the early middle ages, many more of the rounds close to the edges of medieval field systems may have been in rough ground in the earlier part of the period. This suggests that a large area of fields was abandoned at the end of the Roman period when the settlement pattern was restructured. The early medieval fields lay close to their associated settlements in the new 'core' settlement areas. The HLCs also show that although small patches of rough ground and woodland were scattered between the settlements and fields, the large continuous expanses generally lay at the margins of areas of settlements and fields. These areas had important economic roles as pasture, fuel production, and mineral extraction, but were not zones where permanent settlements occurred. Their economic role in part may have been inherited from the landscape organisation of previous periods, but the absence of settlements was probably an early medieval development.

Developments similar to those in Cornwall also took place in Wessex in the late sixth and seventh centuries. In Devon a number of prehistoric settlements were reoccupied in the post-Roman period but abandoned shortly afterwards. In Somerset some high-status post-Roman sites like South Cadbury and Cadbury Congresbury were apparently occupied in the late Roman period but deserted in the sixth century. In Wiltshire occupation at several Romano-British downland sites continued into the post-Roman period, but ceased between the fifth and seventh centuries. Evidence from excavations suggests that from the sixth or seventh centuries onwards the most densely occupied areas were in or close to the valley bottoms. This is also suggested by research and fieldwork in the middle Avon valley on the Wiltshire/Hampshire border (Light et al. 1994) and on the Polden Hills in Somerset (Aston & Gerrard 1999).

Finds of the Roman-British period were generally distributed over a more extensive area than those of the early and central middle ages. Field survey suggests that considerable areas of former arable land were put down to rough grazing in Wessex in the early part of the middle ages, as they were in Cornwall (e.g. Fowler 2000: 233; McOmish et al. 2002). This evidence and the information from Anglo-Saxon charter boundary clauses suggests that zones of rough grazing, woodland and marshland were distributed in large, fairly coherent blocks that were peripheral to the newly refocused areas of settlement and cultivation in Wessex.

In both Cornwall and Wessex, however, early churches were generally sited centrally within the core agricultural land. This commonly meant a position overlooking the most valuable resources, the watermeadow and the arable of the lower valley sides. In Wessex, royal estates were physically organised in broadly the same way, with the royal vill and church at the centre surrounded by fields and meadows, and the largest areas of rough grazing and woodland in peripheral zones.

Burials and Sacred Sites in the Wider Landscape

In the wider landscape away from the major ecclesiastical centres there were a range of minor ritual and religious foci, including burial sites, holy wells, and (in the later part of the period) monumental stone crosses. It seems very likely that some such sites perpetuated the locations of pre-Christian ritual places. Holy wells and springs occur in both Cornwall and Wessex; although the veneration of many of these may have begun in the early or even later medieval periods, it is probable that some have their origins as sacred sites in the Iron Age or Romano-British past. Likewise, in both Cornwall and Wessex there are burial grounds that are not adjacent to churches but have produced archaeological evidence for use spanning the Roman period and early middle ages. New cemeteries were also founded away from churches after the conversion to Christianity, and it appears that the church authorities did not interfere with ordinary community burial grounds until stricter customs governing burial (and the collection of burial taxes) were introduced in the later pre-Conquest period.

In the wider landscape, there were variations in burial practice across the South West during the early middle ages. However, there is no need to link these differing practices to differing forms of Christianity, and there were continuities from pre-Christian practice in both areas. In Cornwall burials in both cists and simple dug graves occur from the Romano-British period through to the later middle ages. Such burial practices are paralleled at eighth-century cemeteries in Wessex, for example in Dorset at sites in the Isle of Purbeck like Ulwell (Cox 1988). Also in Wessex, burials with grave goods overlap the conversion period in parts of Wiltshire, Dorset and Somerset. The Christian church may not have laid down strict codes relating to burial practice until the later pre-Conquest period: the secondary barrow burial in the graveyard of Ogbourne St Andrew church (Wiltshire) shows that burial rites involving monumental display could be employed in the later ninth century (Semple 2002). The range of late Anglo-Saxon burials found at many church sites, including simple dug graves with or without coffins, slab- or plaster-lined graves, and charcoal burials shows that a range of burial customs was allowed within communities.

In both Cornwall and Wessex there were forms of elite burial that continued into the conversion period but had their origins in the pre-Christian past. Religious identity and elite ideology have commonly been studied through burial practice, and the religious agenda of the so-called 'conspicuous' burials has been extensively questioned (Williams 1997; Carver 2002b; Semple 2003). However, in the seventh and eighth centuries even those with ambiguous symbolic content seem to have been intimately linked by their geographical positions to the construction of a new Christian landscape. In the late sixth and seventh centuries cemeteries and burial sites in central Wessex with distinctively 'Anglo-Saxon' grave goods became increasingly distant from contemporary settlement sites. At the same time there was an increase in the number of 'isolated' burials, where one or two individuals are buried on their own, typically in barrows, accompanied by a rich array of grave goods. These burials were normally sited in distinctive topographical positions, for example on high downland hilltops and plateaux (Eagles 2001; Semple 2003). Whether they are the burials of 'pagans' or Christians, the location of many such barrows close to routes of communication suggests that the monuments were intended to act as prominent markers (Semple

2003). Such burials probably stood in the rough grazing land at the edges of territorial units that were centred on newly established elite centres, particularly churches. The kinds of boundaries they marked are hinted at by their relationships with later land divisions.

In Cornwall the use of inscribed stones may have extended from the late Antique period (when conversion to Christianity first began) through to the time Anglo-Saxon political control was established. Mark Handley has suggested that the way these monuments were used changed over time, and has argued convincingly that whilst earlier inscribed stones were often burial markers, the later examples were associated with land ownership, or both land and burial (Handley 1998). The most intensive period of use of stones associated with land ownership was probably the time when the early medieval settlement pattern was being established in the sixth century. The Cornish examples presented in Chapter 6 show that inscribed stones were commonly located in marginal zones on the borders of early medieval farmland.

It has been argued that both inscribed stones and barrow burials may have had more to do with displaying personal or political power than with religious or ideological changes (Knight 1999; Semple 2003). Even if this is the case, such power was being exercised in a landscape that was increasingly being defined in relation to settled areas that were focused on Christian ecclesiastical and/or royal centres. Whether the people commemorated by them were pagans or Christians remains unclear; within the conversion-period landscape they 'defended' newly formalised territories.[1] Their locations were probably linked to a 'Christianised' way of ordering the landscape that put the church at the centre of an area of settled fields, surrounded by a boundary zone of uncultivated land. 'Conspicuous' burials in both Cornwall (sixth to seventh centuries) and Wessex (seventh to eighth centuries) were placed at visible points in this margin.

The symbolic vocabulary of the seventh-century barrows and even of some inscribed stones may have been ambiguous, but this was not the case with another monument type that was probably used to mark certain boundaries later in the early medieval period. Stone crosses bearing distinctive decoration of the later Saxon period are found in both Wessex and Cornwall. In Wessex the vast majority are associated with the sites of major churches, as are many in Cornwall. However, there is a significant sub-set that are not located at or near churches, but stand in isolated sites in the wider landscape. A consideration of the Anglo-Saxon charter references to these monuments suggests that many of them may have acted as boundary markers for important ecclesiastical estates. This interpretation is supported by the earliest known locations of many of the crosses (particularly in Cornwall and western Wessex) which are commonly close to the borders of the medieval settled land and the rough grazing ground. Examples from Cornwall include the possible ring of crosses around St Neot in Cornwall, where four or five monuments appear to have stood on important routeways across the rough ground close to the point where they re-entered the settled landscape. There is a relatively large number of crosses in Cornwall compared to Wessex, and it is possible that this relates to the greater density of major land-holding churches: many of the crosses in both areas may have been set up to mark out ecclesiastical

---

[1] For Irish comparisons see Charles-Edwards 1976; Ó Carragáin 2003.

land that was in danger of being appropriated by increasingly voracious secular landholders from the ninth century onwards.

The use of crosses also suggests that the 'conversion' of the wider landscape to a Christian scheme was becoming increasingly complex in the later Saxon period. Although this process began in the sixth and seventh centuries with the establishment of churches and royal centres and the re-focusing of the pattern of secular settlements, it continued to develop into late Saxon times and beyond. Unlike barrows, stone crosses were resoundingly Christian monuments, and their establishment as permanent features of the landscape showed that it was claimed as part of a Christian world. It is significant that by the later Saxon period, the everyday meaning of the barrows had also changed from places of burial for the social elite to places that were viewed with fear and suspicion (Semple 1998). The conversion of the landscape may have been a process that took several centuries, but by the eleventh century there can be little doubt that Christianity had an institutional grip on the structure of the south-western countryside.

An important part of this process was the establishment of increasing numbers of minor churches in both Cornwall and Wessex. In both areas the foundation of minor churches and chapels probably began when major ecclesiastical communities established chapels on distant parts of their estates in the eighth or ninth centuries, but by the tenth and eleventh centuries it was most commonly secular lords who were establishing small churches on their own land. These new churches acted as ecclesiastical centres for smaller territories than the earlier foundations, but in many ways they fulfilled similar functions and they were probably founded according to a model provided by the existing early ecclesiastical centres. In Wessex, for example, this may be suggested by the close juxtaposition of many estate churches and manorial centres. These minor churches and chapels fragmented the existing networks of ecclesiastical organisation, but in so doing they transformed and reproduced them at a smaller scale in local landscapes all over south-west England.

Dedications to the Saints

Oliver Davies has argued that there were significant differences in Christian religious practice between the 'Celtic' and 'Anglo-Saxon' regions of Britain (O. Davies 1996). The later medieval church dedications of the South West are one sphere where differences are immediately apparent (Padel 2002). In Cornwall, as in Wales, most churches are dedicated to 'Celtic' saints, many of them local Cornish figures. In Wessex, by contrast, the majority of church dedications are to universal saints, even though in the later Saxon period some 'Celtic' saints were imported to provide church dedications in England from Cornwall and the Brittonic world in general (Pearce 1973; Orme 1996a).

Nevertheless, the use of local saints in Cornwall need not be regarded as a simple expression of 'Celtic' identity in opposition to the rest of Britain or Europe. Oliver Padel has argued that the cults of Celtic saints in the west were an intensely *local* phenomenon, and that the saints were strongly linked to their localities (Padel 2002: 351-3). An important element of this was the way that over the course of the early middle ages saints had become closely intertwined with the formation of Brittonic place-names. The names of saints to whom churches were dedicated were used in place-names in a similar way to the many personal names included in the place-names of secular settlements (ibid. 2002).

The veneration of local saints could be part of local political processes as well as local social life. Such processes took place not only in the 'Celtic' lands, but in Wessex too, as Barbara Yorke has suggested. In middle Saxon Wessex, saints favoured by certain political factions may have replaced others favoured by their rivals who had suffered political and military defeats (Yorke 2002). Even so, in Wessex there were local saints whose cults were limited to specific locations, such as Humbert of Stokenham and Ermund of Stoke Fleming in the South Hams of Devon (Orme 1995, 1996a: 24). Blair has suggested that English local saints (as opposed to universal ones) were once relatively widespread, particularly in the pre-Viking period, and that very many minster churches would have housed the cults of local saints. He argues that the lack of local saints in England may be partly a reflection of the differences in the ways place-names were formed in the English and Brittonic languages (see also Padel 2002: 312-14), and partly due to the desire of minster churches in England to centralise cult practice (Blair 2002: 468-9; this may also relate to the differences in secular elite control over religious sites in the two regions discussed below). Nevertheless, Blair maintains that in both Brittonic and English areas

> saints were the object of popular, strongly localised devotion which involved their incorporation into myth-making, and were used to identify and explain landmarks scattered through the landscapes where their cults were based.
>
> (Blair 2002: 486)

The apparent differences may have been more the result of linguistic, political and institutional arrangements after the first centuries of Christianity in Britain than of a fundamental gulf in the nature of Christianity between the two regions; as Blair argues, there was probably a 'basic continuum in the local cult practices of Brittonic and English societies' (ibid. 486). The difficulty of using ethnicity as an explanatory mechanism for some of the subtle differences outlined here is considered further below.

Estates and Administrative Structures

Some of the more significant differences between the churches of Wessex and Cornwall lie in the relationships to secular elite settlements and administrative structures between the seventh and tenth centuries. The earliest churches of Wessex were most commonly located very close to royal vills, and in many cases royal estate centres and churches probably formed different parts of the same complexes from the seventh to the eleventh centuries (around 70% of royal vills in Wessex were probably less than 1km or so from the nearest important ecclesiastical centre). In Cornwall, however, the picture is more complicated. The example of Tintagel shows that post-Roman royal centres and religious sites could form part of the same complex (AD c.300-600). However, in the subsequent early medieval period (AD c.600-900) the available evidence suggests a significant change so that churches in Cornwall were established on sites that were distant from royal secular centres. This distance may suggest a greater degree of independence from royal control for the churches of Cornwall in comparison to most of those in contemporary Wessex. In the later pre-Conquest period (c.AD 900-1050), however, the freedoms which Cornish ecclesiastical communities had acquired began to be eroded by the establishment of new royal centres at or close to important church sites, and also by the increasing numbers of local churches.

The relative independence of major early medieval Cornish churches may also be reflected in the kinds of estates they held. Domesday Book records a very unusual concentration of ecclesiastical communities in Cornwall whose land was free from the payment of geld: the produce of the estate was not diverted to the secular elite in the form of tax. Nevertheless, Domesday Book and various charters also show how the estates of Cornish churches were increasingly being encroached upon in the late Saxon period. It seems likely that the structure of ecclesiastical estates in Cornwall was deliberately being brought into line by the new political masters from Wessex.

The relationships between ecclesiastical centres and the secular administrative structures of the later Saxon period also suggests closer links between royal power and ecclesiastical structures in Wessex than in Cornwall. In Wessex, important churches were often central to the early medieval hundreds administered for secular purposes from adjacent royal vills. As recent research on Wiltshire and Dorset has argued, early units of pastoral responsibility (minster *parochiae*) and hundreds commonly shared the same boundaries (Pitt 1999; Hall 2000). Changes in the patterns of hundredal administration may have led to changes in ecclesiastical structures, once again emphasising the importance of the links between royal and religious administration. In Cornwall, however, it is much less easy to see a close correlation between secular and ecclesiastical administrative units during the early middle ages. The available evidence does not suggest that even in the tenth or eleventh centuries there was much coincidence between hypothetical areas of ecclesiastical pastoral responsibility and the Domesday hundreds. It seems likely that this reflects the relative independence of important Cornish religious communities from the secular power structures of the pre-Saxon period.

Explaining the Differences

Ethnicity

Some recent attempts to explain the differences between the early Christianity of the 'Celtic' western Britain and the Anglo-Saxon kingdoms have appealed to ethnicity as the guiding force. The inscribed stones of Cornwall provide one example: they have been described as 'a manifestation of something called *Britishness*... the planned exploitation... of an exclusive intellectual heritage' (Thomas 1998: 198-9). Olson has observed that the 'Insular Celtic' lands remained free of the regularising influence of the Benedictine Rule for an unusually long time, but that 'monasticism was a dynamic force in early medieval Christianity and nowhere more so, it would seem, than in the Celtic regions of Atlantic Europe' (Olson 1989: 1-3). Oliver Davies has suggested the existence of 'a particular type of spirituality...among the Christians of early medieval Wales' (O. Davies 1996: 5). The case for the early Cornish church as part of a wider 'Celtic Church' was expounded by Taylor (1916: 50-8) and has been current in popular publications and parish histories ever since (e.g. Canner 1982: 5-6). Hughes and Davies have discussed this preoccupation with the 'Celtic Church' and have shown clearly that it has little basis in the evidence (Hughes 1981; Davies 1992). Not only is there no evidence for a 'Celtic Church' with any institutional structure, but there were significant differences between different regions within the Celtic-speaking lands which Davies attributes to local political differences. In addition, she demonstrates that aspects of 'Celtic Christian' life such as monastic bishops and monastic federations were not specific to 'Celtic' areas, but had clear parallels elsewhere in the Europe, including Anglo-Saxon England (Davies 1992: 13-18).

Although the idea of an ethnically based 'Celtic Church' has been discarded by many scholars, the notion of a 'Celtic' Christianity is more persistent. This idea suggests a form of Christianity existed which was special because it reflected certain traits characteristic of 'Celtic' people as a whole, even if it was not organised on a formal basis across the Celtic-speaking lands. Its exponents, such as Oliver Davies, suggest a range of characteristics that distinguish 'Celtic' Christianity from other forms, including

> the central role of the Christian poet, a special emphasis upon the doctrine of the Triune God, an unusually positive attitude towards the natural world and a deeply felt sense of community.
>
> (O. Davies 1996: 5)

Davies suggests that these special elements had their origins in the dialogue between the earliest Christianity of the Celtic world and the 'primal elements' of 'tribal Celtic religion' (ibid. 5-6, 143-4). Other work has continued to emphasise these characteristics; for example, Low argues that early Irish Christianity was particularly oriented towards the natural world (Low 2002), and Atherton has suggested that 'Celtic' influences—often fantastical and otherworldly—can be identified in Old English poetry in opposition to the 'practical and down to earth' Anglo-Saxon elements (Atherton 2002: 80-1).

The use of these supposed characteristics of 'Celtic' peoples to explain certain historical structures has been criticised on the grounds that they are over-generalisations and pre- (or mis-) conceptions. James has stated the case for 'Celtic' identity as an essentially modern construction, and it is clear that there was no overarching ethnic self-awareness in antiquity across the regions now regarded as 'Celtic' (James 1999). Patrick Sims-Williams has evaluated the reliability of some of the model's elements (such as the supposed Celtic love of nature) and has suggested that post-medieval and modern political motivations are largely behind the maintenance of this pan-Celtic identity (Sims-Williams 1986, 1998a; see also I. Bradley 1999: 225-8).

Whilst this work has shown that some of the supposed 'Celtic' traits may rest more on modern imagination than in early medieval culture, it is also clear that the use of categories of ethnicity to explain historical developments is fraught with problems. Sims-Williams has shown how genetic, linguistic and cultural connections have been confused and often deliberately equated where no true equivalence exists (Sims-Williams 1998b). There is surely no one-to-one relationship between ethnicity and culture (including material culture; Jones 1997: 88), let alone between genetics, language and ethnicity (see also Cole 1997). Ethnicity may be expressed in different ways by the same ethnic groups at different times and in different places depending on historical circumstances (Jones 1997: 122-3). This means that a contextual approach is necessary which provides 'thick descriptions' and detailed historical analysis of particular situations; it is hard to use 'ethnicity' as part of an explanatory framework without a clear understanding of its manifestations in specific contexts. As Hines has observed, culture, identity and politics are intimately related spheres, 'like boxers in a three-cornered fight. Each responds to the other' (Hines 2000: 84). His paper uses ethnic identity (which he locates particularly in the use of different languages; see also Ward-Perkins 2000b: 524) to explain the emergence of British Wales and Anglo-Saxon England in opposition to one another in the early middle ages. However, it does not discuss in detail the ways ethnicity related to politics in the context of the early middle ages, and dismisses the contribution of politics on the grounds that 'the polities and kingships of the relevant time were too weak and unstable to have caused the changes' (Hines 2000: 102). This entails a rather limited conception of 'politics', and ignores the fact that it is an active force at local geographical scales and in societies not organised on the basis of 'states'. As a result, 'ethnicity' is largely conflated with 'culture' and 'identity', which makes it too general to be used as an explanatory mechanism on its own.

'Ethnicity' needs to be used cautiously in relation to the early middle ages, and it must be rooted in detailed discussions of individual contexts. This is not to deny that Christianity in some or all of the Celtic-speaking lands may have had elements that distinguished it in some ways from its insular or continental neighbours. It seems likely that Christianity in Cornwall and Wales would have been influenced by pre-Christian religion, but the nature of that influence is hard to perceive, particularly when previous belief systems are so poorly understood. Complicated processes were at work, for example the creation of local and regional political identities at a scale below that of the whole 'Celtic' or 'Brittonic' world. Burial practices provide a good example. They varied considerably across the south-west peninsula, with similarities and differences both within and between Cornwall and Wessex. There are few changes in burial customs that could be explained in terms of the construction of new ethnic identities alone; some, such as the emergence of enclosed burial grounds, may have had more to do with the cultural influence of one area on the other than ethnically based confrontation between them (Gittos 2002: 205-7). Rather than broad ethnic divisions, the variability of evidence relating to mortuary practice suggests that burials were used to construct identities for both the living and dead on more local scales (Lucy 1998). A better explanation for the differences between ecclesiastical structures in Cornwall and Wessex may be that different social and political groups in different areas were using and adapting a new religious ideology in slightly different ways at different times (Davies 1992). As one of the 'boxers' in Hines' three-cornered fight, politics (and ideology) would have contributed to the construction of 'ethnicity' (Hines 2000: 84); explaining the differences between Cornwall and Wessex in terms of local and regional identities and political developments is more convincing than using a straightforward 'pan-Celtic' ethnicity in opposition to an 'Anglo-Saxon' identity.

Political Structures

The most important early medieval churches were largely the province of the social elite in both western Britain and Anglo-Saxon England, and churches were endowed by and probably staffed by members of the social elite in both Cornwall and Wessex. As Carver has argued, different forms of religious institutions can relate to the different political structures under which they develop, and religious ideology can be actively used by royal authorities to enhance their own power (Higham 1997; Carver 1998a). The evidence considered here for differences between Cornish churches and those of Wessex (and elsewhere, e.g. parts of Wales: Charles-Edwards 1970-2; Jenkins 1988) suggest that the political contexts for the development of churches developed differently, and at different rates, in Cornwall and Wessex. After an initial period in Cornwall when churches and secular elite centres were located side by side (fifth to sixth centuries), there followed a long period when major ecclesiastical centres appear to have existed relatively independent of direct royal control (sixth to tenth centuries).

In Wessex, most churches were also initially established adjacent to royal centres (probably in the seventh and eighth centuries), and many of them seem to have been considered part of the royal estate; here, in contrast to Cornwall, direct royal control seems to have been maintained over a core group of early ecclesiastical establishments throughout the early medieval period. In both regions, however, developments in local lordship brought about changes in church organisation in later phases. Firstly, the independent monasteries that had been founded by the Wessex elite began to set up secondary churches on the estates that had been granted to them, and a similar process may have taken place in Cornwall (e.g. Tintagel and Minster). Secondly, and most importantly, minor lords began to establish small estate churches in great numbers from perhaps the ninth century in Cornwall and the tenth in Wessex, further boosting their growing political power and diminishing the influence of the earlier churches. The apparent differences between the two areas can therefore partly be considered the result of similar trajectories of ecclesiastical development running their courses over slightly different timescales: in both areas ecclesiastical systems were initially very closely linked to royal power, but changed as increasingly localised units of lordship assumed greater political importance.

The Church in the Landscape: Developing a Model

The subtle differences in the relationships between churches and secular elites in Cornwall and Wessex during the early middle ages are probably attributable to the adaptation of Christian ideology to different political contexts by secular leaders. Thus local lords advanced their positions through founding local churches, and the Wessex elite of the tenth century took land and power from the primary Cornish monasteries for themselves. Whilst the differences are important, there were also great similarities between Cornwall and Wessex that make it possible to develop a tentative general model to help explain the organisation of early medieval landscapes across south-west England. This model suggests that the ideology of ecclesiastical centres played a central role in the development of the landscape. It places south-west England squarely in a wider European tradition. The changes in the landscape of the conversion period were fundamental. They included the re-focusing of the settled area, the development of new kinds of estates and the drawing of more formal boundaries around territorial units. Nevertheless, elements of earlier patterns of landscape organisation are virtually always incorporated into later ones, and early medieval Britain was no exception in this respect. One of the earliest strata of landscape organisation recognisable in the English landscape (and probably the Cornish landscape too) is the so-called 'folk-region' or early *regio*. The evidence of charters, hundreds and hundred meeting-place names suggest that these *regiones* formed the geographical basis for many later hundreds and therefore kingdoms (Hooke 1986; Bassett 1989; Klingelhofer 1992; Meaney 1993).

The nature of the landscapes within the early *regiones* was rather different to those of the middle Saxon period. This is suggested not only by the settlement patterns, but also by the surviving evidence from the pre-Christian period relating to the nature of early sites with central-place functions like sacred foci and meeting-places. In Anglo-Saxon England, burial complexes and assembly areas of the pre-Christian period seem to have been extensive and dispersed across the landscape, often encompassing numerous small foci scattered across relatively large tracts of land (Semple 2002, 2004). Other interpretations based mainly on place-names also suggest sites like meeting-places and shrines were found throughout the landscape rather than being concentrated in a few central locations (Wilson 1985; Meaney 1993, 1995;). In Cornwall, possible pre-Christian sacred sites like fogous and standing stones are also dispersed throughout the landscape. As in pagan Anglo-Saxon England, evidence is lacking in the far west for clearly defined religious centres in the pre-Christian period. The change from the *regiones* of the post-Roman period to the multiple estates of the middle Saxon era was a change that encompassed settlements, ritual sites, and the distribution of resources in the wider landscape.

Many landscape historians and archaeologists recognise that these changes in the way the landscape was organised reflect social developments and changes in power structures. Even Tom Williamson's discussion, which stresses the contribution of environmental factors to the local distinctiveness of different medieval landscapes, reflects that:

> The steady development of a more hierarchical society in the course of the Saxon period, with the development of 'multiple estates' and their subsequent fragmentation into a mosaic of local lordships, was perhaps the driving force in landscape change
>
> (Williamson 2003: 182)

The contention of the present discussion is that to a large extent it was the influence of an ideology bound up specifically with *Christianity* that shaped many of the fundamental changes in landscape organisation between the folk-*regiones* of the earliest middle ages and the multiple estates of the first medieval states. A close parallel is suggested by recent work in Scandinavia. Here, as in Britain, late Iron Age landscapes were based around areas of settlement with networks of scattered sacred sites, meeting-places and farms (including elite residences) (Brink 1999: 434-5). After the conversion to Christianity, the orientation of the landscape changed so that churches became the new foci. The earlier scattering of elite residences and meeting-places was replaced with a new hierarchically ordered landscape in which churches acted as the chief central places (Brink 1993: 42; Fabech 1999a: 469-71).

Some scholars have questioned the power of ideologies (including Christianity) to influence the physical landscape in this way. Nancy Gauthier, for example, has argued that a specifically Christian ideology was not the guiding factor behind the location of churches in late Antique Gaul. Instead, she regards their placement as solely controlled by practical considerations such as the availability of suitable plots of land (Gauthier 1999: 199). Similarly, Guy Halsall considers economic and social necessity to have been behind the wide-scale abandonment of Metz in the fifth century, rather than the kind of ideological conflict about living in towns envisaged by Carver (Carver 1993; Halsall 1996: 245-6). Although economic factors can have a great influence, belief systems and religious ideologies can also help define the form of the landscape (Ch. 1, 3-5). The fact that early Christian landscapes were not totally different to their predecessors is not problematic: new ideologies are normally in recursive relationships with their contexts, particularly where monuments are concerned (e.g. D. Edwards 1999). Earlier forms of landscape organisation commonly influence later layouts. In early Christian Europe and the Mediterranean, old pagan sacred landscapes were adapted to accommodate the new Christian ideology rather than being completely refigured (Orselli 1999: 186; Caseau 1999). A reinvented Christian ideology of settlement emerged from the new contexts that were created.

'Holy Cities' and Medieval Landscapes

Blair and Gem have called the ecclesiastical centres which stood at the heart of such landscapes 'Holy Cities', a term that recognises their ultimate origins in the urban civilisation of the Roman Empire (Blair 1996a; Gem 1996). Their model regards such ecclesiastical centres as central to the ideological self-understanding of contemporary societies:

> The buildings [of the churches] were a microcosm of society as a whole, an actualization of society understanding itself as a single community bound together in its religious beliefs: in short a holy city.
>
> (Gem 1996: 1)

Furthermore, the influence of the 'Holy Cities' reached out beyond the bounds of their individual precincts, leading to the establishment of Christian sites throughout the wider landscape (Blair 1996a: 10-12). As a way of structuring the landscape this model can be traced from its origins in the fourth-century Mediterranean world, and other landscapes influenced by the same Christian ideology can be recognised across Britain and Europe in the early middle ages and beyond (Howe 2002). Roymans has explained the form of the later medieval landscape in parts of the southern Netherlands and northern Belgium according to a similar model, where various sources suggest that the landscape was mentally and physically divided into two main zones. The first, inner, zone comprised the fields and settlements, and had the church at its heart. It was 'Christian, civilised and cultural' (Roymans 1995: 18). The outer zone on the other hand contained the heaths, marshes and forests, and was the realm of malevolent supernatural creatures: 'dangerous, uncivilised, rough and ... dominated by evil beings' (ibid. 13). There are clearly strong resonances between Roymans' model and the landscape of early medieval south-west Britain discussed in preceding sections.

There is some debate about when Christianity first developed a 'topographical sense'. Some scholars argue that it had always existed, reproduced in stories about the location of the tomb of Christ and other traditions linked to biblical events (Howe 1997: 65-7). Others consider the idea of Christian sacred space to have been developed primarily during the fourth century, when the growth of the cult of martyrs meant that the histories, tombs and relics of particular saints became linked to particular places (Markus 1994: 269-71). It is clear that the sacredness of certain places became increasingly well-established in the Christian tradition over the course of the fourth and fifth centuries. In particular, Christian buildings and other foci were established in Mediterranean towns. In the later fourth and early fifth centuries, the sacred topographies of cities like Rome, Constantinople, Antioch and Jerusalem were transformed by a succession of new churches (Liebeschuetz 2001: 29-43; Ward-Perkins 2000a).

Both great centres and provincial towns were provided with churches in this way, and new sacred topographies were created throughout the cities of the Mediterranean world. In the eastern Mediterranean and elsewhere Christian churches replaced the earlier pagan cults and sometimes appropriated their buildings or locations, as for example in the cities of Asia Minor (Bayliss 1999; Harl 2001). These changes in late Antique urban settlement structure were a central part of the broader social and ideological readjustments that accompanied the coming together of *Romanitas*[2] and Christianity (Turner 1998: 3; Brogiolo 1999: 120-5). The idea of the 'Holy City' was present in Biblical texts (e.g. in the Revelation of St John 21:2), although the Christian idea of the *civitas dei* ('city of God') probably represented a spiritual community rather than physically urban places, at least until the later fourth century (e.g. Augustine's *City of God*; Markus 1992: 139-155; 1994; *cf.* Gem 1996: 1). The Roman city on the other hand had always been a solid entity, and a keystone of the Roman conception of the world (Alcock 1993: 129-30). When the nature of cities changed between the fourth and eighth centuries, maintaining fewer administrative functions and significantly lower population densities, it was their episcopal and ecclesiastical function that remained (Bouras 1981; Haldon 1999: 13). Late Antique 'Holy Cities' were just as much a characteristic of the western Roman Empire as of the east. In Italy, Gaul and Spain cities developed in similar ways, with contraction of the occupied area accompanied by the development of groups of ecclesiastical buildings (Harries 1992; Brogiolo 1999; Liebeschuetz 2001).

Christianised 'Holy Cities' did not only develop around the rim of the Mediterranean, but also in more distant parts of the Roman world. Ward-Perkins has argued that the form of great Christian centres such as Constantinople provided a direct model for Christian towns in both east and west, not only in the fifth and sixth centuries but also in later times (Ward-Perkins 2000a). He suggests this influence may have extended to even the greatest complexes of early medieval Europe. For example, he regards the juxtaposition of palace and palace chapel in Charlemagne's Aachen as a direct echo of the imperial palace and Hagia Sofia in Constantinople (Ward-Perkins 2000a: 335-8). In northern Gaul the spatial and social development of countless towns like Poitiers, Tours, Nantes and Langres was clearly related to the establishment and development of ecclesiastical complexes from the later fourth century onwards (**Plate 13a & b**; Guigon 1997; Galinié 1999; Knight 1999).

Whether such developments significantly affected Britain in the fourth century is not clear. Jeremy Knight has contrasted the situation in Gaul with that of

---

[2] *Romanitas:* 'the notion of belonging politically or emotionally (or both) to a universal order and culture associated in one way or another with the Roman Empire' (Turner 1998: 1).

Britain, which he characterises as being 'like a geological fault, between the late Roman world and the early medieval world' (Knight 1992: 49). Christianity was practised in late Roman Britain (Thomas 1981b), and in Wales and western England a few examples such as St Mary-de-Lode in Gloucester suggest there were occasional examples of institutional continuity (Bassett 1992). However, there is little evidence to suggest such continuity between the Roman period and the early middle ages was the norm (Bell 1998).

Making a Christian Landscape: 'Holy Cities' in Early Medieval Britain

It was not until the kingdoms of Britain were converted to Christianity between the fifth and seventh centuries that the ideology of the 'Holy City' made a significant impact on the insular world. Peter Brown has made it clear that these 'cities' should not be seen as faintly barbarous or provincial reflections of the 'real' Christian civilisation centred on Rome:

> Many Irishmen and Saxons carried with them 'a Rome in the Mind.' The 'Romans' (as they called themselves) often strove to bring that distant Rome to their own region. They did this through the transfer of relics, through styles of art and building, and through following distinctive ecclesiastical customs. But they did this very much on their own terms. Their efforts were perceived as having brought to their own region a 'microcosm' of a worldwide Christianity. They did not aim to subject the 'periphery' of the local Christianities of the British Isles to a 'center' situated in Rome...Rather, they strove to cancel out the hiatus between 'center' and 'periphery' by making 'little Romes' available on their home ground.
>
> (Brown 2003: 15)

Examples such as Canterbury and York show that sometimes ecclesiastical centres could develop so that their layouts were very similar to those of their continental exemplars (Morris 1986; Blair 2005: 66). It might be objected that there were very few places in Britain between the fifth and eighth centuries—perhaps even none—that could be described as 'urban' in the modern sense; how could the 'Holy City' have functioned without an urban centre as its base? Some recent discussions of the so-called 'monastic towns' of Ireland have highlighted the fact that these settlements were not urban by modern or later medieval standards, and have questioned how appropriate this terminology is (Valante 1998; Graham 1998).[3]

The idea of 'monastic towns' in Britain and Ireland is partly based on documentary sources that describe the sites of churches using vocabulary like *civitas*, which in continental Europe might normally refer to the seats of bishops.[4] The idea that early medieval *civitates* were focused on towns has been questioned not only for Ireland and Britain, but also in Europe where scholars have pointed to the mismatch between the expectations aroused by the documents and the reality revealed by archaeology (Brogiolo 1999: 251; Gauthier 1999: 203-5).

---

[3] *cf.* J. Bradley 1999.
[4] For examples see Campbell 1979; J. Bradley 1999: 136; Charles-Edwards 2000: 119-20; Diaz 2000.

Others have shown how places that may have been described as 'urban' fell short of that mark because the range of activities they accommodated was not compliant with the models developed by historical geographers and archaeologists for detecting 'urban' status (e.g. Hodges 1982: 20-8; Halsall 1996; Graham 1998). Such objections risk taking the documentary evidence and the excavated material out of context, and interpreting them according to the standards of later (or earlier) periods. As Martin Carver has pointed out, the early middle ages are 'not a good period in which to employ the old-fashioned notion of "type-sites" to argue historical process from archaeological data' (Carver 2000).

There was considerable adaptation of existing models at this time. As a result, it may have been possible for the *idea* of the town to be incorporated into a society's ideology and political system, even in the absence of places that were 'urban' in the strict sense. As noted above, ideologies are in recursive relationships with pre-existing structures, including their political, social, and monumental or physical contexts. Newly introduced religious ideologies combine with pre-existing elements to create new contexts, as happened in the cities of the Mediterranean during the fourth century. Sharpe has observed that the absence of urban settings was irrelevant to whether or not an episcopal structure could be established in early medieval Ireland (1984: 243-4). Likewise, pre-existing towns were not necessarily required for the idea of the Christian 'Holy City' to become established in Cornwall or Wessex: where ruined Roman towns or forts could be reinhabited and adapted to suit new ideas they sometimes were, but this was not a pre-condition for the establishment of churches. It was the new church complexes, rather than the old Roman towns, that were acting as central places in the landscape of south-west Britain.

This, then, is the first element in the model: the major ecclesiastical centre, an important focus for spiritual, political and economic life. In both Cornwall and Wessex churches were established by the social elite shortly after they had been converted to Christianity. Unlike the majority of contemporary secular settlements, these churches were founded as permanent centres and were venues for a large range of activities. These included not only rituals associated with their religious function such as the provision of burial and baptism, but also trade and exchange associated with craftworking, the consumption of raw materials, and the collection and disposal of revenues from their associated estates. Even if they were not 'urban' in the Roman or modern sense, they would have stood apart from all other sites in the landscape in the imaginations of contemporary people.

The second element in the model is the territory surrounding the ecclesiastical centre. Recent economically and environmentally minded discussions have highlighted the importance of considering 'central places' like towns and monasteries in the context of surrounding territories or 'microregions' with which they normally had close relationships (e.g. Halsall 1996; Horden & Purcell 2000: 89-122). In the same way that Roman towns had functioned as central places for many economic and social activities, the monasteries and other churches which were in many cases their successors maintained similar relationships, sometimes through the direct control of temporal resources such as rural estates (e.g. Balzaretti 1996). Almost all high-status churches in the South West lay at the heart of major agricultural estates which were either held directly by the ecclesiastical community itself or were associated with royal estate centres located nearby. The churches were normally close to the geographical centres of such estates and as such were surrounded by agricultural land. Churches were normally sited within the richest agricultural land in positions that were prominent and visible, though not normally spectacular. Within the settled land lay numerous farms and settlements, some of which were held directly by members of the ecclesiastical communities, some by tenants of the ecclesiastical or royal estate, and some as small independent estates.

In parallel with these economic relationships were ideological links, which were just as crucial to the establishment and maintenance of the medieval Christian countryside. In both the eastern and western parts of the former Roman Empire, major towns became the seats of bishops, who administered pastoral care to the surrounding regions from cathedral churches that were normally located within the old city walls.[5] As Diaz has written:

> The church, an eminently urban phenomenon and imitator of the monarchic forms of civil power and their organisational schemes, assimilated the *civitas* into the bishop's see and its *territorium* to the diocese, to the point that, over time, *civitas* would become a synonym of *urbs episcopalis.*
>
> (Diaz 2000: 8)

The major churches of the late Antique west were therefore located at the centre of their territories, as the Roman cities of the empire had been before them. The episcopal model of the Roman world was adapted in early medieval Britain so that each kingdom had its bishop. As a result bishops were less plentiful here than in Italy or Gaul. Nevertheless, ecclesiastical centres still developed territorial responsibilities, their rights enforced over *parochiae* that were served by the religious communities. In some areas, perhaps those where royal power was strongest, like Wessex, such territories normally shared common boundaries with units of secular administration in the early middle ages.

At various points in the settled and farmed landscapes surrounding major churches, there were scattered minor religious foci. Whilst some of these were newly created, others were incorporated into the Christian religious landscape from earlier sacred landscapes. In Gaul, the acts of saints during their lives gave a kind of 'sanctity' after their deaths to the whole region associated with an ecclesiastical centre, not just the central church where their relics eventually came to rest (Pietri 1997). In south-west Wales, the territory of St David's incorporated various burial grounds and ritual centres, not only by appropriating them physically through the construction of chapels, but also mentally by working them into stories and traditions associated with the saint (James 1993). Over the course of the early middle ages, pre-existing ritual sites in south-west Britain may have been incorporated into the Christian landscape by a similar power of ecclesiastical centres to reach out and 'convert' their territories.

Outside the core areas of ecclesiastical and royal estates in both Cornwall and Wessex there were other secular settlements. Whilst these may have been located in areas with long histories of settlement, they were often on poorer agricultural land away from the principal river valleys. Many of these formed the nuclei of

---

[5] e.g. in the Byzantine world (Haldon 1999), northern Italy (Wataghin 2000: 211), southern Gaul (Loseby 1992) and Spain (Diaz 2000: 7-8).

minor estates that became increasingly important in the later part of the early middle ages, a process that occurred not only in Britain but also elsewhere in Europe at around the same time (Wickham 1990: 487). As more and more land was reclaimed from the rough ground or woodland and granted to thegns between the ninth and eleventh centuries, the number and size of these estates increased, placing increasing pressure on the core areas of settlement. The holders of these estates also increased their power over their land by founding their own estate churches, creating new multi-function centres in imitation of the older royal and/or ecclesiastical centres.

At the margins of these territories were areas of different resources, such as rough grazing ground, woodland, marsh and moor (e.g. Bodmin Moor, **Plate 16)**. Although small patches of these resources often occurred within the core settlement zones, the largest coherent blocks were commonly distributed around their edges. Though the form of such areas looks 'natural' to the modern eye, they have been created as a result of continuous use by people over thousands of years (Rackham 1986: 286; Caseldine 1999). In a similar way, the ideological value of the 'waste' in the middle ages was different to its value in the present day. The medieval conception of the rough ground as a perilous zone was part of a Christian way of seeing the landscape. Early medieval hagiographers made the spiritual achievements of early saints and monastic founders throughout Europe seem all the more impressive by setting them in fearful areas of woodland, marsh or heath (Howe 2002). This remained the case even when the reality was rather more comfortable. As Wickham has noted, the *horrendum desertum* ('dreadful waste') where the monastery of Fulda was established and the *silva densissima* ('thickest forest') of San Vincenzo al Volturno are 'pious topoi': in reality both were located on the sites of Roman villas amidst cultivated land (Wickham 1990: 481-4). Such literary uses do not weaken the idea of the marginal rough ground as a dangerous zone in the early middle ages, but rather served to reinforce it. Heaths and margins inhabited by terrifying beings are found not only in Anglo-Saxon literature (Semple 1998) but also in documents like the Anglo-Saxon charters of the Crediton area. The banishment of dead criminals to this zone was another way these ideas were further strengthened in late Anglo-Saxon England (Reynolds 1997). The tradition of the waste as a fearful place continued to be developed in Christian spiritual life into the twelfth century and beyond by monastic communities (Menuge 2000). Gallows, where criminals were executed, were still located in marginal positions in northern Europe during the later middle ages, where the rough ground continued to be feared as a dangerous place inhabited by evil supernatural beings (Roymans 1995).

The final element in the model of a Christian landscape is therefore the dangerous margins of the woodland, water, heath, moor and marsh. This zone was not normally the location of permanent settlements in early medieval south-west Britain, and between the fifth and seventh centuries in Cornwall and the sixth and eighth centuries in Wessex, there was a distinct re-focusing of the core settled area away from this marginal land. Permanent re-settlement from the ninth century onwards was accompanied by the establishment of new settlements and fields and the construction of new thegnly residences with minor churches, which drew the ancient margins into the 'Christian' landscape.

Thus although different types of Christian institutions were established at different times in Cornwall and in Wessex over the course of the early middle ages, the general patterns of development or 'trajectories' observable in both areas are very similar. The earliest churches were major royal foundations in both areas, but by the tenth century there was a great proliferation of local churches controlled by local lords. The subtle differences are probably attributable to the different political circumstances in each area, and the times when certain groups were able to use and maintain different sorts of church foundations to their own political advantage. The main difference between the influence exerted in the landscape by the earliest monasteries as compared with the latest estate chapels was probably one of scale, itself largely proportional to the power of the churches' founders. Despite this, the relationship between the church and its surrounding landscape was a recurring pattern across the south-western peninsula, suggesting an existing 'grammar' being reused by landholders and church founders in both Cornwall and Wessex. From the conversion period onwards, the 'ideology of settlement' that helped shape the early medieval landscape encompassed a Christian view of the world: the countless churches across the landscape of Cornwall and western Wessex became pivotal points for a Christian landscape of holy places, settlements, fields and wilder boundary zones.

Bibliography

Abrams, L., 1994. 'An early Anglo-Saxon charter including the Polden estate' in M. Aston and M. Costen (eds), *The Shapwick Project: a Topographical and Historical Study. The Fifth Report*, (Bristol: Dept for Continuing Education, University of Bristol), 72-75.

Adams, J., 1957. 'The mediæval chapels of Cornwall', *Journal of the Royal Institution of Cornwall* n.s. 3 (1), 58-65.

Adams, J., 1959-61. 'Berry Tower, Bodmin', *Devon and Cornwall Notes and Queries* 28, 243-246.

Aitchison, N., 1994. *Armagh and the Royal Centres in Early Medieval Ireland: Monuments, Cosmology and the Past*, (Woodbridge: Boydell).

Alcock, L., 1995. *Cadbury Castle, Somerset: The Early Medieval Archaeology*, (Cardiff: University of Wales Press).

Alcock, S., 1993. *Graecia Capta: The Landscapes of Roman Greece*, (Cambridge: Cambridge University Press).

Aldred, A., 2001. 'Somerset and Exmoor National Park Historic Landscape Characterisation Project, 1999-2000', unpublished report (2 vols), (Taunton: English Heritage/Somerset County Council).

Allan, J., 1994. 'Medieval pottery and the dating of deserted settlements on Dartmoor', *Devon Archaeological Society Proceedings* 52, 141-147.

Allan, J., C. Henderson and R. Higham, 1984. 'Saxon Exeter' in J. Haslam (ed.), *Anglo-Saxon Towns in Southern England*, (Chichester: Phillimore), 385-414.

Altenberg, K., 2003. *Experiencing Landscapes: A Study of Space and Identity in Three Marginal Areas of Medieval Britain and Scandinavia*, Lund Studies in Medieval Archaeology 31 (Stockholm: Almqvist & Wiksell International).

Anderson, O., 1939. *The English Hundred Names: The South-Western Counties*, (Lund: University of Lund).

Andren, A., 1998. *Between Artefacts and Texts: Historical Archaeology in Global Perspective*, (New York: Plenum).

Appleton-Fox, N., 1992. 'Excavations at a Romano-British round; Reawla, Gwinnear, Cornwall' *Cornish Archaeology* 31, 69-123.

ApSimon, A. and E. Greenfield, 1972. 'The excavation of Bronze Age and Iron Age settlements at Trevisker, St Eval, Cornwall', *Proceedings of the Prehistoric Society* 38, 302-381.

Ashbee, P., 1996. 'Halangay Down, St Mary's, Isles of Scilly: excavations 1964-1977', *Cornish Archaeology* 35, 3-201.

Aston, M., 1986. 'Post-Roman central places in Somerset' in E. Grant (ed.), *Central Places, Archaeology and History*, (Sheffield: Dept of Archaeology and Prehistory, University of Sheffield), 49-77.

Aston, M., 1994a. 'Medieval settlement studies in Somerset' in M. Aston and C. Lewis (eds), *The Medieval Landscape of Wessex*, Oxbow Monograph 46 (Oxford: Oxbow Books), 219-237.

Aston, M., 1994b. 'More regressive map analysis of Shapwick parish' in M. Aston and M. Costen (eds), *The Shapwick Project: A Topographical and Historical Study. The Fifth Report*, (Bristol: University of Bristol), 19-26.

Aston, M., 2000a. *Monasteries in the Landscape*, (2nd edn, Stroud: Tempus).

Aston, M., 2000b. 'Monasteries in Somerset' in C. Webster (ed.), *Somerset Archaeology: Papers to Mark 150 Years of the Somerset Archaeological and Natural History Society*, (Taunton: Environment and Property Dept, Somerset County Council), 99-104.

Aston, M. and C. Gerrard, 1999. "Unique, traditional and charming". The Shapwick project, Somerset', *Antiquaries Journal* 79, 1-58.

Aston, M., M. Martin and A. Jackson, 1998. 'The potential for heavy metal soil analysis on low status archaeological sites at Shapwick, Somerset', *Antiquity* 72, 838-846.

Atherton, M., 2002. 'Saxon or Celt? Caedmon, "The Seafarer" and the Irish tradition' in M. Atherton (ed.), *Celts and Christians*, (Cardiff: University of Wales Press), 79-99.

Attenborough, F., 1922. *The Laws of the Earliest English Kings*, (Cambridge: Cambridge University Press).

Auduy, M., B. Dix and D. Parsons, 1995. 'The tower of All Saints' church, Earls Barton', *Archaeological Journal* 152, 73-94.

Austin, D., R. Dagett and M. Walker, 1980. 'Farms and fields in Okehampton Park, Devon: the problems of studying medieval landscape', *Landscape History* 2, 39-57.

Austin, D., G. Gerrard and T. Greeves, 1989. 'Tin and agriculture in the middle ages and beyond: landscape archaeology in St Neot parish, Cornwall', *Cornish Archaeology* 28, 5-251.

Balzaretti, R., 1996. 'Cities, *emporia* and monasteries: local economies in the Po valley, *c.* AD 700-875' in N. Christie and S. Loseby (eds), *Towns in Transition: Urban Evolution in Late Antiquity and the Early Middle Ages*, (Aldershot: Scolar Press), 213-234.

Barker, G., 1995. *A Mediterranean Valley: Landscape Archaeology and* Annales *History in the Biferno Valley*, (London: Leicester University Press).

Barker, K., 1980. 'The early Christian topography of Sherborne', *Antiquity* 54, 229-231.

Barker, K., 1984. 'Sherborne in Dorset: an early ecclesiastical settlement and its estate', *Anglo-Saxon Studies in Archaeology and History* 3, 1-33.

Barnatt, J., 1999. 'Peak National Park: a changing landscape' in G. Fairclough (ed.), *Historic Landscape Characterisation: 'The State of the Art'* (London: English Heritage), 41-50.

Barnes, G., 1999. 'Buddhist landscapes of east Asia' in W. Ashmore and B. Knapp (eds), *Archaeologies of Landscape*, (Oxford: Blackwell), 101-123.

Bassett, S., 1989. 'In search of the origins of Anglo-Saxon kingdoms' in S. Bassett (ed.), *The Origins of Anglo-Saxon Kingdoms*, (Leicester: Leicester University Press), 3-27.

Bassett, S., 1992. 'Church and diocese in the west midlands: the transition from British to Anglo-Saxon control' in J. Blair and R. Sharpe (eds) *Pastoral Care Before the Parish*, (London: Leicester University Press), 13-40.

Bassett, S., 1998. 'The origins of the parishes of the Deerhurst area' Deerhurst Lecture 1997 (Deerhurst: Friends of Deerhurst Church).

Bayliss, R., 1999. 'Usurping the urban image: the experience of ritual topography in the late antique cities of the Near East', in P. Baker et al. (eds) *TRAC98, Proceeding of the 8th Annual Theoretical Roman Archaeology Conference (Leicester 1998)*, (Oxford: Oxbow), 59-71.

Bearman, R., 1994. *Charters of the Redvers Family and the Earldom of Devon 1090-1217*, Devon and Cornwall Record Society, n.s. 37 (Exeter: Devon and Cornwall Record Society).

Bell, R., 1996. 'Bath Abbey: some new perspectives', *Bath History* 6, 7-24.

Bell, T., 1998. 'Churches on Roman buildings: Christian associations and Roman masonry in Anglo-Saxon England', *Medieval Archaeology* 48, 1-18.

Bender, B., 1993. 'Introduction: landscape – meaning and action' in B. Bender (ed.), *Landscape: Politics and Perspectives*, (Oxford: Berg), 1-17.

Bennet, J., 1998. 'The Linear B archives and the kingdom of Nestor' in J. Davis (ed.), *Sandy Pylos: An Archaeological History from Nestor to Navarino*, (Austin: University of Texas Press), 111-133.

Biek, L., 1994. 'Tin ingots found at Praa Sands, Breage, 1974', *Cornish Archaeology* 33, 57-70.

Bintliff, J., 1991. 'The contribution of an *Annaliste*/structural history approach to archaeology' in J. Bintliff (ed.), *The* Annales *School and Archaeology*, (London: Leicester University Press), 1-33.

Bitel, L., 1990. *Isle of the Saints: Monastic Settlement and Christian Community in Early Ireland*, (Cork: Cork University Press).

Blair, J., 1983. 'Wimborne Minster: the early development of the town', *Archaeological Journal* 140, 37-8.

Blair, J., 1985. 'Secular minster churches in Domesday Book' in P. Sawyer (ed.), *Domesday Book: a Reassessment*, (London: Arnold), 104-142.

Blair, J., 1987. 'Local churches in Domesday Book and before' in J. Holt (ed.), *Domesday Studies*, (Woodbridge: Boydell), 265-278.

Blair, J., 1988a. 'Minster churches in the landscape' in D. Hooke (ed.) *Anglo-Saxon Settlements*, (Oxford: Blackwell), 35-58.

Blair, J., 1988b. 'Introduction: from minster to parish church' in J. Blair (ed.), *Minsters and Parish Churches: the Local Church in Transition 950-1200*, Oxford Committee for Archaeology Monograph 17 (Oxford: Oxford University Committee for Archaeology), 1-19.

Blair, J., 1991. *Early Medieval Surrey: Landholding, Church and Settlement before 1300*, (Stroud: Sutton).

Blair, J., 1992. 'Anglo-Saxon minsters: a topographical review' in J. Blair and R. Sharpe (eds) *Pastoral Care Before the Parish*, (London: Leicester University Press), 226-266.

Blair, J., 1994. *Anglo-Saxon Oxfordshire*, (Stroud: Tempus).

Blair, J., 1995a. 'Palaces or minsters? Northampton and Cheddar reconsidered', *Anglo-Saxon England* 24, 97-121.

Blair, J., 1995b. 'Anglo-Saxon pagan shrines and their prototypes', *Anglo-Saxon Studies in Archaeology and History* 8, 1-28.

Blair, J., 1995c. 'Debate: ecclesiastical organisation and pastoral care in Anglo-Saxon England', *Early Medieval Europe* 4, 193-212.

Blair, J., 1996a. 'Churches in the early English landscape: social and cultural contexts' in J. Blair and C. Pyrah (eds) *Church Archaeology: Research Directions for the Future*, Council for British Archaeology Research Report 104 (York: CBA), 6-18.

Blair, J., 1996b. 'The minsters of the Thames' in J. Blair and B. Golding (eds), *The Cloister and the World: Essays in Medieval History in Honour of Barbara Harvey*, (Oxford: Oxford University Press), 5-28.

Blair, J., 1997. 'Saint Cuthman, Steyning and Bosham', *Sussex Archaeological Collections* 135, 173-192.

Blair, J., 1999. 'Bath' in M. Lapidge, J. Blair, S. Keynes and D. Scragg (eds), *The Blackwell Encyclopaedia of Anglo-Saxon England* (Oxford: Blackwell), 54.

Blair, J., 2002. 'A saint for every minster? Local cults in Anglo-Saxon England' in A. Thacker and R. Sharpe (eds), *Local Saints and Local Churches in the Early Medieval West*, (Oxford: Oxford University Press), 455-486.

Blair, J., 2005. *The Church in Anglo-Saxon Society*, (Oxford: Oxford University Press).

Blair, J. and N. Orme, 1995. 'The Anglo-Saxon minster and cathedral at Exeter: twin churches?' *Friends of Exeter Cathedral Annual Report* 65, 24-26.

Blair, J., and R. Sharpe, 1992. 'Introduction' in J. Blair and R. Sharpe (eds), *Pastoral Care Before the Parish*, (London: Leicester University Press), 1-12.

Boddington, A., 1996. *Raunds Furnells. The Anglo-Saxon Church and Churchyard*, (London: English Heritage).

Bouras, C., 1981. 'City and village: urban design and architecture', *Acts of the 16th International Byzantine Congress* Vol. 31, (Vienna), 611-653.

Bowen, E., 1969. *Saints, Seaways, and Settlements in the Celtic Lands*, (Cardiff : University of Wales Press).

Bradley, I., 1999. *Celtic Christianity: Making Myths and Chasing Dreams*, (Edinburgh: Edinburgh University Press).

Bradley, J., 1994. 'Killaloe: a pre-Norman borough?', *Peritia* 8, 170-179.

Bradley, J., 1999. 'Urbanization in early medieval Ireland' in C. Karkov, K. Wickham-Crowley and B. Young (eds), *Spaces of the Living and the Dead: An Archaeological Dialogue*, American Early Medieval Studies 3 (Oxford: Oxbow), 133-147.

Bradley, R., 1993. *Altering the Earth: the Origins of Monuments in Britain and Continental Europe*, (Edinburgh: Society of Antiquaries of Scotland).

Bradley, R., 1998. *The Significance of Monuments: On the Shaping of Human Experience in Neolithic and Bronze Age Europe*, (London: Routledge).

Bradley, R., 2000a. *An Archaeology of Natural Places*, (London: Routledge).

Bradley, R., 2000b. 'Mental and material landscapes in prehistoric Britain' in D. Hooke (ed.), *Landscape: The Richest Historical Record*, (Amesbury: Society for Landscape Studies Supplementary Series 1), 1-11.

Braudel, F., 1972. *The Mediterranean and the Mediterranean World in the Age of Philip II*, (2nd edn, London: Collins).

Brink, S., 1993. 'Kyrkan organisevar bygden', *Jamten* (for 1993), 40-48.

Brink, S., 1998. 'The formation of the Scandinavian parish, with some remarks regarding the English impact on the process' in J. Hill and M. Swan (eds), *The Community, the Family and the Saint: Patterns of Power in Early Medieval Europe*, International Medieval Research 4 (Turnhout: Brepols), 19-44.

Brink, S., 1999. 'Social order in the early Scandinavian landscape' in C. Fabech and J. Ringtved (eds), *Settlement and Landscape*, (Moesgård: Jutland Archaeological Society), 423-439.

Britnell, W., 1990. 'Capel Maelog, Llandrindod Wells, Powys: excavations 1984-87', *Medieval Archaeology* 34, 27-96.

Brogiolo, G., 1999. 'Ideas of the town in Italy during the transition from antiquity to the middle ages' in G. Brogiolo and B. Ward-Perkins (eds), *The Idea and Ideal of the Town between Late Antiquity and the Early Middle Ages*, (Leiden: Brill), 99-126.

Brook, D., 1992. 'The early church east and west of Offa's Dyke' in N. Edwards and A. Lane (eds), *The Early Church in Wales and the West*, Oxbow Monograph 16 (Oxford: Oxbow), 77-89.

Brooke, C., 1982 'Rural ecclesiastical institutions in England', *Settimane di Studio del Centro Italiano di Studi sull'Alto Medioevo* 28, 685-711.

Brown, P., 2003. *The Rise of Western Christendom: Triumph and Diversity, AD 200-1000*, 2nd edition (Oxford: Blackwell).

Bruce-Mitford, R., 1997. *Morgan Porth: a Settlement of the Late Saxon Period on the North Cornish Coast*, (London: English Heritage).

Burrow, I., 1981. *Hillfort and Hill-Top Settlement in Somerset in the First to Eighth Centuries A.D.*, British Archaeological Reports (British Series) 91 (Oxford: BAR).

Byock, J., 2001. *Viking Age Iceland*, (London: Penguin).

Cambridge, E., 1984 'The early church in County Durham: a reassessment', *Journal of the British Archaeological Association* 137, 65-85.

Cambridge, E. and D. Rollason, 1995. 'The pastoral organisation of the Anglo-Saxon church: a review of the "Minster Hypothesis"', *Early Medieval Europe* 4, 87-104.

Campbell, E., 1996 'The archaeological evidence for external contacts: imports, trade and economy in Celtic Britain A.D. 400-800' in K. Dark (ed.), *External Contacts and the Economy of Late Roman and Post-Roman Britain*, (Woodbridge: Boydell), 83-96.

Campbell, J., 1979. 'Bede's words for places' in P. Sawyer (ed.), *Names, Words and Graves: Early Medieval Settlement*, (Leeds: School of History, University of Leeds), 34-54.

Canner, A., 1982. *The Parish of Tintagel: Some Historical Notes*, (Tintagel: Tintagel PCC).

Carlyon, P., 1982. 'A Romano-British site at Kilhallon, Tywardreath: excavation in 1975', *Cornish Archaeology* 21, 155-170.

Carmichael, D., 1994. 'Places of power: Mescalero Apache sacred sites and sensitive areas' in D. Carmichael, J. Hubert, B. Reeves and A. Schande (eds), *Sacred Sites, Sacred Places* (London: Routledge), 89-98.

Carr, J., 1985. 'Excavations on the Mound, Glastonbury, Somerset, 1971', *Proceedings of the Somerset Archaeological and Natural History Society* 129, 37-62.

Carr, R., A. Tester and P. Murphy, 1988. 'The middle-Saxon settlement at Staunch Meadow, Brandon', *Antiquity* 62, 71-77.

Carver, M., 1989. 'Kingship and material culture in early Anglo-Saxon East Anglia', in S. Bassett (ed.), *The Origins of Anglo-Saxon Kingdoms*, (Leicester: Leicester University Press), 141-158.

Carver, M., 1993. *Arguments in Stone: Archaeological Research and the European Town in the First Millennium*, Oxbow Monograph 29 (Oxford: Oxbow).

Carver, M., 1996. 'Transitions to Islam: urban roles in the east and south Mediterranean, fifth to tenth centuries AD' in N. Christie and S. Loseby (eds), *Towns in Transition: Urban Evolution in Late Antiquity and the Early Middle Ages*, (Aldershot: Scolar Press), 184-212.

Carver, M., 1998a. 'Conversion and politics on the eastern seaboard of Britain: some archaeological indicators' in B. Crawford (ed.), *Conversion and Christianity in the North Sea World*, (St Andrews: University of St Andrews), 11-40.

Carver, M., 1998b. *Sutton Hoo: Burial Ground of Kings?* (London: British Museum Press).

Carver, M., 2000. 'Town and anti-town in first millennium Europe' in A. Buko and P. Urbanczyk (eds), *Archeologia w Teorii i w Praktyce*, (Warsaw), 373-396 .

Carver, M., 2001. 'Why that? Why there? Why then? The politics of early medieval monumentality' in H. Hamerow and A. MacGregor (eds), *Image and Power in the Archaeology of Early Medieval Britain*, (Oxford: Oxbow Books), 1-22.

Carver, M., 2002a. 'Marriages of true minds: archaeology with texts' in B. Cunliffe, W. Davies and C. Renfrew (eds), *Archaeology: the Widening Debate*, (Oxford: Oxford University Press), 465-496.

Carver, M., 2002b. 'Reflections on the meanings of monumental barrows in Anglo-Saxon England' in S. Lucy and A. Reynolds (eds), *Burial in Early Medieval England and Wales*, Society for Medieval Archaeology Monograph 17 (Leeds: Society for Medieval Archaeology), 132-143.

Carver, M., 2003. 'Introduction: northern Europeans negotiate their future' in M. Carver (ed.), *The Cross Goes North: Processes of Conversion in Northern Europe, AD 300-1300*, (Woodbridge: Boydell), 3-13.

Caseau, B., 1999. 'Sacred landscapes' in G. Bowersock, P. Brown and O. Grabar (eds), *Late Antiquity: a Guide to the Postclassical World*, (Cambridge, Massachusetts: Harvard University Press), 21-59.

Caseldine, C., 1999. 'Environmental setting' in R. Kain and W. Ravenhill (eds), *Historical Atlas of South-West England*, (Exeter: University of Exeter Press), 25-34.

Caseldine, C. and J. Hatton, 1994. 'Into the mists? Thoughts on the prehistoric and historic environmental history of Dartmoor', *Devon Archaeological Society Proceedings* 52, 35-47.

CAU, 1998a. 'St Austell north-east distributor road', *Archaeology Alive 6: A Review of Work by the Cornwall Archaeological Unit 1997-98*, 37-38.

CAU, 1998b. 'Round-up for 1997-8' *Archaeology Alive 6: A Review of Work by the Cornwall Archaeological Unit 1997-98*, 7-19.

Chadwick, O., 1954. 'The evidence of dedications in the early history of the Welsh church' in N. Chadwick (ed.), *Studies in the Early History of Britain*, (Cambridge: Cambridge University Press), 173-188.

Champion, T., 1977. 'Chalton,' *Current Archaeology* 59, 364-369.

Charles-Edwards, T., 1970-2. 'The seven bishop-houses of Dyfed', *Bulletin of the Board of Celtic Studies* 24, 247-262.

Charles-Edwards, T., 1976. 'Boundaries in Irish Law' in P. Sawyer (ed.), *Medieval Settlement, Continuity and Change*, (London: Edward Arnold), 83-87.

Charles-Edwards, T., 2000. *Early Christian Ireland*, (Cambridge: Cambridge University Press).

Chavarría, A. and T. Lewit, 2004. 'Archaeological research on the late Antique countryside: a bibliographical essay' in W. Bowden, L. Lavan and C. Machado (eds), *Recent Research on the Late Antique Countryside*, (Leiden: Brill), 3-51.

Clark, J., J. Darlington and G. Fairclough, 2004. *Using Historic Landscape Characterisation*, (London: English Heritage/Lancashire County Council).

Cole, D., 1997. 'The Cornish: identity and genetics – an alternative view', *Cornish Studies* n.s. 5, 21-29.

Coleman, S. and J. Elsner, 1995. *Pilgrimage: Past and Present in the World Religions*, (London: British Museum Press).

Colgrave, B. (ed.), 1956. *Felix's Life of St Guthlac*, (Cambridge: Cambridge University Press).

Constable, G., 1982. 'Monasteries, rural churches and the *cura animarum* in the early middle ages', *Settimane de Studio del Centro Italiano di Studi Sull'Alto Medioevo* 28, 349-389.

Corcos, N., 1984. 'Early estates on the Poldens and the origins of settlement at Shapwick', *Proceedings of the Somerset Archaeological and Natural History Society* 127, 47-54.

Corcos, N., 2001. 'Churches as pre-historic ritual monuments: a review and phenomenological perspective from Somerset', *Assemblage* 6, http:// www.shef.ac.uk/~assem/issue6/index .htm, (last consulted 15/12/01).

Cornwall County Council, 1994. 'Cornwall HLC 'types' maps' (Unpublished historic landscape characterisation maps, Cornwall Archaeological Unit, Cornwall County Council, Truro).

Cornwall County Council, 1996. *Cornwall Landscape Assessment 1994*, (Truro: Cornwall County Council).

Costen, M., 1992a. 'Dunstan, Glastonbury and the economy of Somerset in the tenth century' in M. Ramsey, M. Sparks and T. Tatton-Brown (eds), *St Dunstan: His Life, Times and Cult*, (Woodbridge: Boydell), 25-44.

Costen, M., 1992b. *The Origins of Somerset*, (Manchester: Manchester University Press).

Costen, M. 1994. 'Settlement in Wessex in the tenth century: the charter evidence' in M. Aston and C. Lewis (eds), *The Medieval Landscape of Wessex*, (Oxford: Oxbow Monograph 46), 97-107.

Cox, P., 1988. 'A seventh-century inhumation cemetery at Shepherd's Farm, Ulwell near Swanage, Dorset', *Proceedings of the Dorset Natural History and Archaeological Society* 110, 37-45.

Cox, P., 1999. 'Archaeological Investigations Undertaken During the Installation of a new Surface Water Drainage System at St Bartholomew's Church, Shapwick, Dorset', Unpublished report, AC Archaeology.

Cramp, R., 1975. 'Anglo-Saxon sculpture of the Reform period' in D. Parsons (ed.), *Tenth Century Studies*, (London: Phillimore), 184-199.

Cramp, R., 2006. *Corpus of Anglo-Saxon Stone Sculpture, Vol 7: The South West of England*, (London: British Academy).

Creighton, O. and J. Freeman, 2006 (forthcoming). 'Castles and the medieval landscape' in S. Turner (ed.), *Medieval Devon and Cornwall: Shaping the Ancient Countryside*, (Macclesfield: Windgather Press).

Crumley, C., 1999. 'Sacred landscapes: constructed and conceptualised' in W. Ashmore and B. Knapp (eds), *Archaeologies of Landscape: Contemporary Perspectives*, (Oxford: Blackwell), 269-276.

Cubitt, C., 1995. *Anglo-Saxon Church Councils c.650-c.850*, (London: Leicester University Press).

Cuissard, C., 1881-3. 'Vie de Saint Paul de Léon en bretagne d'après un manuscrit de Fleury-sur-Loire conservé à la bibliotheque publique d'Orléans', *Revue Celtique* 5, 413-460 .

Cunliffe, B., 1975. *Excavations at Portchester Castle. Vol. 2: Saxon*, (London: Society of Antiquaries).

Cunliffe, B., 1997. *The Ancient Celts*, (Oxford: Oxford University Press).

Daniels, R., 1988. 'The Anglo-Saxon monastery at Church Close, Hartlepool, Cleveland', *Archaeological Journal* 145, 158-210.

Dark, K., 2000. *Britain and the End of the Roman Empire*, (Stroud: Tempus).

Dark, K., 2001. *Byzantine Pottery*, (Stroud: Tempus).

Darlington, R., 1955. 'A history of Wiltshire' in B. Pugh and E. Crittall (eds), *Victoria County History of Wiltshire 2*, (Oxford: Oxford University Press), 24-34.

Darvill, T., C. Gerrard and B. Startin, 1993. 'Identifying and protecting historic landscapes', *Antiquity* 67, 563-574.

Darvill, T., 1997 'Landscapes and the archaeologist' in K. Barker and T. Darvill (eds), *Making English Landscapes*, (Oxford: Oxbow Monograph 93), 70-91.

Darvill, T., 1999 'The historic environment, historic landscapes, and space-time-action models in landscape archaeology' in P. Ucko and R. Layton (eds), *The Archaeology and Anthropology of*

Landscape: Shaping Your Landscape, (London: Routledge), 104-118.

Davey, N., 1964. 'A pre-Conquest church and baptistery at Potterne', *Wiltshire Archaeological and Natural History Magazine* 59, 116-123.

Davey, N., 1990. 'Medieval timber buildings at Potterne', *Wiltshire Archaeological and Natural History Magazine* 83, 57-69.

David, P., 1947. *Études Historiques sur la Galice et le Portugal du VIe au XIIe Siècle*, (Lisbon: Institut Français au Portugal).

Davies, J., 1998. 'The Book of Llandaff: a twelfth-century perspective', *Anglo-Norman Studies* 21, 31-46.

Davies, J., 2002. 'The saints of south Wales and the Welsh church' in A. Thacker and R. Sharpe (eds), *Local Saints and Local Churches in the Early Medieval West*, (Oxford: Oxford University Press), 361-395.

Davies, O., 1996. *Celtic Christianity in Early Medieval Wales*, (Cardiff: University of Wales Press).

Davies, W., 1978. *An Early Welsh Microcosm*, (London: Royal Historical Society).

Davies, W., 1982. 'The Latin charter-tradition in Western Britain, Brittany and Ireland in the early medieval period' in D. Whitelock, R. McKitterick and D. Dumville (eds) *Ireland in Early Medieval Europe: Studies in Memory of Kathleen Hughes*, (Cambridge: Cambridge University Press), 258-280.

Davies, W., 1992. 'The myth of the Celtic Church' in N. Edwards and A. Lane (eds), *The Early Church in Wales and the West*, Oxbow Monograph 16 (Oxford: Oxbow Books), 12-21.

Davies, W., 1996. ''Protected space' in Britain and Ireland in the middle ages' in B. Crawford (ed.) *Soctland in Dark Age Britain*, (St Andrews: St John's House Papers 6), 1-19.

Davies, W., 1998. 'Charter-writing and its uses in early medieval Celtic societies' in H. Pryce (ed.), *Literacy in Medieval Celtic Societies*, (Cambridge: Cambridge University Press), 99-112.

Davis, J., 1998. 'Glimpses of Messenia past' in J. Davis (ed.), *Sandy Pylos: an Archaeological History from Nestor to Navarino*, (Austin: University of Texas Press), xxix-xliii .

Davis, J., S. Alcock, J. Bennet, Y. Lolos and C. Shelmerdine, 1997. 'The Pylos regional archaeological project. Part I: overview and survey', *Hesperia* 66 (3), 391-509.

Diaz, P., 2000. 'City and territory in Hispania in late Antiquity' in G. Brogiolo, N. Gauthier and N. Christie (eds), *Towns and their Territories between Late Antiquity and the Early Middle Ages*, (Leiden: Brill), 3-35.

Doble, G., 1937. *Pontificale Lanaletense*, Henry Bradshaw Society Vol. 74 (London).

Doble, G., 1960. *The Saints of Cornwall, Part 1: Saints of the Land's End District*, (Truro: Dean and Chapter of Truro).

Doble, G., 1962. *The Saints of Cornwall, Part 2: Saints of the Lizard District*, (Truro: Dean and Chapter of Truro).

Doble, G., 1964. *The Saints of Cornwall, Part 3: Saints of the Fal*, (Truro: Dean and Chapter of Truro).

Doble, G., 1965. *The Saints of Cornwall, Part 4: Saints of the Newquay, Padstow and Bodmin District*, (Truro: Dean and Chapter of Truro).

Doble, G., 1970. *The Saints of Cornwall, Part 5: Saints of Mid-Cornwall*, (Truro: Dean and Chapter of Truro).

Doble, G., 1997. *The Saints of Cornwall, Part 6: Saints of North Cornwall*, (Felinfach: Llanerch Publishers).

Dommelen, P. v., 1999. 'Exploring everyday places and cosmologies' in W. Ashmore and B. Knapp (eds), *Archaeologies of Landscape: Contemporary Perspectives*, (Oxford: Blackwell), 277-285.

Dudley, D. and E. Minter, 1965. 'The excavation of a medieval settlement at Treworld, Lesnewth', *Cornish Archaeology* 5, 44-52.

Dymond, R., 1856. 'Devonshire fields and hedges', *Journal of the Bath* and *West of England Society* 4, 132-148.

Eagles, B., 2001. 'Anglo-Saxon presence and culture in Wiltshire c.AD450-c.675' in P. Ellis (ed.), *Roman Wiltshire and After: Papers in Honour of Ken Annable*, (Devizes: Wiltshire Archaeological and Natural History Society), 199-233.

Edmonds, E., M. McKeown and M. Williams, 1975. *British Regional Geology: South-West England*, (London: HMSO).

Edwards, D., 1999. 'Christianity and Islam in the Middle Nile: towards a study of religion and social change in the long term' in T. Insoll (ed.), *Case Studies in Archaeology and World Religion: The Proceedings of the Cambridge Conference*, British Archaeological Reports International Series S755 (Oxford: BAR), 94-104.

Edwards, N., 1999. 'Viking-influenced sculpture in north Wales: its ornament and context', *Church Archaeology* 3, 5-16.

Edwards, N. and A. Lane, 1992. 'The archaeology of the early church in Wales: an introduction' in N. Edwards and A. Lane (eds), *The Early Church in Wales and the West*, Oxbow Monograph 16 (Oxford: Oxbow), 1-11.

English Nature, 2005. 'Ancient woodland inventory (provisional) for England', http://www.english-nature.org.uk/pubs/gis (last consulted 20 May 2005).

Entwistle, R., M. Fulford and F. Raymond, 1994. *Salisbury Plain Project 1993-94 : Interim Report*, (Reading: University of Reading).

Everson, P., 1977. 'Excavations in the vicarage garden at Brixworth, 1972', *Journal of the British Archaeological Association* 130, 55-122.

Exeter Archaeology, forthcoming. 'A prehistoric, Roman and medieval site at Cleave Hill, East Devon', unpublished report (Exeter: Exeter City Council).

Fabech, C., 1999a. 'Centrality in sites and landscapes' in C. Fabech and J. Ringtved (eds), *Settlement and Landscape*, (Moesgård: Jutland Archaeological Society), 455-473.

Fabech, C., 1999b. 'Organising the landscape. A matter of production, power and religion', *Anglo-Saxon Studies in Archaeology and History* 10, 37-47.

Fairbrother, J., 1990. *Faccombe Netherton. Excavations of a Saxon and Medieval Manorial Complex*, British Museum Occasional Paper 74 (London: British Museum).

Fairclough, G.J., Lambrick, G. and Hopkins, D. 2002. 'Historic Landscape Characterisation in England and a Hampshire case study' in G. Fairclough and S. Rippon (eds), *Europe's Cultural Landscape: Archaeologists and the Management of Change*, (Brussels and London: Europae Archaeologiae Consilium and English Heritage), 69-83.

Fairclough, G., G. Lambrick and A. McNab (eds), 1999. *Yesterday's World, Tomorrow's Landscape: The English Heritage Landscape Project 1992-94*, (London: English Heritage).

Faith, R., 1997. *The English Peasantry and the Growth of Lordship*, (London: Leicester University Press).

Farley, A. (ed.), 1783-1816. Domesday Book, *Associated Texts, Introduction and Indices*, (London: Record Commission).

Farmer, D. (ed.), 1990. *Bede: Ecclesiastical History of the English People*, (Harmondsworth: Penguin).

Fasham, P. and R. Whinney, 1991. *Archaeology and the M3*, Hampshire Field Club and Archaeological Society Monograph 7 (Winchester: Hampshire Field Club/Trust for Wessex Archaeology).

Faulkner, N., 2000. *The Decline and Fall of Roman Britain*, (Stroud: Tempus).

Faull, M., 1984. 'Late Anglo-Saxon settlement patterns in Yorkshire' in M. Faull (ed.), *Studies in Late Anglo-Saxon Settlement*, (Oxford: Oxford University Department for Continuing Education), 129-142.

Fawtier, R., 1912. *La Vie de Saint Samson: Essai de Critique Hagiographique*, (Paris: Champion).

Feinman, G., 1997. 'Thoughts on new approaches to combining the archaeological and historical records', *Journal of Archaeological Method and Theory* 4, 367-377.

Fellows-Jensen, G., 1995. 'Scandinavian settlement in Yorkshire - through the rear-view mirror' in B. Crawford (ed.), *Scandinavian Settlement in Northern Britain*, (London: Leicester University Press), 170-186.

Février, R.-A., 1996. 'Poitiers: Baptistère Saint-Jean' in L. Maurin *et al.*, *Les Premiers Monuments Chrétien de la France*, (Paris: Ministère de la Culture/Picard éditeur), 290-301.

Finberg, H., 1951. *Tavistock Abbey: A Study in the Social and Economic History of Devon*, (Cambridge: Cambridge University Press).

Finberg, H., 1953a. 'Sherborne, Glastonbury and the expansion of Wessex', *Transactions of the Royal Historical Society* 5ᵗʰ series, 3, 101-124.

Finberg, H., 1953b. *The Early Charters of Devon and Cornwall*, Dept of English Local History, Occasional Papers 2 (Leicester: University College of Leicester) .

Finberg, H., 1964a. *The Early Charters of Wessex*, (Leicester: Leicester University Press).

Finberg, H., 1964b. 'The making of a boundary' in H. Finberg, *Lucerna: Some Studies on Problems in the Early History of England*, London: Macmillan, 161-180.

Finberg, H., 1969a. 'The open field in Devon' in H. Finberg, *West-Country Historical Studies*, (Newton Abbot: David & Charles), 129-151.

Finberg, H., 1969b. 'Fact and fiction from Crediton' in H. Finberg, *West-Country Historical Studies*, (Newton Abbot: David & Charles), 29-69.

Flanagan, D., 1984. 'The Christian impact on early Ireland: place-name evidence' in M. Richter (ed.), *Irland und Europa: Ireland and Europe*, (Stuttgart: Klett-Cotta), 25-51.

Flatrès, P., 1949. 'La structure agraire ancienne du Devon et du Cornwall et les enclôtures des XIIIe et XIVe siècles', *Annales de Bretagne* 56, 130-134.

Fleming, A. 1998. *The Dartmoor Reaves*, (London: Batsford).

Fleming, R., 1985. 'Monastic lands and England's defence in the viking age', *English Historical Review* 395, 247-265.

Fletcher, R., 1997. *The Conversion of Europe: From Paganism to Christianity, 371-1386 AD*, (London: Harper Collins).

Fleuriot, L., 1980. *Les Origines de la Bretagne*, (Paris: Payot).

Flobert, P., 1997. *La Vie Ancienne de Saint Samson de Dol*, (Paris: CNRS).

Foot, S., 1989. 'Parochial ministry in early Anglo-Saxon England: the role of monastic communities', *Studies in Church History* 26, 43-54.

Ford, S., 1987. *East Berkshire Archaeological Survey*, Occasional Paper 1, Dept of Highways and Planning, Berkshire County Council (Reading: Berkshire County Council).

Foster, S., 1987. 'A gazetteer of the Anglo-Saxon sculpture in historic Somerset', *Proceedings of the Somerset Archaeological and Natural History Society* 131, 49-80.

Fowler, P., 2000. *Landscape Plotted and Pieced. Landscape History and Local Archaeology in Fyfield and Overton, Wiltshire*, (London: Society of Antiquaries).

Fowler, P. and C. Thomas, 1962. 'Arable fields of the pre-Norman period at Gwithian', *Cornish Archaeology* 1, 61-84.

Fox, A., 1961. 'Archaeology and early history', *Transcactions of the Devonshire Association* 93, 79-80.

Fox, A., 1995. 'Tin ingots from Bigbury bay, South Devon', *Devon Archaeological Society Proceedings* 53, 11-23.

Fox, H., 1972. 'Field systems of east and south Devon, part 1: east Devon', *Transactions of the Devonshire Association* 104, 81-135.

Fox, H., 1973. 'Outfield cultivation in Devon and Cornwall: a reinterpretation' in M. Havinden (ed.), *Husbandry* and *Marketing in the South-West*, Exeter Papers in Economic History 8 (Exeter: University of Exeter), 19-38.

Fox, H. 1991. 'Farming practice and techniques: Devon and Cornwall', in E. Miller (ed.), *The Agrarian History of England and Wales, Vol. III, 1348-1500*, (Cambridge: Cambridge University Press), 303-323.

Fox, H. and O. Padel, 1998. *Cornish Lands of the Arundells of Lanherne*, Devon and Cornwall Record Society n.s. 41 (Exeter: Devon and Cornwall Record Society).

Fredengren, C., 2002. *Crannogs*, (Bray: Wordwell Books).

Frodsham, P. and C. O'Brien (eds), 2005. *Yeavering: People, Power and Place*, (Stroud: Tempus).

Fulford, M., 1989. 'Byzantium and Britain: a Mediterranean perspective on post-Roman Mediterranean imports in Western Britain and Ireland', *Medieval Archaeology* 33, 1-6.

Fyfe, R., 2006 (forthcoming). 'Palaeoenvironmental perspectives on the development of the medieval landscape' in S. Turner (ed.), *Medieval Devon and Cornwall: Shaping the Ancient Countryside*, (Macclesfield: Windgather Press).

Fyfe, R., A. Brown and S. Rippon, 2004. 'Characterising the late prehistoric, 'Romano-British' and medieval landscape, and dating the emergence of a regionally distinct agricultural system in South West Britain', *Journal of Archaeological Science* 31, 1699-1714.

Gage, J., 1834. 'The Anglo-Saxon ceremonial of the dedication and consecration of churches', *Archaeologia* 25, 235-274.

Gaimster, M. and J. Bradley, 2001. 'Medieval Britain and Ireland in 2000', *Medieval Archaeology* 45, 233-379.

Galinié, H., 1999. 'Tours from an archaeological standpoint' in C. Karkov, K. Wickham-Crowley and B. Young (eds), *Spaces of the Living and the Dead: An Archaeological Diaologue*, American Early Medieval Studies 3 (Oxford: Oxbow), 87-105.

Gauthier, N., 1999. 'La topographie chrétienne entre idéologie et pragmatisme' in G. Brogiolo and B. Ward-Perkins (eds), *The Idea and Ideal of the Town between Late Antiquity and the Early Middle Ages*, (Leiden: Brill), 195-209.

Geake, H., 2002. 'Persistent problems in the study of conversion-period burials in England' in S. Lucy and A. Reynolds (eds), *Burial in Early Medieval England and Wales*, Society for Medieval Archaeology Monograph 17 (Leeds: Society for Medieval Archaeology), 144-155.

Geary, B., S. West and D. Charman, 1997. 'The landscape context of medieval settlement on the south-western moors of England. Recent palaeoenvironmental evidence from Bodmin Moor and Dartmoor', *Medieval Archaeology* 41: 195-209.

Gelling, M., 1978. *Signposts to the Past*, (London: Dent).

Gelling, M., 1984. *Place-names in the Landscape*, (London: Dent).

Gelling, M., 1998. 'Place-names and landscape' in S. Taylor (ed.), *The Uses of Place-Names*, St John's House Papers 7, St Andrews (Edinburgh: Scottish Cultural Press), 75-100.

Gem, R., 1996. 'Church buildings: cultural location and meaning' in J. Blair and C. Pyrah (eds), *Church Archaeology: Research Directions for the Future*, Council for British Archaeology Research Report 104 (York: CBA), 1-6.

Gent, T. and H. Quinnell, 1999a. 'Excavations of a causewayed enclosure and hillfort on Raddon Hill, Stockleigh Pomeroy', *Devon Archaeological Society Proceedings* 57, 1-75.

Gent, T. and H. Quinnell, 1999b. 'Salvage recording on the Neolithic site at Haldon Belvedere', *Devon Archaeological Society Proceedings* 57, 77-104.

Gerrard, C., 1995. 'Excavations in the Church Field (4016), Shapwick, 1993; a preliminary report' in M. Aston and C. Gerrard (eds), *The Shapwick Project: an Archaeological, Historical and Topographical Study. The Sixth Report*, (Bristol: Dept for Continuing Education, University of Bristol), 89-110.

Gerrard, C., 2000. 'The Shapwick Project, 1989-99' in C. Webster (ed.), *Somerset Archaeology:*

Papers to Mark 150 Years of the Somerset Archaeological and Natural History Society, (Taunton: Environment and Property Dept, Somerset County Council), 31-38.

Gerrard, S., 1997. *Dartmoor*, (London: Batsford/English Heritage).

Gerrard, S., 2000. *The Early British Tin Industry*, (Stroud: Tempus).

Gibb, J., 1975. 'The Anglo-Saxon cathedral at Sherborne', *Archaeological Journal* 132, 71-110.

Gilchrist, R. and R. Morris, 1993. 'Monasteries as settlements: religion, society and economy A.D.600-1050' in M. Carver (ed.), *In Search of Cult: Archaeological Investigations in Honour of Philip Rahtz*, (Woodbridge: Boydell), 113-118 .

Gilmour, B., 1979. 'The Anglo-Saxon church at St Paul-in-the-Bail, Lincoln', *Medieval Archaeology* 23, 214-218.

Gittos, B. and M. Gittos, 1991. 'The surviving Anglo-Saxon fabric of East Coker church', *Proceedings of the Somerset Archaeological and Natural History Society* 135, 107-111 .

Gittos, H., 2002. 'Creating the sacred: Anglo-Saxon rites for consecrating cemeteries' in S. Lucy and A. Reynolds (eds), *Burial in Early Medieval England and Wales*, Society for Medieval Archaeology Monograph 17 (Leeds: Society for Medieval Archaeology), 195-208.

Given, M. and B. Knapp, 2003. *The Sydney Cyprus Survey Project: Social Approaches to Regional Archaeological Survey*, Monumenta Archaeologica 21 (Los Angeles: University of California, Los Angeles).

Given, M., A. Knapp, N. Meyer, T. Gregory, V. Kassianidou, J. Noller, L. Wells, N. Urwin, H. Wright, 1999. 'The Sydney Cyprus Survey Project: an interdisciplinary investigation of long-term change in the north central Troodos, Cyprus', *Journal of Field Archaeology* 26, 19-39.

Godden, D., S. Hamilton-Dyer, M. Laidlaw and L. Mepham, 2002. 'Excavation of Saxon pits at Tidworth, 1999', *Wiltshire Archaeological and Natural History Magazine* 95, 240-248.

Gold, A., 1988. *Fruitful Journeys. The Ways of Rajasthani Pilgrims*, (Berkeley: University of California Press).

Gover, J., 1948. '*The place-names of Cornwall*', (unpublished typescript, Royal Institution of Cornwall Courtney Library).

Gover, J., A. Mawer and F. Stenton, 1932. *The Place-Names of Devon*, English Place-Names Society vols 8 and 9 (Nottingham: EPNS).

Gover, J., A. Mawer, and F. Stenton, 1939. *The Place-Names of Wiltshire*, English Place-Name Society Vol. 16 (Cambridge: Cambridge University Press).

Graham, A. and S. Davies, 1993. *Excavations in Trowbridge, Wiltshire, 1977 and 1986-1988*, Wessex Archaeology Report 2 (Salisbury: Wessex Archaeology).

Graham, B., 1993. 'Early medieval Ireland: settlement as an indicator of economic and social transformation, c.500-1100' in B. Graham and L. Proudfoot (eds), *An Historical Geography of Ireland*, (London: Academic Press), 19-57.

Graham, B., 1998. 'The town and the monastery: early medieval urbanization in Ireland, AD 800-1150' in T. Slater and G. Rosser (eds), *The Church in the Medieval Town*, (Aldershot: Ashgate), 131-154.

Greene, D. and F. O'Connor (eds and trans), 1967. *A Golden Treasury of Irish Poetry AD 600 to 1200*, (London: Macmillan).

Griffith, F., 1994. 'Changing perceptions of the context of prehistoric Dartmoor', *Proceedings of the Devon Archaeological Society* 52, 85-99.

Grundy, G., 1919. 'The Saxon land charters of Wiltshire', *Archaeological Journal* 2nd series 26, 143-301.

Grundy, G., 1920. 'The Saxon land charters of Wiltshire', *Archaeological Journal* 2nd series 27, 8-126.

Grundy, G., 1933. 'Dorset Charters', *Proceedings of the Dorset Natural History and Archaeological Society* 55, 239-268.

Grundy, G., 1934. 'Dorset Charters', *Proceedings of the Dorset Natural History and Archaeological Society* 56, 110-30.

Grundy, G., 1935a. *The Saxon Charters and Field Names of Somerset* (Taunton: Somerset Archaeological and Natural History Society); also as 8 parts, published with *Proceedings of the Somerset Archaeological and Natural History Society*, 73-80 (1927-34), same page numbers.

Grundy, G., 1935b. 'Dorset Charters', *Proceedings of the Dorset Natural History and Archaeological Society* 57, 114-139.

Grundy, G., 1936. 'Dorset Charters', *Proceedings of the Dorset Natural History and Archaeological Society* 58, 103-136.

Grundy, G., 1937. 'Dorset Charters', *Proceedings of the Dorset Natural History and Archaeological Society* 59, 95-118.

Grundy, G., 1938. 'Dorset Charters', *Proceedings of the Dorset Natural History and Archaeological Society* 60, 75-89.

Grundy, G., 1939. 'Dorset Charters', *Proceedings of the Dorset Natural History and Archaeological Society* 61, 60-78.

Guigon, P., 1997. *Les Eglises du Haut Moyen Age en Bretagne, Tome I*, Les Dossiers du Centre

Régional d'Archéologie d'Alet Supplément T (Alet: CeRAA).

Guthrie, A., 1954. 'Dark age sites at St Ives', *Proceedings of the West Cornwall Field Club* 1(2), 73-75.

Guthrie, A., 1960. 'Hellesvean dark age house', *Proceedings of the West Cornwall Field Club* 2(4), 151-153.

Guthrie, A., 1969. 'Excavation of a settlement at Goldherring, Sancreed, 1958-1961', *Cornish Archaeology* 8, 5-39.

Hadley, D., 1997. '*And they proceeded to plough and support themselves*: the Scandinavian settlement of England', *Anglo-Norman Studies* 19, 69-96.

Haldon, J., 1999. 'The idea of the town in the Byzantine Empire' in G. Brogiolo and B. Ward-Perkins (eds), *The Idea and Ideal of the Town between Late Antiquity and the Early Middle Ages*, (Leiden: Brill), 1-23.

Hall, M., 1999. 'Subaltern voices? Finding the spaces between things and words' in P. Funari, M. Hall and S. Jones (eds), *Historical Archaeology: Back from the Edge*, (London: Routledge), 193-203.

Hall, T., 2000. *Minster Churches in the Dorset Landscape*, British Archaeological Reports (British Series) 304 (Oxford: Archaeopress).

Halsall, G., 1996. 'Towns, societies and ideas: the not-so-strange case of late Roman and early Merovingian Metz' in N. Christie and S. Loseby (eds), *Towns in Transition: Urban Evolution in Late Antiquity and the Early Middle Ages*, (Aldershot: Ashgate), 235-261.

Hamerow, H., 1991. 'Settlement mobility and the 'Middle Saxon shift': rural settlements and settlement patterns in Anglo-Saxon England', *Anglo-Saxon England* 20: 1-17.

Handley, M., 1998. 'Early medieval inscriptions of western Britain: function and sociology' in J. Hill and M. Swan (eds), *The Community, the Family and the Saint: Patterns of Power in Early Medieval Europe*, (Turnhout: Brepols), 339-361.

Harl, K., 2001. 'From pagan to Christian in cities of Roman Anatolia during the fourth and fifth centuries' in T. Burns and J. Eadie (eds), *Urban Centers and Rural Contexts in Late Antiquity*, (East Lansing: Michigan State University Press), 301-322.

Harlow, M. and W. Smith, 2001. 'Between fasting and feasting: the literary and archaeobotanical evidence for monastic diet in Late Antique Egypt', *Antiquity* 75, 758-768.

Harries, J., 1992. 'Christianity and the city in late Roman Gaul' in J. Rich (ed.), *The City in Late Antiquity*, (London: Routledge), 77-98.

Harris, D., 1980. 'Excavation of a Romano-British round at Shortlanesend, Kenwyn, Truro', *Cornish Archaeology* 19, 63-75.

Harvey, D., 1997. 'The evolution of territoriality and societal transitions', *Landscape History* 19, 13-23.

Harvey, D. and R. Jones, 1999. 'Custom and habit(us): the meaning of traditions and legends in early medieval western Britain', *Geografiska Annaler B* 81 , 223-233.

Hase, P., 1988. 'The mother churches of Hampshire' in J. Blair (ed.), *Minsters and Parish Churches: the Local Church in Transition 950-1200*, (Oxford: Oxford University Committee for Archaeology), 45-66.

Hase, P., 1994. 'The church in the Wessex heartlands' in M. Aston and C. Lewis (eds) *The Medieval Landscape of Wessex*, (Oxford: Oxbow Monograph 46), 47-81.

Haslam, J., 1980. 'A middle Saxon iron smelting site at Ramsbury, Wiltshire', *Medieval Archaeology* 24, 1-68.

Heaton, M., 1992. 'Two mid-Saxon grain-driers and later medieval features at Chantry Field, Gillingham, Dorset', *Proceedings of the Dorset Natural History and Archaeological Society* 114, 97-126.

Henderson Calendar 5 Henderson, C., n.d. *Calendar 5*, (unpublished manuscript, Royal Institution of Cornwall Courtney Library, Truro).

Henderson EC Henderson, C., n.d. *Materials for a Parochial History of East Cornwall*, (unpublished manuscript (*c.*1924-1933), Royal Institution of Cornwall Courtney Library, Truro).

Henderson, C., 1929. 'Notes on the parish of St Neot' in G. Doble, *St Neot*, Cornish Saints Series 21 (Shipston-on-Stour), 39-59.

Henderson, C., 1931. 'The topography of the parish of St Keverne', *Annual Report of the Royal Cornwall Polytechnic Society* n.s. 7, 49-75.

Henderson, C., 1958. 'The ecclesiastical history of the 109 parishes of west Cornwall', *Journal of the Royal Institution of Cornwall* n.s. vol. 3 pt. 2, 211-382.

Henderson, C. and P. Bidwell, 1982. 'The Saxon minster at Exeter' in S. Pearce (ed.), *The Early Church In Western Britain and Ireland: Studies Presented to C.A. Ralegh Radford*, British Archaeological Reports British Series 102 (Oxford: BAR), 145-175.

Herring, P., 1986. 'An exercise in landscape history. Pre-Norman and medieval Brown Willy and Bodmin Moor, Cornwall' 3 vols, unpublished MPhil thesis, University of Sheffield.

Herring, P., 1993. *An Archaeological Evaluation of St Michael's Mount: a Report to the National Trust*, (Truro: Cornwall Archaeological Unit).

Herring, P., 1996. 'Transhumance in medieval Cornwall' in H. Fox (ed.) 1996 *Seasonal Settlement*, University of Leicester Vaughan Paper 39 (Leicester), 35-45.

Herring, P., 1998. *Cornwall's Historic Landscape: Presenting a Method of Historic Landscape Character Assessment*, (Truro: Cornwall Archaeological Unit).

Herring, P., 1999a. 'Cornwall: how the Historic Landscape Characterisation methodology was developed' in G. Fairclough (ed.), *Historic Landscape Characterisation: 'The State of the Art'*, (London: English Heritage), 15-32.

Herring, P., 1999b. 'Farming and transhumance at the turn of the second millennium (Part 1)', *Cornwall Association of Local Historians. Journal* Spring 1999, 19-25.

Herring, P., 1999c. 'Farming and transhumance at the turn of the second millennium (Part 2)', *Cornwall Association of Local Historians. Journal* Summer 1999, 3-8.

Herring, P., 2000. *St Michael's Mount, Cornwall. Reports on Archaeological Works, 1995-1998*, (Truro: Cornwall County Council).

Herring, P., 2004. 'Cornish uplands: medieval, post-medieval and modern extents' in I. Whyte and A. Winchester (eds), *Landscape, Economy and Society in Upland Britain*, Society for Landscape Studies Supplementary Series 2 (Birmingham: SLS), 37-51.

Herring, P., 2006a (forthcoming). 'The fields of Brown Willy, Bodmin Moor: a case study' in S. Turner (ed.), *Medieval Devon and Cornwall: Shaping the Ancient Countryside*, (Macclesfield: Windgather Press).

Herring, P., 2006b (forthcoming). 'The medieval strip fields of Cornwall' in S. Turner (ed.), *Medieval Devon and Cornwall: Shaping the Ancient Countryside*, (Macclesfield: Windgather Press).

Herring, P. and D. Hooke, 1993 'Interrogating Anglo-Saxons in St Dennis', *Cornish Archaeology* 32, 67-75.

Herring, P. and N. Johnson, 1997. 'Historic landscape character mapping in Cornwall' in K. Barker and T. Darvill (eds), *Making English Landscapes*, (Oxford: Oxbow Monograph 93), 70-91.

Herschend, F., 1993. 'The origin of the hall in southern Scandinavia', *Tor* 25, 175-199.

Higham, N., 1997. *The Convert Kings: Power and Religious Affiliation in Early Anglo-Saxon England*, (Manchester: Manchester University Press).

Hill, D., 1981. *An Atlas of Anglo-Saxon England* (Toronto: University of Toronto Press).

Hill, P., 1997. *Whithorn* and *St Ninian: the Excavation of a Monastic Town, 1984-91*, (Stroud: Sutton).

Hinchcliffe, J., 1986. 'An early medieval settlement at Cowage Farm, Foxley near Malmesbury', *Archaeological Journal* 143, 240-259.

Hines, J., 2000. 'Welsh and English: mutual origins in post-Roman Britain?' *Studia Celtica* 34, 81-104.

Hingeston-Randolph, F., 1889. *The registers of Walter Bronescombe (A.D. 1257-1280) : and Peter Quivil (A.D. 1280-1291), Bishops of Exeter: With Some Records of the Episcopate of Bishop Thomas de Bytton (A.D. 1292-1280): Also the Taxation of Pope Nicholas IV, A.D. 1291, Diocese of Exeter*, (London and Exeter).

Hinton, D., 1987. 'Minsters and royal estates in south-east Dorset', *Proceedings of the Dorset Natural History and Archaeological Society* 109, 50-54.

Hinton, D., 1992. 'The inscribed stones in Lady St Mary church, Wareham', *Proceedings of the Dorset Natural History and Archaeological Society* 114, p.260.

Hinton, D., 1994. 'The archaeology of eighth- to eleventh-century Wessex' in M. Aston and C. Lewis (eds), *The Medieval Landscape of Wessex*, Oxbow Monograph 46 (Oxford: Oxbow Books), 33-46.

Hinton, D., 1998. *Saxons and Vikings*, (Wimborne: Dovecote Press).

Hirst, F., 1936. 'Excavations at Porthmeor, 1933-5', *Journal of the Royal Institution of Cornwall* 24, 1-81.

Hockey, F., 1976. *Beaulieu, King John's Abbey: A History of Beaulieu Abbey, Hampshire, 1204-1538*, (London: Pioneer Publications).

Hodder, I., 1986. *Reading the Past*, (Cambridge: Cambridge University Press).

Hodges, R., 1982. *Dark Age Economics: The Origins of Towns and Trade AD 600-1000*, (London: Duckworth).

Hollinrake, C. and N. Hollinrake, 1997. 'Archaeological evaluations in Carhampton, 1993-1995' Unpublished report for Somerset County Council, Somerset Sites and Monuments Register.

Hooke, D., 1981. *Anglo-Saxon Landscapes of the West Midlands: The Charter Evidence*, British Archaeological Reports British Series 95 (Oxford: BAR).

Hooke, D., 1986. 'Territorial organisation in the Anglo-Saxon west midlands: central places, central areas' in E. Grant (ed.), *Central Places, Archaeology and History*, (Sheffield: Dept of Archaeology and Prehistory, University of Sheffield), 79-93.

Hooke, D., 1988. 'Regional variation in southern and central England in the Anglo-Saxon period and its relationship to land units and settlement' in D. Hooke (ed.), *Anglo-Saxon Settlements*,

(Oxford, Blackwell), 123-152.

Hooke, D., 1994a. *Pre-Conquest Charter Bounds of Devon and Cornwall*, (Woodbridge: Boydell).

Hooke, D., 1994b. 'The administrative and settlement framework of early medieval Wessex' in M. Aston and C. Lewis (eds), *The Medieval Landscape of Wessex*, Oxbow Monograph 46 (Oxford: Oxbow Books), 83-95.

Hooke, D., 1998. *The Landscape of Anglo-Saxon England*, (London: Leicester University Press).

Hooke, D., 1999. 'Saxon conquest and settlement' in R. Kain and W. Ravenhill (eds), *Historical Atlas of South-West England*, (Exeter: University of Exeter Press), 95-104.

Hope-Taylor, B., 1977. *Yeavering: An Anglo-British Centre of Early Northumbria*, (London: HMSO).

Horden, P. and N. Purcell, 2000. *The Corrupting Sea. A Study of Mediterranean History*, (Oxford: Blackwell).

Horner, W., 2001. 'Secrets of the sands', *Devon Archaeological Society Newsletter* 79, 1, 8-9.

Hoskins, W., 1960. *The Westward Expansion of Wessex*, (Leicester).

Hostetter, E. and T. Howe (eds), 1997. *The Romano-British Villa at Castle Copse, Great Bedwyn*, (Bloomington: Indiana University Press).

Howe, J., 1997. 'The conversion of the physical world. The creation of a Christian landscape' in J. Muldoon (ed.), *Varieties of Religious Conversion in the Middle Ages*, (Gainesville: University Press of Florida), 63-78.

Howe, J., 2002. 'Creating symbolic landscapes: medieval development of sacred space' in J. Howe and M. Wolfe (eds), *Inventing Medieval Landscapes: Senses of Place in Western Europe*, (Gainesville: Florida University Press), 208-223.

Howlett, D., 1998. 'Literate culture of 'Dark Age' Britain', *British Archaeology* 33, http://www.britarch.ac.uk/ (last consulted 08/09/01).

Hughes, K., 1981. 'The Celtic Church: is this a valid concept?' *Cambridge Medieval Celtic Studies* 1, 1-20.

Hull, P. (ed.), 1962. *The Cartulary of St Michael's Mount*, Devon and Cornwall Record Society n.s. vol. 5 (Torquay: Devon and Cornwall Record Society).

Hull, P. (ed.), 1987. *The Cartulary of Launceston Priory: Lambeth Palace MS. 719*, Devon and Cornwall Record Society n.s. vol. 30 (Torquay: Devon and Cornwall Record Society).

Hurley, V., 1982. 'The early church in the south-west of Ireland: settlement and organisation' in S. Pearce (ed.), *The Early Church In Western Britain and Ireland: Studies Presented to C.A. Ralegh Radford*, British Archaeological Reports British Series 102 (Oxford: BAR), 297-332.

Hutchinson, G., 1979. 'The bar-lug pottery of Cornwall', *Cornish Archaeology* 18, 81-103.

ICS Index Institute of Cornish Studies *Cornish Place-Name Index'*, (unpublished manuscript copy, held by Cornwall Archaeological Unit, Truro).

Insley, C., 1998. 'Charters and episcopal scriptoria in the Anglo-Saxon south-west', *Early Medieval Europe* 7, 173-197.

Isbell, H. (ed. and trans.), 1971. *The Last Poets of Imperial Rome*, (Harmondsworth: Penguin).

James, E., 2001. *Britain in the First Millennium*, (London: Arnold).

James, H., 1992. 'Early medieval cemeteries in Wales' in N. Edwards and A. Lane (eds), *The Early Church in Wales and the West*, Oxbow Monograph 16 (Oxford: Oxbow), 90-103.

James, H., 1993. 'The cult of St David in the middle ages' in M. Carver (ed.), *In Search of Cult: Archaeological Investigations in Honour of Philip Rahtz*, (Woodbridge: Boydell), 105-112.

James, S., 1999. *The Atlantic Celts: Ancient People or Modern Invention?* (London: British Museum Press).

Jenkins, P., 1988. 'Regions and cantrefs in early medieval Glamorgan', *Cambridge Medieval Celtic Studies* 15, 31-50.

Johns, C. and P. Herring, 1996. *St Keverne Historic Landscape Assessment*, (Truro: Cornwall Archaeological Unit).

Johns, C., 1995. 'Treharrock, St Kew' *Cornish Archaeology* 34, 205-206.

Johnson, M., 1999. 'Rethinking historical archaeology' in P. Funari, M. Hall and S. Jones (eds), *Historical Archaeology: Back from the Edge*, (London: Routledge), 23-36.

Johnson, N., 1999. 'Context, meaning and consequences: using the map in Cornwall' in G. Fairclough (ed.), *Historic Landscape Characterisation: 'The State of the Art'*, (London: English Heritage), 117-122.

Johnson, N. and P. Rose, 1982. 'Defended settlement in Cornwall: an illustrated discussion' in D. Miles (ed.) *The Romano-British Countryside: Studies in Rural Settlement and Economy*, British Archaeological Reports British Series 103.i (Oxford: BAR), 151-208.

Johnson, N. and P. Rose, 1994. *Bodmin Moor: an Archaeological Survey. Vol. 1: The Human Landscape to c.1800*, (London: English Heritage).

Johnston, D., C. Moore and P. Fasham, 1998/9. 'Excavations at Penhale Round, Fraddon, Cornwall, 1995-6', *Cornish Archaeology* 37-8, 72-120.

Jones, A., 2000/1. 'The excavation of a multi-period site at Stencoose, Cornwall', *Cornish Archaeology* 39-40, 45-94.

Jones, G., 1976. 'Multiple estates and early settlements' in P. Sawyer (ed.) *Medieval Settlement*, (London: Edward Arnold), 11-40.

Jones, G., 1985. 'Multiple estates perceived', *Journal of Historical Geography* 11, 352-363.

Jones, R., 1998. 'The formation of the *cantref* and the commote in medieval Gwynedd', *Studia Celtica* 32, 160-177.

Jones, R. and M. Page, 2003. 'Characterizing rural settlement and landscape: Whittlewood Forest in the middle ages', *Medieval Archaeology* 47, 53-83.

Jones, S., 1997. *The Archaeology of Ethnicity*, (London: Routledge).

Jope, E. and R. Threlfall, 1956. 'A late dark-ages site at Gunwalloe', *Proceedings of the West Cornwall Field Club* 1 (4), 136-140.

Kalligas, H., 1990. *Byzantine Monemvasia: the Sources*, (Monemvasia: Akroneon).

Kelly, S., 1990. 'Anglo-Saxon lay society and the written word' in R. McKitterick (ed.), *The Uses of Literacy in Early Medieval Europe*, (Cambridge: Cambridge University Press), 36-62.

Kelly, S. (ed.), 1996. *Charters of Shaftesbury*, British Academy Anglo-Saxon Charters 5 (London: British Academy).

Kepecs, S., 1997a. 'Introduction to new approaches to combining the archaeological and historical records', *Journal of Archaeological Method and Theory* 4, 193-198.

Kepecs, S., 1997b. 'Native Yucatan and Spanish influence: the archaeology and history of Chikinchel', *Journal of Archaeological Method and Theory* 4, 307-329.

Keynes, S. and M. Lapidge (ed. and trans.), 1983. *Alfred the Great: Asser's Life of King Alfred and Other Contemporary Sources*, (Harmondsworth: Penguin).

King, H., 1994. '1994.196: Clonmacnoise - High Crosses', *Excavations.ie: Database of Irish Excavation Reports*, available http://www.excavations.ie (last consulted 25th May 2005).

Kjølbye-Biddle, B., 1986. 'The 7th century minster at Winchester interpreted' in L. Butler and R. Morris (eds), *The Anglo-Saxon Church: Papers on History, Architecture and Archaeology in Honour of Dr HM Taylor*, Council for British Archaeology Research Report 60 (London: CBA), 196-209.

Klaeber, F., 1950. *Beowulf and the Fight at Finnsburg*, (Boston: Heath).

Klingelhofer, E., 1992. *Manor, Vill and Hundred: the Development of Rural Institutions in Early Medieval Hampshire*, Studies and Texts 112 (Toronto: Pontifical Institute of Medieval Studies).

Knapp, B., 1992a. 'Archaeology and *Annales*: time, space and change' in B. Knapp (ed.), *Archaeology, Annales, and Ethnohistory*, (Cambridge: Cambridge University Press), 1-21.

Knapp, B. (ed.), 1992b. *Archaeology, Annales, and Ethnohistory*, (Cambridge: Cambridge University Press).

Knapp, B. and W. Ashmore, 1999. 'Archaeological landscapes: constructed, conceptualized, ideational' in W. Ashmore and B. Knapp (eds), *Archaeologies of Landscape: Contemporary Perspectives*, (Oxford: Blackwell), 1-30.

Knight, J., 1992. 'The early Christian inscriptions of Britain and Gaul: chronology and context' in N. Edwards and A. Lane (eds) *The Early Church in Wales and the West*, Oxbow Monograph 16 (Oxford: Oxbow), 45-50.

Knight, J., 1996. 'Seasoned with salt: insular–gallic contacts in the early memorial stones and cross slabs' in K. Dark (ed.), *External Contacts and the Economy of Late Roman and Post-Roman Britain*, (Woodbridge: Boydell), 109-120.

Knight, J., 1999. *The End of Antiquity: Archaeology, Society and Religion AD235-700*, (Stroud: Tempus).

Lake 1 Polsue, J., 1867-73. *Lake's Parochial History of the County of Cornwall, Vol. 1*, (Truro: W. Lake).

Lake 3 Polsue, J., 1867-73. *Lake's Parochial History of the County of Cornwall, Vol. 3*, (Truro: W. Lake).

Lambrick, G., 1999 'Hampshire: historic landscape character and the community' in G. Fairclough (ed.), *Historic Landscape Characterisation: 'The State of the Art'*, (London: English Heritage), 51-66.

Lang, J., 1984. 'The hogback: a Viking colonial monument', *Anglo-Saxon Studies in Archaeology and History* 3, 85-176.

Langdon, A., 1896. *Old Cornish Crosses*, (Truro: Joseph Pollard).

Langdon, A., 1996. *Stone Crosses in East Cornwall*, (Truro: Federation of Old Cornwall Societies).

Lapidge, M. and M. Herren, 1979. *Aldhelm – the Prose Works*, (Cambridge: Brewer).

Lapidge, M. and J. Rosier (trans.), 1985. *Aldhelm: the Poetic Works*, (Cambridge: DS Brewer).

Lapidge, M., J. Blair, S. Keynes and D. Scragg (eds), 1999. *The Blackwell Encyclopaedia of Anglo-Saxon England*, (Oxford: Blackwell).

Lawson Jones, A., 2001. 'Bear's Down to Ruthvoes, Cornwall. Archaeological Watching Brief', unpublished report, Cornwall Archaeological Unit No. 2001 R007, (Truro: CAU).

Lawson Jones, A., 2002. 'Tremough Campus, Penryn. Phase 1 Excavations and Landscaping Works', unpublished report, Cornwall Archaeological Unit No. 2002 R017, (Truro: CAU).

Leach, P., 1994. *Ilchester Volume 2: Archaeology, Excavation and Fieldwork to 1984*, (Sheffield: John R. Collis).

Leach, P. and P. Ellis, 1993. 'The medieval precinct of Glastonbury Abbey – some new evidence' in M. Carver (ed.), *In Search of Cult: Archaeological Investigations in Honour of Philip Rahtz*, (Woodbridge: Boydell), 119-124.

Leech, R., 1981. 'The Excavation of a Romano-British Farmstead and Cemetery on Bradley Hill, Somerton, Somerset', *Britannia* 12, 177-252.

Leech, R., 1986. 'The Excavation of a Romano-Celtic temple and a later cemetery on Lamyatt Beacon, Somerset', *Britannia* 17, 259-328.

Lewis, C., P. Mitchell-Fox and C. Dyer, 1997. *Village, Hamlet and Field*, (Manchester: Manchester University Press).

Lewit, T., 2003. 'Vanishing villas: what happened to élite rural habitation in the West in the 5th–6th c ?', *Journal of Roman Archaeology* 16, 260-274.

Liebeschuetz, J., 2001. *Decline and Fall of the Roman City*, (Oxford: Oxford University Press).

Light, A., A. Schofield and S. Shennan, 1994. 'The Middle Avon Valley Survey: a study in settlement history', *Proceedings of the Hampshire Field Club and Archaeological Society* 50, 43-101.

Lister, J. and G. Walker, 1986. *Cornwall Inventory of Ancient Woodland (Provisional)*, (Peterborough: Nature Conservancy Council).

Lobb, S. and P. Rose, 1996. *Archaeological Survey of the Lower Kennet Valley, Berkshire*, Wessex Archaeology Report 9 (Salisbury: Wessex Archaeology).

Longley, D., 2001. 'Medieval settlement and landscape change on Anglesey', *Landscape History* 23, 39-59.

Longley, D., 1997. 'The royal courts of the Welsh princes of Gwynedd, AD 400-1283' in N. Edwards (ed.), *Landscape and Settlement in Medieval Wales*, Oxbow Monograph 81 (Oxford: Oxbow), 41-54.

Loseby, S., 1992. 'Bishops and cathedrals: order and diversity in the fifth century urban landscape of Southern Gaul' in J. Drinkwater and H. Elton (eds), *Fifth Century Gaul: a Crisis of Identity*, (Cambridge: Cambridge University Press), 144-155.

Loveluck, C., 1998. 'A high-status Anglo-Saxon settlement at Flixborough, Lincolnshire', *Antiquity* 72, 146-161.

Low, M., 2002. 'The natural world in early Irish Christianity: an ecological footnote' in M. Atherton (ed.), *Celts and Christians*, (Cardiff: University of Wales Press), 169-203.

Lowe, B., 1987. 'Keynsham Abbey: excavations 1961-1985', *Proceedings of the Somerset Archaeological and Natural History Society* 131, 81-156.

Loyn, H., 1984. *The Governance of Anglo-Saxon England AD 500-1087*, (London: Arnold).

Lucy, S., 1998. *The Early Anglo-Saxon Cemeteries of East Yorkshire. An Analysis and Reinterpretation*, British Archaeological Reports British Series 289 (Oxford: BAR).

Lucy, S. and A. Reynolds, 2002. 'Burial in early medieval England and Wales: past, present and future' in S. Lucy and A. Reynolds (eds), *Burial in Early Medieval England and Wales*, (London: Society of Medieval Archaeology), 1-23.

Lund, N., 1976. 'Personal-names and place-names: the persons and the places', *Onoma* 19, 468-485.

Maddicott, J., 1989 'Trade, industry and the wealth of King Alfred', *Past and Present* 123, 3-51.

Markus, R., 1992. *The End of Ancient Christianity*, (Cambridge: Cambridge University Press).

Markus, R., 1994. 'How on earth could places become holy? Origins of the Christian idea of holy places', *Journal of Early Christian Studies* 2 (3), 257-271.

Markus, R., 1997. *Gregory the Great and his World*, (Cambridge: Cambridge University Press).

McNab, A. and G. Lambrick, 1999. 'Conclusions and recommendations' in G. Fairclough, G. Lambrick and A. McNab (eds), *Yesterday's World, Tomorrow's Landscape: the English Heritage Landscape Project 1992-94*, (London: English Heritage), 54-59.

McOmish, D., D. Field and G. Brown, 2002. *The Field Archaeology of the Salisbury Plain Training Area*, (London: English Heritage).

Meaney, A., 1964. *A Gazetteer of Early Anglo-Saxon Burial Sites*, (London: Allen & Unwin).

Meaney, A., 1993. 'Gazetteer of hundred and wapentake meeting-places of the Cambridgeshire region', *Proceedings of the Cambridge Antiquarian Society* 82, 67-92.

Meaney, A., 1995. 'Pagan English sanctuaries, place-names, and hundred meeting-places', *Anglo-Saxon Studies in Archaeology and History* 8, 29-42.

Meaney, A., 1997. 'Hundred meeting-places in the Cambridge region' in A. Rumble and A. Mills (eds), *Names, Places and People: An Onomastic Miscellany in Memory of John McNeal Dodgson*, (Stamford: Paul Watkins), 195-240.

Meaney, A., 1999. 'Paganism' in M. Lapidge, J. Blair, S. Keynes and D. Scragg (eds), *The Blackwell Encyclopaedia of Anglo-Saxon England*, (Oxford: Blackwell), 351-352.

Menuge, N., 2000. 'The foundation myth: Yorkshire monasteries and the landscape agenda', *Landscapes* 1(1), 22-37.

Miles, H. and T. Miles, 1973. 'Excavations at Trethurgy, St Austell: interim report', *Cornish Archaeology* 12, 25-30.

Millett, M. and S. James, 1983. 'Excavations at Cowdery's Down, Basingstoke, Hampshire, 1978-81', *Archaeological Journal* 140, 151-279.

Millett, M., F. Queiroga, K. Strutt, J. Taylor and S. Willis, 2000. 'The Ave Valley, northern Portugal: an archaeological survey of Iron Age and Roman settlement', *Internet Archaeology* 9,(http://intarch.ac.uk/journal/issue9/ millett_index.html; consulted 29/3/01).

Mills, A., 1977. *The Place-Names of Dorset, Part 1*, English Place-Name Society Vol. 52 (Nottingham, EPNS).

Mills, A., 1980. *The Place-Names of Dorset, Part 2*, English Place-Name Society Vol. 53 (Nottingham EPNS).

Mills, A., 1989. *The Place-Names of Dorset, Part 3*, English Place-Name Society Vols 59-60 (Nottingham EPNS).

Monk, M., 1998. 'Early medieval secular and ecclesiastical settlement in Munster' in M. Monk and J. Sheehan (eds), *Early Medieval Munster: Archaeology, History and Society*, (Cork: Cork University Press), 33-52.

Moraes Farias, P. de, 1999. 'Tadmakkat and the image of Mecca: epigraphic records of the work of the imagination in 11th century west Africa' in T. Insoll (ed.), *Case Studies in Archaeology and World Religion: The Proceedings of the Cambridge Conference*, British Archaeological Reports International Series S755 (Oxford: BAR), 105-115.

Moreland, J., 1992. 'Restoring the dialectic: settlement patterns and documents in medieval central Italy' in B. Knapp (ed.), *Archaeology, Annales and Ethnohistory*, (Cambridge: Cambridge University Press), 112-129.

Moreland, J., 1998. 'Through the looking glass of possibilities: understanding the middle ages', *Forschungen des Instituts für Realienkunde des Mittelalters und der Frühen Neuzeit: Diskussionen und Materialien* 3, 85-116.

Moreland, J., 2001. *Archaeology and Text*, (London: Duckworth).

Morris, C., 1984. 'Aspects of Scandinavian settlement in Northern Britain: a review', *Northern History* 20, 1-22.

Morris, C. and R. Harry, 1997. 'Excavations on the lower terrace, Site C, Tintagel Island 1990-1994', *Antiquaries Journal* 77, 1-144.

Morris, C., C. Batey, K. Brady, R. Harry, P. Johnson and C. Thomas, 1999. 'Recent work at Tintagel', *Medieval Archaeology* 43, 206-215.

Morris, I., 2000. *Archaeology as Cultural History*, (Oxford: Blackwell).

Morris, R., 1986. 'Alcuin, York, and the *alma sophia*' in L. Butler and R. Morris (eds), *The Anglo-Saxon Church: Papers on History, Architecture and Archaeology in Honour of Dr HM Taylor*, Council for British Archaeology Research Report 60 (York: CBA), 80-89.

Morris, R., 1989. *The Church in the Landscape*, (London: Dent).

Munby, J. (ed.), 1982. *Domesday Book 4: Hampshire*, (Chichester: Phillimore).

Musty, J., 1969. 'The excavation of two barrows, one of Saxon date, at Ford, Laverstock, near Salisbury, Wiltshire', *Antiquaries Journal* 49, 98-117.

Mytum, H., 1992. *The Origins of Early Christian Ireland*, (London: Routledge).

Nelson, J., 1983 'The church's military service in the ninth century: a contemporary comparative view?' *Studies in Church History* 20, 15-30.

Nenk, B., S. Margeson and M. Hurley, 1995. 'Medieval Britain and Ireland in 1994', *Medieval Archaeology* 39, 180-293.

Nowakowski, J. and C. Thomas, 1992. *Grave News from Tintagel: an Account of a Second Season of Archaeological Investigation at Tintagel Churchyard*, (Truro: Cornwall Archaeological Unit).

Oake, M. and S. Shennan, 1985. 'The Saxon and medieval periods' in S. Shennan, *Experiments in the Collection and Analysis of Archaeological Survey Data: The East Hampshire Survey*, (Sheffield: Dept of Archaeology and Prehistory, University of Sheffield), 89-103.

O'Brien, L., 2002. 'Anglo-Saxon varieties', *The Archaeologist* 44, 20-21.

Ó Carragáin, T., 2003. 'A landscape converted: archaeology and early church organisation on Iveragh and Dingle' in M. Carver (ed.), *The Cross Goes North: Processes of Conversion in Northern Europe, AD 300-1300*, (Woodbridge: Boydell), 127-152.

Ó Floinn, R., 1995. 'Clonmacnois: art and patronage in early medieval Ireland' in C. Bourke (ed.), *From the Isles of the North: Early Medieval Art in Ireland and Britain*, (Belfast: HMSO), 251-260.

Okasha, E., 1993 *Corpus of Early Christian Inscribed Stones of South-West England*, (London: Leicester University Press).

Okasha, E. and A. Preston-Jones, in prep. *Corpus of Anglo-Saxon Stone Sculpture, Supplementary Volume: Cornwall*, (London: British Academy).

Olson, L., 1982 'Crantock, Cornwall as an early monastic site' in S. Pearce (ed.) *The Early Church in Western Britain and Ireland*, British Archaeological Reports British Series 102 (Oxford: BAR), 177-186.

Olson, L., 1988. 'Cornish rural religious processions', *Australian Celtic Journal* 1, 22-29.

Olson, L., 1989. *Early Monasteries in Cornwall*, (Woodbridge: Boydell).

Olson, L. and C. O'Mahoney, 1994. 'Lammana, West Looe: CK Croft Andrew's excavations of the chapel and Monks House, 1935-6', *Cornish Archaeology* 33, 96-129.

Olson, L. and O. Padel, 1986. 'A tenth-century list of Cornish parochial saints', *Cambridge Medieval Celtic Studies* 12, 33-71.

Olson, L. and A. Preston-Jones, 1998/9. 'An ancient cathedral of Cornwall? Excavated remains east of St Germans church', *Cornish Archaeology* 37-38, 153-169.

O'Neil, B., 1933. 'The Roman villa at Magor farm, near Camborne, Cornwall', *Journal of the British Archaeological Association* 39, 116-175.

O'Neil, H. 1964. 'Excavation of a Celtic hermitage on St Helen's, Isles of Scilly, 1956-58', *Archaeological Journal* 121, 40-69.

Orme, N., 1991. 'From the beginnings to 1050' in N. Orme (ed.), *Unity and Variety: A History of the Church in Devon and Cornwall*, Exeter Studies in History 29 (Exeter: University of Exeter Press), 1-22.

Orme, N. (ed.), 1992. *Nicholas Roscarrock's Lives of the Saints of Devon and Cornwall*, Devon and Cornwall Record Society n.s. 35 (Exeter).

Orme, N., 1995. 'Two unusual Devon saints', *The Devon Historian* 51, 12-13.

Orme, N., 1996a. *English Church Dedications*, (Exeter: University of Exeter Press).

Orme, N., 1996b. 'Church and chapel in medieval England', *Transactions of the Royal Historical Society*, 6th series, 6, 75-102.

Orme, N., 1999. 'The church from *c*.1300 to the Reformation' in R. Kain and W. Ravenhill (eds), *Historical Atlas of South-West England*, (Exeter: University of Exeter Press), 212-219.

Orme, N., 2000. *The Saints of Cornwall*, (Oxford: Oxford University Press).

Orselli, A., 1999. 'L'idée chrétienne de la ville: quelques suggestions pour l'antiquité tardive et le haut moyen âge' in G. Brogiolo and B. Ward-Perkins (eds), *The Idea and Ideal of the Town between Late Antiquity and the Early Middle Ages*, (Leiden: Brill), 181-193.

Padel, O., 1978. 'Two new pre-Conquest charters for Cornwall', *Cornish Studies* 6, 20-27.

Padel, O., 1985. *Cornish Place-Name Elements*, (Nottingham: English Place-Name Society vols56-7).

Padel, O., 1987. 'Predannack or Pradnick, in Mullion', *Cornish Studies* 15, 11-14.

Padel, O., 1988. *A Popular Dictionary of Cornish Place-Name Elements*, (Penzance: Alison Hodge).

Padel, O., 1999. 'Place-names' in R. Kain and W. Ravenhill (eds), *Historical Atlas of South-West England*, (Exeter: University of Exeter Press), 88-94.

Padel, O., 2002. 'Local saints and place-names in Cornwall' in A. Thacker and R. Sharpe (eds)., *Local Saints and Local Churches in the Early Medieval West*, (Oxford: Oxford University Press), 303-360.

Page, W., 1915. 'Some remarks on the churches of the Domesday survey', *Archaeologia* 2nd series 16, 61-102.

Palliser, D., 1996 'Review article: the minster hypothesis: a case study', *Early Medieval Europe* 5, 207-214.

Pantos, A., 2004. 'The location and form of Anglo-Saxon assembly places: some 'moot points" in A. Pantos and S. Semple (eds), *Assembly Places and Practices in Medieval Europe*, (Dublin: Four Courts Press), 156-180.

Parker Pearson, M., K. Godden, Ramilisonina, Retsihisatse, J. Schwenninger and H. Smith, 1999. 'Lost kingdoms: oral histories, travellers' tales and archaeology in southern Madagascar' in P. Funari, M. Hall and S. Jones (eds), *Historical Archaeology: Back from the Edge*, (London: Routledge), 233-254.

Payton, P., 1999. 'The retreat of the Cornish language' in R. Kain and W. Ravenhill (eds), *Historical Atlas of South-West England*, (Exeter: University of Exeter Press), 267-268.

Pearce, S., 1973. 'The dating of some Celtic dedications and hagiographical traditions in south-western Britain', *Transactions of the Devonshire Association* 105, 95-120.

Pearce, S., 1978. *The Kingdom of Dumnonia*, (Padstow: Lodenek Press).

Pearce, S., 1982. 'Church and society in south Devon, AD 300-700', *Devon Archaeological Society Proceedings* 40, 1-18.

Pearce, S., 1985. 'The early church in the landscape: the evidence from North Devon', *Antiquaries Journal* 142, 255-275.

Pearce, S., 2004. *South-western Britain in the Early Middle Ages*, (London: Leicester University Press).

Penhallurick, R., 1986. *Tin in Antiquity*, (London: Institute of Metals).

Penna, L., 1968. 'Perran Sands', *Cornish Archaeology* 7, 82.

Pestell, T., 2004. *Landscapes of Monastic Foundation: The Establishment of Religious Houses in East Anglia, c.650-1200*, (Woodbridge: Boydell).

Peters, F., 1990. 'The possible use of West Penwith menhirs as boundary markers', *Cornish Archaeology* 29, 33-42.

Petts, D., 1998. 'Landscape and cultural identity in Roman Britain' in R. Laurence and J. Berry (eds), *Cultural Identity in the Roman Empire*, (London: Routledge), 79-94 .

Petts, D., 2001. 'Burial, religion and identity in sub-Roman and early medieval Britain, AD 400-800', Unpublished PhD thesis, University of Reading.

Petts, D., 2002a. 'Cemeteries and boundaries in western Britain' in S. Lucy and A. Reynolds (eds), *Burial in Early Medieval England and Wales*, Society for Medieval Archaeology Monograph 17 (Leeds: Society for Medieval Archaeology), 24-46.

Petts, D., 2002b. 'The reuse of prehistoric standing stones in western Britain? A critical consideration of an aspect of early medieval monument reuse', *Oxford Journal of Archaeology* 21(2), 195-209.

Petts, D. and S. Turner, forthcoming. 'Multiple churches and ecclesiastical complexes in early medieval Celtic Britain' in N. Edwards (ed.), *The Archaeology of the Celtic Churches*, (Leeds: Society for Medieval Archaeology).

Picken, M., 1965-7. 'The names of the hundreds of Cornwall', *Devon and Cornwall Notes and Queries* 30, 36-40.

Picken, M., 1982-6. 'Light on Lammana', *Devon and Cornwall Notes and Queries* 35, 281-286.

Pietri, L., 1997. 'Grégoire de Tours et la géographie du sacré' in N. Gauthier and H. Galinié (eds), *Grégoire de Tours et l'Espace Gaulois*, (Tours: La Simarre), 111-114.

Pine, J., 2001. 'The excavation of a Saxon settlement at Cadley Road, Collingbourne Ducis, Wiltshire', *Wiltshire Archaeological and Natural History Magazine* 94, 88-117.

Pitt, J., 1999. 'Wiltshire minster *parochiae* and West Saxon ecclesiastical organisation' Unpublished PhD thesis, University of Southampton.

Pollard, J. and A. Reynolds, 2002. *Avebury: The Biography of a Landscape*, (Stroud: Tempus).

Pollard, S., 1966. 'Neolithic and Dark Age settlements on High Peak, Sidmouth', *Proceedings of the Devon Archaeological Exploration Society* 23, 35-59.

Potts, R., 1974. *A Calendar of Cornish Glebe Terriers 1673-1735*, (Exeter: Devon and Cornwall Record Society n.s.19).

Preston-Jones, A., 1984. 'The excavation of a long-cist cemetery at Carnanton, St Mawgan, 1943', *Cornish Archaeology* 23, 157-178.

Preston-Jones, A., 1987. 'Road widening at St Buryan and Pelynt churchyards', *Cornish Archaeology* 26, 153-160.

Preston-Jones, A., 1992. 'Decoding Cornish churchyards' in N. Edwards and A. Lane (eds), *The Early Church in Wales and the West*, (Oxford: Oxbow Monograph 16), 104-124.

Preston-Jones, A., 1999. 'Pre-Norman sculpture in Cornwall' Unpublished paper delivered at the University of Durham, April 1999.

Preston-Jones, A. and A. Langdon, 2001. 'St Buryan crosses', *Cornish Archaeology* 36 (for 1997), 107-128.

Preston-Jones, A. and E. Okasha, 1997. 'Hiberno-Saxon sculpture in Penwith, Cornwall', Unpublished report prepared for the Committee of the British Academy of the *Corpus of Anglo-Saxon Stone Sculpture in England*.

Preston-Jones, A. and P. Rose, 1986. 'Medieval Cornwall', *Cornish Archaeology* 25, 135-185.

Quinnell, H., 1986. 'Cornwall during the Iron Age and the Roman period', *Cornish Archaeology* 25, 111-34.

Quinnell, H., 1993. 'A sense of identity: distinctive Cornish stone artefacts in the Roman and post-Roman periods', *Cornish Archaeology* 32, 29-46.

Quinnell, H., 2004. *Trethurgy*, (Truro: Cornwall County Council).

Quinnell, H. and D. Harris, 1985. 'Castle Dore: the chronology reconsidered', *Cornish Archaeology* 24, 123-132.

Rackham, O., 1986. *The History of the Countryside*, (London: Dent).

Rahtz, P., 1971. 'Excavations on Glastonbury Tor, Somerset 1964–6', *Archaeological Journal* 127, 1-81.

Rahtz, P., 1976. 'The building-plan of the Anglo-Saxon monastery of Whitby Abbey' in D. Wilson (ed.), *The Archaeology of Anglo-Saxon England*, (Cambridge: Cambridge University Press), 459-462.

Rahtz, P., 1979. *The Saxon and Medieval Palaces at Cheddar*, British Archaeological Reports British Series 65 (Oxford: BAR).

Rahtz, P., 1991. 'Pagan and Christian by the Severn Sea' in L. Abrams and J. Carley (eds), *The Archaeology and History of Glastonbury Abbey*, (Woodbridge: Boydell), 3-37.

Rahtz, P., 1993. *Glastonbury*, (London: Batsford/English Heritage).

Rahtz, P., 1999. 'Royal sites' in M. Lapidge, J. Blair, S. Keynes and D. Scragg (eds), *The Blackwell Encyclopaedia of Anglo-Saxon England* (Oxford: Blackwell), 399-401.

Rahtz, P., and S. Hirst, 1974. *Beckery Chapel 1967-8* (Glastonbury: Glastonbury Antiquarian Society).

Rahtz, P. S, Hirst, S. Wright, 2000. *Cannington Cemetery*, Britannia Monograph Series 17 (London: Society for the Promotion of Roman Studies).

Rahtz, P., A. Woodward, I. Burrow, A. Everton, L. Watts, P. Leach, S. Hirst, P. Fowler and K. Gardener, 1992. *Cadbury Congresbury 1968-73: A Late/Post-Roman Hilltop Settlement in*

Somerset, British Archaeological Reports (British Series) 223 (Oxford: BAR).

Ralegh Radford, C., 1935. 'Tintagel: the castle and Celtic monastery, interim report', *Antiquaries Journal* 15, 401-419.

Ralegh Radford, C., 1951. 'Report on the excavations at Castle Dore', *Journal of the Royal Institution of Cornwall* n.s.1 (Appendix), 1-119.

Ralegh Radford, C., 1962. 'The Celtic monastery in Britain', *Archaeologia Cambrensis* 111, 1-24.

Ralegh Radford, C., 1973-6. 'The church of St Germans', *Journal of the Royal Institution of Cornwall*, new series 7, 190-196.

Ratcliffe, J., 1994. *Fieldwork in Scilly, July 1993*, (Truro: Cornwall Archaeological Unit).

Rattue, J., 1995. *The Living Stream: Holy Wells in Historical Context*, (Woodbridge: Boydell).

Ravenhill, W., 1967. 'Cornwall' in H. Darby and R. Welldon Finn (eds), *The Domesday Geography of South-West England*, (Cambridge: Cambridge University Press), 296-347.

Ravenhill, W. and O. Padel (eds), 1991. *Joel Gascoyne's Map of Cornwall 1699*, Devon and Cornwall Record Society n.s. 34 (Exeter: DCRS).

RCHM, 1970. *The County of Dorset. Volume 2: South-East. Part I-III*, (London: HMSO).

Reichel, O., 1939. 'The church and the hundreds in Devon', *Transactions of the Devonshire Association* 71, 331-342.

Reynolds, A., 1997. 'The definition and ideology of Anglo-Saxon execution sites and cemeteries' in G. De Boe and F. Verhaege, *Death and Burial in Medieval Europe: Papers of the Medieval Europe 1997 Conference* 2, (Zellik: IAP), 34-41.

Reynolds, A., 1998. 'Anglo-Saxon law in the landscape', Unpublished PhD thesis, University of London.

Reynolds, A., 1999. *Later Anglo-Saxon England: Life and Landscape*, (Stroud: Tempus).

Reynolds, A., 2002. 'Burials, boundaries and charters in Anglo-Saxon England: a reassessment' in S. Lucy and A. Reynolds (eds), *Burial in Early Medieval England and Wales*, (London: Society of Medieval Archaeology), 171-194.

Reynolds, A., 2003. 'Boundaries and settlements in later sixth- to eleventh-century England', *Anglo-Saxon Studies in Archaeology and History* 12, 98-136.

Reynolds, A., B. Sudds, S. Semple and R. Edmunds, forthcoming. *The Medieval Village of Yatesbury: Excavations 1991-1998*.

Reynolds, A. and S. Turner, 2003. 'Excavations at Holy Trinity, Buckfastleigh, Spring 2002', *Society for Medieval Archaeology Newsletter* 28, 5-6.

Reynolds, P., 1950. 'Muchelney Abbey' *Archaeological Journal* 107, 120-121.

Richards, J., 1991. *Viking Age England*, (London: Batsford/English Heritage).

Riley, H. and R. Wilson-North, 2001. *The Field Archaeology of Exmoor*, (London: English Heritage).

Rippon, S., 1994. 'Medieval wetland reclamation in Somerset' in M. Aston and C. Lewis (eds), *The Medieval Landscape of Wessex*, Oxbow Monograph 46 (Oxford: Oxbow Books), 239-253.

Rippon, S., 1997. *The Severn Estuary: Landscape Evolution and Wetland Reclamation*, (Leicester: Leicester University Press).

Rippon, S., 2004a. *Historic Landscape Analysis: Deciphering the Countryside*, Council for British Archaeology Practical Handbook 16 (York: CBA).

Rippon, S., 2004b. 'Making the most of a bad situation? Glastonbury Abbey, Meare, and the medieval exploitation of wetland resources in the Somerset Levels', *Medieval Archaeology* 48, 91-130.

Rippon, S., M. Martin and A. Jackson, 2001. 'The use of soil analysis in the interpretation of an early historic landscape at Puxton in Somerset', *Landscape History* 23, 27-38.

Rodwell, W., 1982. 'From mausolea to minster: the early development of Wells Cathedral' in S. Pearce (ed.), *The Early Church In Western Britain and Ireland: Studies Presented to C.A. Ralegh Radford*, British Archaeological Reports British Series 102 (Oxford: BAR), 49-61.

Rodwell, W., 2001. *Wells Cathedral: Excavations and Structural Studies, 1978-93*, English Heritage Archaeological Report 21, 2 vols (London: English Heritage).

Rodwell, W. and K. Rodwell, 1982. 'St Peter's church, Barton-on-Humber, excavation and structural study, 1978-81', *Antiquaries Journal* 62, 283-315.

Rose, P., 1994 'The historic landscape' in N. Johnson and P. Rose (eds) *Bodmin Moor: An Archaeological Survey* 1: *The Human Landscape to c.1800*, (London: English Heritage), 77-115.

Rose, P. and N. Johnson, 1983. 'Some cropmark enclosures in Cornwall', *Cornish Archaeology* 22, 99-106.

Rose, P. and A. Preston-Jones, 1995. 'Changes in the Cornish countryside, AD400-1100' in D. Hooke and S. Burnell (eds) *Landscape and Settlement in Britain AD400-1066*, (Exeter: University of Exeter Press), 51-68.

Roymans, N., 1995. 'The cultural biography of urnfields and the long-term history of a mythical landscape', *Archaeological Dialogues* 2(1), 2-24.

Rumble, A., 2001. 'Edward the Elder and the churches of Winchester and Wessex' in N. Higham and D. Hill (eds), *Edward the Elder 899-924*, (London: Routledge), 230-247.

Rushton, N., 1997. 'Parochialization and patterns of patronage in 11th-century Sussex', *Sussex Archaeological Collections* 137, 133-152.

Saunders, A., 1977. 'Excavations at Launceston Castle 1970-76: interim report', *Cornish Archaeology* 16, 129-137.

Saunders, A. and D. Harris, 1982. 'Excavation at Castle Gotha, St Austell', *Cornish Archaeology* 21, 109-153.

Saunders, C., 1972. 'The excavations at Grambla, Wendron, 1972: interim report', *Cornish Archaeology* 11, 50-52.

Sawyer, P., 1957-8. 'The density of the Danish settlement in England', *University of Birmingham Historical Journal* 6, 1-17.

Sawyer, P., 1968 *Anglo-Saxon Charters: An Annotated List and Bibliography*, (London: Royal Historical Society).

Sawyer, P., 1983. 'The royal *tun* in pre-Conquest England' in P. Wormald, D. Bullough and R. Collins (eds), *Ideal and Reality in Frankish and Anglo-Saxon Society*, (Oxford: Basil Blackwell), 273-299.

Schweiso, J., 1976. 'Excavations at Threemilestone round, Kenwyn, Truro', *Cornish Archaeology* 15, 50-67.

Scott, I., 1999. 'Romsey Abbey: Benedictine nunnery and parish church' in G. Keevill, M. Aston and T. Hall (eds), *Monastic Archaeology*, (Oxford: Oxbow), 150-160.

Semple, S., 1998. 'A fear of the past: the place of the prehistoric burial mound in the ideology of middle and later Anglo-Saxon England', *World Archaeology* 30(1), 109-126.

Semple, S., 2002. 'Anglo-Saxon attitudes to the past: a landscape perspective' Unpublished DPhil thesis, University of Oxford.

Semple, S., 2003. 'Burials and political boundaries in the Avebury region, north Wiltshire', *Anglo-Saxon Studies in Archaeology and History* 12, 72-91.

Semple, S., 2004. 'Locations of assembly in early Anglo-Saxon England' in A. Pantos and S. Semple (eds), *Assembly Places and Practices in Medieval Europe*, (Dublin: Four Courts Press), 135-154.

Semple, S. and H. Williams, 2001. 'Excavations on Roundway Down', *Wiltshire Archaeological and Natural History Magazine* 94, 236-239.

Shanks, M. and C. Tilley, 1987. *Re-Constructing Archaeology: Theory and Practice*, (Cambridge: Cambridge University Press).

Sharpe, R., 1984. 'Some problems concerning the organization of the church in early medieval Ireland', *Peritia* 3, 230-270.

Sharpe, R., 1995. *Adomnán of Iona: Life of St Columba*, (London: Penguin).

Sharpe, R., 2002. 'Martyrs and local saints in late antique Britain' in A. Thacker and R. Sharpe (eds), *Local Saints and Local Churches in the Early Medieval West*, (Oxford: Oxford University Press), 75-154.

Simpson, S., F. Griffith and N. Holbrook, 1989. 'The prehistoric, Roman and early post-Roman site at Hayes Farm, Clyst Honiton', *Devon Archaeological Society Proceedings* 47, 1-28.

Sims-Williams, P., 1986. 'The Visionary Celt: the construction of an ethnic preconception', *Cambridge Medieval Celtic Studies* 11, 71-96.

Sims-Williams, P., 1998a. 'Celtomania and Celtoscepticism', *Cambrian Medieval Celtic Studies* 36, 1-35.

Sims-Williams, P., 1998b. 'Genetics, linguistics and prehistory: thinking big and thinking straight', *Antiquity* 72, 505-527.

Small, D., 1999. 'The tyranny of the text: lost social strategies in current historical period archaeology in the classical Mediterranean' in P. Funari, M. Hall and S. Jones (eds), *Historical Archaeology: Back from the Edge*, (London: Routledge), 122-135 .

Smith, I., 1996. 'The origins and development of Christianity in north Britain and southern Pictland' in J. Blair and C. Pyrah (eds), *Church Archaeology: Research Directions for the Future*, Council for British Archaeology Research Report 104 (York: CBA), 19-42.

Snead, J. and R. Preucel, 1999. 'The ideology of settlement: ancestral Keres landscapes in the northern Rio Grande' in W. Ashmore and B. Knapp (eds), *Archaeologies of Landscape*, (Oxford: Blackwell), 169-197.

Somerscales, M., 1957. 'A dark age site on Phillack Towans near Hayle', *Proceedings of the West Cornwall Field Club* 2(1), 8-14.

Speake, G., 1989. *A Saxon Bed Burial on Swallowcliffe Down*, (London: English Heritage) .

Stancliffe, C., 1979. 'From town to country: the Christianization of the Touraine 370-600', *Studies in Church History* 16, 43-59.

Startin, W., 1982. 'Halligye fogou: excavations in 1981', *Cornish Archaeology* 21, 185-186.

Stenton, F., 1971. *Anglo-Saxon England* (3rd edition, Oxford: Oxford University Press).

Stocker, D., 1993. 'The early church in Lincolnshire' in A. Vince (ed.) *Pre-Viking Lindsey*, (Lincoln: City of Lincoln Archaeology Unit), 1-22.

Stokes, W. (ed. and trans.), 1905. *The Martyrology of Oengus: Félire Óengusso Céli dé*, Henry Bradshaw Society Vol. 29 (London: Harrison and Sons).

Stummann Hansen, S. and D. Waugh, 1998. 'Scandinavian settlement in Unst, Shetland: archaeology and place-names' in S. Taylor (ed.), *The Uses of Place-Names*, St John's House Papers 7, St Andrews (Edinburgh: Scottish Cultural Press), 120-146.

Svensson, O., 1987. *Saxon Place-Names in East Cornwall*, Lund Studies in English 77 (Lund: Lund University Press).

Swanton, M. (ed.), 1996. *The Anglo-Saxon Chronicle*, (London: Dent).

Talbot, C. (ed. and trans.), 1954. *Anglo-Saxon Missionaries in Germany*, (London: Sheed and Ward).

Taylor, H., 1968. 'Anglo-Saxon sculpture at Knook', *Wiltshire Archaeological and Natural History Magazine* 63, 54-57.

Taylor, H. and J. Taylor, 1965. *Anglo-Saxon Architecture*, 2 vols (Cambridge: Cambridge University Press).

Taylor, T., 1916 (facsimile reprint, 1995). *The Celtic Christianity of Cornwall*, (Felinfach: Llanerch).

Thacker, A., 2002. '*Loca sanctorum*: the significance of place in the study of the saints' in A. Thacker and R. Sharpe (eds), *Local Saints and Local Churches in the Early Medieval West*, (Oxford: Oxford University Press), 1-43.

Thomas, A. and N. Holbrook, 1994. 'Llandough', *Archaeology in Wales* 34, 66-68.

Thomas, C., 1956. 'Evidence for post-Roman occupation of Chun Castle, Cornwall' *Antiquaries Journal* 41, 89-92.

Thomas, C., 1958. *Gwithian: Ten Years' Work*, (Camborne: West Cornwall Field Club).

Thomas, C., 1959. 'Imported pottery in dark age western Britain', *Medieval Archaeology* 3, 89-111.

Thomas, C., 1963. 'Unpublished material from Cornish museums: 2. Gunwalloe pottery, Helston Museum', *Cornish Archaeology* 2, 60-64.

Thomas, C., 1964a. 'Settlement-history in early Cornwall. 1: The antiquity of the hundreds', *Cornish Archaeology* 3, 70-79.

Thomas, C., 1964b. 'Minor sites in the Gwithian area (Iron Age to recent times)', *Cornish Archaeology* 3, 37-62.

Thomas, C., 1965. 'The hillfort at St Dennis', *Cornish Archaeology* 4, 31-15.

Thomas, C., 1966. 'The character and origins of Roman Dumnonia' in C. Thomas (ed.), *Rural Settlement in Roman Britain*, (London: CBA Research Report 7), 74-98.

Thomas, C., 1967. 'Fenton Ia chapel, Troon', *Cornish Archaeology* 7, 78-79.

Thomas, C., 1968a. 'Grass-marked pottery in Cornwall' in Coles and Simpson (eds) *Studies in Ancient Europe*, (Leicester), 311-332.

Thomas, C., 1968b. 'Merther Uny, Wendron', *Cornish Archaeology* 6, 78-79.

Thomas, C., 1971a. *The Early Christian Archaeology of North Britain*, (Oxford: Oxford University Press).

Thomas, C., 1971b. *Britain and Ireland in Early Christian Times, AD 400-800*, (London: Thames and Hudson).

Thomas, C., 1973. 'Parish churchyard, Phillack', *Cornish Archaeology* 12, 59.

Thomas, C., 1980. 'Hermits on islands or priests in a landscape?', *Cornish Studies* 8, 28-44.

Thomas, C., 1981a. *A Provisional List of Imported Pottery in Post-Roman Western Britain and Ireland*, (Redruth: Institute of Cornish Studies Special Report 7).

Thomas, C., 1981b. *Christianity in Roman Britain to AD500*, (London: Batsford).

Thomas, C., 1985. *Exploration of a Drowned Landscape: Archaeology and History of the Isles of Scilly*, (London: B.T. Batsford).

Thomas, C., 1988. 'Christians, chapels, churches and charters – or, "Proto-parochial provisions for the pious in a peninsula" (Land's End)', *Landscape History* 11, 19-26.

Thomas, C., 1993. *Tintagel: Arthur and Archaeology*, (London: Batsford/English Heritage).

Thomas, C., 1994. *And Shall These Mute Stones Speak? Post-Roman Inscriptions in Western Britain*, (Cardiff: University of Wales Press).

Thomas, C., 1998. *Christian Celts: Messages* and *Images*, (Stroud: Tempus).

Thomas, C., 1999. *Penzance Market Cross: A Cornish Wonder Re-wondered*, (Penzance: Penlee House Museum).

Thomas, J., 1996. *Time, Culture and Identity: An Interpretive Archaeology*, (London: Routledge).

Thomson, W., 1995. 'Orkney farm-names: a re-assessment of their chronology' in B. Crawford (ed.), *Scandinavian Settlement in Northern Britain*, (London: Leicester University Press), 42-62.

Thorn, C. and F. Thorn (eds), 1979a. *Domesday Book 10: Cornwall*, (Chichester: Phillimore).

Thorn, C. and F. Thorn (eds), 1979b. *Domesday Book 6: Wiltshire*, (Chichester: Phillimore).

Thorn, C. and F. Thorn (eds), 1980. *Domesday Book 8: Somerset*, (Chichester: Phillimore).

Thorn, C. and F. Thorn (eds), 1983. *Domesday Book 7: Dorset*, (Chichester: Phillimore).

Thorn, C. and F. Thorn (eds), 1985. *Domesday Book 9: Devon*, 2 vols, (Chichester: Phillimore).

Thorn, F., 1986. 'The identification of Domesday places in the south-western counties of England', *Nomina* 10, 41-60.

Thorn, F., 1999. 'Agriculture and rural settlement in 1086: evidence of the Domesday Book' in R. Kain and W. Ravenhill (eds), *Historical Atlas of South-West England*, (Exeter: University of Exeter Press), 269-272.

Thorpe, C., 1997. 'Ceramics', 74-82 in R. Harry and C. Morris, 'Excavations on the Lower Terrace, Site C, Tintagel Island 1990-94', *Antiquaries Journal* 77, 1-143.

Thorpe, C., 2000. 'Imported Mediterranean wares' in P. Herring, *St Michael's Mount, Cornwall. Reports on Archaeological Works, 1995-1998*, (Truro: Cornwall County Council), 95-97.

Thorpe, C., 2003. 'Mullion Church, Cornwall: Archaeological Watching Brief', Unpublished report, Cornwall Archaeological Unit No. 2003 R004, (Truro: CAU).

Tilley, C., 1994. *A Phenomenology of Landscape*, (Oxford: Berg).

Timby, J., 2001. 'The pottery' in J. Pine, 'The excavation of a Saxon settlement at Cadley Road, Collingbourne Ducis, Wiltshire' *Wiltshire Archaeological and Natural History Magazine* 94, 88-117 at 96-102.

Todd, M., 1983. 'Lammana', *Cornish Archaeology* 22, 122-123.

Todd, M., 1987. *The South West to AD 1000*, (London: Longman).

Tourtellot, G., M. Wolf, S. Smith, K. Gardella and N. Hammond, 2002. 'Exploring heaven on earth: testing the cosmological model at La Milpa, Belize', *Antiquity* 76, 633-634.

Trudgian, P., 1987. 'Excavation of a burial ground at St Endellion, Cornwall', *Cornish Archaeology* 26, 145-152.

Turner, D., 1998. 'Ruminations on Romanisation in the east: or, the metanarrative in history', *Assemblage* 4, http://www.shef.ac.uk/assem/4/, (last consulted 3 April 2006).

Turner, S., 2000. 'Aspects of the development of public assembly in the Danelaw', *Assemblage* 5, http://www.shef.ac.uk/assem/5, (last consulted 3 April 2006).

Turner, S., 2002-3. 'A medieval cross from Lidwell, Stoke Climsland', *Cornish Archaeology* 41-42, 161-164.

Turner, S., 2003a. 'Christianity and the landscape of early medieval south-west Britain', unpublished PhD thesis, University of York.

Turner, S., 2003b. 'Making a Christian landscape: early medieval Cornwall' in M. Carver (ed.), *The Cross Goes North: Processes of Conversion in Northern Europe, AD 300-1300*, (Woodbridge: Boydell and Brewer), 171-194.

Turner, S., 2003c. 'Boundaries and religion: the demarcation of early Christian settlements in Britain', *Anglo-Saxon Studies in Archaeology* and *History* 12, 50-57.

Turner, S., 2004a. 'The changing ancient landscape: south-west England AD *c.*1700-1900', *Landscapes* 5 (1), 18-34.

Turner, S., 2004b. 'Coast and countryside in "Late Antique" south-west England, AD *c.*400-600' in J. Gerrard and R. Collins (eds), *Debating Late Antiquity in Britain, AD 300-700*, (Oxford: BAR British Series 365), 25-32.

Turner, S., 2005. 'Devon historic landscape characterisation: methods, classification and preliminary analysis', unpublished report (Exeter: English Heritage/Devon County Council).

Turner, S., 2006 (forthcoming) 'Churches, chapels and crosses: the medieval Christian landscape' in S. Turner (ed.), *Medieval Devon and Cornwall: Shaping the Ancient Countryside*, (Macclesfield: Windgather Press).

Turner, S. and J. Gerrard, 2004. 'Imported and local pottery from Mothecombe: some new finds amongst old material at Totnes museum', *Devon Archaeological Society Proceedings* 62, 171-175.

Tweddle, D., 1983. 'Anglo-Saxon sculpture in south-east England before *c.*950' in F. Thompson (ed.), *Studies in Medieval Sculpture*, (London: Society of Antiquaries), 18-40.

Valante, M., 1998. 'Reassessing the Irish "monastic town"', *Irish Historical Studies* 31 (121): 1-18.

Wade, K., 1980. 'A settlement site at Wicken Bonhunt, Essex', in D. Buckley (ed.), *Archaeology in Essex to AD 1500*, Council for British Archaeology Research Report 34 (London: CBA), 96-102.

Ward-Perkins, B., 2000a. 'Constantinople: a city and its hinterland' in G. Brogiolo, N. Gauthier and N. Christie (eds), *Towns and their Territories between Late Antiquity and the Early Middle Ages*, (Leiden: Brill), 325-345.

Ward-Perkins, B., 2000b. 'Why did the Anglo-Saxons not become more British?' *English Historical Review* 115, 513-533.

Wataghin, G., 2000. 'Christianisation et organisation ecclésiastique des campagnes: l'Italie du nord aux IVe – VIIe siècles' in G. Brogiolo, N. Gauthier and N. Christie (eds), *Towns and their Territories between Late Antiquity and the Early Middle Ages*, (Leiden: Brill), 209-234.

Watts, L. and P. Leach, 1996. *Henley Wood, Temples and Cemetery*, Council for British Archaeology Research Report 99 (York: CBA).

Weaver, F., 1909. *A Cartulary of Buckland Priory in the County of Somerset*, Somerset Record Society Volume 25 (Taunton: Somerset Record Society).

Weddell, P., 2000. 'The excavation of a post-Roman cemetery near Kenn', *Devon Archaeological Society Proceedings* 58, 93-126.

Wedlake, W., 1958. *Excavations at Camerton, Somerset*, (Camerton: Camerton Excavation Club) .

Wedlake, W., 1982. *The Excavation of the Shrine of Apollo at Nettleton, Wiltshire 1956-71*, (London: Society of Antiquaries) .

Welinder, S., 2003. 'Christianity, politics and ethnicity in early medieval Jämtland, mid Sweden' in M. Carver (ed.), *The Cross Goes North: Processes of Conversion in Northern Europe, AD 300-1300*, (Woodbridge: Boydell), 509-530.

Wheeler, M., 1943. *Maiden Castle Dorset*, (London: Society of Antiquaries).

Whitelock, D., 1979. *English Historical Documents: Volume 1 A.D. c.500-1042*, (2nd edn, London: Eyre Methuen).

Whitelock, D., M. Brett and C. Brooke (eds), 1981. *Councils and Synods with Other Documents Relating to the English Church, I: AD 871-1204, Pt 1: 871-1066*, (Oxford: Oxford University Press).

Wickham, C., 1990. 'European forests in the early middle ages: landscape and land clearance', *Settimane di Studio del Centro Italiano di Studi sull'Alto Medioevo* 36, 479-545.

Williams, A., 1992. 'A bell-house and a burh-geat: lordly residences in England before the Norman Conquest' in C. Harper-Bill and R. Harvey (eds), *The Ideals and Practice of Medieval Knighthood*, (Woodbridge: Boydell), 221-240.

Williams, H., 1997. 'Ancient landscapes and the dead: the reuse of prehistoric and Roman monuments as early Anglo-Saxon burial sites', *Medieval Archaeology* 41, 1-32.

Williams, J., M. Shaw and V. Denham, 1988. *Middle Saxon Palaces at Northampton*, (Northampton: Northampton Development Corporation).

Williamson, T., 1993. *The Origins of Norfolk*, (Manchester: Manchester University Press).

Williamson, T., 2002. *The Transformation of Rural England: Farming and the Landscape, 1700-1870*, (Exeter: University of Exeter Press) .

Williamson, T., 2003. *Shaping Medieval Landscapes*, (Macclesfield: Windgather Press).

Wills, J., 1999 'Cotswolds AONB: characterisation, classification and GIS' in G. Fairclough (ed.), *Historic Landscape Characterisation: 'the State of the Art'*, (London: English Heritage), 33-40.

Wilson, D., 1985. 'A note on OE *haerg* and *weoh* as place-name elements representing different types of pagan Saxon worship sites', *Anglo-Saxon Studies in Archaeology* and *History* 4, 179-183.

Winterbottom, M., (ed. and trans.), 1978. *Gildas: The Ruin of Britain and Other Documents*, (Chichester: Phillimore).

Wormald, P., 1999. *The Making of English Law: King Alfred to the Twelfth Century*, (Oxford: Blackwell).

Wormald, P., 2001. '*On tha wæpnedhealfe:* kingship and royal property from Aethelwulf to Edward the Elder' in N. Higham and D. Hill (eds), *Edward the Elder 899-924*, (London: Routledge), 264-279.

Yeoman, P., 1997. 'Pilgrims to St Ethernan: the archaeology of an early saint of the Picts and Scots' in G. DeBoe and F. Verhaeghe (eds), *Religion and Belief in Medieval Europe*, Papers of the Medieval Europe Brugge Conference, Vol. 4 (Zellick: IAP), 79-88.

Yorke, B., 1995. *Wessex in the Early Middle Ages*, (London: Leicester University Press).

Yorke, B., 1999. 'The reception of Christianity at the Anglo-Saxon royal courts' in R. Gameson (ed.), *St Augustine and the Conversion of England*, (Stroud: Sutton), 152-173.

Yorke, B., 2002. 'Remembering and forgetting: early Anglo-Saxon saints of Wessex', unpublished paper given at the University of Exeter History Seminar, 31st October 2002.

Yorke, B., 2003. 'The adaptation of the Anglo-Saxon royal courts to Christianity' in M. Carver (ed.), *The Cross Goes North: Processes of Conversion in Northern Europe, AD 300-1300*, (Woodbridge: Boydell), 243-257.

Index